Studies on the Turkic World

Studies on the Turkic World

A Festschrift for Professor Stanisław Stachowski on the Occasion of His 80th Birthday

Edited by
Elżbieta Mańczak-Wohlfeld
Barbara Podolak

Jagiellonian University Press

This volume was supported by the Jagiellonian University
Institute of Oriental Philology

PROOFREADER AND TYPESETTER
Kamil Stachowski

TECHNICAL EDITOR
Mirosław Ruszkiewicz

COVER DESIGN
Anna Sadowska

Cover: Map *Natolia quæ olim Asia Minor*, 17th century
Courtesy of Jagiellonian Library

First edition, Kraków 2010

WYDAWNICTWO UNIWERSYTETU JAGIELLOŃSKIEGO

www.wuj.pl

ISBN 978-83-233-3015-8

Jagiellonian University Press
Editorial Offices:
Michałowskiego St. 9/2, 31-126 Cracow
Phone: +48 12 631 18 80, +48 12 631 18 82, Fax: +48 12 631 18 83
Distribution: Phone: +48 12 631 01 97, Fax: +48 12 631 01 98
Cell Phone: +48 506 006 674, e-mail: sprzedaz@wuj.pl
Bank: PEKAO SA, IBAN PL80 1240 4722 1111 0000 4856 3325

St. Stachowski

Tabula Gratulatoria

José Andrés Alonso de la Fuente
Aleksandr Anikin
Teresa Bela
Zofia Berdychowska
Ireneusz Bobrowski
Anna Bochnakowa
Anna Bolek
Bernt Brendemoen
Jerzy Brzozowski
Renata Bura
Elżbieta Chrzanowska-Kluczewska
Özlem Civelek
Renata Czekalska
Musa Duman
Marcel Erdal
Adam Fałowski
Victor Friedman
Stefan Georg
Jordanka Georgiewa-Okoń
Marta Gibińska
Elżbieta Górska
Mária Ivanics
Juha Janhunen
Sławomira Kaleta-Wojtasik

Matthias Kappler
Józef Kąś
Éva Kincses Nagy
Maria Kłańska
Dariusz Kołodziejczyk
Kazimierz Korus
Jadwiga Kowalikowa
Anna Krasnowolska
Agnieszka Kuczkiewicz-Fraś
Janina Labocha
Jens Peter Laut
Ugo Marazzi
Halina Marlewicz
Maria Maślanka-Soro
Zygmunt Mazur
Barbara Mękarska
Jan Michalik
Jadwiga Miszalska
László Nagy
Irina Nevskaya
Anna Niżegorodcew
Piotr Nykiel
Mehmet Ölmez
Maryla Papierz
Walery Pisarek
†Krystyna Pisarkowa
Marzanna Pomorska
Gisela Procházka-Eisl
Jacek Rapak
Volker Rybatzki
Anna Sawicka
Wolfgang Scharlipp
Denis Sinor
Mirosław Skarżyński
Barbara Sosień
Krystyna Stamirowska
Jerzy Styka
Lidia Sudyka

Stanisław Śnieżewski
Marcela Świątkowska
Semih Tezcan
Alexander Vovin
Jadwiga Waniakowa
Halina Waszkielewicz
Stanisław Widłak
Hubert Wolanin
István Zimonyi

Contents

Invitation to Discussion

Prezento de la scienca agado de prof. d-ro habil. Stanislao Stachowski

Stanislao Stachowski naskiĝis la 21-an de oktobro 1930 en Jeziora apud Grodno. Tie li frekventis, komence polan, poste bjelorusan bazlernejojn, kaj dum la dua mondmilito li lernis en konspiraj klasoj. Post la milito la estonta lingvisto translokiĝis kun siaj gepatroj al Tomaszów Mazowiecki, kie, en 1851, li finis mezlernejon.

La ligoj de prof. Stanislao Stachowski kun Jagelona Universitato datas ekde la jaro 1951-a, en kiu li ekstudis serbo-kroatan filologion. Jam tiam li montris intereson pri lingvoj aliaj ol la slavaj, tial li kromstudis turkan lingvistikon. La magistriga laboraĵo de la estonta profesoro, pri fremddevenaj sufiksoj en la serbo-kroata lingvo, estis publikigita en 1961. La grandan intereson pri la publikaĵo pruvas tri recenzoj, aperintaj en Parizo, Budapeŝto kaj Skopjo.

Tuj post magistriĝo Stanislao Stachowski eklaboris en la Katedro de Slava Filologio kiel, laŭvice, anstataŭanto de asistanto, asistanto kaj alt-asistanto.

La doktorigan disertaĵon, preparatan komence sub gvido de prof. d-ro Tadeo Lehr-Spławiński kaj post ties morto direktatan de prof. d-ro Stanislao Urbańczyk, li defendis en 1967. Jam laŭ la titolo de la disertaĵo *Język górnołużycki w „De originibus linguae Sorabicae" A. Frencla (1693–1696)* (*La soraba lingvo en „De originibus linguae Sorabicae" de A. Frencel (1693–1696)*) videblas, ke la esplorintereso de la Jubileanto direktiĝis al alia slava lingvo ol tiu, kiu estis la objekto de lia universitata studado.

Kvin jarojn poste Stanislao Stachowski finverkis sian habilitigan disertaĵon, kiu estis publikigita la postan jaron, t.e. en 1973. Ĝi koncernis ne nur la slavan lingvistikon, sed ankaŭ la turkan: la titolo de la laboraĵo estis *Fonetyka zapożyczeń osmańsko-tureckich w języku serbsko-chorwackim* (*La fonetiko de la osmanturkaj pruntaĵoj en la serba-kroata lingvo*). Tiu tute nova kaj malsama esplorintereso faris, ke la tiama habilita doktoro estis nomumita docento (en 1974) kaj transigita al la Instituto de Orienta Filologio (Sekcio de Turkologio), kie li laboris ĝis sia emeritiĝo, en 2000.

Surbaze de tri partoj de la jam tute dediĉita al orientaj studoj libro, titolita *Studien über die arabischen Lehnwörter im Osmanisch-Türkischen* (*Studoj pri la arabaj leksikaj pruntaĵoj en la osmanturka lingvo*) (1975, 1977, 1978), de la verko *Słownik górnołużycki Abrahama Frencla (1693–1699)* (*Soraba vortaro de Abraham Frencel (1693–1699)*), publikigita en 1978, kaj de multnombraj artikoloj Stanislao Stachowski iĝis, en 1983, titola profesoro pri humanistiko. Enpostenigo de Stanislao Stachowski kiel ordinara profesoro de Jagelona Universitato, en 1992, kronis lian sciencan aktivadon.

Jam la cititaj kelkaj laboraĵoj, kiuj estis bazo por la avancado de Stanislao Stachowski, montras lian vastan esplorkampon. Tamen, rigardante la verkaron de la Jubileanto eblas rimarki, ke liaj interesoj koncernas tri terenojn de la lingvistiko: la slavan, turkan kaj balkanan. Ja, kvankam ili diferencas, kunligas ilin leksikologia aliro, precipe esplorado de rilatoj inter leksikunuoj apartenantaj al diversaj lingvaj grupoj. Kiel montras la troviĝanta en la sekvaj paĝoj listo de la laboraĵoj de prof. Stanislao Stachowski, la profesoro dediĉis al tiuj temoj 19 librojn kaj ĉ. 70 artikolojn, recenzojn kaj malpli grandajn verkojn. La ecoj de la tuta verkaro de prof. Stanislao Stachowski estas granda precizeco, precipe pri fontoj de la priskribata leksiko, elstara metodologia ilaro kaj trafeco de la proponataj solvoj.

Prof. Stanislao Stachowski plurfoje restadis eksterlande, i.a. realigante 10-monatan sciencan staĝon en Zagrebo (1959/60), kaj malpli longajn studrestadojn en Prago, Budapeŝto kaj Moskvo. Li faris ankaŭ malpli longajn prelegvojaĝojn al, ekz., Budisino, Skopjo, Minsko, Sofio, Vilno, Peĉo, Segedo. Lia prelegado estis tre bone akceptita. Li partoprenis ankaŭ multajn landajn kaj eksterlandajn konferencojn.

Prof. Stanislao Stachowski estas membro de pluraj sciencaj komisionoj: la Komisiono pri Slavologio de la filio de la Pola Scienc-Akademio (PAN) en Krakovo ekde 1969, kaj ekde 1996 – Honora Membro de tiu filio; la Lingvistika Komisiono de la sama filio, ankaŭ ekde 1969; la Orientstuda Komisiono de la filio de la Pola Scienc-Akademio en Krakovo ekde 1969, kaj en la jaroj 1987–1989 ties prezidanto. En 1984 li iĝis membro de la Komitato de Orient-Sciencoj de la Pola Scienc-Akademio, en 1987–1989 li apartenis al la Prezidantaro de la komitato kaj en 1996–1998 li estis ties vic-prezidanto. En 1990 Stanislao Stachowski membriĝis en la Societas Uralo-Altaica.

Priparolante la sciencan aktivadon de la profesoro, oni ne prisilentu lian ĉefredaktadon de la revuoj *Folia Orientalia*, ekde 1987; *Prace Językoznawcze* (*Lingvistikaj Laboraĵoj*) – parto de *Zeszyty Naukowe* (*Sciencaj Kajeroj*) de Jagelona Universitato, ekde 1988; la serio *Studia Turcologica Cracoviensia*, kies ne nur ĉefredaktoro, sed ankaŭ fondinto li estas.

La sfero de la kursoj, kiujn prof. Stanislao Stachowski ofertis al la studentaro de Jagelona Universitato estas impona: ĝi koncernas la historian kaj komparan lingvistikon de lingvoj slavaj, tjurkaj, de la rumana, ankaŭ de la hungara. La kursoj estis destinitaj al studentoj de diversaj filologioj: slava, pola, rusa, turka, rumana kaj hungara. Rezulto de tiuj diversspecaj okupoj estis magistrigo de pli ol 40 studentoj ne nur de turkologio, sed ankaŭ de hungarologio, kio – konsiderante la specifecon de la studoj – estas granda nombro. La kvar doktorigaj disertaĵoj verkitaj sub lia gvido koncernas la turkan lingvistikon. Se temas pri formado de profesiuloj, menciindas ankaŭ la partopreno de la profesoro en kelkaj doktorigoj kaj habilitigoj kiel recenzanto.

La prezentitaj imponaj sciencaj kaj didaktikaj atingoj permesas konsideri la Jubileanton kiel grandan erudiciulon kaj eminentan lingviston, kio estis rimarkita de landaj aŭtoritatoj kaj honorigita per multaj premioj: tri Triagradaj Premioj de la Ministro de Edukado kaj Superaj Lernejoj (1967, 1974 kaj 1979), du premioj de la Rektoro de Jagelona Universitato (1991 kaj 1995) kaj du distingoj: La Ora Kruco por Meritoj (1976) kaj la Kavalira Kruco de la Ordeno de Renaskiĝo de Pollando (1986).

Malgraŭ la granda aktiveco en la scienca kaj didaktika kampoj prof. Stanislao Stachowski trovis tempon ankaŭ por universitataj administraj taskoj. Dufoje, dum 1981–1984 kaj 1989–1991, li estis vic-direktoro de la Instituto de Orienta Filologio, kaj dum 1991–1994 ties direktoro. Krome, en 1987 li estis komisiita de la Rektoro de Jagelona Universitato formi memstaran Katedron de Hungara Filologio, kiun li estris dum 1989–1991. Sendube, la sciencaj, didaktikaj kaj organizaj atingoj envicigas prof. Stanislao Stachowski inter la plej elstarajn polajn lingvistojn, kies alta pozicio estas rekonata ne nur en Pollando, sed ankaŭ eksterlande.

Elżbieta Mańczak-Wohlfeld
(Tradukis Maria Majerczak)
Krakovo, 2010

Publications of Prof. Stanisław Stachowski

Abbreviations

ABS	=	*Acta Baltico-Slavica*, Warszawa–Białystok.
AOH	=	*Acta Orientalia Academiae Scientiarum Hungaricae*, Budapest.
BSLP	=	*Bulletin de la Société de Linguistique de Paris*, Paris.
BSS	=	*Beiträge zur sorbischen Sprachwissenschaft*, Bautzen.
Ètim.	=	*Ètimologija*, Moskva.
FO	=	*Folia Orientalia*, Kraków.
MJ	=	*Makedonski Jazik*, Skopje.
MS	=	*Monografie Slawistyczne*, Wrocław–Warszawa–Kraków.
MT	=	*Materialia Turcica*, Göttingen.
OLZ	=	*Orientalistische Literaturzeitung*, Berlin.
PrJ	=	*Zeszyty Naukowe UJ. Prace Językoznawcze*, Kraków.
RO	=	*Rocznik Orientalistyczny*, Warszawa.
RS	=	*Rocznik Slawistyczny*, Kraków.
SEC	=	*Studia Etymologica Cracoviensia*, Kraków.
SFPS	=	*Studia z Filologii Polskiej i Słowiańskiej*, Warszawa.
SSH	=	*Studia Slavica Academiae Scientiarum Hungaricae*, Budapest.
STC	=	*Studia Turcologica Cracoviensia*, Kraków.
UAJb-NF	=	*Ural-altaische Jahrbücher. Neue Folge*, Wiesbaden.
ZfS	=	*Zeitschrift für Slawistik*, Berlin.

Books

1961

1. *Przyrostki obcego pochodzenia w języku serbochorwackim*, Kraków, 163 pp.
   Rev.: Jašar-Nasteva O., *MJ* 13–14 (1962–63), 279–282.
   Hazai G., *SSH* 10 (1964), 472–473.
   Vaillant A., *BSLP* 58/2 (1963), 179–180.

1966

2. *Słownik do górnołużyckiego Katechizmu Warychiusza (1597)*, Warszawa–Kraków, 119 pp.
   Rev.: Müller K., *ZfS* 12 (1967), 599–605.

1967

3. *Język górnołużycki w „De originibus linguae Sorabicae" Abrahama Frencla (1693–1696)* (= *MS* 11), Wrocław–Warszawa–Kraków, 189 pp.
4. *Studia nad chronologią turcyzmów w języku serbsko-chorwackim* (= *PrJ* 18), Kraków, 82 pp.

1969

5. *Wyrazy serbsko-chorwackie w „Thesaurus Polyglottus" H. Meginsera (1603)* (= *MS* 19), Wrocław–Warszawa–Kraków, 168 pp.

1971

6. *Studia nad chronologią turcyzmów w języku bułgarskim* (= *PrJ* 33), Kraków, 104 pp.
   Rev.: Kostov K., *ZfS* 18 (1973), 923–926.

1973

7. *Fonetyka zapożyczeń osmańsko-tureckich w języku serbsko-chorwackim* (= *MS* 23), Wrocław–Warszawa–Kraków–Gdańsk, 241 pp.
   Rev.: Šimundić M., *Dometi* 1974/5, 102–107.

1975

8. *Studien über die arabischen Lehnwörter im Osmanisch-Türkischen*, I: *A–İ*, Wrocław–Warszawa–Kraków–Gdańsk, 145 pp.
   Rev.: Johanson L., *OLZ* 73 (1978), 374–379.

1977

9. *Studien über die arabischen Lehnwörter im Osmanisch-Türkischen*, II: *K–M*, Wrocław–Warszawa–Kraków–Gdańsk, 246 pp.
   Rev.: Johanson L., *OLZ* 76 (1981), 385–386.

1978

10. *Słownik górnołużycki Abrahama Frencla (1693–1696)* (= *MS* 40), Wrocław–Warszawa–Kraków–Gdańsk, 246 pp.

1981

11. *Studien über die arabischen Lehnwörter im Osmanisch-Türkischen, III: N–T*, Wrocław–Warszawa–Kraków–Gdańsk–Łódź, 147 pp.
Rev.: Johanson L., *OLZ* 85 (1990), 577.

1986

12. *Studien über die arabischen Lehnwörter im Osmanisch-Türkischen, IV: U–Z und Nachträge*, Wrocław–Warszawa–Kraków–Gdańsk–Łódź, 113 pp.
Rev.: Johanson L., *OLZ* 85 (1990), 577.

1992

13. *Türkische Lehnwörter im serbischen Dialekt von Pirot* (= *PrJ* 111), Kraków, 78 pp.

1996

14. *Historisches Wörterbuch der Bildungen auf* -cı ‖ -ıcı *im Osmanisch-Türkischen* (= *STC* 2), Kraków, 197 pp.

1998

15. *Osmanlı Türkçesinde yeni farsça alıntılar sözlüğü – Wörterbuch der neupersischen Lehnwörter im Osmanisch-Türkischen*, İstanbul, 303 pp.

2000

16. *Index der türkischen Wörter* [= vol. 6 of: Franciscus à Mesgnien Meninski, *Thesaurus Linguarum Orientalium Turcicæ-Arabicæ-Persicæ. Lexicon Turcico-Arabico-Persicum*, Stachowski S., Ölmez M. (eds.)], İstanbul, 96 pp.

2002

17. *Lexique turc dans le Vocabulaire de P.F. Viguier (1790)*, Kraków, 322 pp.

2005

18. *Glosariusz turecko-polski*, Kraków, 330 pp.

2007

19. *Słownik historyczny turcyzmów w języku polskim*, Kraków, l + 514 pp.

Articles

1963

1. Z historii dialektu czarnogórskiego – *SFPS* 4, 155–170.
2. Czasowniki serbochorwackie o osnowie tureckiej – *Studia linguistica in honorem Th. Lehr-Spławiński*, Państwowe Wydawnictwo Naukowe, 265–268.
3. Die osmanisch-türkischen Lehnwörter im Serbokroatischen und ihre Bedeutung für die historische Phonetik des Osmanisch-Türkischen – *FO* 4, 154–170.

1964

4. Studien über den osmanisch-türkischen Wortschatz. I – *FO* 5, 75–88.

1965

5. Studien über den osmanisch-türkischen Wortschatz. II – *FO* 6, 41–54.
6. Zametki po metodologii ètimologičeskich issledovanij tureckich zaimstvovanij v serbsko-chorvatskom jazyke – *Ètim. 1964* [1965], 56–71.

1966

7. Studien über den osmanisch-türkischen Wortschatz. III – *FO* 7, 75–89.
8. Słowniczek serbsko-turecki z r. 1631 – *Sprawozdania z posiedzeń Komisji Nauk Orientalistycznych Oddziału PAN w Krakowie* I, 113–15.
9. Dialekt turecki w Albanii XVII w. – *Sprawozdania z posiedzeń Komisji Nauk Orientalistycznych Oddziału PAN w Krakowie* I, 85–7.

1967

10. Der türkische Dialekt des 17. Jhs. in Albanien – *FO* 8 (1966) [1967], 179–195.
11. Turcizmy v slovare Ja. Mikali – *Ètim. 1965* [1967], 196–210.

1968

12. Osmanisch-türkische Wörter im Wörterbuch von P. S. Pallas (1787–1789) – *FO* 9, 53–68.
13. Die Turzismen in dem *Slavenoserbskij Leksikon* aus dem J. 1790 – *Slavica* 8, 231–236.
14. Słowotwórstwo rzeczowników w języku górnołużyckim XVII wieku – *BSS*, 180–191.

1969

15. Przyczynek do chronologii turcyzmów w języku serbsko-chorwackim – *SFPS* 8, 303–309.
16. Beiträge zur Chronologie der albanischen Turzismen – *FO* 10, 48–55.

1970

17. Ein türkisches Wörterverzeichnis aus dem J. 1688 – *FO* 11, 259–264.

1971

18. Źródła staropolskie do historii języka osmańsko-tureckiego – *Sprawozdania z posiedzeń Komisji Nauk Orientalistycznych Oddziału PAN w Krakowie* 17/I, 68–69.

1972

19. Beiträge zur Geschichte der griechischen Lehnwörter im Osmanisch-Türkischen – *FO* 13, 267–298.

1973

20. Studien über die neupersischen Lehnwörter im Osmanisch-Türkischen, I (*abad–çükündür*), *FO* 14 (1972–1973), 77–118.

1974

21. Studien über die neupersischen Lehnwörter im Osmanisch-Türkischen, II (*dar–hünkâr*), *FO* 15, 87–118.

1975

22. Studien über die neupersischen Lehnwörter im Osmanisch-Türkischen, III (*ibrişim–nümayan*), *FO* 16, 145–192.

1976

23. Studien über die neupersischen Lehnwörter im Osmanisch-Türkischen, IV (*orospu–pürhuni*), *FO* 17, 141–173.

1977

24. Studien über die neupersischen Lehnwörter im Osmanisch-Türkischen, V (*raf–süvāri*), *FO* 18, 87–118.

1978

25. Studien über die neupersischen Lehnwörter im Osmanisch-Türkischen, VI (*şād*–ümidvār), *FO* 19, 93–126.

1979

26. Studien über die neupersischen Lehnwörter im Osmanisch-Türkischen, VII (*vay!–zürümbād*), *FO* 20, 31–55.
27. Slawische Wörter in der türkischen Sprache des 17. Jahrhunderts – *SSH* 25, 363–370.

1983

28. Die türkischen Lehnwörter im Talyschischen – Bednarczuk L., Czapkiewicz A. (eds.), *Studia Indo-Iranica*, Wrocław–Kraków, 147–181.

1986

29. Wyrazy albańskie w Słowniku P. S. Pallasa (1787–1789) – *ABS* 17, 237–253.

1987

30. Zapożyczenia weneckie w tekstach czarnogórskich XVI–XVIII wieku – *Slawistyczne studia językoznawcze*, Wrocław, 363–392.

1988

31. Das osmanisch-türkische Wortgut bei J. Leunclavius (1591) – *PrJ* 78, 127–150.

1990

32. Przyczynek do historii słownictwa dialektu czarnogórskiego – *SSH* 36, 357–362.

1992

33. Balkanischer Einfluß auf dem Wortschatz des Judenspanischen – *Estudios Hispanicos* 2 (= *Acta Universitatis Wratislaviensis* 1370), Wrocław, 101–113.

1993

34. Arabische Lehnwörter im Codex Cumanicus – *PrJ* 113, 103–112.

1994

35. Geschichte des osmanisch-türkischen *pınar* 'Quelle' – *RO* 49, 185–190.
36. Nieznane źródła do historii słownictwa arabskiego – *Studia orientalia Thaddaeo Lewicki oblata*, Kraków, 65–71.

1995

37. Studien zur türkischen Wortgeschichte (1) – *STC* 1, 185–209.
38. Osmanisch-türkische und tatarische Lehnwörter im Polnischen und ihre Bedeutung für die türkische Wortgeschichte – Kellner-Heinkele B., Stachowski M. (eds.), *Laut- und Wortgeschichte der Türksprachen. Beiträge des Internationalen Symposiums, Berlin, 7. bis 10. Juli 1992*, Wiesbaden, 155–171.
39. Die Rolle des Griechischen in der Geschichte des Osmanisch-Türkischen – Smoczyński W. (ed.), *Analecta Indoevropaea Cracoviensia* I. *Safarewicz memoriae dicata*, Kraków, 377–385.
40. Turzismen im Dushami-Dialekt des Albanischen – *AOH* 48 [= Dávid G., Vásáry I. (eds.), *Studia Orientalia Prof. Susannae Kakuk septusgennariae dedicta*], 465–472.

1996

41. Zur Geschichte des osmanisch-türkischen *zıbın* 'eine Art Obergewand' – *SEC* 1, 117–124.

1997

42. Arabisches Lehngut im türkischen Dialekt von Edirne – *RO* 50, 243–250.
43. Zur Geschichte des osmanisch-türkischen *pabuç* 'schaftloser Schuh, Pantoffel' – Kellner-Heinkele B., Zieme P. (eds.), *Studia Ottomanica. Festgabe für Gy. Hazai*, Wiesbaden, 181–192.
44. Turcyzmy w języku ukraińskiej prozy pamiętnikarskiej pierwszej połowy XVIII wieku – Bolek A., Fałowski A., Zinkiewicz-Tomanek B. (eds.), *Słowianie Wschodni. Między językiem a kulturą*, Kraków, 151–157.
45. Turcyzmy w dialektach serbsko-chorwackich (1) – *PrJ* 118, Kraków, 87–102.

1998

46. Zum Wortschatz der türkischen Mundarten Mazedoniens – *STC* 5 [= Stachowski M. (ed.), *Languages and Culture of Turkic Peoples*], 255–262.
47. Ein bulgar-türkisches Lehnwort in den slawischen Sprachen (*varkoč* 'Haarzopf') – Laut J.P., Ölmez M. (eds.), *Bahşı Ögdisi. Festschrift für*

Klaus Röhrborn anläßlich seines 60. Geburstags, Freiburg–İstanbul, 379–389.

1999

48. Turcyzmy w dialektach serbsko-chorwackich (2) – *PrJ* 119, 111–117.
49. Słownictwo pochodzenia orientalnego w utworach Adama Mickiewicza – Kurzowa Z., Cygal-Krupowa Z. (eds.), *Mickiewicz i Kresy. Rozprawy przedstawione na międzynarodowej sesji naukowej w Krakowie, 4–6 grudnia 1997*, Kraków, 230–246.
50. Słownictwo polskie w *Dykcjonarzu tureckim* Marcina Paszkowskiego (1615) – Brzezina M., Kurek H. (eds.), *Collectanea Linguistica in honorem Casimiri Polański*, Kraków, 243–253.
51. Das Suffix *-rak* in der osmanisch-türkischen Sprachgeschichte – *MT* 20, 59–71.

2000

52. François à Mesgnien Meninski ve *Thesaurus Linguarum Orientalium* – Franciscus à Mesgnien Meninski, *Thesaurus Linguarum Orientalium. Turcicæ-Arabicæ-Persicæ. Lexicon Turcico-Arabico-Persicum*, Stachowski S., Ölmez M. (eds.), 1, İstanbul 2000, xiii–xxii.
53. François à Mesgnien Meninski und sein *Thesaurus Linguarum Orientalium* – Franciscus à Mesgnien Meninski, *Thesaurus Linguarum Orientalium. Turcicæ-Arabicæ-Persicæ. Lexicon Turcico-Arabico-Persicum*, Stachowski S., Ölmez M. (eds.), 1, İstanbul 2000, xxiii–xxxiv.
54. Przyczynek do historii wyrazów polskich pochodzenia zachodnio-europejskiego – Wróbel H. (ed.), *Studia z filologii słowiańskiej ofiarowane profesor Teresie Zofii Orłoś*, Kraków, 237–241.
55. Turcyzmy w tekstach słowiańsko-rumuńskich 1. połowy XVII w. – Stępniak-Minczewa W., Boryś W. (eds.), *Sъkrovište slovesьnoje. Studia slawistyczne ofiarowane Profesorowi Jerzemu Ruskowi na 70. urodziny*, Kraków, 195–198.

2002

56. Slawizmy rumuńskie w słowniku łac.-rum.-węg. zwanym *Lexiconem Marsilianum* (1687–1700) – Rusek J., Boryś W., Bednarczuk L. (eds.), *Dzieje Słowian w świetle leksyki. Pamięci Profesora Franciszka Sławskiego*, Kraków 2002, 463–475.

2003

57. Turcyzmy w gwarze macedońskich wsi Suche i Wysoka w Soluńskiem – *PrJ* 121, 271–305.

2004

58. Wyrazy polskie w *Burattino Veridico* Giuseppe Misellego – Świątkowska M., Sosnowski R., Piechnik I. (eds.), *Maestro e Amico. Miscellanea in onore di Stanisław Widłak – Mistrz i Przyjaciel. Studia dedykowane Stanisławowi Widłakowi*, Kraków, 351–356.

2005

59. Osm.-tur. *yapunca* 'eine Art Mantel, Gewand' – *RO* 58/1 [= *Opera altaistica Stanislao Kałużyński octogenario dicata*], 204–207.
60. Turcyzmy w dialektach serbskich i chorwackich. 3. Turcyzmy w gwarze baczkich Buniewców – *PrJ* 112, 189–202.

2006

61. Osmanisch-türkisch *yoġurt* 'geronnene Milch, Joghurt' – Krasnowolska A., Maciuszak K., Mękarska B. (eds.), *In the Orient where the gracious light... Satura orientalia in honorem Andrzej Pisowicz*, Kraków, 185–189.
62. Źródła obce do historii słownictwa polskiego – Koniusz E., Cygan S. (eds.), *Staropolszczyzna piękna i interesująca* 1, Kielce, 53–67.

Reviews

1965

1. Škaljić A., *Turcizmi u narodnom govoru i narodnej književnosti Bosne i Hercegovine*, I–II, Sarajevo 1957 – *RS* 24, 162–171.

1966

2. Németh J., *Die Türken von Vidin. Sprache, Folklore, Religion*, Budapest 1965 (= *Bibliotheca Orientalis Hungarica* XIII) – *FO* 8, 243–247.

1979

3. Scherner B., *Arabische und neupersische Lehnwörter im Tschuwaschischen. Versuch einer Chronologie ihrer Lautveränderungen*, Wiesbaden 1977 – *FO* 20, 304–307.

1987

4. Podolsky B., *A Greek Tatar-English Glossary*, Wiesbaden 1985 – *FO* 24, 287–290.

1991

5. Seewann G. (ed.), *Historische Bücherkunde Südosteuropa* II, *Neuzeit*, 1: *Osmanisches Reich – Makedonien – Albanien*, München 1988 – *OLZ* 86/5–6, 544–547.

1993

6. Johanson L., *Linguistische Beiträge zur Gesamtturkologie*, Budapest 1991 – *FO* 29, 319.

1995

7. Prokosch E., *Osmanische Grabinschriften. Leitfaden zu ihrer sprachlichen Erfassung. Mit einem Anhang über seldschukische, Tavāʾi-fü-l-Mülük, frühosmanische, moderne zweisprachige und karamanische Grabinschriften*, Berlin 1993 – *OLZ* 90/1, 73–75.

1996

8. Zieme P., *Religion und Gesellschaft im Uigurischen Königreich von Qočo. Kolophone und Stifter des alttürkischen buddhistischen Schrifttums aus Zentralasien*, Opladen 1992 – *UAJb-NF* 14, 291–293.
9. Schubert G., *Kleidung als Zeichen. Kopfbedeckungen im Donau-Balkan-Raum*, Berlin 1993 – *OLZ* 91/2, 206–210.

Eulogies

1969

1. Sesja naukowa w związku z trzydziestoleciem zgonu Aleksandra Brücknera (31 V 1969) – *Studia Historyczne* 12/4 (47), 651–652.

1979

2. Die dem 30. Jahrestags des Todes von Prof. T. Kowalski gewidmete wissenschaftliche Sitzung – *FO* 20, 311–312.

1991

3. Śp. doc. dr hab. Tadeusz Pobożniak (1910–1991) – *Informacja nr 8/132 Sekretarza ds. prasowych UJ z dnia 8 marca 1991 r.*, 8.

Editorial work

1987

1. *Folia Orientalia*, journal of The Commission on Oriental Studies of the Polish Academy of Sciences in Kraków, editorship since volume 24 (1987) till volume 39 (2003).

1990

2. *Zeszyty Naukowe Uniwersytetu Jagiellońskiego – Prace Językoznawcze*, journal of the Faculty of Philology of the Jagiellonian University, Cracow, editorship since volume 102 (1990) till volume 122 (2005).

1995

3. *Studia Turcologica Cracoviensia*, Turcological series, foundation and editorship since volume 1 (1995) (last volume: 11 (2008)).

On Prof. Stanisław Stachowski

1. Stachowski Stanisław – *Dictionary of International Biography. A Biographical Record of Contemporary Achievement*, [26]1998, Cambridge, 437.
2. Stachowski Stanisław – Kawka T., *Leksykon I Liceum Ogólnokształcącego im. Jarosława Dąbrowskiego w Tomaszowie Mazowieckim 1903–1998. Sławni absolwenci, nauczyciele i rodzice uczniów szkoły*, Tomaszów Mazowiecki 1998, 117.

In print

1. Glosy włoskie w tekstach polskich z końca XVI w. – [FS M. Świątkowska].
2. Lista zestawień polskich turcyzmów F. Menińskiego (1680) – [FS M. Strycharska-Brzezina].
3. Warstwy etymologiczne turcyzmów polskich – [Sesja Polsko-Rusycystyczna Uniwersytetu Pedagogicznego, Kraków, grudzień 2009].
4. Słownik historyczno-etymologiczny turcyzmów w języku polskim, ca. 500 pp.

Articles

Studies on the Turkic World
A Festschrift for Professor St. Stachowski on the Occasion of His 80th Birthday
edited by E. Mańczak-Wohlfeld and B. Podolak, Kraków 2010: 3–22

Anna Dybo (Moskva)

Bulgars and Slavs: Phonetic Features in Early Loanwords

The earliest divergence of the Proto-Turkic language unity is the division into the 'Bulgar' and 'Common Turkic', or 'Standard Turkic' groups. A number of arguments (the dating of the Old Chinese loans into Proto-Turkic; different glottochronological calculations) force us to place this division into the time space on the boundary of the Christian Age, no later than the 3rd century A.D. The only offspring of the Bulgar branch still alive is Modern Chuvash, but the earlier stages of the proper Bulgar phonetic history are still reconstructable on the basis of the data of the early loans from the languages of the Bulgar group into other languages. The Bulgar loans into Hungarian, numbering about 400 words, are the most informative material for this topic.

Below are the phonetic features of the Bulgar group compared to the Standard Turkic ones.[1]

1) The development of the Proto-Turkic *λ, **lč*, **ř* into the Proto-Bulgar **l*, **lč*, **r*, (Danube and Volga Bulgar *l*, *lč* > *č*, *r*) but into Standard Turkic **š*, **š*, **z*;
2) The change **s* > *š* in the Proto-Bulgar before the Proto-Turkic **i*, **ı*, **ia*;
3) The lack of the voicing of the PT **t*- > ST **d*- before voiced obstruents, *λ, **r* and **ř*;
4) The Bulgar development *-*δ*- > *j* in stems containing *r*, and *-*δ*- > -*r*- in other contexts (chronologically, this process will be placed after the

[1] The last version of the PT reconstruction we are proceeding from appeared in Дыбо 2007, 5–64.

coincidence of *r and *ř in Bulgar, cf. Chuv. *xujər* 'bark' < PT **Kaδɨř*, ST *kadɨz*);

5) The preservation of the glide initials of the falling diphthongs in Bulgar and their disappearance in ST.

The Bulgar loanwords in Hungarian can be divided into two groups. In the first group the assumed appearance of the Turkic prototypes is very close to the Proto-Turkic stage (excluding the 'Bulgar palatalization': the change *s- > š- before *i, *ï). In the second group the prototypes appear to be extremely similar to the prototypes of Danube Bulgar loanwords in the South Slavic languages. So, the first group should be considered among 'the Pre-Conquest Layer' (Róna-Tas 1988, 752)—these were the loans occurring in the territory of Volga-Kama (or, as A. Róna-Tas now prefers to believe (Róna-Tas 2005, 436–438), Don-Kuban) area (5–7th centuries A.D.). The other group of the Bulgar loans in Hungarian are, apparently, the loans from the Danube Bulgar, which were acquired in the territory near present-day Hungary; the adaptation rules for their phonetics in Hungarian are almost identical to the adaptation rules of early Slavic loans, which appeared in Hungarian in the time period 'chronologically near to the Hungarian conquest of the Lower Danube region (895–900 A.D.)'—see Хелимский 2000, 422.

The recently collected material of Turkic loans in Slavic languages allows us to assert that two categories of Bulgar loanwords in Slavic can be distinguished: **1)** Words borrowed from the language of Danube Bulgars into the South Slavic languages (not to the Proto-Slavic, as it was considered earlier since it is chronologically impossible). These words incorporated into the Old Church Slavonic language spread into East Slavic and partly also into West Slavic languages with the literary language of the Slavic world. On historical grounds these loans should be dated as early as 8–9 A.D. **2)** Words borrowed from the language of Volga Bulgars into the East Slavic languages (on the Volga trade route) and partially spread on to the West Slavic languages, mostly to Polish. These borrowings should, apparently, be dated later, after the rise of the Volga Bulgar state.

Below I will examine the early Turkic loans into Slavic languages, focusing on the reflexes of the first syllable vowels.

I. 'Danube Bulgar' loanwords in Slavic, reflecting PT **a*, **ā*

The adaptation of *a* of the source language in early Slavic loanwords as *o* or *a* according to the primary brevity/length (cf. the similar reflection of Danube Bulg. *a*, *ā* from PT **ä, *ǟ* below) is, apparently, related to the existence of the indistinctive feature of vowel length in the Proto-Slavic and Early Slavic phonemic inventory. PSl. **a, *u, *y, *ě, *i* and nasalized **ǫ* and **ę* were long, PSl. **o, *e, *ъ, *ь* were short. Cf. the reflexes of first syllable Slavic vowels in Old Hungarian (Хелимский 2000, 422, Table 1):

Slavic	Old Hungarian	Slavic	Old Hungarian
**a* [ā]	*ā*	**y* [ȳ, ū]	*ī, i, ū*
**o* [o]	*å*	**i* [ī]	*ī, i*
**ě* [ē]	*ē*	**ь* (weak) > Ø	Ø
**e* [ɛ]	*a*	**ь* (strong) [i]	*i*
**u* [ū]	*ū, u*	**ǫ* [ũ]	*un*
**ъ* (weak) > Ø	Ø	**ę* [ĩ]	*in*
**ъ* (strong) [u]	*u*		

PT short **a* > Dan.-Bulg. **a* > Slavic *o*

**kovъčegъ:* Rus. *ковчéг*, Ukr. *ковчéг*, ORus., OChSl. ковъчегъ *κιβωτός, θήκη*, Bulgarian *ковчéг*, Srb.-Croat. *кȍвчêг* 'box, chest' (Фасмер II 272–273). PT **Kapyrčak* 'box, coffin' (ЭСТЯ 1997, 276); cf. Hung. *koporsó* 'coffin', fixed after 1372; *kaporsó, koparsó* (MNyTESz 2, 566), a Bulgar loan by *s* < **č*.

**doxtorъ* 'pillow': RusChSl. and OChSl. дохъторъ (Zogr.), дъхъторъ (Supr.) *προσκεφάλαιον*. Traditionally compared with OBulg. **ǯa/oɣδor*, Chuv. *śъDar, śïDar* 'pillow, bed' (Федотов 2, 158–159), incorrectly by Räsänen (VEWT 127), to the Mong. *ǯoɣdar* 'bunch of camel wool for stuffing pillow'. More reasonable would be to relate the Bulg. (and Chuv.) word to Turkic **jat-kur: *jat-* 'to lie' + *-kUr* deverb. noun of desire/supposition (cf. Щербак, Имя, 171–172). Cf. OT *jatuɣ* 'bunks', *jatuq* 'felt carpet' (cf. OChSl. ѧтъхѵльница 'cloister hotel' with the Kipchak reflex of PT **j-*, see Дыбо 2008a).

**tojagъ* 'cudgel, staff', ORus. *тояга* (Uspenskij Sbornik, XII cent.), ChSl. *тоягъ* (m.), *тояга* (f.), Bulgarian *тоя́га* (Младенов 636), Srb.-Croat. *тȍјага*, Chernogor. *тȍљага* (Фасмер IV 91). PT **daja-k* 'staff' (or rather **daj-n-a-k,* that is a derivate form of a reflexive verb), Chuv. *toja*, Yak. *tajax, taɟax*, Dolg. *tajax, tańak*, Tofa *daɟaq, tajaq,* OUig., QrqUig. *tajaq*, Tur. *dajak*, Az. *dajaG*, Trkm. *tajaq*, Tat. *tajak* (EDT 568, TMN 2, 445, Щербак 1997, 152). From PT **daja-* 'to prop up, to lean (smth.)', Refl. **daja-n-* 'to lean' (VEWT 455, EDT 567, ЭСТЯ 1980, 125–127, Федотов 2, 259–260).

**klobukъ* 'cap', Rus. *клобýк*, Ukr. *клобýк*, ORus., ChSl. *клобоукъ* (since the 12th cent.), Srb.-Croat. *клȍбӯк* 'cap, hat', Sloven. *klobúk* 'hat, helmet, base of roof timbers', Czech *klobouk* 'hat', Slovak *klobúk*, Polish *kłobuk, kobłuk* 'a high cap, klobuk', HSorb., USorb. *kłobuk*, Polab. *klüöbük* (Фасмер 2, 252, ЭССЯ 10, 61–62). PT **Kalpak* 'cap, hat' (ЭСТЯ 1997, 234–235). The voicing $p > b$ is remarkable. Cf. Hung. *kalpag* 'fur cap' (MNyTESz 1, 330), since 1653. The Hung. form is considered to be a Turkish loan (i.e. later than the 14th cent.), but cf. the final *-g* (not *-k*), which implies an earlier layer of loans.

**bojanъ* n.p., ORus. *Боян*, an ancient narrator in the 'Igor's tale', Bulgarian *Боян* (Фасмер I 203). The Turkic *Bajan*, name of an Avar khan in the 7th cent., of a Bulgar prince in the 8th cent. Considering the existence of such Turkic name, the Slavic etymology (M. Vasmer: 'The most evident relation is to *бой* 'fight''; but the affix is unknown) appears unlikely. The Turkic name is mostly related to the **bāj* 'wealthy', Chuv. *poj-* 'to be rich', Participle *poj-an* 'rich', Yak. *bāj*, Dolg. *bāj, bājdak, bājdïk*, Tuv. *baj*, Khakas *paj*, SarygUig. *pȧj*, OT *baj* (Orkhon, Yeniss., OUig.), QrqUig. *baj* (MK, QB), Chag. *baj*, Uzbek *bɔj*, MUig. *baj*, Tur., Gagauz, Az. *baj*, Trkm. *bāj*, Karaite, Kumyk, Balqar *baj*, Tat. *baj, bajtaq*, Bashq. *baj*, Nogai, Kazakh, Karakalpak, Kirgiz *baj*, Altai *baj, bajtaq* (EDT 384, VEWT 56, TMN 2, 259, ЭСТЯ 1978, 27–29, 36, СИГТЯ 2000, 304, 332, Федотов 1, 440). The derivational verification of the etymology forces us to suppose in this case a *-*γan* participle from the verb **bāj-* 'to grow rich'. But the tracing of the earliest occurrences in this case poses a problem. From the phonetic point of view it could be a Mongolian form (Turkic > Mongolian *bajan* 'rich' (KWb 29, Щербак 1997, 103), borrowed in modern (or late medieval) Turkic languages, particularly, as personal name: Kazakh, Altai *Bajan* etc.); then we have here the only reliable Mongolian loan in Danube Bulgar (cf. below about *хоругвь*). If we try to trace them to a Turkic form segment-by-segment, in congruence with the Modern Chuvash form, we should expect **bojxanъ* or **bojganъ* rather than **bojanъ* (cf. a Danube Bulgar title recorded in Greek, 9th cent.: *Βαγαΐνος*; The modern Slavic title *ban* (Bulg., Srb.-Croat. *бан*, Czech *bán*) is rather a loanword from Hung. *bán* 'a commander of a boundary fortress' etc.: the etymological dictionaries of Hungarian propose a Srb.-Croat. loan, but the first occurrence of the Hungarian word is dated by 1138 A.D., and at this time such contraction in Slavic is improbable; in the Old Hungarian, on the other hand, even a voiceless guttural could be dropped in the

intervocalic position). Apparently, the Turkic name shall be connected with another appelative, PT **baj* 'holy, blessed', Yak. *bajanaj* 'a name of a deity', QrqUig. *bajat* 'god' (MK—Argu, KB, Бор.ЛТ), Chag. *bajat* 'god' (Abush., Sangl.), Tur. *bajat* 'god', Trkm. *bajna-* 'be blessed, enjoy', Kirghiz *baj terek* 'Arbor mundi', Altai *baj-lu* 'sacred', *maj-* 'first component of some theonyms', *baj terek* 'Arbor mundi' (EDT 385, VEWT 56–57, TMN 2, 379, Аникин 109, 125–126); a Proto-Altaic etymology exists, see EDAL. Such Turkic forms as *bajat* formally are relic plural forms, the singulative/collective of which should be exactly like **bajan*, cf. Erdal 1991, 82, 91. The Yakut derivative is a vocative form from **bajan*, the Trkm. form is a denominative verb with *-a-*.
Cf. the borrowing in the East Slavic, apparently from Volga Bulgar, with the same reflex of the first vowel: only ORus. *Хопужьское море* 'Caspian sea', (the Pskov II Chronicle, in the hagiography of Alexandr Nevski), *Хупожское* id. (I Sophian Chronicle, 1242). Cf. Tur. *kapu* 'gate', also about the gate of Derbent (Temirkapu), and ORus. *Дербеньское море* 'Caspian sea'; see details in Vasmer, ZfslPh 24, 28, Фасмер IV 261. The PT derivatives from **kap-* 'to close' meaning 'gate, door' are as follows: **1)** **kap-ïg*; Orkh. *qapyγ*, OUig. *qapaγ*,[2] QrqUig. *qapuγ* MK, Middle Uig. *qapuγ* (Tafs.), Cuman. *kabak*, OKipch. *qapy, qapu* (Hou., AH) Modern Uig. *qapuq*, Tur. *kapı*, Az., Trkm. *Gapy*, Karaite, Kumyk, Nogai, Karakalpak *qapy*; **2)** Probably, **kap-gu* is reflected in the Middle Uig. *qapu* (Tafs.), Chag. *qapu* (if these are not Oghuz forms); **3)** **kap-ga*, *qapγa* MK, IM, Tat. *kapka* (> Chuv. *χapχa*) and similarly in other Kipchak and Karluk languages; see ЭСТЯ 1997, 274–275, TMN 3, 370–371, EDT 583. In Chuv. we have only one genuine derivative of **kap-*: *xobъ* 'lid, cover'. The Hung. form *kapu* 'gate', since 1009 (Lig. MNyTK 1, 10, MNyTESz 2, 367), could be derived from Osmanlï-Tur. *kapu* (as Doerfer supposed; so the short narrow vowel in the end could be explained, otherwise, in the case of **kap-ï*, it should be lost or, in the case of **kap-ïg*, become long. Cf. Hung. *kapucsi* 'door-keeper', since 1522, probably from Tur.), but early fixation contradicts such possibility. The Hung. word reflects either **kap-ïg* with an unclear development of the final vowel (final *-ïK* should become *-ú*), or **kap-gu* (else unattested; with a natural development *γ* > *v* > Ø after *p*). In both cases a Bulgar source is most likely; the first one agrees better with the ORus. form, but, finally, different Bulgar (Danube and Volga) dialects could have different derivates.

2 About the details of spelling of this word in Old Uigur see Erdal 1991, 190.

PT long *ā > Dan.-Bulg. *ā > Slavic *a*

samъčьjь* 'butler', OChSl. самъчии *ὁ οἰκονόμος, ὁ μειζότερος* (Фасмер III 554–555). Borrowed from OBulg. **sām-čï*, an agentive noun from the noun PT **sā-m*, Bulg. > Hung. *szám* 'cipher' (MNyTESz 3, 667), since 1086, Chuv. *sum* 'figure, counting', a name from PT **sā(j)-* 'to count, to believe', as a Refl. **sā-n-* (Chuv. *su-, sъv-*, Refl. *sun-*, Yak. *ā-x-*, Trkm. *sāj-*; Bulg. > Hung. *szán-* 'to pity' (MNyTESz 3, 672), since 1372), cf. Tur., Tat., Qazaq *san*, Trkm. *sān* 'figure, counting, quantity' (VEWT 390, EDT 781–782, ЭСТЯ 2003, 132–134, Федотов 2, 53). Apparently, the Modern Bulgarian *самсур* 'boor, lout' belongs here as a Dan. Bulg. loanword (sā-m* 'figure, respect' + *-*sUř* 'without', Chuv. *-sъr*, Standard Turkic *-sIz*).

**šaranъ*, South. Rus. dial. *шара́н* 'young sazan, carp', Ukr. *шара́н* id., Bulgarian *шера́н, шара́н*, Srb.-Croat. *ша̀ран*, Polish *szaran* (Фасмер IV 407–408). PT **siāř-an*, Bulg. **šāran*, Tuv., Khakas *sazan*, Uzbek dial. *sazan*, Tur., Gagauz, Az. *sazan*, Trkm. *sāzan*, Kumyk *sazan*, Bashq. *haδan, saδan* (dial.), Kazakh, Kirghiz *sazan* (VEWT 406, СИГТЯ 2000, 179, ЭСТЯ 2003, 147–148). Here two different ways of borrowing are possible for South and East Slavic languages.

Old Bulgarian *шатъръ*, Bulgarian *ша́тър, ша́тра*, ORus. **шатъръ* (G.Sg. *ни шатра имяше* in the chronicle tale about Svyatoslav), *шатоp* (Lavrentyevskaya Chronicle, in the hagiography of Boris and Gleb; Novgorodskaya I Chronicle; the form has a cleared-up *ъ), Ukr. *шатор*, Serbian ChSl. *шатьръ σκηνή* (apparently from a manuscript written by 'odnoyerovaya' orthography, i.e. the change ъ to ь is pure graphic), Srb.-Croat. *ша̂тра* 'counter, shop', Czech *šatr*, Polish *szatr* m., *szatra* f. 'Gypsy tent'. The ORus. forms as *шатеръ* (Georgiy Amartol, Lavrentyevskaya Chronicle), Instr. Pl. *шатьры* (Ipatyevskaya Chronicle), *шатерныи* (Novgorodskaya I Chronicle) represent a ChSl. loanword from a Serbian 'odnoyerovaya' form, possibly just through the Serbian source of the Georgiy Amartol; from the ChSl. form descended the Modern Rus. *шатёр, шатра́*. See Фасмер IV 413, Младенов 692, Skok. From PT (?), ST **čātur*. Bulg. **ćātur* > Hung. *sátor* 'tent' (MNyTESz 3, 500), since 1150 (as a placename), either 1200. Hung. > Srb.-Croat. *ша̀тор* 'tent', Slovenian *šátor*, Slovak *šiator*. Some researchers regard the Hung. word as a Slavic loan. Indeed the *o* in the second syllable could reflect the Slavic cleared-up *ъ, and the long *á* could reflect both the Turkic length and the Slavic *a*, see the table of Хелимский 2000, 422. So, we can suppose either the borrowing in Hung. from Early Bulgar and in Old Bulgarian (= OChSl.) from Danube Bulgar, or Danube Bulgar > Old Bulgarian > Hung.; the second hypothesis seems to be too complicated (somehow or otherwise, the South Slavic and Slovac forms with *-o-* are borrowed from Hung.). In other Turkic languages we have Tuv. *čadyr* 'wigwam, shelter', Tuv. dial. *čadyr* 'summer kitchen' (Сегл. РНДХР 153), Tofa *čadyr* 'reindeer enclosure' (Рас. 74); Khakas *sadyr* 'tent' (Верб. 283—Abakan), Shor *šadyr* id. (Верб. 441, Р IV 972); QrqUig. *čatyr*, *čašyr* (Oghuz), *čačyr* MK 'tent' (two last forms are obviously re-borrowings from Mongolian); LateOUig. (14th cent.) *kün čatyry* (Lig.VSOu 150) 'parasol, tent' (lit. 'sun *čatyr*'), Middle Uigur *čatyr* (IM 24) 'tent', *čadyr* (Бор.ЛТ 355) 'tent'; Middle Kipchak *čatyr* (CC 74) 'tent' (Abû H. 27), 'parasol' (Ettuhf. 161) 'izar (woman veil)'; Khorazm Turkic *čadyr* 'tent'; Chag. *čadir* 'fabric tent' (as opposed to the tent made with sticks and felt, the latter one is *ak öj* or *alaču*) Sangl.; Uzbek *čådir* 'tent; curtain; veil', Modern Uigur *čedir* 'roof, attic; tent'; Osmanli *čadyr* 'tent'; Tur. *čadyr* 'yurta, tent', Gagauz *čadyr* 'tent, parasol', Az. *čadyr* 'tent'; Trkm. *čādyr* 'tent'; Crimean Karaite *čadyr* 'tent', Trokai Karaite *čatyr* 'cottage'; Galich Karaite 'wagon, tent'; Kumyk *čatyr* 'tent, shelter', QBalqar *čatyr* 'tent', Tatar *čatyr* 'tent' (borrowed to Chuv. *čatər* 'tent, shed; curtain'), Bashq. *satyr* 'tent; *botanical* umbel', Nogai *šatyr* 'tent; cobweb', Karakalpak *šatyr* 'tent', Kazakh *šatyr* 'tent; roof'; Kirghiz *čatyr* 'tent; parasol; shed; roof', Altai *čadyr* 'tent; curtain; bark jurt', Teleut *šatyr* (Верб. 445).

For a description of the reality, denoted by *čadyr* in Turkic languages of South Siberia, see e.g. Пот. ОИА 309: 'conic tent made with poles and covered by larch bark' (cf. *čadyr ajyl* 'bark jurt'—Верб. 421). Turkic > Middle Mongolian *čačir* SH 25 'tent' (from a form where labial harmony already took its effect on the (–)-labiality, and *-y-* in the second syllable was interpreted as *i*), Khalkha *цацар* etc. See VEWT 101; EDT 403b; TMN III № 1042, СИГТЯ 2000, 497 and the works cited there. Normally the word is derived from Modern Persian *čādur, čādir, čādar* 'tent; veil', Middle Persian *čādur* 'veil' [čʾtwl] (CPD 21), cf. also Modern Persian *čatr* 'parasol (especially as a symbol of royal power); tent' (Гаф. 1, 132, Fazl. 201). The last form is most likely an Indian loanword, which came across the East Turkestan (Sanskr. *chattra* 'parasol' existing since Brahmanas; especially a royal parasol (under such parasols Indian kings marched off to campaign); *figuratively* umbellates; kind of mushroom) > Prakrit *chatta*, Panjabi *chatrī*, Lahnda *chattar* 'parasol' (Turner № 4972), derived from *chad-* 'to cover', Mayr. 1, 558).

Neither the corresponding root, nor the affix *-tra* are very popular in Iranian languages, cf. Аб. I 292; Цаболов 1, 224; ОИЯ. The form and meaning of the Proto-Turkic word could be adequately explained from the Modern Persian *čādur* (except the devocalization of the intervocalic resonant), but such explanation is poor from the point of view of the time depth; supposing a Middle Persian source is not good from the point of view of the meaning. It is possible that the meaning of the Modern Persian word was affected by the Turkic word, but most probably, the Modern Persian is a borrowing from Turkic, reflecting the Oghuz vocalization ($t > d$ after $\bar{a}$).[3] The Ossetic *catyr* 'tent' is also from Turkic (Аб. I 292). On the other hand, the development of the meaning 'tent' through 'royal tent' from 'royal parasol' seems quite possible. There are no other fixations of the word in Middle Iranian. For the Proto-Turkic form the voiceless *t* after the long *ā* (which vocalizes the *t* in Oghuz and Karluk languages) must be reconstructed by regular rules. We can suppose that the word was borrowed in PT from an unknown Middle Iranian language, where it would be either an etymon of Sanskrit *chattra*, i.e. Iranian **čad- + -tra* with a substitutive length, or an Indian loanword. Anyway, in the Saka Khotanese language a genuine name for royal parasol is attested: *śāhauja* 'parasol' < **sāyača-* < **sk'ai-* 'shadow' [Bailey 398], and it served as a source for QrqUig. *čowač* [MK] 'royal parasol' (EDT 395). Besides it, we have in Khotanese a word borrowed from Buddhist Hybrid Sanskrit, *kṣąttra* 'parasol' (*ysarrnā kṣąttra, śāhaujä, pale* 'golden parasols, canopies, banners' [K 48.3.2]). The same is the origin of Tocharian B *kṣātre* (~ *kṣāttre*) (n. [m.sg.]) 'umbrella', as D. Adams explains, 'from BHS **kṣattra-*, a hyper-Sanskritism of the more usual *chattra-*'. So, as early as 5–7th century A.D., the object was quite popular among Indo-European peoples of Eastern Turkestan; probably it appeared on the verge of our era in the Turkic-Iranian contact zone as such Indian loanword was emerging. Otherwise, we have to regard the Turkic word as genuine,[4] but, maybe, contaminated in Turkic languages of Central Asia with Modern Persian borrowing from Indian *čatr* 'parasol; tent' and also with Modern Persian (reflecting

[3] Cf. the supposition of K.G.Menges about Middle Persian [č'twl] being borrowed from Turkic (ВЭ 182–183).

[4] But by phonetical reasons (vowel length) not from Turkic **čat-* 'to come together at an acute angle (about beams)' (despite Németh J. Rev. of Brockelmann C. *Osttürkische Grammatik—OLZ*, 1953 № 5/6, 267); from the last a name with *-ma*: *čatma* 'nomade tent, shelter' is derived: СИГТЯ 2000, 499.

Middle Persian; also from Indian?) *čādur* 'veil'. Cf. TM **č/šita*: Evenki *čita, tita* 'birch bark', Lamut *titīk* 'shelter' (borrowed in Yakut *titīk* 'summer cattle-shed'), Negidal *tita* 'reed mat', Orok *čita, tita* 'bedding made of birch-bark; cover for a jurt made of birch-bark', Nanai *čita* 'reed mat' ССТМЯ 2, 189. Both the PT and the PTM words may have descended from PA ***č/šiat'V*.

? RusChSl. *брачина* (since the 12th cent.) 'a kind of silk fabric', OSerb. *брачинъ* id. (15–16th cent.) (Фасмер I 208–209). PT **bārčun*: OUig. Buddh. *barčyn*, QrqUig. *barčyn* QB, IbnM 'silc brocade'; further Xwarazm Turkic *barčyn* (Nahc-al-Faradis), Middle Kipchak *barčyn* (Abû H.) id., see EDT 357–358 (where a Tochar etymology is evidently false). From Turkic (phonetically from Bulgar) Hung. *bársony* 'brocade, velvet' is borrowed. New Turkic languages: only Chuv. *purśən / porśəm* 'silk fabric', Chuv. (late Volga Bulgar?) > Rus. *бурсá* 'Persian silk fabric' (Фасмер I 208–209) and in Volga-Finnic languages: Mari *порсын, парсын*, Udmurt *буртчин* etc. (Федотов 1, 447). Turkic is from Middle Persian *abrēšom* [*'plyš(w)m*, Manichean *'bryšwn*] 'silk' (CPD 4), Persian *abrēšum* < **abi-raiš-* 'to spin', see Аб. I 132, Цаболов 1 15–16. The Persian word is borrowed in many languages with the same meaning. The Modern Persian word is the source for Turkish *ibiršim*, and Modern Uigur (R: Tarantschi) *äbrišin* 'silk', cf. Persian *berīšem*. Formally **bārčun* could be a loanword in Proto-Turkic, connected with early stages of the Silk Road functioning. Indeed, as early as by Sasanide Empire (since 224 A.D.) Iran received floss in abundance and there were many textile mills; by August (27 B.C.–14 A.D.) Persian silk, probably through Parthians, reached Rome. Another possibility is to assume a layer of 'bazaar loanwords' (exposed to the phonetic adaptation) in Early Bulgar from Turkic languages of Central Asia. The primary length of the first vowel is confirmed by the length in Hungarian (see Дыбо 2009); also cf. the long vowel in the Middle Persian source. For Slavic form, the *-ч-* is unclear, cf. Hung. *-s-* = Bulgar *-ś-* (regular reflexes of PT **č* except the position before **i*, **ï*, cf. самъчии above, Hung. *ács* 'carpenter' from **ạgač-čï*). Maybe, not from Bulgar, but from some Kypchak dialect?

The complicated case is OChSl. халѫга 'fence, enclosure', *φραγμός*, RusChSl. *халуга* 'paling, fence' (Yuryevskoe ev., in 1119), also 'street' (Efremovskaya Kormchaya; see Срезн. III, 1359), Rus. dial. *халýжина* 'long switch', Ukr. *халýга* 'seaweed', Blr. *халýга* 'twig-maid shelter', Srb.-Croat. *xàлуга* 'weed, thicket, cleft', Slovenian *halóga* 'thicket, bushes; seaweed', OCzech *chalužník* 'highway robber' (Фасмер IV 218–219).

As a possible source for this word we propose the Danube Bulgar reflex of PT *(h)ā/ala-ŋ '(forest) glade, copse, water meadow': Bulg. *halaŋ-uk > Chuv. *olъх* 'water meadow', Yak. *alās* (< *(h)alaŋ-ač), *alï̄* (< *(h)alaŋu), Dolg. *alïn, alï*, Tuv. *alāk* (*(h)alaŋ-uk),[5] QrqUig. *alaŋ* (MK), Chag. *alaŋ* (Pav. C.); Tur. *alan*, Trkm. *alaŋ*, Karaite *alaŋ*, Tat. *alan*, Nogai, Kazakh, Karakalpak *alaŋ* (EDT 147; ЭСТЯ 1974, 134–135, Федотов 2, 277). Yak. *alās* > Rus. Sib. *alás* (Аникин 80–81). PT < PA *p'ā̀là, EDAL. But the length/shortness of the first *a in Proto-Turkic is not verifiable for this word. The Trkm. and Yakut forms may have been secondarily shortened. For Yakut it is normal in a polysyllabic word, see Stachowski 1992, 42–45. For Turkmen cf. the shortening of a derivate with the same affix: *ȫl* 'damp', *öleŋ* 'meadow'. M. Erdal (Erdal 1991, 160–161) proposes to consider *öleŋ* as a Mongolian loanword but such hypothesis is not obligatory. Another case of PT *h-, remaining in Danube Bulgar, reflecting PA *p'- is Slavic *xorǫgy, -ъve* 'banner, gonfalon', see below.

A marginal case is ORus., ChSl. *бълванъ, болванъ, блаванъ* (12th cent.) (Срезн. 1, 197–198), Ukr. *боввáн* 'idol; a lump', Belorus. *балвáн* 'post, pole', Middle Bulgarian *балванъ* (12th cent.) 'statue' (Mi. LP. 11), Bulgarian, Macedonian *балван*, Srb.-Croat. *ба̀лван, бо̏ва̄н* 'idol, beam', Slovenian *balvân* 'idol, beam, lump', *bolvân* 'idol, lump', Czech *balvan* 'lump', Slovak *bolvan*, Polish *bałwan* 'big stone, lump'. As Proto-Slavonic prototypes the forms *bъlvanъ and *bal(ъ)vanъ were proposed (the latter one appeared in several languages as a result of vowel assimilation from *bъlvanъ) (Фасмер I 186–187, ЭССЯ 3, 121). We point out that the assertion, that the protoform *bъlvanъ explains most of Slavic forms, is absolutely wrong: such protoform can explain only East Slavonic (with ORus.) and a part of Slovenian forms.[6] The East Slavonic

[5] Tuv. *alandï, alaŋgï* 'thawed patch', as also Trkm. *āla* 'plain dappled by small sandy plots', Tur. dial. *ala* 'fallow plots on the ploughed field', regarding their meaning, are rather derived from *āla 'variegated', see e.g. Татаринцев I 93.

[6] For the diversity of reflexes of *ъl cf. ORus. *вълна*, OChSl. влъна, Bulgarian *вълнá*, Czech *vlna*, Polish *wełna* 'wave'; Ukr. *вóвна*, Belorus. *вóўна*, ORus. *вълна ἔριον*, Bulgarian *вълна*, Srb.-Croat. *ву̑на*, Slovenian *vólna*, Czech *vlna*, Slovak *vlna*, Polish *wełna*, High Sorbian *wołma*, Lower Sorbian *wałma* 'sheep wool'; Ukr. *полк*, ORus. *пълкъ*, OChSl. плъкъ *φάλαγξ, παράταξις* (Supr.), Bulgarian *пълк*, Srb.-Croat. *пу̑к* 'народ, толпа', Czech, Slovak *pluk* 'куча', Polish *pułk* 'полк', High Sorbian *połk* 'полк', Ukr. *вовк*, ORus. *вълкъ*, OChSl. влькъ, Bulgarian *вълк*, Srb.-Croat. *ву̑к*, Slovenian *vôłk*, Czech, Slovak *vlk*, Polish *wilk*, High Sorbian *wjelk*, Lower Sorbian *wel'k* 'волк'.

**bъlvanъ* is supported by East Baltic **búlvānos* > Lithuanian *bulvõnas*[7] 'eiserner Knopf am Peitschenende, rundes Ding, Blase, großer Knoten', Lettish *bũlvāns* 'ausgestopfter Vogel, um Wildherbeizuziehen, Lockvogel'; Lithuanian *balvõnas* 'Gott, Abgott, Götze, Götzenbild', also 'Ölgotze, stumpfsinniger Mensch', was borrowed later from early West Russian *bolvan*, see Fraenkel I 33, 64. In Hung. we have *bálvány* 'idol', since 1001 (MNyTESz 1, 234). The word is related to OT *bAlbal* 'a stone pillar in the funeral complex, idol' (EDT 333). The etymology of the Turkic word is extremely difficult. OT may be a Mongolian loan, from Early Mongolian **bari-βal* > Written Mongolian *barimal* 'sculpture', however, see the critique of the hypothesis in Дыбо 2007, 182–183 (Mong. *barimal* is rather a Khalkha innovation). The impossibility of the hypotesis of Radlow about a Chinese origin for *balbal* was demonstrated by K. Menges (Менгес ВЭ 88–89). The Turkic word has an unrepresentative structure which suggests a secondary rebuilding as a reduplication. So, to explain Slavic and Hungarian borrowings a PT form like **balba-n* should be found. We can detect some evidence of such form in Chuv. *popla* 'игра в чушки' (Аш. IX, 291). The game *чушки* or *городки* consists of throwing a bat at one or several wooden cylindrical bars vertically placed in a square, somehow marked on the ground. These bars are named *чушки* or *рюхи* in Russian; probably, *popla* was their Chuvash name (with a metathesis). If we accept this cognate, another may be Yakut *balbaax* 'длинная смерзшаяся глыба навоза (*balbaax saax*), кислого молока (*balbaax tar*), квашеной рыбы и т.п. в большом объеме' (Пек. I 350) ('a long frozen lump of dung, sour milk, fermented fish, etc. in large quantities'). Cf. dial. *balbān, balbār* 'ice-cellar' (ДСЯС 47), probably contaminated or borrowed from Russian *подвал* 'cellar'. In Popov's etymological dictionary (Попов 2003, 115–116) the word is, following Kałużyński II 72, etymologized from Yakut *балбай-* 'to seem too wide and soft', a descriptive verb related to ideophone *балк* 'sound of a falling big piece of jelly-like matter'; the semantical derivation would be rather good for 'dung', but not for 'frozen matter'.[8] Also it can be a derivate with similative **-gak*

7 The position of stress in Lithuanian is probably the result of influence from *balvõnas*.

8 This descriptive word family may be borrowed from Mongolian, but possible Mongolian sources of descriptive words also do not have appropriate meanings for *balbaax*; these are Khalkha *balba-* 'to beat, to knock', *balba-la-* 'to smash to pieces', *balba-gar* 'squat; tattered, shapeless (garment)', *balba-lʒa-* 'to swing; to shake; to pulsate'; Buryat *balbaj-* 'to be plump, to expand', *balbagar* 'plump; shaking',

from some **balba*, as OT *qadïzγaq* 'callosity' from *qadïz* 'bark' and OT *müŋüzgäk* 'hard skin on hands' from *müŋüz* 'horn' (Erdal 1991, 74). The word *балбааччы* 'аляповатый, неуклюжий, неотесанный, грубой отделки, топорной работы / аляповато, некрасиво, грубо' ('crude, coarse, clumsy / coarsely, crudely') is etymologized by Popov as **balbal-sïg* 'alike to *balbal*' following Менгес ВЭ 89. But it is phonetically impossible: *-s-* in clusters does not give *-č-* in Yakut, cf. e.g. *-tar* as an affix of Conditionalis. According to Дьячковский 2, 63, *-čč-* can descend from *-lč-*, *-nč-*, *-rč-*, *-sč-*, *-tč-* or *-kč-*. So *балбааччы* may be derived from Yakut *balbaax* by the adverbial affix *-čï* (probably < locative **-ču* (Erdal 1991, 108)), which mostly forms adverbs from verbal stems (*olorču* 'vertically', *kïtarčï* 'until smth. is red').

If these words are really related to **balban* 'statue', then it should be noted that the stem tends to contaminate with Turkic *balaban* 'big, massive', see ЭСТЯ 1978, 50, also Аникин РЭС 2, 112–113. The result of such contaminaton may be the same descriptive verb *балбай-* in Yakut and Oyrot (borrowed to Mongolian from Middle Turkic?) and such derivates as Tatar dial. *balban* 'too plump, heavy'. Kirg. *balbal* mentioned by Менгес ВЭ 87 (following Melioranskiy), 'a small plot edged by a low cob wall', is probably borrowed from Persian *pulvān* 'a such cob wall' id., derived from Persian *pul* 'bridge'. There is a possibility to attach this word to Turkic *balbal* (it would not be so bad from the semantic point of view, since enclosures were characteristic for Old Turkic and pre-Turkic funeral complexes). Persian *pul* is from **pr̥tu-* 'bridge' (Horn 72, Расторгуева 1990, 108, Эдельман 1986, 179, Цаболов II, add Sogdian *prtʾw* [*partaw*] 'bench' Harib 7238) and Proto-Iranian *-rt-* > cerebral consonants in South East Iranian languages, as in Khotanese Saka, where it is regular *-ḍ-* (Эдельман 1986, 179). But *-ḍ-* regularly substitutes Turkic *-l-* , when Turkic words are spelled in Khotanese texts. If we would suppose a Pre-Khotanese reflex of ***pr̥tu-āna-* 'related to the bridge' (about the affix see ОИЯ 1981, 305), it would be something like *päḍvan* and could mean 'funeral enclosure', so, such a word could be a source for Turkic **balba-n*. Cf. also an Altaic etymology for Turkic **balba-n* in EDAL. The Ket *bal'be-ś*^{6} 'cross; idol' ('object of prayer') cited by Menges is not related to the Turkic word, as it is a derivate

---

balba- 'to mash', *balbal-* 'to smash to pieces'. Undoubtely from *balbaj-* in Yakut *balbaččï* is derived: *balbaččï olor* 'to sit, having a plump body spreading widely' (Харитонов 1954, 213).

from Yeniss. **baŕ-* (~ -r_1-) 'to pray', cf. Ket *bal'bɛt*[6], *balvɛt*[6] 'to pray', lit. 'to make a prayer' CCE 206.

So, rather, we shall accept diverse Bulgar sources for Slavic forms; the primary quality/quantity of the first vowel cannot be verified yet.

II. Danube loanwords in Slavic, containing PT *ä, *ā̈

Evidently, both Old Bulgar languages, Volga Bulgar and Danube Bulgar, changed PT **ä* > *a*; the result of this change we observe now in all dialects of Modern Chuvash. At the same time the primary length opposition retained up to a certain moment, judging by loanwords in Slavic.

PT short *ä > Dan.-Bulg. *a > Slav. *o*

Srb.-ChSl. *огаръ* 'foxhound', Srb.-Croat. *ȍгар*, Slovenian *ogar, -rja*, Czech *ohař*, Polish *ogar*, Lower Sorbian *hogoŕ* (Фасмер III 117), ORus. *огаръ* 'foxhound, greyhound', under 1520, in a document dealing with Poland, probably a Polish loanword, see Stachowski 1995, 104. Despite Vasmer's opinion, it is unlikely that ORus. *огаръ* 'a kind of ship' is related (*ѽгары трегребныя* 'trieras' (Иос. Флав. 225, 233, Acc. Pl.); M. Vasmer relates it with the name of foxhound through the feature of swiftness, cf. Greek *δρόμων* 'a swift sailer', but the last is a light ship, and the trieras are not). PT **äker* 'hound', Bulgar > Chuv. *agar jïtti*, Shor *eger*, Chag. *iger* (Буд.), Kumyk *eger*, QBalqar *eger* 'hound, greyhound, foxhound', Tatar (Sib.), Bashq. *igɛr* 'a hybrid of a wolf and a dog', Altai *eger* (VEWT 38, 23). From Danube Bulgar descends also Hung. *agár* 'foxhound' (MNyTESz 1: 101), since 1193. An earlier loanword from Ancient Bulgar is Ossetic *egar* 'foxhound'. Avar *эгер* is probably borrowed from Kumyk. Ingush *эр* 'greyhound, foxhound', Chechen *эре* id. (*d*-class) are not necessarily related (but it will be useful to ascertain the reflexes of Bulgar *-k-* in the borrowings to the Proto-Chechen-Ingush). Kabardinian *ħaǵer* is also cited (Аб. I 411) (after Корш 1913, *hager* 'foxhound'); the status of this form is unclear. The Kabardinian-Russian Dictionary does not contain such word; only *ħa* 'dog', (orthographically *хъэ*) is found there; 'foxhound' is *самыр*, 'greyhound' is compounded *хъэджэафэ*. See in particular Stachowski 1995 about the problem of Tur. *zogar*, Srb.-Croat. *за̏гар* id., Middle Greek *ζαγάριον* etc. (cf. for this Megrelian *зогор* 'dog'); but it seems to be evident that in Hung. and Slav. we have, nevertheless, a Danube Bulgar loan (Dan.-Bulg. **ager*?). The interpretation of Bulgar front vowel as a back one in the second syllable can be caused by the guttural, cf. in the first syllable: *кънига* 'book': PT **kün-ig*; *кържыга* 'litter': PT **kürk* 'fur, cover', but *тьма* '10,000': PT **tümen* id.

? Rus. *коври́га* 'a round-loaf of bread' (Avvakum 265), Belorus. *каврі́га*, ORus. *коврига* id., Lavrentyevskaya Chronicle, under 1075 and others (Срезн. I, 1242), Bulgarian *коври́г* 'pasty' (> Romanian *covrig* (Младенов 244)). Фасмер II 272. (?) Turkic **gäbrek* > Tur. *gevrek* 'a kind of pita', Gagauz 'biscuit' (from Tur. is borrowed Bulg. *гевре́к* 'bagel'). This old etymology, as Vasmer thinks, runs across some phonetic difficulties; but they can be removed if we treat a Danube Bulgar form (**kavrek*) as the source. The Turkic word means a type of bread only in Middle Kipchak *kewrek* 'biscuit' (AH), 'ship biscuit' (Bulg.), Turkish and Gagauz (Chuv. *кавринкке* 'round-loaf' is probably from Russian). Reflexes in other languages are as follows: Yak. *кэбирэх* 'fragile, brittle', Dolg. *кэбирэк* 'lacerated, ragged', Tuv. *хээрэк* 'fragile, of poor quality', Shor (Kondoma) *kebrek* (Верб. 168), Khakas *kibərek* 'fragile, brittle, unstable', QrqUig. *kevrek* (MK) 'fragile (a k. of timber)', Uzbek *кyврак* 'crispy' (about fruits, vegetables), Az. *kövräk* 'friable, crumbly', Tat. dial. (Sib.) *köjräk* 'fragile, toasted', Bashk. dial. *köjrök* 'fragile' (timber, for example) (БТДҺ 150), Kazakh *küjrek* 'unstable'. See EDT 690, ЭСТЯ 1980, 7; a derivate from **geber-* 'break', Trkm. *güjür-*, Kirghiz *küjrö-*. The shortness of the vowel is confirmed (not too reliably) by Yakut and Dolgan forms and quite reliably by Turkmen form (*-*ā̈b*- should give -*ā̈v*-, cf. Trkm. *gā̈vüš* 'cud').

Cf. also the Volga Bulgar loanword in East Slavic: Rus. *ковёр*, Gen. -*вра́*, Ukr. *ко́вер*, ORus. *ковьръ* (The Tale about Boris and Gleb in Lavrentyevskaya Chronicle and others) 'carpet'. Romanian *covor*, Lithuanian *kaũras, kaurà* borrowed from Slavic (Фасмер II 270–271). Alongside with these forms, cf. Czech *koberec, kober*, Polish *kobierzec*, Bulg. *гу́бер* id.: for West Slavic forms with -*b*- a Danube Bulgar origin is possible (cf. OChSl. боубрегъ: PT **bögrek* > **bövrek* 'kidney'); but the Bulgarian form (particularly -*ý*-) is not explicable in that case and should be treated as a loanword from an unknown source. Ultimately from PT **gäbir* or **gäbüř* 'carpet', Danube Bulgar, Volga Bulgar (Old Chuvash) **kavər*, Tuv. *xevis*, Khakas *kibəs*, Shor *kemis*, SarygUig. *γïγïs* 'carpet' (Тен. ССЮЯ); QrqUig. *keviz, köwüz* (MK), Chag. *kebiz* (MA), Middle Kipchak *köwüz* (CCum.), *kevüz* (AH); Tur. dial. (Kipchak) *köüz*, Kumyk dial. (Qaytaγ) *guuz*, Balkar *küwüz, küjüz*, Bashk. *köjöð*, Noghai *küjiz*, Altai, Teleut, Qumandy, Tuba *kebis* (EDT 692,

ЭСТЯ 1997, 83). Quoted by Vasmer Qazaq *kijiz*, Tat. *kijez* mean 'felt' and belong to another etymon: PT **kiδiz* 'felt'. Turkic > Mongolian *kebis* (> Manchu *kebisu* etc., see ССТМЯ 1, 444) 'carpet', Kalmuck *kews*; see Clark 1980, 39.

PT long *ä > Dan.-Bulg. *ā > Slav. *a*

OChSl. капь f. *εἴδωλον* 'appearance', *εἰκών* 'statue, idol', капнште (borrowed in Rus. *кáпище*) 'heathen temple', Bulgarian *кáпище* (Фасмер II 185–186, Младенов 231). From Danube Bulgar **kāp* < PT **g̈āp* 'form, exemple, image', Early Bulgar > Hung. *kép* (ɛ̄/ē̆) (unaltering length) 'appearance, portrait' (MNyTESz 2: 447–448), since 1315[9]; Volga Bulgar > Chuv. *kap*; Yak. *kiep*, Trkm. *g̈āp* (EDT: 686, VEWT: 253, ЭСТЯ 1997: 44–45). From Chuvash Mari *kap* 'body, figure', Komi *kab* 'boot-tree' are borrowed.

The reflection of the Bulgar vowel length opposition, descending from the ProtoTurkic opposition, also appears in the words borrowed into Slavic in some other cases. Most clearly one can see it on the examples of PT **o*, **ö*. Cf.:

PT **o*: **1)** OChSl. хоржгъı: PT **horuŋgu* 'flag' > Danube Bulgar **horъŋgu* EDT 362; **2)** OChSl. сокачнн 'butcher': PT **sok-* 'to slaughter' + **-či* > Danube Bulgar **soqъčə* (EDT 805, СИГТЯ 2000, 396); **3)** (from Volga Bulgar) East Slavic *воръ*: PT **ogrï* 'thief' (Early or Danube Bulgar **ovrъ* > Hung. *or*, *orv* (MNyTESz 2, 1096), since 1131; Volga Bulgar > Chuv. *vъrъ* 'thief') (EDT 90, ЭСТЯ 1974, 412–414, TMN 2, 77–78).

PT **ō*: **1)** OChSl. ваıатн (borrowed in Rus. *ваять*) 'to sculpture, to carve'. If not from *вить* 'to weave', then: PT **ōj-* 'to carve, to chisel, to dig up' > Danube Bulgar **vāj-* (ЭСТЯ 1974, 425–428, 434); **2)** Slavic **kvarъ* 'harm, damage' (South Slavic, Slovak, Gutsul) (ЭССЯ 13: 150) (intra-Slavic derivation, suggested there, is unconvincing): PT **kōr* 'harm, loss, damage', Danube Bulgar **qvār* > Hung. *kár* 'harm' (Lig. MNyTK 1: 3–4, MNyTESz 2: 370), since 1019; (EDT: 641–642, 645–646, ЭСТЯ 2003: 73–74, Федотов 2: 369); **3)** Slavic **tvarogъ* 'cottage cheese' (Фасмер IV 31–32): PT **dōrak* 'cheese', Danube Bulgar **tvāraq*, Volga Bulgar > Chuv. *tъvara*; Early Bulgar > Hung. *túró*

[9] On the difference of vowel reflexes in Hungarian loans from Early Bulgar and Danube Bulgar see Дыбо 2009.

'cottage cheese' (MNyTESz 3: 1005; TMN 3, № 1195, VEWT: 490, ЭСТЯ VIII); **4)** (From Volga Bulgar) ORus. *ватага* 'шатер' (only East Slavic) (Фасмер I 278): PT **ōtag* 'tent, nomade dwelling', Volga Bulgar **vātaγ* (EDT 46, VEWT 366, ЭСТЯ 1974, 484–487, TMN 2, 66–67, Дыбо 2008).

PT **ö*: **1)** Rus. ChSl., Serbian ChSl. *боубрьгъ, боубрекъ* (Bulgarian *бӯбрек*, Srb.-Croat. *бȕбрег*): PT **bögrek* > (?) Danube Bulgar **buvrek* > **bubrek* (*-br-* under the ifluence of the initial *b*-, cf. Modern Turkish *böbrek*) 'kidneys' (EDT 328, TMN 2, 353, ЭСТЯ 1978, 205–207, СИГТЯ 2000, 278); Volga Bulgar > Chuv. *püre* 'kidneys' (contracted); **2)** Rus. ChSl., Bulg. ChSl. *курълъкъ σχῆμα, τύπος* 'appearance, form, shape', RusChSl. *курилъ τύπος* 'form', 'mould' (rederivation? A late Novgorod form, 16th cent., with the Novgorod shift *ъ* > *u*) (Фасмер II 425, Срезневский 1, 1380, 1378): Turkic **görüg-lük* > (?) Danube Bulgar **kurəv/jlək* 'shape, appearance' from **gör-* 'to see' (EDT 743, ЭСТЯ 1980, 81) (cf. slightly otherwisely by Pritsak UAJb., 29, 1957, 212–213).

PT **ȫ*: **1)** OChSl. вєрнга *ἄλυσις* (South Slavic, Russian): PT **ȫr-ük* (from PT **ȫr-* 'to weave' > Hung. *ver-*), cf. Chuv. *vər-en* 'thigh rope' (ЭСТЯ 1974, 544–546; **2)** (From Volga Bulgar) Rus. *бирю́к* 'lone wolf; unsociable person': PT **bȫrö* 'wolf' > Bulgar **bire-g* > West Ossetian *berœg*, East Ossetian *birœg* (Аб. I 262–263); Volga Bulgar > Mari *pirə, pirəg* 'wolf'. A different reflex we can see in Serbian Church Slavic *колимогъ*, ORus. ChSl. *колимагъ* 'tent', West Slavic, Rus. 'a kind of vehicle' (Фасмер II 291): PT **gȫl-* 'to harness' > OUig. *kölüŋü* 'vehicle' (EDT 719). Probable, as in the case of OChSl. ѧтъχѵльница 'cloister hotel' (see above), it is an Old Kipchak, not a Bulgar, loanword.

Literature

Аб.: Абаев В.И. *Историко-этимологический словарь осетинского языка.* I–V. Москва–Ленинград, 1958–1995.

Абуш.: Вельяминов-Зернов В.В. *Словарь джагатайско-турецкий.* Санкт-Петербург, 1868.

Аникин: Аникин А.Е. *Этимологический словарь русских диалектов Сибири. Заимствования из уральских, алтайских и палеоазиатских языков.* Москва–Новосибирск, 2000.

Ашм.: Ашмарин Н.И. *Словарь чувашского языка.* 1–17. Казань–Чебоксары, 1928–1950.

Бор.ЛТ: Боровков А.К. *Лексика среднеазиатского тефсира XII–XIII веков.* Москва, 1963.

БТДҺ: *Диалектологический словарь башкирского языка.* Уфа, 2002.

Буд.: Будагов Л. *Сравнительный словарь турецко-татарских наречий.* I. Санкт-Петербург, 1869; II. Санкт-Петербург, 1871.

Верб.: Вербицкий В. *Словарь алтайского и аладагского наречий тюркского языка.* Казань, 1884.

Гаффаров: Гаффаров М.А. *Персидско-русский словарь.* I. Москва, 1914; II. Москва, 1927; Переизд.: I–II. 1974.

Дыбо 2007: Дыбо А.В. Лингвистические контакты ранних тюрков. Лексический фонд. Пратюркский период. Москва, *Восточная литература*, 2007.

Дыбо 2008: Дыбо А.В. Материальный быт ранних тюрок. Жилище // *Природное окружение и материальная культура пратюркских народов.* Москва, 2008.

Дыбо 2008a: Дыбо А.В. К кыпчакским заимствованиям в славянских языках // *Материалы международной науч-практ. конф.* Россия и Башкортостан: история отношений, состояние и перспективы. Уфа, 2007.

Дыбо 2009: Дыбо А.В. Вокализм раннетюркских заимствований в венгерском. // *E. Helimskii in memoriam.* Wiesbaden, 2009.

ЗКВ: *Записки коллегии востоковедов.*

Корш 1913: Корш Ф.Е. Несколько лингвистических данных для исторической этнографии Восточной Европы // *Сборник в честь 70-летия проф. Д.Н.Анучина.* Москва, 1913.

Менгес ВЭ: Менгес К.Г. *Восточные элементы в «Слове о полку Игореве».* Ленинград, 1979.

Младенов: Младенов С. *Етимологически и правописен речник на българския книжовен език.* София, 1941.

ОИЯ 1981: *Основы иранского языкознания. Древне- и среднеиранские языки.* Москва, 1981.

Попов 2003: Попов Г.В. *Этимологический словарь якутского языка.* I. Новосибирск, 2003.

Пот. ОИА: Потапов Л.П. *Очерки по истории алтайцев.* Новосибирск, 1948.

Р: Радлов В.В. *Опыт словаря тюркских наречий: В 4-х томах.* Санкт-Петербург, 1899–1911.

Рас. ФиЛ: Рассадин В.И. *Фонетика и лексика тофаларского языка.* Улан-Удэ, 1971.

Расторгуева 1990: Расторгуева В.С. *Сравнительноисторическая грамматика западноиранских языков.* Москва, 1990.

Сегл. РНДХР: Сегленмей С.Ф. Особенности речи населения Дзун-Хемчакского района // *Вопросы тувинской филологии.* Кызыл, 1983.

СИГТЯ 2000: *Сравнительно-историческая грамматика тюркских языков: Лексика.* Москва, 2000.

Срезн.: Срезневский И.И. *Материалы для словаря древнерусского языка по письменным памятникам.* I–III. Санкт-Петербург, 1893–1912.

ССЕ: Старостин С.А. Сравнительный словарь енисейских языков // *Кетский сборник.* Москва, 1995.

ССТМЯ: *Сравнительный словарь тунгусо-маньчжурских языков.* I–II. Ленинград, 1975–1977.

Фасмер: Фасмер М. *Этимологический словарь русского языка. В 4-х томах.* Москва, 1964–1973.

Федотов: Федотов М. Р. *Этимологический словарь чувашского языка.* 1–2. Чебоксары, 1996.

Харитонов 1954: Харитонов Л.Н. *Типы глагольной основы в якутском языке.* Москва–Ленинград, 1954.

Хелимский Е.А. Венгерский язык как источник для праславянской реконструкции и реконструкции славянского языка в Паннонии. // Е.А. Хелимский. *Компаративистика, уралистика.* Москва, Языки русской культуры, 2000: 416–432.

Цаболов: Цаболов Р.Л. *Этимологический словарь курдского языка.* Т. I. Москва, 2001. Т. II (*в печати*).

Щербак, Имя: Щербак А.М. *Очерки по сравнительной морфологии тюркских языков: Имя.* Ленинград, 1977.

Щербак (1997): Щербак А. М. *Ранние тюркско-монгольские языковые связи (VIII-XIV вв.).* СПб, 1997.

Эдельман 1986: Эдельман Д. И. *Сравнительная грамматика восточноиранских языков. Фонология.* Москва, 1986.

ЭССЯ: *Этимологический словарь славянских языков.* Под ред. О.Н. Трубачова. Москва, 1974–.

ЭСТЯ 1974: Севортян Э.В. *Этимологический словарь тюркских языков. Общетюркские и межтюркские основы на гласные.* Москва, 1974.

ЭСТЯ 1978: Севортян Э.В. *Этимологический словарь тюркских языков. Общетюркские и межтюркские основы на букву «Б».* Москва, 1978.

ЭСТЯ 1980: Севортян Э.В. *Этимологический словарь тюркских языков. Общетюркские и межтюркские основы на «Г», «Д».* Москва, 1980.

ЭСТЯ 1997: *Этимологический словарь тюркских языков: Общетюркские и межтюркские основы на буквы «К», «Қ»* / Авт. сл. статей Л.С. Левитская, А.В. Дыбо, В.И. Рассадин. Москва, 1997.

ЭСТЯ 2000: *Этимологический словарь тюркских языков: Общетюркские и межтюркские основы на букву «Қ»* / Авт. сл. статей Л.С. Левитская, А.В. Дыбо, В.И. Рассадин. Москва, 2000.

ЭСТЯ 2003: *Этимологический словарь тюркских языков: Общетюркские и межтюркские основы на буквы «Л», «М», «Н», «П», «С»* / Авт. сл. статей Л.С. Левитская, Г.Ф. Благова, А.В. Дыбо, Д.М. Насилов, Е.А. Поцелуевский. Москва, 2003.

ЭСТЯ VIII: *Этимологический словарь тюркских языков: Общетюркские и межтюркские основы на буквы «Т», «Ч»* / Авт. сл. статей Л.С. Левитская, Г.Ф. Благова, А.В. Дыбо, Д.М. Насилов, Е.А. Поцелуевский. Рукопись.

Abû H AH: Caferoğlu A. *Abû-Hayyân. Kitâb al-Idrâk li-lisân al-Atrâk.* İstanbul, 1931.

AOH = *Acta Orientalia Academiae Scientiarum Hungaricae.*

Bailey: Bailey H.W. *Dictionary of Khotan Saka.* Cambridge etc., 1979.

Bulg.: Zajączkowski A. *Słownik arabsko-kipczacki.* Warszawa, 1954.

CAJ = *Central Asiatic Journal.*

CCum: *Codex Cumanicus* / Ed. G. Kuun. Budapestini, 1880.

Clark 1980: Clark L.V. Turkic Loanwords in Mongol. I: The Treatment of non-initial *s, z, š, č* // *CAJ.* 1980 24, № 1–2.

CPD: MacKenzie D.N. *A Concise Pahlavi Dictionary.* London, 1971.

EDAL: Starostin S.A., Dybo A.V., Mudrak O.A. *An Etymological Dictionary of Altaic Languages.* Leiden, 2003.

EDT: Clauson G. *An Etymological Dictionary of Pre-Thirteenth-Century Turkish.* Oxford, 1972.

Erdal (1991): Erdal M. *Old Turkic Word Formation.* I–II. Wiesbaden, 1991.

Ettuh.: *Ettuhfet-üz-zekiyye fil-lūgat-it-türkiyye* / çeviren Besim Atalay. İstanbul, 1945.

Fazl.Fazl-i-Ali: Fazl-i-Ali. *A Dictionary of the Persian and English Languages.* New Delhi, 1979.

IM: **1)** Battal Aptullah. *İbnü-Mühenna lûgati.* İstanbul, 1934. **2)** Мелиоранский П.М. *Араб филолог о турецком языке.* Санкт-

Петербург, 1900. **3)** Малов С.Е. Ибн-Муханна о турецком языке // ЗКВ. Ленинград, 1928. III, 2.

KWb: Ramstedt G.J. *Kalmückisches Wörterbuch.* Helsinki, 1935.

Lig. MNyTK: Ligeti L. *A magyar nyelv török kapcsolatai és ami körülöttük van.* I. Budapest, 1977; II. Budapest, 1979.

Lig. VSOu: Ligeti L. Un vocabulaire sino-ouigour des Ming. Le "Kao-ch'ang-kouan yi-chou" du bureau des traducteurs // *AOH.* 1966. XIX, 2–3.

Mayr.: Mayrhofer M. *Kurzgefasstes etymologisches Wörterbuch der Altindischen.* Heidelberg, 1953–1979.

MK: словарь Махмуда Кашгарского (см.: EDT)

MNyTESz: *A magyar nyelv történeti-etimológiai szótára.* I–III. Budapest, 1967–1976.

OLZ = *Orientalische Literaturzeitung.*

Pav. C.: Pavet de Courteille M. *Dictionnaire turc-oriental.* Paris, 1820.

Róna-Tas A. Turkic influence on the Uralic languages. // Sinor D. (ed.) *The Uralic languages: Description, History and Foreign Influences.* Leiden e.a., 1988: 742–780.

Róna-Tas (2005): Róna-Tas A. Néhány megjegyzés faneveinkről (Bükk, dió, gyertyán, gyümölcsény, gyürüfa, éger, kőris, mogyoró, tölgy). // *Magyar Nyelv.* 2005: 419–438. Budapest.

Sangl.: Sanglax. *A Persian Guide to the Turkish Language by Muhammad Mahdī Xān: Facsimile Text with an Introduction and Indices by sir G. Clauson.* London, 1960.

Skok: Skok P. *Etimologijski rječnik hrvatskoga ili srpskoga jezika*, I–IV. Zagreb, 1971–1974.

Stachowski: Stachowski M. *Dolganischer Wortschatz.* Kraków, 1993.

Stachowski (1995): Stachowski M. Problem orientalnych etymologii polskiego *ogar* i węgierskiego *agár.* // *Studia z Filologii Polskiej i Słowiańskiej*, 32. SOW, Warszawa 1995: 103–115.

TMN: Doerfer G. *Türkische und mongolische Elemente im Neupersischen.* Wiesbaden, I. Wiesbaden, 1963; II. Wiesbaden, 1965; III. Wiesbaden, 1967.

Turner: Turner R.L. *A Comparative Dictionary of the Indo-Arian Languages.* Fasc. I–IV. London, 1962–1964.

VEWT: Räsänen M. *Versuch eines etymologisches Wörterbuchs der Türksprachen.* Helsinki, 1969.

Studies on the Turkic World
A Festschrift for Professor St. Stachowski on the Occasion of His 80th Birthday
edited by E. Mańczak-Wohlfeld and B. Podolak, Kraków 2010: 23–32

Henryk Jankowski (Poznań)

The Consonants *ž* ~ *ǯ* in Kazakh

Kazakh, beside Yakut, is one of the most dispersed Turkic languages.[1] The territory of Kazakhstan stretches over 2.7 million km^2 and substantial Kazakh minorities inhabit China and Mongolia. Although large lands in Kazakhstan lie uninhabited, the distances between extreme territories are very large. Quite surprisingly most researchers insist that Kazakh is a relatively homogeneous language with few dialect differences.[2]

1. Distribution of *ж* in Standard Modern Kazakh

In Modern Kazakh, *ж* (pronounced *ž* or *ǯ*) occurs mostly in word initial and medial. In the initial the number of words with *ж* is very high, since it has emerged from the change *y-* → *ž* ~ *ǯ*. This change in Kazakh is regular and it includes almost all words, except for some compounds.[3] In the medial between vowels *ж* appears rarely in genuine words, e.g. *әже* 'grandmother', *ожау* 'ladle', but the number of loanwords with *ж* in this position is also relatively low, e.g. *ажар* 'complexion; countenance',

1 If we neglect the problem of Siberian Tatars.

2 Radloff (1870: xiv, xviii), Баскаков (1960: 169), Benson, Svanberg (1988: 95). The homogeneity of language was variously explained. Some researchers pointed to the mobility of the Kazakhs, relative social homogeneity, and marriages between distant couples (cf. Olcott 1987: 11).

3 Exceptions are mostly some adverbs composed of demonstrative pronouns and nouns which once had *y-* in the initial and this *y-* may still be retained, e.g. *бүяқ* ~ *бүжақ* (Жанпейісов ed. 2002: 154; Сарыбаев, Қалиев 2002: 43) 'this side; this way', *биыл* [bïyïl] 'this year'.

қожа 'member of social class pretending to be descendants of Muhammad', both of Arabic origin. In the final, *ж* is very rare and it is encountered in loanwords, e.g. *тaж* 'crown' (an Iranian loanword) and *келемеж* 'mockery' (a word of quite complicated origin).

The consonants *ž* ~ *ǧ*, although not very frequently, may occur in the medial after or before a consonant, if another adjacent sound is a vowel. These consonants are usually [r l n]: (a) *-рж-*, e.g. *абыржы-* 'to be astonished', *тыржи-* [tïržïy] 'to sulk', *ыржыңда-* 'to grin'; (b) *-лж-*, e.g. *жылжы-* 'to move', including loanwords, e.g. *олжа* 'booty' (a Mongolian loanword); (c) *-нж-*, e.g. *кенже* 'the youngest child; the last-borne young', including loanwords, e.g. *күнжіт* 'sesame' (an Iranian loanword) or *жанжал* 'scandal' (an Arabic loanword).

In addition to this, *ž* ~ *ǧ* may be preceded by a consonant in compounds, such as *біржақты* 'one-sided' ← *бір* 'one' + *жақты* 'sided', *темiржол* 'railway' ← *темір* 'iron' + *жол* 'road' or syncopated words as a result of vowel deletion, e.g. *аржағы* 'that side' ← *ары жағы*.

2. The alternation of *ž* ~ *ǧ*

Standard descriptive grammars of Kazakh describe the consonant *ж* as an apical fricative [ž], IPA [ʒ], a weak counterpart of *ш* [š], IPA [ʃ]. However, it is obvious that many Kazakhs pronounce this consonant [ǧ], IPA [ʤ]. This fact is seldom reported in grammars and language descriptions. For instance, Kajdarov shows many vowel and consonant alternations, among which he assigns a special place to the alternation of *ж* ~ *дж* and *ш* ~ *ч*, both in word initial (Қайдаров 1997: 247). In another place of his grammatical sketch, Kajdarov says that *дж-* and *ч-* initials are typical of Eastern Dialect (Қайдаров 1997: 254). Unfortunately, this explanation is not satisfactory, for it does not include all cases. Before examining this question, we should see what has been established or supposed in the existing studies so far. An important clue to this question may be how the Kazakhs noted this consonant before the transition to the current Cyrillic script.

When we read old manuscripts written in Arabic characters, we see that the authors and copyists employed the letter ج, which probably represents *ǧ*, e.g. جكت [ǧigit] 'young man', جاودان [ǧawdan] 'from a foe', جير [ǧer] '(he) eats' (Исин 2001: 20).[4] Because they employed other Persian letters

[4] The poems edited by Isin are quite old and the copies are dated to the beginning of the 19th century. It is important to note at this point that the Soviet allegations that the Kazakh written literature was created in the Soviet period are untrue.

such as those for the consonants *p* and *č*, we can take for sure that they could also make use of the Persian letter for *ž*. The letter ج was also employed in Kazakh printed publications for which we have examples from the years 1913–1928, e.g. جيرگه [ǧerge] in Yaʿqub Dulatof's (Mircaqıb Dulatulı, later Mircaqıp Dulatulı[5]) *Azamat* from 1913 (Dulatof 1913) and Baytursınulı's works (e.g. Baytursınulı 1928). However, on the front page of Baytursınulı's textbook published in 1928, the title 'new practical aid' written in Arabic characters is also provided in a Latin transcription as "ʒaṇa qural" (in the modern standard spelling *Жаңа құрал*), which suggests the pronunciation [ʒ]. The tradition of employment of the letter ج in private writings and correspondence of some Kazakh intellectuals continued to exist at least in the 1930s, after the official shift to the Latin-based alphabet, see for example the copy of a letter by Baytursınulı of 1932 to Dulatulı, published in 2004 (Дулатұлы 2004: 412).

Naturally, the use of the letter ج does not make its pronunciation clear. It is possible that the Kazakh intellectuals had just chosen a letter more familiar to the Turkic tradition, and it could have been pronounced variously according to the dialect of a speaker and the distribution within word sequence, as also observed by Omarbekov (Омарбеков 1992: 26).[6]

Reliable publications of Kazakh language material started to appear in the 19th century. The first to mention are Kazakh texts published by Il'minskij in 1861.[7] Since this publication is unavailable to us, we have to refer to the materials published by Radloff and his dictionary where he employed Il'minskij's texts.[8] In the dictionary, Radloff recorded all relevant

---

Radlloff's opinion about it is contradictory. On the one side he says that there is no genuine literary Kazakh language, for nearly all teachers are Tatars, on the other he reports that he had employed written books from which the Kazakhs recited and sang songs (Radloff 1870: xix).

5 The Kazakh names and titles of Kazakh publications are transcribed from Arabic and Cyrillic into a system predominantly based on Modern Turkish.

6 At this point it should be mentioned that in the first Kazakh books and periodicals printed in the Kazakh centres the Kazakh consonant [ʃ] was also written traditionally by the letter چ, e.g. *Bastawıç ekinçi cıl oqılatın qırağat kitabı* 'a reader for the second class of elementary schools' (Dulatulı 1926, title page), as in the first Kazakh books published in Kazan affected by the Tatar orthography, although it was later replaced by ش [ʃ].

7 Н. И. Ильминскій. 1861. *Матеріалы для изученія Киргизскаго нарѣчія*. Казань.

8 Two tales recorded by Il'minskij were republished by Radloff in 1870 (see Radloff 1870: xviii) and Il'minskij's lexical material was included in Radloff's dictionary (Radloff 1893: iii).

Kazakh words with the letter *ǧ* (џ) in the initial.[9] However, in the medial Kazakh words are written with the letter *ж*, i.e. *ā̆жä* 'grandmother' (Radloff 1983: 914), *ожау* 'small scoop with a short handle' (Radloff 1983: 1154), *олжа* 'booty; income' (Radloff 1983: 1095), the two latter words being written exactly as in the modern spelling. The verb 'to grin' is recorded in the form *ыржаі-*, with reference to its Kirghiz equivalent *ырџаі-* (Radloff 1893: 1373), and the word 'the youngest child' is represented as *кенжä* (Radloff 1899: 1083).[10] As for the word-final position, Radloff records the Kazakh words with the letter *ж*, e.g. *тaж* (Radloff 1905: 944). In his Kazakh texts published in 1870, Radloff transcribes the letter *џ* as *dsch* (e.g. Radloff 1870: xxiv, 8), which also shows that it was pronounced *ǧ*. Moreover, Radloff unambiguously demonstrates that the relevant consonant was *ǧ* "џ pronounced dsch".[11] However, Radloff's remark is only valid for Eastern Kazakh. At the same time he observes that Il'minskij in his texts recorded in the western steppes employs the letter *ж* in the place of *џ* (Radloff 1870: xxvi–xxvii). The presence of the sound *ǧ* is supported by what Melioranskij writes in his grammar of Kazakh. Melioranskij employs the same letter as Radloff did, but he remarks that the initial component of the *дж* affricate is not very strong and disappears in the western part of the Kazakh steppe (Меліоранскій 1894: 8–13).

However, Ibrahim (Ibıray) Altınsarin in his Kirghiz (i.e. Kazakh) chrestomathy (Алтынсаринъ 1879), regarded as the first book written by a Kazakh author with Cyrillic characters, employes exclusively the letter *ж* in all positions. Although Altynsarin's orthography is far from being exact, this is an important argument for *ž* [ʒ].

There are valuable texts published by Çağatay in 1961 recorded among the Kazakhs who emigrated from China to Turkey. In the introduction to this publication, Çağatay has discussed the problem of the consonants spelled on the basis of Turkish orthography *c* ~ *j*, i.e. *ǧ* ~ *ž*, but she could not formulate strict rules of the distribution and alternation of these consonants. Instead, she demonstrated a stylistic aspect, observing that the

[9] There are only eleven words beginning with the letter *ž* (*ж*) in his dictionary, all being Troki Karaim and Tatar (Radloff 1911: 1115–1116).

[10] Radloff's findings are contradictory, again. Namely, in the introduction to his texts he says that "ж" is pronounced by the Eastern Kazakhs only in the medial in loanwords, which in the written form had the letter ج (Radloff 1870: xxvii).

[11] "Diejenigen Wörter, die im Altaidialecte auf j, bei den Sagaiern ч und bei der Koibalen auf j anlauten, erhalten im Kirgisischen der Oststeppe den Anlaut џ (sprich dsch), das d als Vorschlag ist ganz deutlich hörbar" (Radloff 1870: xxvi).

Kazakhs pronounce *c* when an educated man is present, but "c ~ j" and sometimes "c ~ d" in an uncontrolled conversation.[12] When she asked what the correct pronunciation should be like, they said that it should be "c" (Çağatay 1961: 6).[13] Therefore, in most cases she introduced the vowel [ʤ] and spelled it *c*. In a vocabulary appended to the texts, most words have *c-* in the initial (Çağatay 1961: 168–170), but four words are spelled with *j-*: *jan, japalaḳ, jin* and *jut* (Çağatay 1961: 174). Three of these words were also provided with the *c-* initial, namely *can, japalaḳ,* and *cut*. However, she also noted other cases of the *j-* initial in the texts, some alternating with *c-*, e.g. *jabuω ~ cabuωın* '(camel) blanket' (Çağatay 1961: 24).

According to Koç, Doğan and Bayniyazov's grammar (2004: 45), the normal Kazakh consonat corresponding to Common Turkic *y-* was once *c-*, but it changed into *j-* as affected by the letter *ж* imposed by the modern writing. Quite interestingly, in contrast to Çağatay these authors maintain that the Kazakhs – except for a few northern dialects – in a free, uncontrolled conversation almost always pronounce this consonant "c", and "j" appears only when they are obliged to use literary pronunciation. They attribute the question of the use of the letter *ж* and its pronunciation *j-* to the political factors. Koç, Doğan and Bayniyazov deliver three proofs, one is Radloff's notation *җ*, the other is the Russian rendering *дж* of this consonant, not *ж*, and the third is Baytursınulı's alleged opinion that ǰ occurs in Russian words. These authors say nothing about the position of this consonant in a word or speech sequence. Despite this sharp critic, Koç, Bayniyazov and Başkapan in their Kazakh-Turkish dictionary write the relevant words with *j* (Коч, Байниязов, Башкапан 2003). In another Kazakh grammar published by a Turkish scholar (Tamir 2007: 435), the author says that the Turkish initial *y-* corresponds to the Kazakh *j-* in all words, but he adds that this consonant is pronounced *c* by the Kazakhs in Mongolia, China and also in many regions in Kazakhstan.

As a result, there is no standardized sign in Turkish transcription system for the Standard Modern Kazakh *ж*. For example, Ercilasun proposed both *c* and *j* for it (Ercilasun 1990).

[12] In fact the alternation *ž ~ d* is also known in some standard Kazakh words, e.g. *ежірей- ~ едірей-* 'to goggle' (Жанпейісов ed. 2002: 154), though in the course of time such pairs usually acquire new meanings, e.g. *бүжыр* 'knoll, hill' ~ *бұдыр* 'pockmarked'.

[13] In the Kazakh dialect of China the normal consonant in the initial is [ʤ], see Bazılhan (Базылхан 1991: 31).

The first – and to the best of our knowledge – the only author to give a correct distribution of the consonants *ž* ~ *ǧ* was Bazılhan. Although his distribution was intended to represent the language of the Kazakhs in Mongolia, it is valid for many variants of Kazakh spoken in Kazakhstan as well. In Bazılhan's opinion, *ж*, i.e. *ž*, is pronounced in the medial after a vowel or between two vowels[14] as well as in the final,[15] while *дж*, i.e. *ǧ*, is pronounced in the initial and in medial after [l n], for which the following examples are delivered: *қалджа* 'dish of hot meat for a woman after childbirth or for the sick', *олджа* 'booty' and *қанджар* 'dagger'.

The alternation *ž* ~ *ǧ* has not escaped the attention of Kazakh linguists, but they regard it as a feature of dialect variation. However, in the first voluminous study on Kazakh dialectology, Amanžolov (1957), who demonstrated many vowel and consonant alternations in three dialects he established, said nothing about the alternation *ž* ~ *ǧ*. Information on these consonants is found in Sarıbayev's introduction to the first Kazakh dialect dictionary. Namely, Sarıbayev says that the affricate *ǧ* is pronounced in word-initial position in Qorday and Uyğır districts of the Almatı province as well as in some districts of the Eastern Kazakhstan province (Сарыбаев 1969: 10). In a study on Kazakh dialectology published in 1979 and its new, revised edition of 2002, Qalıyev and Sarıbayev remark that *ǧ* occurs in the Eastern Dialect in the initial and the medial after [l n]. They provide the same examples as other researchers, i.e. *қалджа*, *олджа* and *қанджар*, and link this feature to the language of Mongolian Kazakhs (Сарыбаев, Қалиев 2002: 43). Their observations are inconsistent, since in another place of their book the same feature is also demonstrated in the Southern Dialect (Сарыбаев, Қалиев 2002: 108). In spite of this, this feature was disregarded in the dictionary (in contrast to the *č*- initial),[16] for the *ǧ*- pronunciation is irregular and vary with *ž*-. The alternation *ž* ~ *ǧ* has attracted Omarbekov's attention who in his study on the geography of Kazakh dialects employed it as a feature characterizing dialect distribution. Two maps in this study show the alternation *ž* ~ *ǧ*, one with the word *джыл* ~ *жыл*, the other with *джоқ* ~ *жоқ* (Омарбеков 1992: 194–195). The area of *дж* is similar in both maps, it includes the territory of South-Eastern Kazakhstan stretching from the

[14] However, all of his examples show *ž* in intervocalic position only, i.e. V—V, in words such as *ажал, ежелден, қыжылдау, кіжілдеу* etc.

[15] No example is delivered for this position.

[16] The same principle was applied in a new dialect dictionary (Әнес, Үдербаев eds. 2007).

river Chu across the Seven River land up to the Altai mountains. On the borders of this territory there is an area of *дж* ~ *ж* variation. Omarbekov considers this alternation a shift from *ж* to *дж* (Омарбеков 1992: 24), accepting therefore the standard language as starting point and implicitly the *ж* stage as original, though he points to the fact that the area of *ж* which covers northern and western Kazakhstan is characteristic as a Turkic feature, not only Kazakh.

Turkology reference books and comparative studies regard the initial Kazakh consonant as *ǧ-* (e.g. Menges 1995: 92). Räsänen does not formulate any opinion, he just refers to Russian and Soviet works (Räsänen 1949: 186).

3. Discussion of the problem in a comparative perspective

Kazakh *ǧ* and *ž* go back to various Old Turkic consonants. In the following, two points will be discussed.

1. *y-* → *ǧ-*

Since there is no clear historical phonetic evidence, we do not know if Old Turkic *y-* has first changed to *ǧ-* or *ž-*.[17] Therefore, it is impossible to trace all stages of the relevant phonetic process. Before going into the discussion of the change *y-* → *ǧ-* and *y-* → *ž-* in Turkic languages, we have to note that these changes are known in many languages of the world. Among Indo-European languages, they are evidenced in the Romance branch. For example, Latin *y-* changed to *ǧ-* in Italian and *ž-* in French.

In Turkic languages, initial *y-* shifted to *ǧ-* in Old Bulgarian, in most northwestern languages such as Karachai, Tatar, Nogai (not literary standard language), northern Crimean Tatar, Karakalpak and Kirghiz, also in southern dialects of Altai, a northeastern language. In Chuvash it changed into *ś-* (via *ǧ-*), in Yakut into *s-* (also via *ǧ-*). In some other northeastern languages it shifted into *č-* (Tuvan, Shor, Khakas). It is to be noted that these changes in some languages are partial and do not embrace all dialects.

In some traditional grammars the change *y-* → *ǧ-* is termed palatalisation (Dauzat 1950: 42). However, this term is inadequate, for both sounds are palatal. A better term is affrication. Affrication may also be called closing,

[17] We believe that there is no need to start the discussion with Proto-Turkic. Some Turkologists derive Old Turkic /j/ from other consonants, e.g. Ščerbak derives it from Proto-Turkic /ϑ/ (Щербак 1970: 159).

as in Lass (1984: 181), who gives Latin /j/ → Italian /ʤ/ and → French /ʒ/, e.g. Latin *maior*, Italian *maggiore*, French *majeur* as an example.

The change *y-* → *ǧ-* is a phonological process that may be regarded as fortition. Also Lass takes closing for fortition. As is well-known, in northwestern Turkic languages initial consonants are typically strong. Therefore, one may explain this process by analogy, i.e. a change from weak to stronger. However, if this is the case we have to ask why *y-* strengthened to *ǧ-* weakened later to *ž-*. The answer seems to be simple. Namely there are also other cases of lenition in the initial position, e.g. *č-* → *š-*, though this occurs in all environments and is not position-depended. Moreover, the change *ǧ-* → *ž-* may be affected by *č-* → *š-*, for it is a similar change.

2. *ǧ* → *ž* / V—V[18]

Medial *-ǧ-* has not developed from *-y-*, but is a continuation of the Proto-Turkic **-č-* from the time before the change *č* → *š*.[19] In contrast to the preceding, this change occurs in all dialects. Medial *-ǧ-* may be retained if it is protected by /l n r/, i.e.

ǧ → ǧ / {l n r} —V

See the examples above like *kenǧe* ~ *kenže* etc. As is evident from the discussion, this change occurs in some dialects, while in others it does not.

Lenition and fortition are little studied in Turkic, although these processes underlie the whole historical development of Turkic sounds. On the phonetic level, it was discussed in many aspects in Bajčura's studies, on the phonetic and phonological levels by Ščerbak (Щербак 1970: 88–89). On the comparative, phonological and historical levels the problem of consonant strength was examined in detail by Johanson (1986, reprinted in 1991). However, Johanson does not discuss the changes relevant to our topic. Traditional Turkic linguistics treats most cases of fortition and lenition as voicedness and voicelessness (Räsänen 1949: 143, Menges 1995: 81). Naturally becoming voiced or voiceless does not exclude lenition and fortition. However, lenition and fortition as notions pertaining to phonological strength are more feasible to explain historical phonological processes.

Summing up, we will argue that the Old Turkic *y-* changed in two stages in Kazakh. The first stage was the change *y-* → *ǧ-*, whereas the second

[18] Final position will not be discussed, as this is not typical of Kazakh, see above.

[19] Except from some complicated cases, such as *ayïr-* * → *aǧïra-* * → *ažïra-* 'to separate; to go apart'.

one was $\check{g}$- $\rightarrow$ $\check{z}$-. The first change achieved its final point in southern and eastern dialects of Kazakh, whereas in central, northern and western dialects it went further and produced the consonant $\check{z}$-, accepted in Modern Kazakh as standard. It must be observed that in the pronunciation of many speakers both consonants may appear in the initial, depending on factors that have not been yet examined.

References

Алтынсаринъ, И. 1879. *Киргизская Хрестоматія.* Оренбургъ: Типографія И. И. Ефимовскаго-Мировицкаго.

Аманжолов, С. А. 1959. *Вопросы диалектологии и истории казахского языка.* Алма-Ата: Наука.

Баскаков, Н. А. 1960. *Тюркские языки.* Москва: Издательство восточной литературы.

Baytursınulı, Aqımet. 1928. *Elib-biy. Caña qural. 3-nşı iret basıluwı.* Qızıl Orda: Qazazğıstan Bilim Ordası.

Базылхан, Б. 1991. *Моңголиядагы қазақтардың тілі.* Улаанбаатар: Өлгий.

Benson, Linda; Svanberg, Ingvar. 1988. "The Kazaks in Xinjiang": Benson, Linda; Svanberg, Ingvar (eds.). 1988. *The Kazaks of China. Essays on an Ethnic Minority.* Uppsala [= Acta Universitatis Upsaliensis, Studia Multiethnica Upsaliensia 5], 1–106.

Çağatay, Saadet. 1961. *Kazakça Metinler.* Ankara: Türk Tarih Kurumu.

Dauzat, Albert. 1950. *Phonétique et grammaire historiques de la langue française.* Paris: Larousse.

Dulatof, Yaʿqub. 1913. *Azamat.* Orenburg: Vaqt Matbaʿası.

Dulatulı, Mircaqıb. 1923. *Oquw qural.* Orınbor: Qazaqstan Baspahanası.

Дулатұлы, Міржақып. 2004. *Бес томдық шыгармалар жинагы. 5. Аудармалар, естеліктер, құжаттар мен деректер.* Алматы: Мектеп.

Әнес, Ғарифолла, Үдербаев, Алмас (eds). 2007. *Диалектологиялық сөздік.* Алматы: Арыс.

Ercilasun, Ahmet B. 1990. *Bugünkü Türk Alfabeleri Anahtar Kitapçığı.* Ankara: Kültür Bakanlığı.

Johanson, Lars. 1991. „Zur Konsonantenstärke im Türkischen“: Johanson, Lars. *Linguistische Beiträge zur Gesamtturkologie.* Budapest: Akadémiai Kiadó, 84–98.

Қайдаров, А. Т. 1997. „Казахский язык”: Тенишев, Э. Р. (ed.). *Языки мира. Тюркские языки.* Бишкек: Кыргызстан, 242–254.

Коч, Кенан; Байниязов, Аябек; Башкапан, Вехби. 2003. *Қазақша-түрікше сөздік. 32 мынға жуық сөзбен сөз тіркестері қамтылған.* Түркістан: Тұран (Koç, Kenan; Bayniyazov, Ayabek; Başkapan, Vehbi. 2003. *Kazak Türkçesi Türkiye Türkçesi Sözlüğü.* Türkistan: Turan).

Koç, Kenan; Doğan, Oğuz; Bayniyazov, Ayabek (eds.). 2004. *Kazak Türkçesi Grameri.* Ankara: Gazi Kitabevi.

Lass, Roger. 1984. *Phonology. An Introduction to Basic Concepts.* Cambridge: Cambridge University Press.

Меліоранскій, П. М. 1894. *Краткая грамматика казакъ-киргизскаго языка* I. С.-Петербургъ.

Menges, Karl H. 1995. *The Turkic Languages and Peoples. An Introduction to Turkic Studies. 2nd, revised Edition.* Wiesbaden: O. Harrassowitz.

Мұсабаев, Ғ. (ed.). 1969. *Қазақ тілінің диалектологиялық сөздігі.* Алматы: Ғылым.

Olcott, Martha Brill. 1987. *The Kazakhs.* Stanford: Hoover Institution Press.

Омарбеков, С. 1992. *География фонетических различий казахской речи.* Алма-Ата: Рауан.

Radloff, W. 1870. *Proben der Volkslitteratur der Türkischen Stämme Süd-Sibiriens.* III. *Kirgisische Mundarten.* St. Pétersbourg.

Radloff, W. 1893–1911. *Versuch eines Wörterbuches der Türk-Dialecte.* I–IV. St. Pétersbourg.

Räsänen, Martti. 1949. *Zur Lautgeschichte der türkischen Sprachen.* Helsinki [= Studia Orientalia 15].

Сарыбаев, Ш. (ed.) 2005. *Қазақ тілінің аймақтық сөздігі.* Алматы: Арыс.

Сарыбаев, Ш.; Қалиев, Ғ. 2002. *Қазақ диалектологиясы.* Алматы: Ғылым.

Щербак, А. М. 1970. *Сравнительная фонетика тюркских языков.* Ленинград: Наука.

Tamir, Ferhat. 2007. “Kazak Türkçesi”: Ercilasun, Ahmet B. (ed.). *Türk Lehçeleri Grameri.* Ankara: Akçağ, 481–542.

Жанпейісов, Ербол (ed.). 2002. *Қазақ грамматикасы. Фонетика, сөзжасам, морфология, синтаксис.* Астана: Қазақстан Республикасы Білім және Ғылым Министрлігі, Байтұрсынұлы Атындағы Тіл Білімі Институты.

Studies on the Turkic World
A Festschrift for Professor St. Stachowski on the Occasion of His 80th Birthday
edited by E. Mańczak-Wohlfeld and B. Podolak, Kraków 2010: 33–42

Michael Knüppel (Göttingen)

Überlegungen zum Problem von Sprachtabus im Alttürkischen

Das aus den ural., alt. und sog. „paläoasiat." Sprachen bekannte und – vor allem für die Arbeit am Wörterbuch – recht leidige Problem der Sprachtabus wurde in der Altturkologie bislang nicht (sieht man einmal von S. Kljaštornyjs Beitrag „Problemy rannej istori plemeni tjurk (ašina)", in dem der Vf. u. a. den Ursprüngen von atü. *börü* ~ *böri* [„Wolf"] nachgeht[1] oder den Überlegungen zu atü. *toġrul* ~ *toġril* ~ *toġan* [„Falke"] oder zu der Metathese *käči* ~ *äkči* [„Ziege"][2] ab) behandelt – um nicht zu sagen gemieden. Seinen Grund hat dies zweifellos schon in dem Umstand, daß die Ermittlung von Sprachtabus – nicht nur im Atü. – mit erheblichen Problemen verbunden sein kann. „Gelingt" die Deutung – etwa durch Erschließen aus dem Kontext oder gar bloßes Erahnen –, so kann man sich häufig bereits glücklich schätzen. Oftmals ist dann jedoch an die Feststellung des durch das betreffende Ersatzwort verdeckte oder gar einer Tabuumformung unterworfene Wort kaum zu denken. Aufgrund der zahlreichen Schwierigkeiten scheint die Auffassung vorzuherrschen, daß man Sprachtabus im Atü. nicht zu entschlüsseln vermag, eben weil Tabuisierungen vorliegen.

Ein Eindruck, der durch den Umstand, daß hier – im Gegensatz zu den Sprachen des nördl. Eurasien – keine geeigneten Vergleichsmöglichkeiten gegeben zu sein scheinen, noch verstärkt wird. Im Falle etwa der tung. oder

[1] Kljaštornyj (1965), 278–281; Räsänen (1969), 84.

[2] Dies vielleicht keine Tabuisierung, da viele Parallelen in anderen Sprachen – möglicherweise Entlehnung. Hierzu ausführlich Menges (1983), dessen Folgerungen – möglicherweise SW-nostratischen Ursprungs – man nicht unbedingt zustimmen muß.

samoj. Sprachen genügt mit ein wenig Glück und Erfahrung häufig schon ein Blick auf die in den zur selben Sprachfamilie gehörenden Sprachen vorliegenden Formen, um Tabuumformungen oder Ersatzwörter zu erkennen (vgl. z. B. Ew. [auch Arman.] *sum-* ~ *sām-* „sterben" [eigentl. „zuschließen" (z. B. die Augen)]; dies Tabuumformung, da sonst *som-* [Lamut., Ulča, Orok., Ma., J̌ü. (Cincius [1975–77], 141: *sə̄m-* „verloren gehen, sterben")]).

Das Atü. steht demgegenüber recht „isoliert" da. Es repräsentiert die früheste uns bekannte Stufe des Türkischen und wir müßten für Vergleiche auf andere, tatsächlich oder vermeintlich „archaische" Turksprachen ausweichen – etwa das Čuvašische, das Jakutische oder das Chaladsch. Eine Vorgehensweise, die in zugleich mehrfacher Hinsicht als problematisch angesehen werden muß: zum einen werden resp. wurden (im Falle des Atü.) diese Sprachen in geographisch recht weit voneinander entfernten Regionen gesprochen und zum anderen weisen die Träger dieser Sprachen aufgrund kaum vergleichbarer Lebensumstände recht unterschiedliche kulturelle Hintergründe auf, die die betreffenden Sprachen geformt haben. Vollkommen verschiedene religiöse Milieus lassen entsprechende Vergleiche ohnehin kaum zu.

Auch die nicht-verwandten, jedoch „unmittelbar benachbarten" Sprachen scheinen im Falle des Atü. wenig geeignet, um zur Aufhellung möglicher Tabuisierungen beizutragen. Hinsichtlich eigensprachlicher Ersatzwörter oder Tabuumformungen ist der Blick in diese Sprachen ohnehin zumeist wenig ergiebig und im Hinblick auf ihre mögliche Funktion als „Gebersprache" von fremdsprachl. Ersatzwörtern ergeben sich hier ganz erhebliche Schwierigkeiten. So haben zum einen die für die Tabuisierung entlehnten Ersatzwörter in den „Gebersprachen" häufig vollkommen andere – oder doch zumindest deutlich abweichende Bedeutungen (vgl. z. B. lamut. *kuturuk* – „Wolf" < jak. *kuturuk* – „Schwanz"[3] oder *nukun* „Vagina" < mo. *nüken* „Loch"[4] etc.) und zum anderen sind die meisten der für das Atü. in betracht kommenden nicht-verwandten „Gebersprachen" (Sogdisch, Tocharisch, Sakisch) ihrerseits noch viel zu ungenügend untersucht, um für derartige vergleichende Untersuchungen herangezogen werden zu können (auch zu Tabuisierungen in den betreffenden Sprachen existieren keine für die Erhellung möglicher Muster oder Vorlagen erforderlichen Voruntersuchungen) – so ist das Problem der Sprachtabus auch für die genannten Sprachen (– ebenso wie etwa auch für das Tibetische –) bislang nicht

3 Doerfer (1993), 17–34 (hier 33 f.).

4 Shirokogoroff (1944/53), col. 191/ Doerfer (2004), Nr. 8140: *nukun* [X.] – „vulva" – „Vulva" < mo. *nüken* – „Loch" (hierzu Doerfer [1988], 237).

behandelt worden. Es scheint also in der Tat geringe Aussichten für eine Aufdeckung von Sprachtabus im Atü. zu geben.

Dennoch gibt es eine Reihe von – wenngleich zugegebenermaßen recht umständlichen – Möglichkeiten den zweifellos auch im Atü. vorhandenen Sprachtabus auf die Spur zu kommen. Mit rein sprachvergleichenden Methoden ist hier freilich wenig zu erreichen. Entscheidend ist vielmehr im Vorfeld möglicher Untersuchungen zu bestimmen, *was* eigentlich genau gesucht werden soll, d. h., zunächst sind die Kategorien von Tabuisierungen zu bestimmen. Generell lassen sich drei solche Kategorien definieren:

1. kultur- resp. religionsspezifische Tabuisierungen, d. h. solche Tabuisierungen, die sich aus einem spezifischen religiösen Kontext erklären, wie etwa die zahlreichen Tabuisierungen von Tiernamen bei den eurasischen Völkern (vor allem Bär, Wolf, Tiger etc.), die sich aus totemistischen Vorstellungen[5] und vor allem den Bezug auf den Komplex der Jagd erklären lassen.[6] Daneben finden sich natürlich auch die Tabuisierungen, die sich aus den Vorstellungen von Unreinheit oder den mit den betreffenden Religionen verbundenen Wertesystemen resp. -vorstellungen verbunden sind, ergeben wie die bis in unsere Tage erhalten gebliebenen Tabuisierungen des Teufels in christl. und muslim. geprägten Gesellschaften (vgl. dt. „der Leibhaftige“ oder „Gott-sei-bei-uns“). Freilich sind es nicht nur rein religiöse Gründe, die hier eine Rolle spielen, sondern zumeist ganze Bündel von religiösen u. sozio-ökonom. Faktoren. So spielen etwa im Weltbild nomadisierender Steppenbewohner auch in religiöser Hinsicht gänzlich andere Vorstellungen eine Rolle, als etwa bei Küstenbewohnern, deren primäre Existenzgrundlage die Fischerei bildet;
2. „verschleppte“ Tabuisierungen. Bei diesen handelt es sich um Tabuisierungen, die aus einer früheren Phase der Geschichte einer Gemeinschaft von Sprechern – nicht selten auch aus einer früheren Sprachstufe – stammen und ihre Bedeutung durch einen Wandel der Lebensumstände, der Sprache – oder gar den Wechsel der Religion – verloren haben und von den Sprechern der betreffenden Sprache i. d. R. nicht mehr verstanden werden. Man denke hier bloß an dt. *Bär*, engl. *bear*, beides geht auf eine gemein-german. Tabuisierung in der ursprüngl. Bedeutung „braun“ zurück (eine Eigenschaft des Tieres, das mit einem solchen Sprachtabu belegt wird – hier die Farbe des Fells – als Ersatzwort zu verwenden, entspricht einem gängigen Muster. Die nicht belegte ursprüngl. german.

[5] Vgl. hierzu etwa Findeisen (1956), 42–52.

[6] Menges (1932).

Bez. für „Bär“ wird zumeist als *$\text{ṛ}k$-t-os ~ *ṛk-s-os [re]konstruiert).[7] Als vergleichbares Bsp. im Türk. wäre das eingangs genannte atü. *börü* ~ *böri* „Wolf“ zu nennen, bei dem es sich nach Kljaštornyj um eine Entlehnung aus einer IE Sprache handelt und das im Atü. als Ersatzwort diente. Später wurde dieses von den Sprechern W-türk. Sprachen nicht mehr verstanden, als die tatsächliche Benennung des Wolfes angesehen und seinerseits mit einem Ersatzwort (*kurt* – eigentl. „Wurm“; auch dies entspricht einem geläufigen Muster – vgl. tung. *kúlikān* ~ *kulíkā* [„Wurm“, eigentl. „Schlange“] als Ersatzwort für „Bär“[8]) abermals tabuisiert;

3. „universelle“ Tabuisierungen, d. h. solche Tabuisierungen, die sich – unabhängig etwa von Sprache oder Religion – in nahezu allen Kulturen, wenngleich in unterschiedlicher Ausprägung, finden. Zu diesen zählen z. B. Tabuisierungen aus den Sphären von Krankheit, Plagen oder Tod sowie der Sphäre der Sexualität. So wurden (und werden z. T. noch immer) in nahezu allen Sprachen des nördl. Eurasien u. Zentralasiens – unabhängig von ihren Verwandtschaftsverhältnissen oder dem kulturgeschichtl. Hintergrund – die Bez.en für Infektionskrankheiten tabuisiert (vgl. etwa die Bez.en für die Pocken in zahllosen Sprachen, in denen selbst das Muster der Tabuisierung übereinstimmt: tung. *am̄īn* [dies eigentl. „Mutter“],[9] kolyma-juk. *comoł-epíe* [= „Urgroßmutter“ oder „große Großmutter“],[10] neu-uig. *čäčäk anesi* [= „Mutter der Pocken (eigentl. „Blume“)“ = Pockenepidemie][11] oder tung. *ilga*, *iłga* [= „Blume“]).[12]
Im Atü. liegt eine solche „universelle“ Tabuisierung vermutlich im Falle der Bez. des „Flohs“ (*börgä* – dies viell. < *börgät* ~ *börgüt* – eigentl. „Adler“; hier sind die Verhältnisse insofern unklar, als auch eine umgekehrte Tabuisierung des Adlers denkbar ist [etwa als Jagdtabu?])[13] vor. Wir haben hier

[7] Menges (1982); ders. (1983), 286 f.

[8] *kúlikān* (cf. Liste Leo Heinen/ [Nachlaß v.] Hans Findeisen, Bonn) ~ *kulíkā* (Vasilevič [1934]; Cincius [1975–7], 428) = „Bär“ (< *kulīn* = „Schlange“ + Diminutiv-Suff. *-kān* = „Wurm“ [Menges (1985), 233]).

[9] Shirokogoroff (1944/53), col. 12/ Doerfer (2004), Nr. 519: *am̄īn* [K.] – „ospa“ – „Pokken“ u. Shirokogoroff (1944/53), col. 16/ Doerfer (2004), Nr. 683: *änin* [U. C.] – „(Blatter) puzaŕ, voldyŕ (ospa ?)“.

[10] Angere (1957), 41.

[11] Menges (1933), 102; ders. (1932); Samojlovič (1915).

[12] Shirokogoroff (1944/53), col. 118 / Doerfer (2004), Nr. 5116: *ilga*, *iłga* [B.] – „cvětok“ – “Blume“.

[13] Die von Roux (1999) vorgeschlagene Tabuisierung *börgüt* ~ *börgät* „Adler“ < *börgä* „Floh“ ist allerdings insofern problematisch, als meist entweder eine Tabuumformung oder ein Tabuwort vorliegt, selten beides zugleich (dies zumeist nur bei Mehrfachta-

wohl ein eigensprachl. Ersatzwort vor uns, das durch die weitverbreitete Tabuisierung von Plagen bedingt ist. „Ungeziefer" und (tatsächliche wie auch vermeintliche) Überträger von Krankheiten (Mücken, Läuse etc.)[14] unterliegen in sehr vielen Kulturen umfangreichen Tabuisierungen.[15]
Im Hinblick auf das Muster, wie auch die Entwicklung liegt im Falle der Tabuisierung der Lepra (und vielleicht auch anderer Hautkrankheiten) eine Analogie zur Tabuisierung des Wolfs im Atü. vor. Die ursprüngl. Bez. ist uns nicht mehr bekannt der „Aussatz" wird im Atü. als *ala* bezeichnet,[16] was ursprüngl. „bunt" bedeutet.[17] Später wurde (wohl ebenfalls im W-türk. Bereich) die Schlange als „bunt, die Bunte" mit *ala* tabuisiert[18] und schließlich wiederum diverse Hauterkrankungen mit Bez. für die Schlange bezeichnet.[19] Auf diesen recht verworrenen Wegen gelangte *ala* als *ăla* ~ *hăla* in der Bedeutung „Drache" schließlich sogar bis ins Serbo-Kroatische.[20]

buisierungen). Zum anderen bereitet der Gegensatz Pl. : Sing. einige Schwierigkeiten (Roux deutet *börgüt* ~ *börgät* „Adler" als *börgä* „Floh" + *-t* [Pl.]).

[14] Häufig wird zwischen bestimmten Tieren und Krankheiten auch ein – etwa religiös begründeter – Zusammenhang hergestellt, ohne daß eine solcher tatsächlich besteht. Man denke hier im Bereich des nordeurasischen Šamānismus nur an die Rolle von Tieren als Helfer der Šamānen oder bestimmter Geister.

[15] Als Beispiel seien hier bloß die Tabuumformungen bei den Bez.en für die „Mücke" in den tung. Sprachen angeführt: Ma. *galman* (Doerfer [2004], Nr. 7243) Mandschu], Oroč. *gamata* ~ *garmakta* (Doerfer [2004], Nr. 7243), Bir. *manmakta* (Doerfer [2004], Nr. 6994), Neg. *monnakta*, *ńanmakta* ~ *nganmakta* (Doerfer [2004], Nrr. 7243 u. 7641). Bei Cincius (1975–77) wird – ohne weiter auf das Problem einzugehen – für alle dort behandelten tung. Sprachen eine Form *ŋanmakta* angegeben (Cincius [1975–77], 657).

[16] So bei Arat (1930), 466, Anm. 48 und ders. (1937); entgegen Röhrborn (1979), 90b kein Druckfehler für „Ausschlag" (vgl. auch Radloff [1893], col. 352 sowie die teilweise nach Radloff erfolgten Anmerkungen bei Arat [1930], 466, Anm. 48).

[17] Vgl. Malov (1932), 143, Z. 5, Zieme (1975), 102, aber auch Arat (1930), 466, Anm. 48 und Röhrborn (1979), 90b.

[18] Noch heute wird in verschiedenen anatolischen Dialekten die Schlange als „bunt, die Bunte" bezeichnet (Knüppel [2009]). Die Tabuisierung der Schlange ist ebenfalls geradezu „regelmäßig", sind die Benennungen für giftige Tiere doch in nahezu dem gesamten zentral- und nordasiatischen Raum umfangreichen Tabus unterworfen (vgl. etwa Knüppel [2007] u. [2008]).

[19] Als Beispiel sei hier bloß die Bezeichnung *yılancık* ~ *yılancuh* zur Bezeichnung von Hautkrankhreiten (bes. der Wundrose [Erysipelas]) in den anatolischen Dialekten genannt (vgl. *Türkiye Halk Ağzından Söz Derleme Dergisi*, III. İstanbul 1942, 1524 f.; *Türkiye'de Halk Ağzından Söz Derleme Dergisi*, XI. Ankara 1979, 4264 f.).

[20] Knüppel (2009).

Es liegt natürlich in der Natur der Sache, daß hier zumeist keine scharfen Abgrenzungen der einzelnen Kategorien möglich sind. So können sich Prozesse des Kulturwandels über Jahrhunderte hinziehen und das Vorliegen „verschleppter“ Tabuisierungen ist dann nicht ohne weiteres festzustellen – ebenso wie dies im Falle eines Nebeneinanders verschiedener Religionen (dies einigermaßen gut untersucht für Šamānismus u. Christentum bei versch. nordeurasischen Völkern) gegeben ist. Man muß sich die Kategorien eher als Mengen und die Übergänge als Schnittmengen derselben vorstellen, denn als deutlich abgrenzbare Einheiten.

Ist – soweit dies eben möglich war – einigermaßen geklärt, nach welcher Kategorie der Tabuisierung gesucht wird, ist es erforderlich, sich dem Muster der möglichen Tabuisierung zuzuwenden – also dem *wie* der Tabuisierung. Dies ist nur möglich durch den Vergleich mit Sprachen und Kulturen, in denen dieselben Gegenstände und Handlungen tabuisiert werden. Grundsätzlich gibt es im zentral- und nordasiatischen Bereich die folgenden Möglichkeiten der Tabuisierung:

1. Tabuumformungen – d. h., lautliche Verfremdungen des zu tabuisierenden Begriffs, der Handlungen oder der Gegenstände. Für das ältere Türk. wäre hier z. B. der Fall der „Verfremdungen“ der Bez. für den Falken *toġrul* ~ *toġril* ~ *toġan* anzusprechen.
2. Ersatzwörter – d. h., Ersatz des Begriffs für eine tabuisierte Handlung oder einen tabuisierten Gegenstand durch ein anderes Wort oder eine Wendung. In diese zunächst recht allgemeine Kategorie gehören auch Euphemismen und Metaphern. Im Falle der Ersatzwörter wiederum können wir grob unterscheiden zwischen (2.1) eigensprachlichen Ersatzwörtern (im Falle der aus dem Atü. gewählten Bsp.e wäre hier etwa *ala* „bunt“ als Ersatz für die Nennung der Lepra genannt) und (2.2) fremdsprachlichen Ersatzwörtern, wie etwa die türk. Tabubez. für den Wolf, *böri̇̈*, die – wie oben ausgeführt – letztlich IE Herkunft ist.[21] Neben der Wahl von fremd- und eigensprachlichen Ersatzwörtern, kann jedoch auch (2.3) der Ersatz durch kindersprachliche Elemente erfolgen. Als kindersprachl. Elemente werden hier solche Wörter (seltener Wendungen) aufgefaßt, die von Kindern in der Kommunikation mit anderen Kindern oder Erwachsenen benutzt werden. Zwar werden kindersprachl. Elemente stets als Bestandteile der eigenen Sprache aufgefaßt, jedoch erfordern sie eine gesonderte Behandlung, da sie unterschiedliche Stu-

[21] Vgl. hierzu zudem Korsch (1912), 199, Hübschmann (1887) [hierzu vgl. Vasmer (1958), 87], Kljaštornyj (1965). Zu *börü* cf. auch Roux (1999), 204 f.; zur Diskussion um die IE Herkunft cf. Doerfer (1963), 333 ff.

fen der kindl. Sprachentwicklung repräsentieren können und bisweilen Züge von sprachl. „Universalien“ aufweisen. Hiervon zu trennen sind Diminutivformen, wenngleich diese auch an kindersprachl. Elemente angefügt werden können. Kindersprachl. Elemente als Ersatz finden sich aus nahliegenden Gründen bes. im Bereich der Bez. primärer Geschlechtsmerkmale: *apaka* [X.] – „Vulva“,[22] *!momo!*, *mōmo*, *mōmei* [K., X.] – „id“.[23] Neben all den genannten Möglichkeiten findet sich (2.4) als weitere Möglichkeit der Tabuisierung natürlich auch das weite Feld der Kombinationen mehrerer der genannten Muster – etwa die Anfügung von bestimmten Suff.en (z. B. Diminutivsuff.) an oder die lautliche Veränderung von Ersatzwörter(n). Gerade innerhalb des Komplexes der „Šamānensprache(n)“ kommt diesen Kombinationen eine besondere Bedeutung zu. Auch die bereits angesprochene Erscheinung von Mehrfachtabuisierungen ist hiervon betroffen.

Es können an dieser Stelle natürlich nur einige Überlegungen mitgeteilt werden – allerdings hofft der Vf. dieser Z.n, mit dem kleinen Beitrag wenigstens einen Anstoß zu einer erforderlichen, ausgedehnteren Behandlung der Thematik zu geben.

Abkürzungen (Sprachen)[24]

Arman. = Armanisch; **Atü.** = Alttürkisch; **Bir.** = Birare; **Dt.** = Deutsch; **Engl.** = Englisch; **Ew.** = Ewenki; **IE** = Indoeuropäisch; **Jak.** = Jakutisch; **J̌ü.** = J̌ürčen; **Juk.** = Jukagirisch; **Lamut.** = Lamutisch; **Ma.** = Mandschu; **Mo.** = Mongolisch; **Neg.** = Negidal; **N-Uig.** = Neu-Uigurisch; **Oroč.** = Oročisch; **Orok.** = Orokisch; **Samoj.** = Samojedisch; **Türk.** = Türkisch; **Tung.** = Tungusisch; **W-Türk.** = West-Türkisch.

Abkürzungen (Literatur)

AoF – „Altorientalische Forschungen“, Berlin.
APAW – „Abhandlungen der Preußischen Akademie der Wissenschaften“, Berlin.

[22] Shirokogoroff (1944/53), col. 17/ Doerfer (2004), Nr. 714.
[23] Shirokogoroff (1944/53), col. 169/ Doerfer (2004), Nr. 7205.
[24] Abkürzungen nach S. M. Shirokogoroffs „Tungus Dictionary“ (1944/53): **B.** = Birare; **K.** = Kumare (Manegirisch); **U. C.** = Urulga nach Castrén; **X.** = Xingan (Chingan-)Tungusisch.

CAJ – „Central Asiatic Journal. International Periodical for the Languages, Literature, History and Archaeology of Central Asia“, Wiesbaden.
MOS – „Münchner Ostasiatische Studien“, München.
MT – „Materialia Turcica“, Bochum, Göttingen.
RO – „Rocznik Orientalistyczny“, Warszawa.
SPAW – „Sitzungsberichte der Preußischen Akademie der Wissenschaften“, Berlin.
TDKY – „Türk Dil Kurumu Yayınları“, Ankara.
UAJb – „Ural-Altaische Jahrbücher. Internationale Zeitschrift für uralische und altaische Forschung“, Wiesbaden.
VOK – „Veröffentlichungen der Orientalischen Kommission, Akademie der Wissenschaften und der Literatur“, Mainz.
WSlJb – „Wiener Slavistisches Jahrbuch“, Wien.

Literatur

Angere, Johannes:
1957 *Jukagirisch-Deutsches Wörterbuch.* Zusammengestellt auf Grund der Texte von W. Jochelson. Stockholm–Wiesbaden.

[Arat], G[abdul] R[ašid] Rachmati:
1930 *Zur Heilkunde der Uiguren* [I]. Berlin [aus SPAW. Phil.-hist. Kl. 1930 (23), 451–473].
1937 *Türkische Turfan-Texte.* VII. Mit sinologischen Anmerkungen von Dr. Wolfram Eberhard. Berlin [APAW. Phil.-hist. Kl. 1936 (12)].

Cincius, Vera Ivanovna:
1975–77 *Sravniteĺnyj slovaŕ tunguso-mańčžurskich jazykov. Materialy k ėtimologičeskomu slovarju.* 2 Bde. Leningrad.

Doerfer, Gerhard:
1963 *Türkische und mongolische Elemente im Neupersischen. Unter Berücksichtigung älterer neupersischer Geschichtsquellen, vor allem der Mongolen- und Timuridenzeit,* I. *Mongolische Elemente im Neupersischen.* Wiesbaden (VOK XVI).
1988 *Grundwort und Sprachmischung. Eine Untersuchung anhand von Körperteilbezeichnungen.* Wiesbaden–Stuttgart (MOS 47).
1993 Nostratismus. Illič-Svityč und die Folgen. In: *UAJb* N. F. 12, 17–34.

2004 *Etymologisch-Ethnologisches Wörterbuch tungusischer Dialekte (vornehmlich der Mandschurei).* Unter Mitarbeit von Michael Knüppel. Hildesheim–Zürich–New York.

Findeisen, Hans:

1956 *Das Tier als Gott, Dämon und Ahne. Eine Untersuchung über das Erleben des Tieres in der Altmenschheit.* Stuttgart.

Hübschmann, Heinrich:

1887 *Etymologie und Lautlehre der ossetischen Sprache.* Straßburg (Sammlung indogermanischer Wörterbücher 1).

Kljaštornyj, Sergej Grigorevič:

1965 Problemy rannej istori plemeni tjurk (ašina). In: *Novoe v sovetskoj archeologii (pamjatii S. V. Kiseleva).* Moskva, 278–281.

Knüppel, Michael:

2007 Zu (Neu-)Uigurisch (*ḳara*) *éşek* „Skorpion". In: *RO* LX (1), 44–47.

2008 Zu (Neu-)Uigurisch (*ḳara*) *éşek* „Skorpion" – eine Ergänzung. In: *RO* LXI (1), 115–119.

2009 Zu serbo-kroatisch *hȁla* ~ *ȁla* „Drache". In: *WSlJb* 55, 183–187.

Korsch, Theodor:

1912 Türkische Etymologien. In: *Festschrift Wilhelm Thomsen zur Vollendung des siebzigsten Lebensjahres dargebracht von Freunden und Schülern.* Hrsg. v. K. Brugmann. Leipzig, 198–201.

Malov, Sergej Ėfimovič:

1932 Ujgurskie rukopisnye dokumenty ekspedicii S. F. Olʹdenburga. In: *Zapiski Instituta Vostokovedenija Akademii Nauk SSSR* 1. Leningrad, 129–149.

Menges, Karl Heinrich:

1932 Jägerglaube und -gebräuche bei altajischen Türken. In: *Le Muséon* N.S. 45, 85–90.

1933 *Volkskundliche Texte aus Ost-Türkistan.* Aus dem Nachlass von N. Th. Katanov, hrsg. von Karl Menges (SPAW 32), Berlin, 1171–1293 [Auch als Separatdruck resp. „Sonderausgabe (aus den SPAW)" herausgebracht; Berlin 1933].

1982 Etymologika. In: *CAJ* 26, 105–118.

1983 Etymologika. In: *MT* 7–8. (1981–1982) 1983 (zugl. Byzantino-Altaica. Festschrift für Hans-Wilhelm Haussig zum 65. Geburtstag), 264–294.

1985 Einiges Material zum Wortaccent im Ewenki-Tungusischen. In: *CAJ* 29 (3–4), 218–241.

Radloff, Friedrich Wilhelm:
1893 *Versuch eines Wörterbuchs der Türk-Dialecte.* I. St. Petersburg.

Räsänen, Martti:
1969 *Versuch eines etymologischen Wörterbuchs der Türksprachen.* Helsinki.

Röhrborn, Klaus:
1979 *Uigurisches Wörterbuch. Sprachmaterial der vorislamischen türkischen Texte aus Zentralasien.* 2: *agrıglan- – anta.* Wiesbaden.

Roux, Jean-Paul:
1999 Die alttürkische Mythologie. In: *Wörterbuch der Mythologie*, VII: Erster Teil: *Götter und Mythen in Zentralasien und Nordeurasien.* Hrsg. von Egidius Schmalzriedt und Hans Wilhelm Haussig†. Stuttgart, 173–277.

Samojlovič, Aleksandr Nikolaevič:
1915 Zapretnye slova v jazyke kazak-kirgizskoj zamužnej ženščiny. In: *Živaja Starina* XXIV, 161–168.

Shirokogoroff, S[ergei] M[ikhailovich]:
1944/53 *A Tungus dictionary*: Tungus-Russian and Russian Tungus. Photogravured from the manuscripts. Hrsg. von Shinobu Iwamura. Tokyo.

Türk Dil Kurumu:
1942 *Türkiye Halk Ağzından Söz Derleme Dergisi*, III. İstanbul.
1979 *Türkiye'de Halk Ağzından Söz Derleme Dergisi*, XI. Ankara (TDKY 211: 11).

Vasmer, Max:
1953–58 *Russisches etymologisches Wörterbuch.* I. Heidelberg 1953; II. 1955; III. 1958 (Indogermanische Bibliothek [Zweite Reihe: Wörterbücher], 352).

Zieme, Peter:
1975 Ein uigurischer Erntesegen. In: *AoF* 3, 109–143.

Studies on the Turkic World
A Festschrift for Professor St. Stachowski on the Occasion of His 80th Birthday
edited by E. Mańczak-Wohlfeld and B. Podolak, Kraków 2010: 43–48

Yong-Sŏng Li (Seoul)

On the Expression of *(ä)dgü kört(ä)či s(ä)n* on the Bilgä Kagan Inscription

The Orkhon Inscriptions are the earliest known records of the Turkic language. The inscriptions of Kül Tigin, Bilgä Kagan and Tuñukuk are the most well-known ones among them. Since Vilhelm Thomsen deciphered the characters on the inscriptions, many scholars tried to interpret the texts of the inscriptions. Most parts of the inscriptions are already well read. But some of them still need more thorough investigations.

I have translated two works of Talat Tekin, *Orhon Yazıtları* (1988) and *Tunyukuk Yazıtı* (1994), into Korean in one volume with the title of 돌궐 비문 연구—퀼 티긴 비문, 빌개 카간 비문, 투뉴쿠크 비문 – [Dolgwəl Bimun Yəngu—Kül Tigin Bimun, Bilgä Kagan Bimun, Tunyukukï Bimun = Researches into the Orkhon Inscriptions – Kül Tigin Inscription, Bilgä Kagan Inscription, Tuñukuk Inscription] (2008).[1] I have found some doubtful readings and suggested different readings for those places.[2]

1 I have already translated these two works of Talat Tekin into Korean together with Prof. Dr. Young-Il Kim entitled 고대 튀르크 비문의 연구 (1993) [Godä Türïkï Bimunïy Yəngu = Researches into the Old Turkic Inscriptions] for *Orhon Yazıtları* (1988) and 고대 튀르크 비문의 연구 (II) — 투뉴쿡 비문 — (1996) [Godä Türïkï Bimunïy Yəngu (II) — Tunyukug Bimun — = Researches into the Old Turkic Inscriptions (II) – Tuñukuk Inscription] for *Tunyukuk Yazıtı* (1994). But the Korean translation of 1993 contains very few annotations by the translators. The version of 2008 has many new annotations by the translator which are not found in the translations of 1993 and 1996.

2 I have already shown the majority of them in the article entitled "Orhon Yazıtları Üzerine Bazı Notlar", M. Ölmez (ed.), *Festschrift in Honor of Talat Tekin* (= *Türk Dilleri Araştırmaları* 18), İstanbul 2008: 207–228.

There is an expression of *(ä)dgü kört(ä)či s(ä)n* on the 14th line of the north side of the Bilgä Kagan Inscription. The part in question of the inscription is as follows:

(1) ...𐰇𐰃:....𐰃𐰼𐰇𐰼𐱅𐰲𐰃𐰾𐰤 (IO 21)

(2) ...𐰃:𐰓𐰏𐰇:𐰚𐰇𐰼𐱅𐰲𐰃𐰾𐰤 (Radloff 1894: 80)
... *ädgü körtäčisin*[3] "... (Um auf diesen Stein aufzeichnen zu lassen), wer von ihnen true mir anhing" (Radloff 1894: 81)

(3) [...] *(ä)dgü kört(ä)čis(ä)n* "tu verras [...]" (Thomsen 1896: 132)

(4) *mäni*[4] *ädgü körtäči-sän* "Du bist bereit mir treu anzuhängen" (Radloff 1897: 154)

(5) *özüŋ ädgü körtäči-sän* "bu auras toi-même du bon temps (littéralement: toi-même tu verras du bien)" (Thomsen 1916: 62)

(6) "... wird es dir gut gehen" (Thomsen 1924: 143)

(7) ...𐰃:𐰓𐰏𐰇:𐰚𐰇𐰼𐱅𐰲𐰃𐰾𐰤 (Orkun 1936: 59)
[*öz(ü)n*[5]] *(ä)dgü kört(ä)čis(ä)n* "İyi (= hayır) göreceksin!" (Orkun 1936: 58)

(8) 𐰇𐰕𐰭:𐰓𐰏𐰇:𐰚𐰇𐰼𐱅𐰲𐰃𐰾𐰤 (Malov 1959: 15)
özüŋ ädgü körtäči-sän "ты сам будешь жить счастливо" (Malov 1959: 19, 24)

(9) *özüŋ ädgü körtäči sän* "you will become better" (Tekin 1968: 247, 281)

(10) 𐰇𐰕𐰭:𐰓𐰏𐰇:𐰚𐰇𐰼𐱅𐰲𐰃𐰾𐰤 (Ergin 1970: 150)
özüŋ ädgü körtäči sän "kendin iyilik göreceksin" (Ergin 1970: 74, 34)

(11) ... *(ä)dgü kört(ä)či s(ä)n* "... iyilik göreceksin" (Tekin 1988: 32, 33)

(12) [...............] *ädgü körtäči sän* "... iyilik göreceksin" (Tekin 2003: 60, 61)

(13) **Ẅzñ** : dgẄ : kẄrtčIsn (Berta 2004: 101)
özẅñ äδγẅ körᴅäči sän (Berta 2004: 137)
"[akkor] tenmagad a jót fogod szolgálni"[6] (Berta 2004: 192)

As mentioned above, most of the researchers regarded *(ä)dgü* as the direct object of the verb *kör-* 'to see'. In front of this *(ä)dgü*, there is

[3] The meaning of *körtäčisin* is given as 'die Schauenden, die in Treue Anhängenden' in Radloff 1894: 113.

[4] "M. Radloff lit à tort *mäni* 'me' (accusatif) au lieu de *özüŋ*; mais sa traduction exigerait de datif *maŋa* (*kör-*, avec le datif, 'obéir à qn.'). La traduction des formes en *–dačï* par „du bist bereit" n'est pas bonne." (Thomsen 1916: 62)

[5] This form must be an editorial error for *öz(ü)ŋ*.

[6] This sentence can be translated into English as "You (Turkic peoples) will serve the good course". I thank Mr. Hyuk-yang Kwon (권혁양) in Szeged for his help to translate this sentence. The Hungarian words *akkor* and *tenmagad* mean 'then, at that time' and 'thyself', respectively.

a word 𐰃N. in the Finnish edition of 1892 and 𐰃... in the 1894 Radloff's edition. Radloff (1897) amended this word as *mäni* (𐰃𐰤𐰢) and translated the sentence in question as "Du bist bereit mir treu anzuhängen" (1897: 154). That is, he translated *(ä)dgü* into the adjective *true* 'faithful'. But according to his translation, the required form of the word before *(ä)dgü* is not *mäni*, but *maŋa*.[7]

According to the Finnish edition of 1892 and Radloff's edition of 1894, the last letter of the word before *(ä)dgü* is 𐰃. This 𐰃 (ï *or* i) may be the last part of 𐰃𐰤𐰃𐰢, that is *mini* 'me' (accusative).[8] The letter N in the Finnish edition of 1892 may be 𐰤 (n). If it is so, the first sentence on the 14th line of the north side of the Bilgä Kagan Inscription can be read as [*mi*]*ni (ä) dgü kört(ä)či s(ä)n* "You (sing.) will see me well" (or "You (sing.) will love me", "You (sing.) will respect me", etc.).

There are expressions in the same structure as *ädgü kör-* in the modern Turkic languages as follows:

- Trk. *iyi gör-* 'to approve; to welcome' (TRS 486b)
- Tkm. *yaġšï gör-* 'to see well; to love, to respect'(TmRS 202a), 'to prefer; to love; to approve' (TmRS 805b)
- Uz. *yaxši kor-* 'to love, to respect'(URS 234b, 576a)
  xuš kor- 'to love, to respect'(URS 234b, 509a)
- Uyg. *yaxši kör-* 'to love, to be in sympathy (with)' (UjRS 770b), 'to be fond of, to love, to fall in love with, to take a liking to' (UyXL 578b)
  xuš kör- 'to be in sympathy (with)'(UjRS 427b), 'to love' (UyXL 134a)
- Krč.-Blk. *igi kör-* 'to see well; to treat kindly; to respect' (KBRS 293b)
- Kzk. *žaqsï kör-* 'to love' (KRS 269b)
- Kkp. *žaqsï kör-* 'to love' (KkRS 215b; RKkS 404b)
- Tat. (dial.) *xuš kür-* 'to be satisfied with, to feel satisfaction; to love, to respect'(TaRS 617a)
- Bšk. *yaqšï kür-* 'to see well' (BRSb 318ab), 'to approve; to treat kindly' (BRSb 834b)
  xuš kür- 'to be satisfied with, to feel satisfaction'(BRSa 608a; BRSb 714b)
- Kyr. *ǰaqšï kör-* 'to love' (KrRS 218b), 'to feel sympathy for, to love' (KrRS 428a)
- Alt. *d'aqšï kör-* 'to love, to treat kindly' (ORS 43b), 'to feel sympathy for, to love' (ORS 92a)

[7] See footnote 4.

[8] Cf. *bini og(u)z(u)g* 'us (lit. *me*), the Oguz' on the 10th line of the Tuñukuk Inscription.

- Xak. *čaxsï kör-* 'to treat kindly, to look after well' (XRSa 314a), 'to see well; to look after well' (XRSb 205a)
- WYug. *yaxṣi kör-* 'to love' (XHC 250b)
- ED **eḏgü:** 'good' in every sense of the word, (of people) 'morally good'; (of things) 'qualitatively good, serviceable'; (of fortune, etc.) 'good'. Older than the more or less synonymous **yaxşı:**, q.v. (51b)

See DBY 130, footnote 12.

Abbreviations and Bibliography

1. Languages

Alt.	Altay	Tkm.	Turkmen
Bšk.	Bashkir	Trk.	Turkish
Kkp.	Karakalpak	Uyg.	modern Uyghur
Krč.-Blk.	Karachay-Balkar	Uz.	Uzbek
Kyr.	Kyrgyz	Xak.	Khakas
Kzk.	Kazakh	WYug.	Western Yugur
Tat.	Tatar		(= Yellow Uyghur)

2. Dictionaries

BRSa Axmerov, K. Z., et al. (eds.), *Baškirsko-russkij slovar'*, Moskva 1958.

BRSb Uraksin, Z. G. (ed.), *Baškirsko-russkij slovar'*, Moskva 1996.

ED Clauson, Sir G., *An Etymological Dictionary of Pre-Thirteenth-Century Turkish*, Oxford 1972.

KBRS Tenišev, E. R. & Sujunčev, X. I. (eds.), *Karačajevo-balkarsko-russkij slovar'*, Moskva 1989.

KkRS Baskakov, N. A. (ed.), *Karakalpaksko-russkij slovar'*, Moskva 1958.

KrRS Judaxin, K. K., *Kirgizsko-russkij slovar'*, Moskva 1965.

KRS Syzdykova, R. G. & Xusain, K. Š. (eds.), *Kazaxsko-russkij slovar'*, Almaty 2001.

ORS Baskakov, N. A. (ed.), *Ojrotsko-russkij slovar'*, Moskva 1947.

RKkS Baskakov, N. A. (ed.), *Russko-karakalpakskij slovar'*, Moskva 1967.

TaRS Golovkina, O. V. (ed.), *Tatarsko-russkij slovar'*, Moskva 1966.

TmRS Baskakov, N. A., et al. (eds.), *Turkmensko-russkij slovar'*, Moskva 1968.

TRS Mustafajev, E. M.-E. & Starostov, L. N. (eds.), *Turecko-russkij slovar'*, Moskva 1977.

URS Akabirov, S. F., et al. (eds.), *Uzbeksko-russkij slovar'*, Moskva 1959.

UjRS Raximov, T. R. (ed.), *Ujgursko-russkij slovar'*, Moskva 1968.

UyXL Šinǰiang dašüe Xänzu tili fakulteti, *Uyġurčä-Xänzučä Luġät*, Ürümči 1982.

XHC Lei, Xuan-chun (ed.), *Xibu Yugu-Han Cidian*, Chengdu 1992 [雷選春 編著, 西部裕固漢 詞典, 成都 1992].

XRSa Baskakov, N. A. (ed.), *Xakassko-russkij slovar'*, Moskva 1953.

XRSb Subrakova, O. V. (ed.), *Xakassko-russkij slovar'*, Novosibirsk 2006.

3. Others

DBY Tekin, Talât, 돌궐 비문 연구 — 퀼 티긴 비문, 빌개 카간 비문, 투뉴쿠크 비문 — [Dolgwəl Bimun Yəngu — Kül Tigin Bimun, Bilgä Kagan Bimun, Tunyukukï Bimun — = Researches into the Orkhon Inscriptions – Kül Tigin Inscription, Bilgä Kagan Inscription, Tuñukuk Inscription], translated and annotated by Yong-Sŏng Li, Seoul 2008.

IO *Inscriptions de l'Orkhon, recueillies par l'expédition finnoise 1890 et publiées par la Société finno-ougrienne*, Helsingfors 1892.

Berta, Á., *Szavaimat jól halljátok..., A Türk és Ujgur rovásírásos emlékek kritikai kiadása*, Szeged 2004.

Ergin, M., *Orhun Âbideleri*, İstanbul 1970.

Malov, S. Je., *Pamjatniki drevnetjurkskoj pis'mennosti mongolii i kirgizii*, Moskva–Leningrad 1959.

Orkun, H. N., *Eski Türk Yazıtları* I, İstanbul 1936.

Radloff, W., *Die alttürkischen Inschriften der Mongolei*, St. Petersburg 1894.

———, *Die alttürkischen Inschriften der Mongolei*, Neue Folge, St. Petersburg 1897.

Tekin, T., *A Grammar of Orkhon Turkic*, Indiana University Publications, Uralic and Altaic Series 69, Bloomington & The Hague 1968.

———, *Orhon Yazıtları*, Türk Dil Kurumu Yayınları 540, Ankara 1988.

Tekin, T., "A New Classification of the Turkic Languages", *Türk Dilleri Araştırmaları* 1 (1991), 5–18.

———, 고대 튀르크 비문의 연구 [Godä Türïkï Bimunïy Yəngu = Researches into the Old Turkic Inscriptions], translated and annotated by Young-Il Kim and Yong-Sŏng Li, Busan 1993. [the Korean translation of *Orhon Yazıtları* (1988)]

———, *Tunyukuk Yazıtı*, Türk Dilleri Araştırmaları Dizisi 5, Ankara 1994.

———, 고대 튀르크 비문의 연구(II) — 투뉴쿡 비문 — [Godä Türïkï Bimunïy Yəngu (II) — Tunyukug Bimun — = Researches into the Old Turkic Inscriptions (II) — Tuñukuk Inscription —], translated and annotated by Young-Il Kim and Yong- Sŏng Li, Daegu 1996. [the Korean translation of *Tunyukuk Yazıtı* (1994)]

———, *Orhon Yazıtları: Kül Tigin, Bilge Kağan, Tunyukuk*, Yıldız Dil ve Edebiyat Dizisi 1, İstanbul 2003. (3rd impression; 1st and 2nd impressions, 1995, 1998)

Thomsen, V., *Inscripntions de l'Orkhon déchiffrées*, Mémoires de la Société Finno-Ougrienne V, Helsingfors 1896.

———, *Turcica, études concernant l'interprétation des inscriptions turques de la Mongolie et de la Sibérie*, Mémoires de la Société Finno-Ougrienne XXXVII, Helsingfors 1916.

———, "Alttürkische Inschriften aus der Mongolei, in Übersetzung und mit Einleitung", translated by Hans Heinrich Schaeder, *ZDMG* 78 (1924), 121–175.

Studies on the Turkic World
A Festschrift for Professor St. Stachowski on the Occasion of His 80th Birthday
edited by E. Mańczak-Wohlfeld and B. Podolak, Kraków 2010: 49–57

Kinga Maciuszak (Kraków)

On the Iranian Honorific Title *bag*, *baγ*, *bay* 'lord, prince'

A possible derivation of the Turkish lordly title *bäg*, later *bey*, from Iranian is, especially for Iranologists, superficially attractive.[1] There are many reasons for this possible loan: **1.** semantic correspondence, **2.** presence of many Persian loanwords, proper names and titles in Turkish; **3.** lack of convincing etymology in Turkish.[2]

It is true that in the Classical Persian period, Turkish (turkicized?) *beg(ī)* (also: *bak*) 'a lord, prince'[3] entered Persian lexicon together with compound names, as a title put after the names of lords, servants and petty officials, e.g.: ***atā-bak***[4] 'lord father (a title given to the governors of Shiraz); a guardian, preceptor, teacher, the prime minister or vizir; honorary title of an amir; name of a Persian dynasty originating from Sa'd bin Zangi' [Steingass 12];

[1] Cf. Sims-Williams, N. *Baga. II. In Old and Middle Iranian*, [in:] *Encyclopaedia Iranica*, ed. Yarshater, E., 1982ff., London/Boston/Henley (www.iranica.com), p. 404.

[2] Cf. Doerfer, G., *Türkische ind mongolische Elemente im Neupersischen*, II, Wiesbaden 1965, pp. 402–6.

[3] **beg** – dominus (*sāhib va xodāvand*). Inde ***begā-begī*** dominus s. princeps principum (*xodāvand va amir-amirān*) in app. [Vullers 302]; **bega** i.q. *beqam* 'domina, matrona' [Vullers 303].

[4] **atā-bak** – vox turc. ex *atā* pater et *bak* pro *beg* dominus comp., ut significet pater dominus, vel. sec. pater magnus (*pedar-bozorg*), quo nomine olim ii, quibus educatio et instructio principum Selgukidarum curae erat, proprie appellabantur; cf. Mirchond's Gesch. der Selguken pg. 73, not 29; 2) custos, instructor, magister (*negāhdārande va adab āmuzande*); 3) minister supremus, princeps; 4) cognomen dynastiae regum Persidis, quae a Sa'd bin Zangi originem ducit; 5) ut *atā-xvāǧe* simil., titulus honorarius Emirorum [Vullers 70].

axta-begī[5] 'grand equerry, master of the horse' [Haim 24]; ***uluq-beg*** 'great prince; name of a king of Parthia and India, grandson of Timur Lang' [Steingass 94], ***andar-beg*** '(admitted) amongst the great, also amongst the higher order of demons' [Steingass 108]; ***dād-beg*** 'an administrator of justice' [Steingass 494], ***daryā-begī*** 'an admiral' [Steingass 517], etc. This word was also loaned into Hindustani, *beg* 'lord, master (Mughal title)', *begam* 'lady of rank; queen; princes' [Kuczkiewicz-Fraś 119].

The question is how and when could this word possibly have entered the Turkic lexicon? The aim of this paper is neither to solve this question (nor to show the potential paths of borrowing), but provide some arguments, i.e. mainly linguistic and textual data from all Iranian languages, where the word is attested. We hope that this material will be taken into consideration by Turkologists.

I. Old Iranian **baga-* (~ 6th–4th B.C.)

The Old Iranian agent noun *baga-*[6] 'distributor, dispenser; the generous one' (< *bag-*: *baj-*: *baxš-* 'to give, distribute, allot; receive portions' < Pr.Ar. **bhag-* : *bhaj-*, cf. OInd. *bhaj-*, *bhága-*, Greek -*φαγος* 'eater', OCS *bogŭ* 'god' < PIE **bhag-* [Pokorny 107, Rastorgueva-Edel'man II: 48–49] was adopted as a name for 'god'.

1. **Avestan** *baga-* occurs in the *Gathas*, in a passage (Yasna 32.8), where it possibly means 'lot, portion, distribution, good fortune'. In *Avesta* much preferred word for 'god, divinity' was *yazata-* 'worshipful' (cf. Middle Iranian Saka dialects: Khotan *gyasta-*, Tumšuq *jezda-*). In the later Avestan texts *baγa-* occurs as a title of divinities (Ahura Mazdā, Māh, Mithra):[7] *aurvaṅtəm ϑwā dāmiδātəm* ***baγō*** *tatašat hvāpå* (Yasna 10.10) „Swift and wise hath the well-skilled **Deity** created thee";[8] ... *taṅčištəm* ***baγanąm*** *asti* (Yasht 10.141) "... he is the most intelligent of the **gods**".[9]

[5] **axta-begī** n.c. summus stabuli magister, stabularius H. Mong. I, 108; cf. *axta-ğī*, *axtā-ğī* [Vullers 72].

[6] Cf. g. *baga-*, j. *baγa-* 'Anteil, Los; bes. günstiges Los, Glück; vom Glück in der Ehe, Eheglück (nur Komp.)' Vd. 2, Y. 32.8, F. 16, Yt. 16.15; im jAw. 'Herr, Gott': Y. 10.10, Yt. 7.5, Yt. 10.141, Y. 70.1 [Bartholomae 921]

[7] "It is arguable whether it should still be understood in the earlier sense of 'dispenser' or already as 'god'" N. Sims-Williams, *Baga. II...*, p. 404.

[8] Mills, L.H., *Sacred Books of the East*, American Edition, 1898.

[9] Darmesteter, J., *Sacred Books of the East*, American Edition, 1898.

2. **Old Persian.** The development of the latter meaning is securely attested in Old Persian where *baga-*, translated by words meaning 'god' in Babylonian (Akkadian *ilu*) and Elamite, is the only generic term for the divinities (primarily for Ahura Mazda and less frequently for Mithra[10]) worshipped by the Achaemenids: ***baga*** *vazraka Auramazdā* 'the great **god** AM' (passim), *Auramazdā ... hya maϑišta* ***bagānām*** 'AM ... who (is) the greatest of **gods**' (Darius 4.1; Xerxes 6.1).
   In OP *baga-* is found also in many compound names: *Bagābigna-* (a Persian, father of Hydarnes) < *baga-* + *ā-bigna* ptc. in *-na-* of an unidentified root; *Bagabuxša-* (an ally of Darius against Gaumata) 'God-freed' < *baga-* + deriv. of root *baug-* 'free', *Bāgayādi-* 'God-worship month' *baga-*, with vriddhi, + *yad-* 'worship' [Kent 199, Mayrhofer 18–19].
3. **Median** **baga-* in compound names: **baga-yāza-* 'God-worship (month)' (Elamic source), **baga-spāda-* 'the army of God' (Akkadian source) [Rastorgueva-Edel'man 49].
4. **Scythian** **baga-*: *Bάγης* [Bages] shortened form of a name, possibly *Baga-dāta* 'God-given' [Abaev 283].

II. Middle Iranian *bag, baγ, bay (4th B.C. – 9/10th C.E.)

Almost all attested Middle Iranian languages retain forms derived from *baga-* in the sense 'god' and 'lord'. These forms are used as honorific titles, not only of gods but also of kings, nobles, and other men of high rank.

1. Middle Persian

a) **bag** [bg, bk'; inscr. bgy, Pers. /'RHY'/, Parth. /'LH'/]; pl. cas. obl. **bagān** ['RHY'-n, bg'n'] as a pl. majestatis: ***ōišān bagān šahpuhrʸ*** (the Persepolis inscription in Pahlavi 2: 8); without the king's name (the Persepolis inscription in Pahlavi 1: 4); ***šmāh bagān*** (addressing the king; passim); as a real pl. 'lords' (of princess, noblemen, etc.)' [Nyberg II: 42].
   In the later Zoroastrian books Pahlavi and Pazand *bag* became *baγ* and occured associated with *yazata-* in the phrase *yazdān baγān* 'gods'.
   – 'god' [bk', a quotation from the above cited Yasna 10.10]; pl. cas. obl. ***bagān*** [bg'n] (opp. to *dēvān*); *garān* ***bagān*** *kōf* 'the mountain of the mountain **gods**'

[10] In fact only in later inscriptions, e.g. Artaxerxes III text form Persepolis: *Mām Auramazdā utā Miϑra baga pātuv* "Me may AM and the god Mithra protect" [Kent 156].

– 'lord; (his) majesty', spoken of the supreme god: **Ohurmazd-bag** 'Ohrmazd, the Lord'; and of kings: **Kāyōs-bag**; **Bag-Pāpak** and **Bag-Artaxšahr**, **Bag-šahpuhr** (*škand-gumānīk Vičār* 10.70), **Bag-Yazdkart** (*Dēnkard* 21), **Bag-Ohurmazd**, **Bag-Xōsrōi**, **Bag-Narsah** (in the Parthian and Persian inscriptions of the Sasanian king Shapur at Hājjiābād, Naqsh-e Rustam, Persepolis, Tāq-e Bastān, etc.):

PATKAR IM MAZDAYASN **BAQ**[11] **ARTAXŠAΘR** ŠĀHĪN ŠĀH ARYĀN KĒ ČIHR HAČ YAZATĀN **PUΘR BAQ PĀPAK** ŠĀH (Naqsh-e Rustam)
"(This is) an image of the Mazdean, **Lord Ardashir**, king of kings, (of) Aryans, whose appearance (is) from deities (*yazatān*), **the son of Lord Papak**, the king."

PATKAR IM MAZDAYASN **BAQ ŠĀHPUHR** ŠĀHĀN ŠĀH ĒRĀN UT ANĒRĀN KĒ ČIHR HAČ YAZATĀN PUΘR MAZDAYASN **BAQ ŌHRMAZD** ŠĀHĀN ŠĀH ĒRĀN UT ANĒRĀN KĒ ČIHR HAČ YAZATĀN NAP **BAQ NARSAH** ŠĀHĀN ŠĀH (Taq-e bastan)
"This is an image of the Mazdean, **Lord Shahpur**, king of kings, (king of) Iran and Non-Iran, whose appearance (is) from deities, son of Mazdean **Lord Ormazd**, king of kings, (king of) Iran and Non-Iran, whose appearance from deities, grandson of **Lord Narses**, king of kings."

Other attested forms: ***pitar-bag*** 'lord father' in the Persepolis inscription in Pahlavi (cf. Tur. *atā-bak*), ***bag (bay) āfrās*** 'petition to the King or a royal person' [*Frahang ī Pahlavīk* XXX.9], ***bagān*** ['RHY'n'] 'gods, lords' [*Frahang ī Pahlavīk* I.10], ***bagīk*** 'lordly, royal' [*Frahang ī Pahlavīk* II.19].

b) ***bay*** [by], pl. ***bayān*** [b''n, b'n] (SW form of *bag*) [= Pers. *buvand* 'wealthy, majestic', cf. also *buvand* 'proud, arrogant'] [*Frahang ī Pahlavīk* XXX.8], mostly in comp.:
– ***Bay-ādur*** (m.) [bg'twr'] – nom à deux divinités, formé des decendants de **Baga* et *ātr-* « Bay (et) ādur » [Gignoux 193];
– ***Bay-ādur-Farrbay*** (m.) [b(g)'twrpl(nbg), bgy(')t)wrplnbg] – nom à deux divinités, formé de *Bay* (< **Baga*) et du nom de feu A.F. « Bay (et) le feu Farrbay ». Ce nom justifie mon interprétation de *baga* comme le nom propre du dieu (correspondant au ved. *Bhaga-*) dans les composés du même type, puisque *baga* est ici *répété*, et ne

[11] In Aramaic version of this inscription: ALHA, Greek: THEOS.

peut donc être considéré comme l'appellatif, dont il n'y aurait pas d'explication plausible" [Gignoux 194].

- ***Bayān-bay*** (m.) [bg'nbg] – ce nom semble être une ancienne épithète, comparable à *šāhān šāh*, et servant probablement à qualifier *Ahura Mazdā*, qui est bien « le dieu des dieux », i.e. le dieu suprême (< **bagā-nām baga-*) [Gignoux 195] – cf. NPers. (< Tur.) ***begā-begī***.
- ***Ohrmazd-bay*** ['whrmyzd-by], ***Bay-zurwān*** [by zrw'n].[12]

Also Turfan Persian had developed *-y-* from *-γ-* in *bay*, pl. *bayān*, adj. *bayānīy*. This *bay* is found in New Persian *bi-doxt* < *bē-duxt* < **baga-duxtā* 'daughter of god' used for the planet Venus.

2. Parthian

a) ***baγ*** [bg], pl. ***baγān*** [bg'n]:
- 'god': ***Ohrmuzd-baγ*** ['whrmyzd-bg]
- 'lord': ***mānī-baγ*** [m'ny bg] 'Lord Mani':

> ryst, ... hw'xšd m'ry m'ny bg', tw mn bwj, bg', tw mn' bwj, 'whrmyzd-bg'.
> *rist, ... huaxšad mār-ā* ***mānī-baγ****, tū man bōž,* ***baγ-ā****, tū man-ā bōž,* ***Ohrmezd-baγ****.*
> "Truly, merciful my lord, Oh **Lord Mani**, you save me, Oh **lord**, you save me, **lord** Ohrmazd."

b) ***bay*** [by] – SW form of *baγ* in a proper name of the Third Messenger ***zēnārēs-bay*** [zyn'rys by]:

> 'pwr'm 'w prystg'n, yzd'n, ... nwg xwrxšyd ... zyn'rys by ... *āfurām ō frēstagān, yazdān, ... nōg xwarxšēd* ... **zēnārēs bay** ...
> "Creation in angels, gods ... ever new sun ... **the Third Messenger**" [Boyce 105].

3. Sogdian

βaγ [βγ] 'God, Lord, king, sir, excellency (in Buddhist Sogdian of the Buddha)' (Budd., Man., Chr.) [Gharib 2543]: *prn'm* ***βγy*** *δ'mδ'nk* "in the name of **God**, the Creator" (the opening words of Mugh Letter 1.I.);[13] *ZKn* ***βγy*** *ZY ZKn myδr' nβ'nty* "by the **Lord** Mithra" (Mugh Letter Nov. 4); pl. ***βaγān*** [βγ''n] [Gharib 2545]; ***βaγāne-piš(ē)*** [βγ''ny BRY] (Chr.) 'husband' [Gharib 2547]; ***rām-rātux-βaγi*** [r'mr'twxβγy] (Man.) 'pace-dispensing god (of Manichaean god, Mother of Life)' [= Pers. *rām-baxš-baq*]

[12] Andreas, F.C., *Mitteliranische Manichaica aus Chinesisch-Turkestan*, II, ed. Henning, W., Sitzungsberichte d. Preuss. Akad. d. Wiss., Phil.-hist. Kl. 1933, VII, pp. 294–363.

[13] Yakubovich, I., *Mugh 1.I revisited*, Studia Iranica 31/2, 2002, pp. 231–53.

[Gharib 8433], ***xurmazda-βaγi*** [xwrmzt'βγy] (Man.) 'Manichaean god, First Man' [= Pers. hormozd-baq] [Gharib 10754], ***zarwā-βaγe/i*** [zrw'βγyy] (Man.) 'god Zurvan, Father of Greatness' [Gharib 11416].

4. Choresmian

(a)βaγīk [(')βγ(y)k] 'doll' < **baga-ka* and ***βaγī*** [βγy] – name of the sixteenth day of the month corresponding to [mtr] (Mitra) [Bailey 390].

5. Bactrian

The Kushan-Bactrian (2nd c. C.E.) ***βαγο*** 'sir, lord' is attested in a famous inscription of Kanishka (Surx-Kotal, north of Kabul): *Ειδο μαλιζο μο Κανηþκο οανινδο* ***βαγολαγγο*** *σιδο-ι* ***βαγο*** *þαο ναμο βαϱγο* "This is the acropolis of Kanishka, the Victorious, **the temple** (*bago-lango* < **baga-dānaka-*), which bears the name of our **lords**, the king" [Mękarska 152]. The same word appears in naming formulae of many letters written in cursive script on leather, cloth or wood, belonging to a period of a century, covering the last years of the Sasanian domination of Bactria (7–8th c.): *βαγο χοηο* 'the noble lord' (*χοηο* = Parth. xwd'wn, Pers. *xodāvand*) [= Sogd. βγw xwt'w/xwβw].[14]

6. Khotan-Saka

The Kotan-Saka had preferred *gyastānu gyastä* 'god of gods' from *yazata*, but also had a word ***vvūvayau-*** < **baga-yauna-* 'of the origin of the *baga*-distributor; i.e. of the royal origin' used as a royal title [Bailey 390].

III. New Iranian

The Middle Iranian ***baq*** 'god' was generally devaluated in Persian 'idol',[15] entered into composition of names[16] (in fact became a suffix) and ultimately

[14] Cf. Sims-Williams, N., *Bactrian letters from the Sasanian and Hephthalite periods*, [in:] *Proceedings of the 5th Conference of the Societas Iranologica Europaea* held in Ravenna, 6–11 October 2003, I: *Ancient and Middle Iranian Studies*, ed. Panaino, A.; Piras, A., Milano 2006, pp. 701–713.

[15] Cf. *faq*, *foq* 'idol, mistress, handsome man or woman'; which according to the Vuller's explanation: **faq**, **foq** (alia forma vocis **baq**) – 1. (dialecto Ferganensium et Transoxaniae) 'idolum' (= P. *bot*); 2. (met.) 'amasius, amica, amicus, dilectus et formosus, pulcer; **foqestān** – 1. 'templum idolicum', 2. 'gynaeceum regium', 3. (met.) 'formosus, pulcer' [Vullers, 684].

[16] **baq** – 2) nom. idoli cuiusdam (*boti*), qua significatione respondet z. *baghō* [...], eadem vox in compositionis apparet, ut *baqdād*, *baqpur* [Vullers 249].

disappeared.[17] Since the Muslim times (new religion, a new name for god), an old Persian word for a suzerain (in a political sense)[18] *xodā* < MP *xwadāy* beacame to be applied in the meaning of 'god'. One also should mention here a very interesting correspondence: when Old Iranian *bag* 'god' became to be applied as a term for 'lord', simultaneously *xwadāy* 'lord' (cf. *nōg purrmāh-āy-ā ud wahār* ... ***xwadāy***-*ā Mānī-ā* "Ever new full moon and spring ... O **lord** Mani") became to mean 'god':

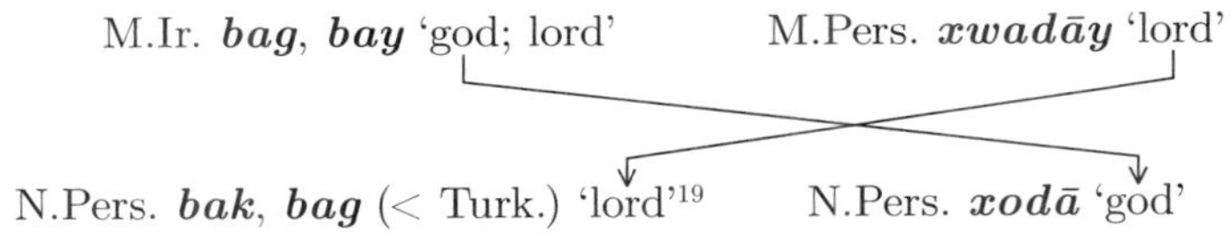

One should also mention here eastern (used in Transoxania and Fergana) dialectal forms with initial *f*:[20] ***faq***, ***foq***, which also entered Persian lexicon, replacing *baq*, *bay*. They are attested in Classical Persian texts in the meaning 'idol, mistress, handsome man or woman' [Steingass 934]. Moreover, old compound name *baq-pur* 'son of god; son of the lord' [Vullers 149] < **baga-putra-*, a calque of Skr. *deva-putra-*? (cf. Parthian *bay-puhr*, Sogd. *βγpwr*, Kushan-Bactrian *bago-pouro*, Turfan Parthian *bay-puhr*) in New Persian *faq-fur*[21] (> Armenian *čen-bakour* 'Chinese emperor', Tur. *far-fur*) was used as the general name of the emperors of China (cf. Chinese imperial title *t'ien-tsï* 'son of heaven').

According to Bailey: "About A.D. 800 Iranian *bay* is present in Kirkut (Qirγiz) *bai*, written by the Chinese sign *buâi* (Matthews, *Chinese-English Dictionary*, no. 4991, modern *pei*) cited in *JA*, 1950, p. 298. The Kirkut adopted the Turkish language only in the 7th–8th centuries".[22]

17 The only remnants of the old Iranian *baga* in Persian, besides compound names, e.g. as: *baq-dād* (other forms: *baq-zāz*, *baq-dāz*, *baq-dān*, *baq-din*, *maq-dān*) 'god-given; the city of Baghdad', *baq-sur* (*baq-šur*) 'name of a town between Herat and Sarakhs', etc. [Steingass 192].

18 Also 'god' but in the Jewish-Christian sense [Nyberg 222].

19 Beside most common *āqā* 'lord, master' also borrowed from Turkish.

20 In Arabic script the initial eastern *β*- [= western *b*-] was expressed by the letter *f* with three dots on it, which in Arabic could be replaced by *f*.

21 **faqfur** (cuius forma primitiva est **baqfur** < e *bag* et *pur*) – 1. 'nomen commune regum Sinensium', 2. 'nom. regis dynastiae Ashkanidarum, qui post Alexandrum sexaginta duos annos regavit', 3. 'nom. regionis in Sina, ubi nitida fictilia conficiuntur'; 4. 'terra pretiosa sinensis, vulg. porcellana'; **faqfuri** (suff. –i) 1. 'ad reges Sinenses pertineus, regius'; 2. 'usitat. ex porcellana' [Vullers 685].

22 Bailey, H.W., *Baga*, [in:] *Encyclopaedia Iranica*, ed. Yarshater, E., 1982ff., London/Boston/Henley (www.iranica.com), p. 403.

In consequence a derivation of the Turk. *beg*, later *bey* from Iranian is quite possible if we take into consideration not Classical Persian but Eastern languages from Sogdiana and Turfan spoken in the Middle Iranian period.

Literature

Abaev, V.I., *Skifo-sarmatskije narečija*, [in:] *Osnovy iranskogo jazykoznanija*, I, *Drevneiranskije jazyki*, Moskva 1979, pp. 272–365.

Andreas, F.C., *Mitteliranische Manichaica aus Chinesisch-Turkestan*, II, ed. Henning, W., Sitzungsberichte d. Preuss. Akad. d. Wiss., Phil.-hist. Kl. 1933, VII, pp. 294–363.

Bailey, H.W., *Dictionary of Khotan-Saka*, Cambrigde 1979.

Bailey, H.W., *Baga*, [in:] *Encyclopaedia Iranica*, ed. Yarshater, E., 1982ff., London/Boston/Henley (www.iranica.com), pp. 403–404.

Bartholomae, Ch., *Altiranisches Wörterbuch*, Strassburg 1904 (1979).

Boyce, M., *A Reader in Manichaean Middle Persian and Parthian*, Acta Iranica, II, 1975.

Darmesteter, J., *Sacred Books of the East*, American Edition, 1898.

Doerfer, G., *Türkishe und mongolische Elemente im Neupersischen*, II, Wiesbaden 1965.

Gharib, B., *Sogdian Dictionary. Sogdian-Persian-English*, Tehran 1995.

Gignoux, Ph., *Iranisches Personennamenbuch*, II: *Mitteliranische Personennamen*, Wien 1986.

Haim, A., *Persian-English Dictionary*, New York 1994.

Kent, P., *Old Persian: Grammar, texts, lexicon*, New Haven 1953.

Kuczkiewicz-Fraś, A., *Perso-Arabic Loanwords in Hindustani*, I: *Dictionary*, Kraków 2008.

Mayrhofer, M., *Iranisches Personennamenbuch*, I: *Die Altiranischen Namen*, Wien 1979.

Mękarska, B., *An attempt at the reconstruction of the Bactrian Language System*, Folia Orientalia XV, 1974, pp. 149–165.

Mills, L. H., *Sacred Books of the East*, American Edition, 1898.

Nyberg, H.S., *A manual of Pahlavi*, I: *Texts*, II: *Ideograms, glossary, abbreviations, index, grammatical survey, corrigenda to part I*, Wiesbaden 1964–1974.

Pokorny, J., *Indogermanisches etymologisches Wörterbuch*, Bern/München 1959–1969.

Rastorgueva, V.C., Edel'man, D.I, *Etimologičeskij slovar' iranskich jazykov*, II: *b–d*, Moskva 2003.

Sims-Williams, N., *Baga. II. In Old and Middle Iranian*, [in:] *Encyclopaedia Iranica*, ed. Yarshater, E., 1982ff., London/Boston/Henley (www.iranica.com), pp. 404–405.

Sims-Williams, N., *Bactrian letters from the Sasanian and Hephthalite periods*, [in:] *Proceedings of the 5th Conference of the Societas Iranologica Europaea* held in Ravenna, 6–11 October 2003, I: *Ancient and Middle Iranian Studies*, ed. Panaino, A.; Piras, A., Milano 2006, pp. 701–713.

Steingass, F., *A Comprehensive Persian-English Dictionary*, London 1892.

Tietze, A., Lazard, G., *Persian Loanwords in Anatolian Turkish*, Oriens, 20, 1967, pp. 125–168.

Utas, B., *Frahang ī pahlavīk* (edited with transliteration, transcription and commentary from the posthumous papers of H. S. Nyberg), Wiesbaden 1988.

Vullers, I.A., *Lexicon Persico-Latinum etymologicum*, Bonn 1855.

Yakubovich, I., *Mugh 1.I revisited*, Studia Iranica 31/2, 2002, pp. 231–253.

Studies on the Turkic World
A Festschrift for Professor St. Stachowski on the Occasion of His 80th Birthday
edited by E. Mańczak-Wohlfeld and B. Podolak, Kraków 2010: 59–67

Tomasz Majtczak (Bochum)

Proto-Turkic Causative in *-*g*-?

Od przybytku głowa nie boli.
(a Polish proverb)

The more the merrier.
(an English proverb of not quite the same meaning)

1. The category of causative is commonly treated in the Turkic languages as one of the elements of voice (diathesis, genera verbi), i.e. it is put on a par with passive, reflexive or reciprocal-cooperative.[1] Unlike the other categories, however, the formation of the causative is far from being automatic and one is inclined to place it in the realm of derivatives rather than among grammatical categories. Thus, for instance, in Modern Turkish the following suffixes are used to build the (more or less) regular

[1] Strictly speaking, the cooperative is not a voice but a manner of action (Aktionsart), since it does not change the syntactic relation between the agent and the patient, i.e. their functioning as the subject and the object in a sentence, which has rightly been pointed out by M. Stachowski (2007, 244/13.1.c). The reciprocal, on the other hand, does introduce a specific relation between the two, namely one wherein several beings perform simultaneously b o t h functions, and hence it can be counted among voices. Yet the problem is that – in contrast to Mongolian for example (cf. Poppe 1974, 62–63/232–234) – in the Turkic languages the cooperative and the reciprocal are usually regarded as one category on the basis of their formal coincidence.

voices of verbs (Ersen-Rasch 2004, 188–193/18.1–18.2; Stachowski 2007, 245–250/13.3–13.4, 257/13.6, 383–384/20.12):

1.1. passive: *-il-*, e.g. *sev-* 'to love' → *sev-il-* 'to be loved'

1.2. passive-reflexive: *-(i)n-*, e.g. *yıka-* 'to wash' → *yıka-n-* 'to be washed, to wash oneself'

1.3. reciprocal-cooperative: *-(i)ş-*, e.g. *vur-* 'to hit' → *vur-uş-* 'to fight each other'.

By contrast, the causative is formed by means of a vast array of morphemes, their choice not being governed by any strict rules – even if it is possible to discern some general tendencies. Taking again Modern Turkish as an example, the suffixes in question are as shown (for some details of their distribution, see Ersen-Rasch 2004, 193–196/18.3; Stachowski 2007, 250–257/13.5):

1.4. causative:

-dir-, e.g. *ye-* 'to eat' → *ye-dir-* 'to feed'
-t-, e.g. *hatırla-* 'to remember, to recollect' → *hatırla-t-* 'to remind'
-it-, e.g. *kork-* 'to fear' → *kork-ut-* 'to frighten, to scare'
-ir-, e.g. *düş-* 'to fall' → *düş-ür-* 'to drop, to let fall'
-er-, e.g. *git-* 'to go' → *gid-er-* 'to remove'
others (isolated), e.g. *em-* 'to suck' → *em-zir-* (~ *em-dir-*) 'to suckle, to nurse'.[2]

2. Old (and Middle) Turkic had at its disposal still greater a set of causative morphemes, which can be listed as follows (Brockelmann 1954, 206–211/151; Erdal 1991, II, 706–847; Gabain 1974, 80–83/155, 161, 165–167; Šervašidze 1986, 38–43; cf. also Räsänen 1957, 153–159):

2.1.

-(u)r-	*-tur-*	*-gur-*
-(X)t-		*-gXt-*
-(X)z-	*-tXz-*	(*-gXz-*).

What made this early Turkic category even less regular than in Modern Turkish is the fact that some verbs combined with more than one suffix (sometimes in different chronological layers, sometimes merely on a synonymous basis), e.g.:

[2] As for the unreliability of any formulated rules, cf. e.g. *seç-* 'to choose' → *seç-tir-* 'to cause to choose' vs *geç-* 'to pass, to go through' → *geç-ir-* 'to move, to transfer', or *ak-* 'to flow' → *ak-ıt-* 'to let flow, to pour' vs *çık-* 'to go out' → *çık-ar-* 'to take out'. That the causative can be an absolutely regular grammatical category is confirmed by Japanese, where it is formed from virtually any verb by means of one suffix only, *-(s)ase-* (synonymous colloquial variant: *-(s)as-*).

2.2. *öl-* 'to die' → *öl-ür-* ~ (later) *öl-dür-* 'to kill'
olur- 'to sit' → *olur-t-* 'to seat'
tut- 'to hold, to grasp' → *tut-uz-* 'to entrust'
amryl- 'to be at peace, to calm down' → *amryl-tur-* 'to calm, to pacify'
bil- 'to know' → *bil-tür-* ~ *bil-tiz-* ~ *bil-düz-* 'to make known, to inform'
bul- 'to find' → *bul-tur-* ~ *bul-duz-* 'to make/let find'
az- 'to go astray, to lose one's way' → *az-gur-* 'to lead astray'
tod- 'to be full/satiated' → *tod-gur-* 'to satiate, to satisfy'
kör- 'to see' → *kör-gür-* ~ *kör-git-* ~ *kör-güt-* ~ (Middle Tk) *kör-güz-* 'to show'
jat- 'to lie down' → *jat-gur-* ~ (Middle Tk) *jat-gyz-* 'to make lie down'.

It seems most reasonable to analyse the formatives *-tur-* and *-tXz-*, together with Modern Turkish *-zir-* (cf. *em-zir-* in 1.4 above) as compound suffixes in which two causative morphemes have been accumulated, i.e. as *-t-ur-*, *-t-Xz-* and *-z-ir-*, respectively, yet not – as might be expected – with a double causative meaning, but with a single one. Such accumulations can be observed at other stages of linguistic development and in other Turkic languages too; in Karaim (KRPS, s.vv.) and Modern Turkish, for instance, one encounters the following derivatives:

2.3. *ax-* 'течь, струиться' → *aγ-yz-* ~ *aγ-yz-dyr-* 'лить, выливать, проливать'
em- 'сосать' → *em-iź-* ~ *em-iź-dir-* 'кормить грудью, давать сосать'
atłan- 'сесть на коня' → *atłan-dyr-* ~ *atłan-γyz-dyr-* 'сажать на коня'

2.4. *de-* 'to say' → (*de-dir-* ~) *de-dir-t-* 'to make/let say'.

The etymologically double-causative nature of *-t-ur-* and *-t-Xz-* was already noticed by G. J. Ramstedt (1912, 28/32, 48–49/59) and it has later been acknowledged by many other scholars. Accumulation of isofunctional morphemes without adding to their meaning is after all nothing unusual among the languages of the world, be it for the phonetic or semantic attrition, or any other reasons. To cite but a few examples without going into details as to the causes for their origin:

2.5. English *children* = *child-re-* (< Middle English *child-re* < late Old English *ćild-ru*; cf. German *Lämm-er* 'lambs') + *-(e)n* (cf. English *ox-en*)

Spanish *conmigo* 'with me' = *con-* (< Latin *cum* 'with') + *-mi-go* (< Latin *mē-cum* 'with me')
Bulgarian *във водата* (< **vъ* + **vъ*) 'in the water' vs *в гората* (< **vъ*) 'in the forest'; *със сол* (< **sъ* + **sъ*) 'with salt' vs *с мене* (< **sъ*) 'with me'
Polish *wniwecz* '[to reduce] to ashes / to rubble' = *w-* (< **vъ* 'into') + *-niwecz* (< **ni-vъ-čь* 'into nothing (*lit.* not-into-what)')
Japanese *kodomo-tachi* 'children' = *ko-domo-* 'child(ren)' (< Old Japanese ko_1-do_2mo 'children' = ko_1- 'child(ren)' + -do_2mo plural) + *-tachi* plural
Japanese *omikuji* 'fortune slip (paper slip drawn at a shrine or temple to tell one's fortune)' = *o-* honorific prefix + *-mi-* honorific prefix + *-kuji* 'lot, lottery, draw, raffle'.[3]

By the same token one could easily analyse Old and Middle Turkic *-gur-*, *-gXt-* and *-gXz-* into *-g-ur-*, *-g-Xt-* and *-g-Xz-*, respectively, the second element of which would be the already mentioned causative formatives in *-(u)r-*, *-(X)t-* and *-(X)z-*.

3. Nonetheless, it does not yet decide the original function of the morpheme **-g-* itself. Thus for G. J. Ramstedt (1912, 19–20/22, 27–28/31) the suffix goes back to proto-Altaic passive – which although not entirely senseless, seems little probable, for causative passive formations are rather closer to simple verbs than to causatives themselves (cf. Modern Turkish *daya-* 'to lean sth against, to base sth on' → *daya-n-* 'to lean against, to be based on' → *daya-n-dır-* 'to lean sth on').

A. v. Gabain (1974, 393/27), on the other hand, interprets this **-g-* as the suffix forming deverbal nouns, involving also *-tur-* in her elucidation:

> Die Entstehung des fakt. *-γur-* ist aus *-γ+u-r-* zu denken, da auch ein *-γut-* belegt ist: *kör-güt-* (Maitr. 36) „erleben lassen" < *-g+ü-t-*; ebenso ist *-tur-* aus *-t+u-r-* entstanden.

One would have to assume here the existence of deverbal substantives in *-g* and *-t* (both attested as such already in Old Turkic, cf. Gabain 1974, 70/109, 75/131), then of verbs formed from these nouns by means of the suffix *-u-* (again, attested in Old Turkic, cf. Gabain 1974, 66/85), and only

[3] Even more expanded is Japanese *omiotsuke* 'soup made from miso (fermented soybean paste) [polite equivalent of *miso-shiru*]' = *o-* honorific prefix + *-mi-* honorific prefix + *-o-* honorific prefix + *-tsuke* 'addition', although an alternative etymology has also been offered (see KKGJ, s.v.).

then would the causative morphemes come into play. Such an etymology, however, requires a long derivational chain, whose individual links are scarcely to be found, if traceable at all.

Lastly, C. Brockelmann explains the *-*g*- very much like A. v. Gabain does, as far as the suffix -*gur*- is concerned, i.e. seeing here the deverbal nominal -*g* (Brockelmann 1954, 206–207/151.c,e). Yet, for reasons not stated explicitly, in -*gXz*- he prefers to single out the gerund, or participle, in -*gu* (Brockelmann 1954, 210/151.k; for -*gu* see, e.g., Gabain 1974, 71–72/115, 117/225). In either case, however, he would like to have the causative morphemes -*(u)r*- and -*(X)z*- attached *directly* to those nominal forms, which in the Turkic languages is simply impossible (not to mention the phonetic discrepancy between the vowels in -*gu* and -*gXz*-).

4. Since all other attempts at explaining the element *-*g*- have failed (or at least remain unconvincing), it seems most advisable to place it among causative suffixes, although unlike the rest of them it was unproductive already at the Old Turkic stage. This idea was for the first time expressed – still with extreme caution – by W. Bang (1919, 16/13);[4] also W. Kotwicz's (1953, 167–168) statement, again not voiced very clearly, can be so interpreted. Some years later I. N. Šervašidze (1986, 41, 43) did not have any more doubts:

> Он [= -*gür*-] является сложным образованием и представляет собой слияние мертвой для стадии языка ТРН [= тюркских рунических надписей] морфемы -*g*- и активного форманта -*ür*- [...]. Суффиксы -*tur*-, -*tür*- и -*tïz*-, равно как и -*gür*-, являются составными: -*tur*-/-*tür*- < -*t*- + -*ur*-/-*ür*-; -*tïz*- < -*t*- + -*ïz*-; -*gür*- < -*g*- + -*ür*-. [...] В этих образованиях явно проступают элементы -*t*-, -*r*-, -*g*-, которые и следует признать древнейшими показателями понудительности.

Of exactly the same opinion is also A. N. Kononov (1980, 181/324.4), and the list of its supporters does not probably end with his name (cf. furthermore Kormušin 1978, 43–53/9–10).

4 The actual passage in W. Bang's article reads (loc. cit.): "A priori wird man also geneigt sein, auch in -*γ°r* und -*γ°z* gehäufte Bildungen zu vermuten, obwohl bei dieser Annahme der erste Komponent vorläufig in Dunkel gehüllt bleibt (vgl. die mongol. Bildungen in Anm. 1)", and in the said footnote he enumerates Mongolian "Faktitivformantien -*ga*, -*ge*, -*lga*, -*lge* und -*gul*, -*gül*".

5. Finally it is worth mentioning that G. J. Ramstedt (1912, 10–16/9–16; 1952, II, 173–175/85) once proposed reconstructing a proto-Altaic causative morpheme of the shape **-ga-* ~ **-ka-*. He was later followed by N. Poppe (1973, 123–128/I.1–3), who modified the reconstruction to **-gā-*. The suffix would be best attested in Mongolian, where *-γa-* ~ *-ge-* forms regularly factitive, or causative, verbs (Kałużyński 1998, 86–88; Poppe 1974, 61–62/223–228):[5]

5.1. *bol-* 'to become' → *bol-γa-* 'to cause to be(come), to make (into)'
sur- 'to learn, to study' → *sur-γa-* 'to teach, to instruct'
una- 'to fall (down/off/out)' → *una-γa-* 'to throw off/down, to overthrow'
bütü- 'to be(come) formed/fulfilled' → *bütü-ge-* 'to fulfil, to materialise'
ködel- 'to move, to be moved' → *ködel-ge-* 'to set in motion, to move'.

In the Tungusic languages it would be documented rather scantily, although one can cite e.g. the following Evenki derivatives in which *-γā-* (~ *-кā-*) is used to convert intransitive verbs into their transitive counterparts (Kormušin 1978, 64–68/13; Poppe 1973, 123–125/I.1; Sunik 1962, 119):

5.2. *уму-* 'установиться, устроиться, образоваться' → *уму-γā-* 'подготовить, собрать, наладить'
мам- 'привыкнуть (*к работе*); научиться, приучиться' → *маму-γā-* ~ *мам-кā-* 'учить, приучать'.

As the Turkic comparandum G. J. Ramstedt (1952, II, 175/85) himself suggested "aktivierendes *-q-* ~ *-k-*", present e.g. in Modern Turkish *ya-k-* 'to light, to ignite, to set on fire' : *ya-n-* 'to burn, to be on fire', cf. further *ya-l-ım* ~ *ya-l-ın* 'flame' (see also Räsänen 1957, 155). One could moreover adduce Old Turkic so-called "intensive verbs" in *-(X)k-*, a category put forth by some scholars (DTS, 660, s.v. *-q-*; Gabain 1974, 82/160; Kormušin 1978, 41–43/8; Tekin 1995, 181/6; cf. Räsänen 1957, 164–165), but almost all these formations are highly questionable (see Erdal 1991, II, 524, 645–651, especially 650–651; 2004, 228–229/408) and they are thus better left out of consideration.

It seems, however, that the proto-Turkic causative **-g-* reconstructed above would be – if accepted – much better a candidate for comparison with the Mongolian and Tungusic suffixes. The credit for the first mention of this idea must again be given to W. Bang (see fn. 4).

[5] To this Classical suffix correspond the Middle Mongolian causative morphemes *-QA-* and *-'A-* ~ *-jA-* (Godziński 1985, 66–67/109–110).

Bibliography

Bang, Willy. 1919. Vom Köktürkischen zum Osmanischen. Vorarbeiten zu einer vergleichenden Grammatik des Türkischen. II: Über einige schallnachahmende Verba. — *Abhandlungen der Preussischen Akademie der Wissenschaften. Philosophisch-historische Klasse* 1919:5.3–36.

Brockelmann, Carl. 1954. *Osttürkische Grammatik der islamischen Litteratursprachen* [*sic*] *Mittelasiens.* Leiden: E. J. Brill, viii + 431 pp.

Clauson, Sir Gerard. 1972. *An etymological dictionary of pre-thirteenth-century Turkish.* Oxford: Clarendon Press, xlviii + 989 pp.

DTS = *Древнетюркский словарь.* Edited by Наделяев, В. М.; Насилов, Д. М.; Тенишев, Э. Р.; Щербак, А. М. Ленинград 1969: Наука, xxxviii + 676 pp.

Erdal, Marcel. 1991. *Old Turkic word formation. A functional approach to the lexicon.* I–II. Wiesbaden: Otto Harrassowitz, xiv + 874 pp. (Turcologica, 7.)

Erdal, Marcel. 2004. *A grammar of Old Turkic.* Leiden – Boston: Brill, xii + 575 pp. (Handbuch der Orientalistik, VIII:3.)

Ersen-Rasch, Margarete I. 2004 (2001). *Türkische Grammatik für Anfänger und Fortgeschrittene*; 2nd edition. Ismaning: Max Hueber, x + 299 pp.

Gabain, Annemarie von. 1974 (1941). *Alttürkische Grammatik*; 3rd edition. Wiesbaden: Otto Harrassowitz, xxiv + 399 pp. (Porta Linguarum Orientalium, Neue Serie, 15.)

Godziński, Stanisław. 1985. *Język średniomongolski. Słowotwórstwo, odmiana wyrazów, składnia* [‘Middle Mongolian. Word formation, inflexion, syntax’]; 1st edition. Warszawa: Wydawnictwa Uniwersytetu Warszawskiego, 271 pp. (Dissertationes Universitatis Varsoviensis, 258.)

Kałużyński, Stanisław. 1998. *Klasyczny język mongolski* [‘Classical Mongolian’]. Warszawa: Dialog, 150 pp. (Języki Azji i Afryki, [8].)

KKGJ = *Kurashi no kotoba gogen jiten* [‘Etymological dictionary of everyday-life words’]. Edited by Yamaguchi, Y. 山口佳紀; 6th impression. Tōkyō 2001 (1998): Kōdansha, 719 pp.

Kononov 1980 = Кононов, Андрей Николаевич. 1980. *Грамматика языка тюркских рунических памятников VII–IX вв.* Ленинград: Наука, 256 pp.

Kormušin 1978 = Кормушин, Игорь Валентинович. 1978. Каузативные формы глагола в алтайских языках. — *Очерки сравнительной морфологии алтайских языков.* Edited by Суник, О. П. et alii. Ленинград: Наука, 10–87.

Kotwicz, Władysław. 1953. Studia nad językami ałtajskimi ['Studies on Altaic languages']. Edited by Lewicki, M. — *Rocznik Orientalistyczny* 16(1950).1–314.

KRPS = *Караимско-русско-польский словарь*. Edited by Баскаков, Н. А.; Зайончковский, А.; Шапшал, С. М. Москва 1974: Русский язык, 688 pp.

MED = *Mongolian-English dictionary*. Compiled by Lessing, F. D. et alii; 3rd reprinting with minor type-corrections. Bloomington 1995 (1960): The Mongolia Society, xv + 1226 pp.

Poppe, Nikolaus. 1973. Über einige Verbalstammbildungssuffixe in den altaischen Sprachen. — *Orientalia Suecana* 21(1972).119–141.

Poppe, Nicholas. 1974 (1954). *Grammar of Written Mongolian*; 3rd impression. Wiesbaden: Otto Harrassowitz, xv + 195 pp. (Porta Linguarum Orientalium, Neue Serie, 1.)

Ramstedt, Gustaf John. 1912. Zur verbstammbildungslehre der mongolisch-türkischen sprachen. — *Journal de la Société Finno-Ougrienne* 28:3.1–86.

Ramstedt, Gustaf John. 1952–1966. *Einführung in die altaische Sprachwissenschaft*. Edited by Aalto, P. Helsinki: Suomalais-Ugrilainen Seura. I: *Lautlehre*, 1957, 192 pp.; II: *Formenlehre*, 1952, 262 pp.; III: *Register*, 1966, 171 pp. (Mémoires de la Société Finno-Ougrienne, 104:1–3.)

Räsänen, Martti. 1957. *Materialien zur Morphologie der türkischen Sprachen*. Helsinki: Societas Orientalis Fennica, 256 pp. (Studia Orientalia, 21.)

Redhouse çağdaş Türkçe-İngilizce sözlüğü. Redhouse contemporary Turkish-English dictionary. Edited by Avery, C. R. et alii; 1st printing. İstanbul 1983: Redhouse, xxii + 455 pp.

Šervašidze 1986 = Шервашидзе, Иван Николаевич. 1986. *Формы глагола в языке тюркских рунических надписей*. Тбилиси: Мецниереба, 136 pp.

Stachowski, Marek. 2007. *Gramatyka języka tureckiego w zarysie* ['Outline of Turkish grammar']. Kraków: Księgarnia Akademicka, 407 pp.

Sunik 1962 = Суник, Орест Петрович. 1962. *Глагол в тунгусо-маньчжурских языках. Морфологическая структура и система форм глагольного слова*. Москва – Ленинград: Издательство Академии наук СССР, 363 pp.

Tekin, Talat. 1995. Relics of Altaic stem-final vowels in Turkic. — *Laut- und Wortgeschichte der Türksprachen. Beiträge des Internationalen*

Symposiums, Berlin, 7. bis 10. Juli 1992. Edited by Kellner-Heinkele, B.; Stachowski, M. Wiesbaden: Harrassowitz, 173–187. (Turcologica, 26.)

TMS = *Сравнительный словарь тунгусо-маньчжурских языков. Материалы к этимологическому словарю.* Edited by Цинциус, В. И. et alii. Ленинград: Наука. I: *А – Ӈ*, 1975, xxx + 672 pp.; II: *О – Э*, 1977, 992 pp.

Studies on the Turkic World
A Festschrift for Professor St. Stachowski on the Occasion of His 80th Birthday
edited by E. Mańczak-Wohlfeld and B. Podolak, Kraków 2010: 69–73

Witold Mańczak (Kraków)

Relations entre les titres turcs *qaγan*, *qan*, *qaγatun*, *qatun*

Alexander Vovin (2007) a consacré à ce problème un long article, qui commence de la façon suivante:

> Enormous amount of ink has been spilled on the etymology of the title *qaγan* 'emperor, supreme ruler' that is found in many Inner Asian languages. The proposed etymologies most invariably tried to explain *qaγan* on the basis of Turkic, Mongolic, or Tungusic, although suggestions involving Iranian, Korean and Chinese are also present. However, none of these attempts won the universal recognition, which probably testifies to the fact that none of them is correct. My intention here is not to review these numerous proposals, but rather to look for an alternative explanation of this title, which does not involve any of the languages mentioned above.

P. 178, on lit ce qui suit:

> Before attempting to etymologize the title *qaγan*, we should ask ourselves a question, what is a *qaγan* in relation to a *qan*. Old Turkic examples may suggest that *qaγan* and *qan* were used interchangeably, e. g. *Bilgä-qaγan* and *Bilgä-qan* [...] This might imply that these two terms are synonymous [...] Regarding the Mongolic tradition, de Rachewiltz pointed out that Cinggis bore only the title *qan* during his life, and that the title *qa'an* was assumed only starting with his successor Ögedei [...] It is nevertheless telling that in the later tradition Cingiis is given the title *qa'an* (presumably posthumously). It is also important that the title *qan* 'ruler' is not attested in the Inner Asian

> languages before the eighth century and in Chinese inscriptions prior to the tenth century [...] Superficially it might seem to give some credibility to Pelliot's hypothesis that *qan* is a contracted form of *qaγan* [...] However, there is a serious counterargument to de Rachewiltz and Pelliot's hypothesis: *-kan* is amply attested on a periphery of Inner Asia in sixth and seventh centuries as a part of the titles of Silla's kings and nobility, for example royal titles [...] *malip-kan* [...] *kese-kan* [...] Furthermore, O[ld] K[orean] *kan* [...] as a nobility title is attested by itself [...] and in a great number of compounds, such as [...] *kak-kan* [...] *kup-kan*, etc. [...] It is important to note that Silla kings never had the title of 'emperor' or 'supreme ruler': they were simply 'kings'. Thus, while the overlapping Old Turkic usage remains to be explained, it appears that Ögedei's title was elevated from *qan* to *qa'an* and the latter title was also 'granted' posthumously to Cinggis. This approach finds its further justification in the previously mentioned fact that both Xianbei and Ruan-ruan rulers were carrying the title *qaγan* and not *qan*. Thus it becomes quite apparent that *qan* is a lesser ruler than *qaγan*, and that *qaγan* is a greater ruler than *qan*. The interpretation of the relationship between the two is then almost self-inviting: *qaγan* is a 'great *qan*'.

Et voici la conclusion de l'article de Vovin:

> Thus, it seems to be quite likely that the ultimate source of both *qaγan* and *qan* can be traced back to Xiong-nu and Yeniseian. The scenario of the transmission of these titles in Inner Asia is probably as follows. The original Xiong-nu terms **qaˀ-Gā* 'great ruler' (? < **qaˀ-qʎ̄j*) and **qʎ̄j* 'ruler' were borrowed initially by Xianbei with further addition of the Mongolic singular *-n* and plural *-d*. Neither *qatun* nor *qaγatun* are attested in Xianbei's usage, but they are attested for Ruan-ruan, so the addition of feminizing suffix *-tu-* must have been a Ruan-ruan creation. Almost nothing is known about the Ruan-ruan language, but the bits and pieces that we have allowed me previously to draw a conclusion that it was an Inner Asian language, unrelated to any other language of this area that are known to us [...]. When Turks borrowed all four titles from their Ruan-ruan masters, they borrowed them as single units, and not as compounds.

A notre avis, la différence entre *qaγan* et *qa'an*, *qan* consiste ne ce que *qaγan* est régulier, tandis que *qa'an* et *qan* s'expliquent par ce que nous appelons un développement phonétique irrégulier dû à la fréquence. Il en est de même pour les formes féminines: *qaγatun* est régulier, alors que la naissance de *qatun* est liée à un développement irrégulier dû à la fréquence.

Depuis de longues années, nous affirmons que, dans toutes les langues, la forme des mots dépend de trois facteurs principaux, non seulement du développement phonétique régulier et du développement analogique, mais aussi du développement phonétique irrégulier dû à la fréquence: les groupes de mots, mots et morphèmes très employés subissent souvent des réductions irrégulières. Par exemple, *God be with you* s'est réduit en *good-bye*. En anglais, il y a 700 dérivés en *-iness* (tel *laziness*), parmi lesquels un seul a subi une réduction irrégulière, à savoir *business* (> [*biznis*]), et *business* est le mot le plus fréquemment usité parmi les dérivés en *-iness*. En polonais, il y a presque 3500 mots en *-ść* (< proto-slave *-*stь*), par exemple *gość* 'hôte', *kość* 'os', *wieść* 'nouvelle' et surtout les innombrables dérivés en *-ość* du type *wielkość* 'grandeur'. Parmi ces 3500 mots en *-ść*, il y a un seul mot qui présente un développement irrégulier, à savoir v. pol. *jeść* 'il est', qui s'est réduit en *jest* (on a ici affaire à une dépalatalisation irrégulière), et *jest* est plus employé que tous les mots où *-ść* a persisté jusqu'à nos jours (Mańczak 2009). En allemand, on dit *geben*, *gegeben*, en anglais on dit *give*, *given*, c'est-à-dire que le suffixe *-n* s'est maintenu au participe, qui est moins employé, et est tombé irrégulièrement à l'infinitif, qui est plus employé (Mańczak 1993). En ce qui concerne le développement phonétique irrégulier dû à la fréquence, nous y avons dédié trois monographies (Mańczak 1969, 1977 et 1987) ainsi que de nombreux articles (pour les langues turques, voir Mańczak 2005).

Parmi les arguments que nous alléguons à l'appui de notre conception, il y en a un qui est le suivant: s'il existe, pour la langue et la période en question, un dictionnaire de fréquence, on peut en user parce que la grande majorité des mots subissant un développement phonétique irrégulier dû à la fréquence se trouve parmi les mots les plus employés. Par exemple, en français moderne, ces mots se présentent comme suit:

1er mille	99	86%
2e mille	9	8%
3e mille	4	3%
4e mille	2	2%
5e mille	1	1%
6e mille	–	

Il est intéressant de noter que, selon le dictionnaire de fréquence de Eaton (1940), esp. *rey*, fr. *roi*, angl. *king* et all. *König* se trouvent parmi les mille mots les plus utilisés dans ces langues.

En outre, il faut attirer l'attention sur le fait que, à côté du développement phonétique irrégulier dû à la fréquence, il existe une autre évolution irrégulière, consistant en des accidents phonétiques connus depuis longtemps sous le nom d'assimilations, dissimilations ou métathèses, en des formes hypercorrectes ou expressives. Toute cette évolution se caractérise par le fait qu'elle a lieu, dans des langues différentes, dans les mots les plus divers. *Chercher* < *cercher* présente une assimilation, *faible* < *flebilem* une dissimilation, *troubler* < **turbulare* une métathèse, tandis que *s* dans *besicles* est hypercorrect et *h* dans *herse* est censé être expressif. Mais il serait difficile de trouver, dans une autre langue indo-européenne, un mot signifiant 'faible' avec une dissimilation, un mot signifiant 'troubler' avec une métathèse ou un mot signifiant 'herse' avec un phonème d'origine expressive. Bref, il n'y a aucun parallélisme entre les irrégularités dites assimilations, dissimilations, métathèses, etc. En revanche, le développement phonétique irrégulier dû à la fréquence a lieu, dans les langues diverses, d'une manière plus ou moins parallèle parce que, malgré les différences qui séparent des communautés linguistiques, les mots les plus fréquents sont partout plus ou moins les mêmes. Par exemple, le verbe signifiant 'parler' présente dans beaucoup de langues des réductions irrégulières, cf. fr. *parler*, it. *parlare* < lat. *parabolare*, des formes de *narrare* devenu en sarde *nárrere* (*nau*, *nas*, *nat*, etc.), lat. *ajo* < **agio* (en face du régulier *adagium*, qui est moins utilisé), angl. *says*, *said* (en regard du régulier *lays*, *laid*, où la diphtongue a persisté), russe dial. *gyt* < *gryt* < *govorit*, a. polonais *pry* < *prawi*, etc.

Or, il est important de noter que le nom du roi, qui est très employé, présente, dans beaucoup de langues, des réductions irrégulières, cf. angl. *king* (< *cyning*), all. *König* (< *kuning*), suédois *kung* (< *konung*), dan. *konge*. Le fait que le suffixe *-ing* s'est maintenu dans néerlandais *koning*, s'explique par l'histoire: pendant plusieurs siècles, les Pays-Bas n'étaient pas gouvernés par un roi. La simplification de la géminée dans le v. h.-all. *kuning* 'roi' (en regard de *kunni* 'race') est due à un fréquent usage. Le nom germanique du roi a été emprunté par d'autres langues, où il a également subi des réductions irrégulières. En lituanien, *kuningas* a été abrégé en *kunigas* et même *kungas* (il en est de même pour le letton *kungs*). En a. polonais *księże* (voc. de *ksiądz*) était réduit en *ksze*. *Książę* 'prince', qui est un dérivé de *ksiądz*, se déclinait à l'origine comme des neutres du type *cielę* 'veau': nom. *książę*, gén. *książęcia*, dat. *książęciu*, etc. La vieille flexion a persisté jusqu'à nos jours au pluriel (qui est moins utilisé que le singulier): nom. *książęta*, gén. *książąt*, dat. *książętom*, etc., mais au singulier il y a aujourd'hui des formes réduites: nom. *książę*, gén. *księcia*, dat. *księciu*, etc. A partir du masculin *kъnędzь*, on a tiré le féminin **kъnęgynji*, qui a subi des réductions irrégulières, cf. polonais *ksieni* 'abbesse', v. tchèque *knieni*, haut-sorabe *knjeni*, bas-sorabe *kněni*, v. russe *knjaini*. La forme régulière a persisté dans le toponyme polonais *Księginki* (évidemment moins employé que l'appellatif *ksieni*). Le monarque s'appelle en russe *gosudar'*, qui est une forme réduite de *gospodar'*. Il en est de même pour russe *car'* < *cěsar'*.

A la lumière de tous ces faits, il est indubitable que les titres *qa'an*, *qan*, *qatun* s'expliquent par un développement phonétique irrégulier dû à la fréquence.

Références

Eaton H. 1940, *Semantic Frequency List for English, French, German and Spanish*, Chicago.

Mańczak W. 1969, *Le développement phonétique des langues romanes et la fréquence*, Kraków.

——— 1977, *Słowiańska fonetyka historyczna a frekwencja*, Kraków.

——— 1987, *Frequenzbedingter unregelmäßiger Lautwandel in den germanischen Sprachen*, Wrocław.

——— 1993, Loss of the final *n* in English, *Kwartalnik Neofilologiczny* 40, p. 21–30.

——— 2005, Développement phonétique irrégulier dû à la fréquence dans les langues turques, *Studia Turcologica Cracoviensia* 10, p. 259–267.

——— 2009, Nieregularny rozwój fonetyczny spowodowany frekwencją a słownik pod redakcją Doroszewskiego, J. Wawrzyńczyk (ed.), *Czterdzieści lat minęło... Nad „Słownikiem Doroszewskiego"*, Warszawa, p. 51–56.

Vovin A. 2007, Once again on the etymology of the title *qaγan*, *Studia Etymologica Cracoviensia* 12, p. 177–187.

Studies on the Turkic World
A Festschrift for Professor St. Stachowski on the Occasion of His 80th Birthday
edited by E. Mańczak-Wohlfeld and B. Podolak, Kraków 2010: 75–94

Michał Németh (Kraków)

North-Western and Eastern Karaim Features in a Manuscript Found in Łuck*

I. Preliminary remarks

As reported in MARDKOWICZ (1933b), a considerable part of the Karaim manuscripts stored in the loft of the *kenesa* in Łuck until the First World War were destroyed during the war and the Russian Revolution in 1917. Luckily for us, some of those manuscripts, mostly private letters and circulars, after having been stored and partly edited in 1933 by Aleksander Mardkowicz,[1] ended up in a private collection and have survived in almost perfect condition to this day.

The majority of the surviving manuscripts is written in Hebrew semicursive script – most of them in the Łuck subdialect of Łuck-Halicz Karaim (hereinafter called, for the sake of brevity, the Łuck Karaim dialect), a smaller part of the collection being written in Troki Karaim. Even though some of the manuscripts display glosses from other dialects, the reader normally has no particular difficulty classifying the manuscript from the linguistic point of view. They are going to be presented in the near future in another, more extensive study. The collection, however, contains

* We are indebted to Prof. Henryk Jankowski (Poznań) for reviewing the present paper and for valuable suggestions. We are grateful also to Dr. Marek Piela (Kraków) for Hebraistic help.

1 We have recently dealt with this part of the collection in NÉMETH (2009) discussing intentional amendments introduced to some of the surviving texts in MARDKOWICZ (1933a).

a document of which we cannot be entirely sure which dialect some of its fragments represent. As it exhibits a number of interesting features, including traces of far-reaching dialect mingling, it undoubtedly deserves a separate presentation.[2]

II. Description of the manuscript

The manuscript is part of Józef Sulimowicz's (1913–1973) collection and can be found under the catalogue number 50^{II} (see the upper-right corner of the sheet). The dark cream-coloured plain sheet of the size of 215 × 165 mm has been folded in four and contains four drafts written in dark brown and black ink. The drafts were ordered by someone who had previously read them (most probably by A. Mardkowicz) and are marked with A, B, C, and D. We copy this order in our transcription as this order follows logically from the arrangement of the four fragments on the sheet. The right and, to some extent, also the left margins of the sheet are somewhat ragged, but the text itself has not been damaged.

It is clear at first glance that the drafts are written by four different hands. Firstly, this transpires from the fact that only the first fragment is vocalised. Secondly, this is especially visible when comparing the shape and the size of the letters (see facsimile provided). The most important differences are: *koph* is considerably different in fragment A and in the rest of the manuscript (where its shape is quite unusual when compared to other Łuck Karaim texts available to us); *tzadhe* and *shin* have different shapes in fragments A, B, and D; and, finally, *daleth* and the final *mem* are shaped differently in parts B and C. The shape of the rest of the letters is simple to such a degree that there are usually only minor differences between them, such as have no value of proof unless an extensive graphological examination is performed. We strongly believe that the above-mentioned dissimilarities in themselves suffice to prove that all of these fragments originate from different authors, even if in terms of handwriting, parts B and C are somewhat similar to each other.

We consider these texts to be drafts because many words have been struck through, amended, or added to the text at a later time. Apart

[2] We are indebted to Mrs Anna Sulimowicz for making access to the digital copy of the manuscript possible.

from this, the signatures of the authors are also missing. The latter fact would support our assumption, especially when seen in the light of the content of line 16.

As far as their content is concerned, all four parts are quite similar to one another and rather simple. In fact, the manuscript is simply a common summons sent to Shemoel the son of Yaakov Simcha by four different people seeking to have their property restored (including jewellery and articles made of gold, silver and copper). Thus, the letter is most probably a result of the authors' joint effort to get their property back.

Our knowledge about the addressee is extremely modest. Based on the information available in the census record list of the census conducted on 8th May 1858 (RS 1858), we can say that Shemoel, the son of Yaakov Simcha, was born around 1826, and his father Yaakov passed away in 1855. Additionally, from another document written most probably in 1868 and containing a list of heads of households in the Karaim community of Łuck, we know that his surname was *Kačor*[3] and that he was still unmarried at that time. Finally, the present manuscript tells us that he was living in a village called in Karaim *Rudecki* (= Pol. *Rudecka*), situated approximately 16 km south-east of Łuck in the municipality of Jarosławicze, in the district of Dubno (SGKP XV/2: 556).

Note that this place name is missing from the list of villages inhabited by Karaims in the second half of the 19th century drawn up and published by MARDKOWICZ (1933c: 22).

Unfortunately, we do not have enough information to say exactly when the manuscript was written. As such, we can merely attempt to establish an approximate date based on the highly fragmentary information about the author's life. Namely, the fact that the creditors deposited their goods with him and addressed the summons to him means probably that he was already independent financially. Consequently, according to Karaim tradition that would mean that either he should have been married by this time or the letter was sent after his father passed away. Based on the dates previously mentioned, we can say then that the letter was most probably written after Yaakov Simcha's death in 1855.

[3] We quote this Karaim surname basing on the list of family names drawn up in KRPS 674–680 – in a transcription.

III. Transcription[4]

A

[1] *ʾhwby*[5] *kmʿ*[6] Šemoeł *b*[7] *ʾhwby ʾḥy*[8] *kmʿ* Jaakov
[2] Simχa[9] *hzqn*[10] *zl*[11]
[3] Kołamen seńi ḱi bojurγajsen berme[12]
[4] ćiringńi baĺašanyj puskaba da belibawny[.]
[5] Ospu ~~nerseł~~[13] eki nerseńi ber bu[14]
[6] ribbiǵe ńepriḿenno[.]

B

[7] *bkpr*[15] Rudeckij Šemoeł ben Jaakov Simχanyn
[8] kołuna b́erǵań ńerśalarimd́ań artyk bir ńerśam

[4] In order to distinguish the Hebrew fragments we have transliterated them with italic letters. The phonetic value of [w] remains a disputable question in the light of Kowalski's (1929: XLIV) remark about Karaim: 'Doch findet man u̯ als individuelle Aussprache, namentlich bei Leuten aus der älteren Generation, auch in der NW-Mundart'. A similar case is that of the voiced uvular [γ], which was most probably pronounced as a velar voiced [h] at that time – at least in the Łuck Karaim dialect. We have left [γ] in the transcription in view of Grzegorzewski's (1903: 5–6) description, in which we can read that this phoneme was still used at the beginning of the 20th century in Halicz by elderly people, more precisely 'bei solchen die aus Troki (oder aus dem Oriente) stammen oder längere Zeit dort zugebracht haben'. Thus, the phonetic realisation of [w] and [γ] differed depending on the speakers' idiolect.

[5] אהובי: Hebr. אֲהוּבִי 'my beloved'.

[6] כמע: The abbreviation stands for Hebr. כְּבוֹד מַעֲלַת 'honourable sir, the Honourable' (see e.g. Baader 1999: 148).

[7] ב̇: An abbreviation of Hebr. בֵּן 'son; the son of'.

[8] אהובי אחי: Hebr. אֲהוּבִי אָחִי 'my beloved kinsman'.

[9] שימחה: The Hebrew name *Simcha* שִׂמְחָה – an orthographical variant written with *yodh* here.

[10] הזקן: Hebr. זָקֵן '1. aged man; 2. scholar' used with Hebrew definite article הַ.

[11] זל: A commonly used abbreviation for Hebr. זִכְרוֹנוֹ לִבְרָכָה 'may his memory be blessed; of blessed memory' (cf. e.g. Baader 1999: 112).

[12] A word has been inked over at the end of line 3 in a manner which makes the reading of it impossible, cf. the facsimile.

[13] נֵרְיסֵיל: Probably the first part of the mistakenly (and erroneously) written word *nersełerni* has been struck through here by the author.

[14] בוּ: Surprisingly, the demonstrative pronoun *bu* appears in this sentence in the role of the definite article. Cf. also the same usage of *bu* in line 14.

[15] בכפר: Hebr. כְּפָר 'village' used with the Hebrew preposition בְּ 'in; within'.

[9] kałmady da bir[16] kurušłuχ[17] ńerśa sakłamadym[.]
[10] Eǵer jałγan sowłasam to *mšpṭ*[18] *ṣʾwʾ*[19] po zakońe[20] borčłum[21][.]

C

[11] Kołamen seńi ḱi bujurγajsen berme bar
[12] nersełerimńi ~~kasjyłaryn~~ ne men berd́im
[13] seńin kołłaryna[.] ~~bir~~ Nemeded́[22] oťatet[-]
[14] memeśḱe[23][.] Baryn berǵin[24] bu[25] ribbińin
[15] kołuna[26][.]

D

[16] *ʾny hḥwtm mṭh mʿyd ʿly ky*[27] *bkpr* Rudecki
[17] Šemoeł ben Jaakov Simχanyn kołuna b́erǵań ńerśa[-]
[18] larimd́ań baška artyk bir ńerśam kałmady
[19] ńi ałtyn ńi ḱuḿuš[28] ńi bakyr[.] Da bir
[20] ńerśa astramadym da *byt dyn*ńiń[29]
[21] bujruγuna *wmlk*nyn[30] ijǵań kišilarińa[.]

16 ביר: The author added the word afterwards to the text, between lines 8 and 9.
17 כורושלוק: This shape of final *koph* is characteristic of Łuck Karaim texts.
18 משפט: Hebr. מִשְׁפָּט 'seat of judgement', here in *status constructus* מִשְׁפַּט.
19 צאוא: Hebr. צַוָּאָה '1. command, order; 2. testament, will'.
20 פו זכוני: < Russ. *по закону* 'in compliance with the law'. The *-u* > *-e* change can probably be explained by contamination with the prepositional case form of Pol. *zakon* 'order, monastery', namely *zakonie*.
21 בורצלום: The abbreviated *-m* COPULA.1.SG ending (< *-myn*) is quite rare in Karaim texts. As far as we know, it has been mentioned only by BERTA (1998: 309).
22 The reading of the word remains somewhat unclear. To justify our reading we must assume that the letter *daleth* is written carelessly and that is why it rather resembles *resh*. Cf. also the word *berd́im* in the previous line, where *daleth* is very similar to *resh*, too.
23 אוטייטיטמיסיסכיא: The word form most probably contains a writing error, as from the morphological point of view the repeated syllable *-me-* cannot be explained.
24 בירגין: A closer examination of the word shows that the author previously wrote an initial *waw* standing for [*v*-], instead of *beth*.
25 בו: The pronoun is used in the role of definite article. Cf. *bu* in line 5.
26 כולונה: The final letter is written somewhat carelessly, cf. the facsimile.
27 Hebr. אֲנִי הַחוֹתֵם מַטָּה מֵעִיד עָלַי כִּי 'I, the undersigned, testify that'.
28 כומוש: We would expect rather כיומיוש here rendering [-́u-] in both syllables, analogically to the notation of [-́o-] < [-ö-] in כיוריה *ḱoŕa* in lines 23 and 24.
29 ביתדין נין: Hebr. בֵּית־דִּין 'law court' with the Karaim genitive suffix attached.
30 ומלך נין: The word form consist of Hebr. וְ 'and' and מֶלֶךְ 'king, sovereign'. A separately written genitive case ending is attached to the latter one.

[22] Jałγan sowłamadym. Eǵer jałγan śoźlaśam[31] da
[23] bir ńerśa sakłasam to *mšpṭ*ka[32] ḱońa
[24] da zakonγa ḱońa borčłu bołurmyn[33][.]

IV. Translation

A

[1] My beloved Shemoel the Honourable, the son of my beloved kinsman of blessed memory Yaakov Simcha
[2] the Honourable [and] the scholar [~ the aged][.]
[3] I ask you to have the kindness to give [back]
[4] the jewellery with the tinplate box and the belt[.]
[5] Give these two particular articles to the
[6] *ribbi* by all means[.]

B

[7–8] Except the articles passed into
Shemoel the son of Yaakov Simcha's hands in the village of Rudecki not even one
[9] left and I did not store even a [single] worthless[34] thing[.]
[10] If I had lied, then an order[35] of the law court[36] [would be enough to state that] in compliance with the law I am [, and not you,] the indebted [~ guilty] one[.][37]

[31] סוזלסים: The letter *zayin* has been written over an original *waw*, which points to the fact that the author originally wanted to use the verb *sowła-* here, too. Probably the author's intention was to improve the text stylistically, reducing the number of words repeated in one sentence. A *yodh* denoting palatality after the word-initial *samekh* might, in fact, be expected here, as it is also used for [-́o-] in the postposition כיוריה *ḱońa*. The lack of it, in this case, can be explained as a result of corrupt amendment. Another possible explanation for such writing would be to interpret the word form as *sözlesem*, see the relevant chapter in the *commentary and conclusions*.

[32] משפט קא: Hebr. מִשְׁפָּט 'seat of judgement' with a separately written dative case suffix.

[33] בולורמין: The author made a significant error by writing the word originally with an initial *o-* (cf. the facsimile, the initial *aleph* and *waw* is clearly legible under *beth*).

[34] Literally: 'one *kuruš*'s worth of something'.

[35] צאוא: Corruptly written Hebr. צַוָּאָה 'command, order'.

[36] משפט: Hebr. מִשְׁפָּט 'seat of judgement', here in *status constructus* מִשְׁפַּט.

[37] The meaning of the last line is somewhat vague.

C

[11] I ask you to have the kindness to give [back] all of
[12] my articles that I passed into
[13] your hands[.] There is nothing to be taken
[14] away[.][38] Pass all [of them back] into the
[15] *ribbi*'s hands[.]

D

[16–17] I, the undersigned, testify that except the articles passed into Shemoel the son of Yaakov Simcha's hands in the village of Rudecki
[18] [there is] not even one [article] left,
[19] either [made of] gold, silver or copper[.] And
[20] I did not hide [away] even a single thing, either,
[21] [according] to the order of the law court and the [order of the] sovereign sent to the people[.]
[22] I did not lie. If I had lied and
[23] stored even a single thing, I would be [, and not you], according to the law court
[24] and in compliance with the law, the indebted [~ guilty] one[.]

V. Commentary and conclusions

It must be stated at the outset that Karaim manuscripts in general – written in any of the dialects – usually reflect different degrees of irregular writing, in parts very irregular. This, being characteristic also of the edited text, makes the assignment of the particular fragments to respective dialects, based on orthographical evidence only, fairly difficult, all the more so as the fragments are very short. Not only that, but the north-western fragments and even eastern Karaim elements occurring in the manuscript compel us to treat the whole document even more cautiously, irrespective of the fact that the addressee was a member of the community in Łuck and that the manuscript was stored and found in that town, too.

Part A

The first, four-line-long Karaim fragment can be conclusively classified, based purely on linguistic evidence, as clearly a south-western type. Already

[38] The translation is uncertain due to difficulties in reading the handwriting.

the first verbal form קוֹלַמְן *kołamen* (3) itself – with the KarŁ. personal ending *-men* as opposed to KarT. *-myn* – is enough to rule out north-western Karaim.[39] Similar morphonological evidence is provided by בוֹיוּרְהַיְיסֵן *bojurγajsen* (3) and בֵּרְמֶה *berme* (3) – as opposed to KarT. *bujurγejsyn* and *b́erḿa*, respectively. Furthermore, based on the word forms פּוּסְקַבָא *puskaba* (4) and אוֹסְפּוּ *ospu* (5) we can rule out eastern Karaim as the language of this particular fragment, too. Given that the distinction between *samekh* used for [s] and *shin* for [š] is retained throughout in the text, we can confidently postulate south-western [s] in those words. Note that the first of these is a loanword from Pol. *puszka* [-š-] 'box', and the second one is an equivalent of KarK. *ušbu* 'this; this particular' (KRPS 587).[40] Finally, an additional piece of evidence supporting the south-western origin of the fragment is the simple fact that the author addressed Shemoel the son of Yaakov Simcha as his kinsman (see lines 1–2), i.e. they possibly belonged to the same community.

Worth mentioning are the rules of spelling of this fragment, more precisely the notation of [e]. Compared to other Łuck Karaim manuscripts, this letter displays a distinct difference when representing this sound in every position.

The notation of medial [-e-] deserves special attention. The most significant difference is the use of *shwa* for indicating both [-e-] and the absence of a vowel, even in Karaim words, cf. קוֹלַמְן *kołamen* (3) and נִירְסֵנִי *nerseńi* (5). As a matter of fact, in Łuck Karaim manuscripts, at least those available to us, medial [-e-] occurs as a realization of *shwa* solely in the case of words of Hebrew-origin, obviously simply because in those words the original spell-

[39] We claim this even though the medial [-e-] as written in the word is quite unusual, namely with *shwa*. Further explanations of this notation will follow below.

[40] Çulha (2006: 115) quotes KarKT. *ušpu*, probably assuming an assimilative *-šb-* > *-šp-* change in respect of the Crimean form. It may well be, however, that the authoress of the latter dictionary misrepresented the data found in KRPS, and ascribed the KarT. form *ušpu* 'this; this particular' also to the eastern dialect. It also remains unclear why Tksh. *öteki* 'the other one; the further; the one over there' is provided as the meaning of the word in the dictionary discussed (Tksh. *işbu* would be much more appropriate). Older Karaim dictionaries and Łuck Karaim texts we have had the opportunity to read so far do not note it. Perhaps it is a mistake? Even Clauson (1972: 254–255), cited by Çulha (2006: 115), does not provide the above-mentioned meaning for compound words containing Tkc. *oš* and *bu* (for the structure and etymology of the pronoun see Stachowski 2007: 172–173). In our text the meaning 'this; these' fits in well with the context. We cannot find the above-mentioned eastern form in Chafuz (1995) and Levi (1996).

ing tended to be retained. This notation has its roots most probably in the tradition of reading Hebrew liturgy and prayers, which was still alive at that time. It fits with the fact that the basic realisation of *shwa* in Hebrew texts was [e] amongst the Karaims in the Crimea and in Lithuania, see HARVIAINEN (1997: 106ff.). There is, in fact, also some evidence allowing us to assume that the same was the case in Halicz (see HARVIAINEN 1997: 109) or even in Łuck (see HARVIAINEN 1997: 112). Consequently, to a certain extent we may treat this notation as an additional piece of evidence showing that the basic realisation of *shwa* in the 19th-century Hebrew current among Łuck Karaims could have been [e], too.

Another curiosity of the fragment is the use of the vowel sign *seghol* (plus a *yodh*, i.e. -ֶי-), in the word בֶּילִיבַבְנִי *belibawny* (4) for rendering [-e-]. This, similarly to the previous notation, is very rare in Karaim manuscripts from Łuck. And again, from the manuscripts available to us, it is clear that *seghol* was used mostly in Hebrew loanwords.

The third vowel sign used for medial [-e-] is *tzere* written without *yodh* after it (see בֵּרְמֶה *berme* in line 3). Even though this was not the most frequent notation in Łuck Karaim manuscripts, it was frequent enough not to be treated here as a peculiarity.

In initial position [e-] appears once: in the word אֵקִי *eḱi* (5), i.e. it is noted with *aleph* with *tzere* (אֵ). It is true that one example is wholly insufficient to be representative. Still, we can say that the notation is unusual when compared to those manuscripts from Łuck we have seen. In those, the vocalised fragments display mostly *aleph* with *tzere* plus *yodh* (-אֵי) – *aleph* with *tzere* is very rare. Hebrew loanwords – in which the original spelling was kept unchanged – and proper names are, of course, an exception here.

We have only one attestation of final [-e] in this part, rendered by *seghol* and *he* (-ֶה) in the word בֵּרְמֶה *berme* (3). In this case we cannot find any analogical example in the materials compared. Both the vowel sign *seghol* in general, and *he* for final [-e], are extremely rare.

The lexicon and the syntax of this short fragment display evident Slavonic, more precisely Polish and Russian influence. Besides the word *puska* (4), already mentioned, two other Slavonic words, namely בַּלִישָׁנִיְ *bal̃ašanyj* (5) and נֵיפְּרִימֵינְנוֹ *ńeprim̃enno* (6), appear here. Surprisingly enough, the letter *yodh* after *lamedh* in the word *bal̃ašanyj* most probably reflects the Russian palatal *l̃* in *бляшный*, which would be a rather interesting influence of Polish orthography, in which the letter *i*, that is to say the graphic equivalent in the Latin alphabet of Hebr. *yodh*, is used for expressing palatality of a prevocalic consonant. If *yodh* stood for *-j-*, we would expect the vowel sign *pattāḥ* to be written underneath it, not after it.[41]

As is usually the case in Łuck Karaim texts, the word order is strongly influenced by Slavonic constructions (SVO). In fact, the whole fragment copies Slavonic syntax and word order, except for the use of the demonstrative pronoun בו *bu* (5) used, on the model of Hebrew, as a definite article. The Hebrew influence in this case is unambiguous; the more so as the pronoun stands before the title *ribbi* – just as in the case of other Hebrew honorifics used with the definite article הַ in Karaim, Hebr. הַזָּקֵן '1. the scholar; 2. the aged' used in line 2 (see *hzqn*) being a good example. What makes the use of the pronoun in question even more interesting is the fact that, to the extent we know, in the grammatical descriptions to date this role has been attributed only to the pronoun *ol* 'that; those' (PRITSAK 1959: 331).

Part B

The most important clue allowing us to identify the language of the second fragment is the notation of the vowels [a] and [e]. In particular, the expression פו זכוני *po zakońe* (10), of Slavonic origin, clearly shows us that final [-e] was written, as expected, with *yodh*. It is important to state that *yodh* is also used in all places where, in each of the three Karaim dialects, there is [e]. Additionally, the conjunction דא *da* (9) confirms that the final *aleph* was used by the author for rendering [-a]. Seen in this light, the word form נירסא *ńerśa* (9) cannot be read but with final [-a] as opposed to KarŁ. *nerse* with [-e]. The same can be said about *aleph* in medial position: it must have been used for [-a-] in the word נירסאלרימדן *ńerśalarimdań* (8), as we cannot see any reason why it would not be noted with *yodh* if it had been pronounced [e]. In any case, it is also clear from the Łuck Karaim manuscripts known to us that medial *aleph* was never used for [-e-]; thus the latter word cannot be interpreted as KarŁ. *nerseƚerimden*. This is the first argument to show that the current fragment should be classified as written in Troki Karaim.

Further, there is another orthographical feature which can be explained only with Troki Karaim morphonology. In such word forms as בירגן *b́erǵań* (8), נירסאלרימדן *ńerśalarimdań* (8), נירסם *ńerśam* (8) and סוולסם *sowłasam* (10) the suffix vowel is not noted, which points to the reading with [-a-], too. It is because the vowel [-e-], expected here if the words were

[41] Such notation was characteristic also of north-western Karaim texts, cf. ZAJĄCZKOWSKI, A. (1931–1932: 184).

written in Łuck Karaim, was nearly always written *plene* in south-western non-vocalised texts, by contrast with [-a-] which was very frequently not noted, both in Łuck and in Troki Karaim manuscripts.

Although our reasoning is corroborated by the handwritten Troki Karaim material available to us, the argumentation presented above does not exclude without any reservation Crimean Karaim as the possible language of this fragment. The crux of the problem is that even though in printed Crimean materials *aleph*, according to SULIMOWICZ (1972: 43) and JANKOWSKI (1997: 4–5) at least, was not used for denoting medial [-e-] or [-ä-], the non-vocalised Crimean manuscript presented by JANKOWSKI (2003: 126–129) gives evidence of such notation.[42] Additionally, [e] was quite frequently not noted word-medially, according to what we can see in JANKOWSKI (1997: 4–5 and 2003: 126–129). But one must also admit that the spelling of the Crimean manuscript presented in JANKOWSKI (2003) is irregular to such a degree that we can find there any kind of orthographic feature.

Regardless of this, if we take a look at the manuscript as a whole, there are some additional hints pointing to the fact that the discussed fragment was written by a Karaim speaking the north-western dialect. As argued below, Part D must be classified as Troki Karaim with some eastern Karaim elements. If so, it seems somewhat more plausible that the manuscript consists of two Łuck Karaim fragments (A and C) and two Troki Karaim fragments (B and D) with eastern Karaim elements (*vide infra*), than to suppose a linguistically mingled document comprising all three dialects at once. We think so, even though in the fragment discussed we can find the word כורושלוק *kurušłuχ*[43] (18), being certainly a trace of Crimean influence, cf. e.g. CTat. *kuruš* 'piaster' (KtRS 372). On the other hand, this lexicological feature might also demonstrate that the author of the present fragment and the author of part D had their roots in the same milieu of Karaims speaking north-western Karaim, interspersed with the Crimean Karaim word. This idea of a 'common language' for these two authors is supported by the verb *sawła-* (19, 22), not listed in any of the existing Karaim dictionaries (nor in those manuscripts known to us), and used only in fragments B and D. Moreover, if we take a closer look at the lexical material of the manuscripts, we can see that in general the lexicon is shared by parts A and C, as opposed to B and D.

[42] The idea that the Crimean Karaim [e] in non-first syllables was pronounced as [a], as suggested by SULIMOWICZ (1972) and (1973), has been, in our opinion, rightly refuted in JANKOWSKI (1994: 109–112).

[43] The [-k] > [-χ] change in Troki is regular (see e.g. KOWALSKI 1929: XXXII).

Part C

The unusual notation of medial and final [e] is a feature characteristic also of this fragment. Firstly, the use of the letter *he* for final [-e], as is the case in the word ברמה *berme* (11), is very rare in the Łuck Karaim texts available to us. But what is more significant for us is that, surprisingly, medial [-e-] is often not noted here, as was the case in the previous fragment, too. A closer examination of the relevant word forms, however, leads to a different conclusion than in the case of part B. The issue here is that the personal endings in the verbal forms קולמן *kołamen* (11) and בויורהייסן *bujurγajsen* (11) would have been noted with an additional *yodh* in both cases if the words had been written in the north-western dialect of Karaim, i.e. if we read here *kołamyn* and *bujurγajsyn*, respectively. This is for the simple reason that [y] was, as far as we know, always written with this letter both in Troki and Łuck Karaim texts, as well as in the Crimean dialect (see e.g. JANKOWSKI 1997: 5, TIRIJAKI 2004: 256). In comparison, we can find corroborating examples where [-e-] is omitted in all dialects, although only a few exists in Łuck Karaim.

Troki Karaim can be neglected here even more conclusively in the light of the word קוללרינא *kołłaryna* (13) – the form in Troki Karaim is *kołłaryja*.

These examples, however, do not exclude Crimean Karaim as the possible language of this fragment. The relation of this dialect to the note of five lines is the more interesting, given the significant error found in the text, which points to an evident eastern Karaim feature. Namely, in line 14 the word בירגין *berǵin* was originally written with initial *waw* which points to the reading with [v-], i.e. points to Crimean influence (cf. KarK. *ver-* 'to give' listed in KRPS 158). The same word, however, dispels the doubt on the dialectal affiliation of the fragment discussed; the imperative suffix *-gyn* does not exist in Crimean Karaim, see PRIK (1976: 144).[44]

The syntax of this portion of the text resembles that of Part A, and, in fact, that of Łuck Karaim texts in general as it clearly copies Slavonic sentence structures. The only exception is, again, the use of the demonstrative pronoun בו *bu* as the definite article (line 14; cf. description of part A). Slavonic influence on the lexicon is represented by only one, corruptly written word: אוטייטיטמימיסכיא *oťatetmemeśke* (13–14).

Part D

The dialectal classification of the last fragment as Łuck Karaim is, similarly to part B, dubious. As will be argued below, it seems very likely that it was written in Troki Karaim.

[44] Cf., however, the manuscript edited by AQTAY (2009: 41), where this suffix is noted.

At first sight, south-western Karaim would seem to be excluded owing to the shape of the letters *shin* and *tzadhe*, which are characteristic rather of manuscripts written in north-western Karaim.[45] We can treat, however, this piece of palaeographical evidence, merely as supportive.

Furthermore, similarly to what has been said above regarding part B, the lack of the letter *yodh* in suffixes, where in Łuck Karaim there would have been a medial [-e-] – juxtaposed to KarT. [-́a-], is, again, a serious argument against classifying this fragment as south-western Karaim, cf.: בירגן *b́erǵań* (17), נירסיהלרימדן *ńerśalarimdań* (17–18) and כישילרינא *kišilarińa* (21). Even though we can find several forms in which the use of *yodh* could suggest medial [-e-], and, consequently, could point to Łuck Karaim word forms (cf. e.g. נירסים *ńerśam* in line 18), we believe that, in these cases, the letter *yodh* could have been used as a diacritic, pointing to a palatal consonant preceding [a]. This phenomenon, as we have already mentioned above, was frequent even in north-western religious texts, and was irregular, too, just as in the case of this fragment, see ZAJĄCZKOWSKI, A. (1931–1932: 184).

Some additional evidence against a Łuck Karaim provenience of this fragment emerges from the clear distinction between the use of the letters *shin* ‹ש› and *samekh* ‹ס›. From the spelling of the words בשקא *baška* (18), כומוש *ḱuḿuś* (19), and כישילרינא *kišilarińa* (21), it is clear that ‹ש› is used only in those cases where the Turkic equivalents of these words have [š], likewise in proper names and appellatives of Hebrew origin. On the other hand, *samekh* ‹ס› is consistently used for [s].

The idea here presented should be supplemented with the fact that we can perceive some Oghuz, most probably Crimean Karaim influence in this fragment, too, which makes this manuscript even more unique. The most significant example here is the word form בולורמין *bołurmyn* (24) written initially as *ołurmyn* (with או-), which is clearly visible in the manuscript (see facsimile). Given such evidence, it seems plausible that the word כו-מוש *ḱuḿuś* (19) should be deciphered rather as *kümüš*[46] (in the light of *waws* used without the expected *yodh* + *waw* combination – i.e. כיומיוש*),

[45] The shape of these letters, visible e.g. in words בורצלו *borčlu* or Hebr. משפט (in the last and last but one lines of the manuscript, respectively; see facsimile), are very similar to those used in the cursive Ashkenazi script from 19th-century Germany, presented by YARDENI (1997: 272, 273).

[46] Or as *kumüš*. The status of the palatal rounded vowels in the first syllable in Crimean Karaim has not been entirely clarified yet (see JANKOWSKI 1994: 112). This applies also to *sözlesem* mentioned below.

and treated as another trace of Crimean influence, or Oghuz influence at least (cf. KarK. *kümüš* 'silver', KRPS 353). The reading of the word סוזלסים *śoźlaśam* (22) might remain an open question for the same reason: one would expect *yodh* + *waw*, rendering [-́o-] in the first syllable like in כיוריה *ḱoŕa* (23, 24). Moreover it could be, in fact, read even as *sözlesem* (or *sozläsäm*), since – as we have mentioned above – based on JANKOWSKI (2003: 128–129) we can say that internal [-e-] (or [ä]) was not always noted in non-vocalised Crimean Karaim texts written in Hebrew script, cf. e.g. KarK. גלן *gelen* or וירמישלר *vermišler* attested in the manuscript presented by JANKOWSKI (2003: 128–129).

VI. The lexicon of the manuscript[47]

1. Appellatives

ałtyn 'gold' (t) ♦ NOM: אלטין [19]

artyk (*with a negative verb*) 'any more; no longer, no more' (t) ♦ ADV: ארטיק [8, 18]

astra- 'to hide' (t) ♦ PRAET.NEG.1.SG: אסטרמדים [20]

bakyr 'copper' (t) ♦ NOM: בקיר [19]

baĺašanyj '*adj.* tin, being made of tinplate' (ł) ♦ NOM: בַלַישָׁנִיְ [4]

- < Pol. *blaszany* id. ↔ Russ. *бляшный* id. The *-a-* in the first syllable is epenthetic.

bar '1. everything, all; 2. (*with possessive suffix*) all' (ł) ♦ NOM: בר [11] ♦ ACC.POSS.3.SG: ברין [14]

baška (*abl.*) 'except' (t) ♦ POSTP: בשקא [18]

belibaw 'belt' (ł) ♦ ACC: בֶילִיבַבְנִי [4]

ber- (ł) ~ **b́er-** (t) 'to give' ♦ INF: ברמה [3] ♦ בֵרְמֶה [11] ♦ IMPER.2.SG: בֵרְ [5] ♦ בירגין [14] ♦ PRAET.1.SG: בירדים [12] ♦ PART.PRAET: בירגן [8, 17]

bir '1. one; 2. (*used with negation*) not a, not even a' (ł, t) ♦ NOM: ביר [8, 9, 13, 18, 19, 23]

bojur- 'to have the kindness' (ł) ♦ OPT.2.SG: בוֹיוּרְהַיְיסֵן [3]

- Karaim dictionaries note *bujur-* only (KSB 17, KRPS 138). The *-o-* in the first syllable should be treated as a result of *u – u > o – u* dissimilation. For a similar example, cf. **ospu**. Cf. also **bujur-**.

boł- 'to be' (t) ♦ FUT.1.SG: בולורמין [24!]

borčłu '1. indebted; 2. guilty' (t) ♦ NOM: בורצלו [24] ♦ COPULA.1.SG: בורצלום [10]

bu *definite article* (ł) ♦ ART.DEF: בו [14!] ♦ בוּ [5!]

[47] The Hebrew lexicon has been already commented on in the footnotes in the transcription, therefore we have decided not to repeat it here.

bujur- 'to have the kindness' (ł) ♦ OPT.2.SG: בויורהייסן [11]
- Cf. **bojur-**.

bujuruk 'order, command' (t) ♦ DAT.POSS.3.SG: בויירוגונה [21]

ćiring 'jewellery' (ł) ♦ ACC: צִירִינְגְנִי [4]

da 'and, too' (ł, t) ♦ CONI: דַ [4] ♦ דא [9, 19, 20, 22, 24]

eǵer 'if' (t) ♦ CONI: אגר [10, 22]

eḱi 'two' (ł) ♦ NOM: אֶקִי [5]

ij- 'to send' (t) ♦ PART.PRAET: אייגין [21]

jałγan 'lying, deceitful' (t) ♦ NOM: יילגן [22] ♦ ילגן [10, 22]
- ~ **sowła-** 'to lie' [10, 22] ♦ ~ **śoźla-** 'to lie' [22!]

kajsy 'which, that' (ł) ♦ ACC: קייסילרין [12]

kał- (t) 'to stay, to remain' ♦ PRAET. NEG.3.SG: קלמדי [9, 18]

ḱi 'to, in order to' (ł) ♦ CONI: כִי [3]

kiši 'man' (t) ♦ DAT.PL.POSS.3.SG: כישילרינא [21]

koł 'hand' (ł, t) ♦ DAT.POSS.3.SG: קולונא [8] ♦ קולונה [15] ♦ קולונא [17] ♦ DAT.PL.POSS.2.SG: קוללרינא [13]

koł- 'to ask; to entreat' (ł) ♦ PRAES. 1.SG: קולמן [11] ♦ קוֹלַמְן [3]

ḱoŕa (*dat.*) 'according to, in respect for' (t) ♦ POSTP: כיוריה [23, 24]

ḱuḿuš 'silver' (t) ♦ NOM: כומוש[19!]

kurušłuχ 'worth (a certain amount of) *kuruš*' (t) ♦ NOM: כורושלוק [9!]
- < CTat. *kuruš* 'piaster' (KtRS 372) with the suffix *-łuk* forming *nomina abstracta* (Zajączkowski, A. 1932: 29–30).

men 'I' (ł) ♦ NOM: מן [12]

ne (*pron.*) 'which' (ł) ♦ NOM: ני [12]

nemede 'nothing' (ł) ♦ COPULA.3.SG: נימידיד [13]

ńepriḿenno 'by all means' (ł) ♦ ADV: נֵיפְּרִימֵינְנוֹ [6]
- < Russ. *непременно* 'by all means, necessarily'. The vowel *-i-* possibly reflects the actual pronunciation of the unaccented Russ. *e*.

nerse (ł) ~ **ńerśa** (t) 'affair, thing' ♦ NOM: נירסא [9] ♦ נירסיה [20, 23] ♦ NOM.POSS.1.SG: נירסים [18] ♦ ני־ רסם [8] ♦ ACC: נִירְסֵנִי [5] ♦ ACC. PL.POSS.1.SG: נירסילריםני [12] ♦ ABL.PL.POSS.1.SG: נירסאלרידן [8] ♦ נירסיהלרידן [17–18]

ńi 'neither, nor' (t) ♦ CONI: ני [19]
- ~ **...** ~ **...** 'neither ... nor ...' [19]
- < Pol. *ni* 'neither, nor', Russ. *ни* id., Ukr. *ні* id.

ospu 'this, this particular' (ł) ♦ PRON: אוֹסְפּוּ [5]
- Karaim dictionaries note only KarŁ. *uspu* 'this, this particular' (KSB 68, KRPS 583). The *u* > *o* change took place most probably due to dissimilation. For a similar example cf. **bojur-**.

po 'according to, on the basis of' (t) ♦ PRAEP: פו [10]
- ~ **zakońe** 'in compliance with the law' [10!].
- < Russ. *no* 'according to, on the basis of'.

puska 'box' ♦ INSTR: פּוּסְקָבָא [4]
- < Pol. *puszka* 'box'.

ribbi '*ribbi*, teacher (*used as a title*)' (ł) ♦ GEN: ריבינין [14] ♦ DAT: רִיבְגֵה [6]
- < Hebr. רַבִּי 'a title given to Jewish religious scholars'.

sakła- 'to store' (t) ♦ PRAET.NEG.1.SG: סקלמדים [9] ♦ COND.1.SG: סקלסם [23]

sen 'you (*thou*)' (ł) ♦ ACC: סיני [11] ♦ סֶנִי [3] ♦ GEN: סנין [13]

sowła- 'to speak' (t) ♦ PRAET.NEG.1.SG: סוולמדים [22!] ♦ COND.1.SG: סוולסם [10!]
- **jałɣan** ~ 'to lie' [10, 22]
- The word could be read also as *sawła-* and *sewłe-*. The latter one is less probable in the light of the lack of *yodh* for noting [-e-]. For comparative data cf. KTkc. *sovła-* 'to speak' (Grunin 1967: 405), M-Kipch. *savła-* 'to speak' and *jałɣan savła-* 'to lie' (Zajączkowski, A. 1968: 101), KarK. *sevle-* 'to speak' (Radloff 1911: 501, s.v. *cäwlä-*).

śoźla- 'to speak' (t) ♦ COND.1.SG: סוזלסים [22!]

to 'then; in that case' (t) ♦ CONI: טו [10, 23]
- < Pol. *to* 'then, in that case', Russ. *то* 'then, in that case'.

zakon 'law' (t) ♦ DAT: זכונגא [24] ♦ RUSS: פו זכוני [10!]
- < Russ. *закон* 'law', Ukr. *закон* 'rule of law'.

2. Proper names

Šemoeł ben Jaakov Simχa ♦ NOM: שמואל בֿ יעקב שמחה [1–2] ♦ GEN: שמואל בן יעקב שמחהנין [7, 17]

Rudecki 'a village, approximately 16 km south-East of Łuck (in the municipality of Jarosławicze, district of Dubno)' ♦ NOM: רודיצקי [16] ♦ רודצקיי [7]
- < Pol. *Rudecka* (see SGKP XV/2: 556).

Rudeckij see **Rudecki**

VII. Abbreviations and symbols

1. Languages

CTat. = Crimean Tatar | **Hebr.** = Hebrew | **KarK.** = Crimean Karaim (E dialect) | **KarŁ.** = Łuck Karaim (SW dialect) | **KarT.** = Troki Karaim (NW dialect) | **M-Kipch.** = Mameluk-Kipchak | **Pol.** = Polish | **Russ.** = Russian | **KTkc.** = Kipchak-Turkic | **Tksh.** = Turkish | **Ukr.** = Ukrainian

2. Grammatical terms

Abl. = Ablativus | **Adv.** = Adverbium | **Acc.** = Accusativus | **Art.def.** = Articulus definitus | **Cond.** = Conditionalis | **Coni.** = Coniunctio | **Dat.** =

Dativus | **Fut.** = Futurum | **Gen.** = Genetivus | **Imper.** = Imperativus | **Inf.** = Infinitivus | **Loc.** = Locativus | **Neg.** = Negatio | **Nom.** = Nominativus | **Opt.** = Optativus | **Part.praet.** = Participium praeteriti | **Pl.** = Pluralis | **Poss.** = Possessivus | **Postp.** = Postpositio | **Praes.** = Praesens | **Praet.** = Praeteritum | **Praep.** = Praepositio | **Pron.** = Pronomen | **Sg.** = Singularis

3. Symbols used in the text

[...] = in transcription and translation: complementary fragments facilitating the reading | **[~ ...]** = alternative translation | **~~abc~~** = in transcription: text lined through by the author | ↔ = contamination | >, < = phonetic development, borrowing | **[!]** = in glossary (after the line number): additional commentary in part III. or V.

VIII. References

AQTAY, G., 2009, *Eliyahu Ben Yosef Qılcı's Anthology of Crimean Karaim and Turkish Literature. Critical Edition with Introduction, Indexes and Facsimile*, 1–2 [1: Introduction, Text and Indexes; 2: Facsimile] (= *Yıldız Dil ve Edebiyat Dizisi* 8), İstanbul.

BAADER, F.H., 1999, *Kurzwort- und Abkürzungslexikon. Hebräisch-Deutsch und Hebräisch-Englisch*, Schömberg.

BERTA, Á., 1998, West Kipchak Languages. – Johanson, L. / Csató, É.Á. (eds.): *The Turkic Languages*, London–New York: 301–317.

CHAFUZ, M.È., 1995, *Russko-karaimskij slovaŕ. Krymskij dialekt*, Moskva.

CLAUSON, G., 1972, *An etymological dictionary of pre-thirteenth-century Turkish*, Oxford.

ÇULHA, T., 2006, *Karaycanın Kısa Sözvarlığı. Karayca–Türkçe Kısa Sözlük* (= *Dil ve Edebiyat Dizisi* 6), İstanbul.

GRUNIN, T.I., 1967, *Dokumenty na poloveckom jazyke XVI v. (sudebnye akty kamenec-podoĺskoj armjanskoj obščiny). Transkripcija, perevod, predislovie, vvedenie, grammatičeskij kommentarij i glossarij*, Moskva.

GRZEGORZEWSKI, J., 1903, Ein türk-tatarischer Dialekt in Galizien. Vokalharmonie in den entlehnten Wörtern der karaitischen Sprache in Halicz. (Mit Einleitung, Texten und Erklärungen zu den Texten). – *Sitzungsberichte der kais*[*erlichen*] *Akademie der Wissenschaften in Wien. Philosophisch-historische Klasse* 146: 1–80.

HARVIAINEN, T., 1997, Three Hebrew Primers, the Pronunciation of Hebrew among the Karaims in the Crimea, and Shewa. – Wardini, E. (ed.):

Built on Solid Rock. Studies in Honour of Professor Ebbe Egede Knudsen on the Occasion of his 65th Birthday April 11th 1997, Oslo: 102–114.

JANKOWSKI, H., 1994, Jak krymscy Karaimowie czytali *pataḥ* i co z tego wynika? – Górska, E. / Ostafin, B. (eds.): *Studia Orientalia Thaddaeo Lewicki oblata. Materiały z sesji naukowej poświęconej pamięci Profesora Tadeusza Lewickiego, Kraków, 17–18 listopada 1993*, Kraków.

JANKOWSKI, H., 1997, A Bible Translation into the Northern Crimean Dialect of Karaim. – *Studia Orientalia* 82: 1–84.

———, 2003, On the Language Varieties of Karaims in the Crimea. – *Studia Orientalia* 95: 109–130.

KOWALSKI, T., 1929, *Karaimische Texte im Dialekt von Troki* (= *Prace Komisji Orjentalistycznej Polskiej Akademji Umiejętności* 11), Kraków.

KRPS = BASKAKOV, N.A. / ŠAPŠAL, S.M. / ZAJONČKOVSKIJ, A. (eds.), 1974, *Karaimsko-russko-poĺskij slovaŕ*, Moskva.

KSB = MARDKOWICZ, A., 1935, *Karaj sez-bitigi. Słownik karaimski. Karaimisches Wörterbuch*, Łuck.

KtRUS = GARKAVEC, A.N. / USEINOV, S.M., 2002, *Krymskotatarsko-russko-ukrainskij slovaŕ*, 1 (A–L), Simferopol̍.

LEVI, B.Z., 1996, *Russko-karaimskij slovaŕ. Krymskij dialekt*, Odessa.

MARDKOWICZ, A., 1933a, Jedi bitik. – *Karaj Awazy* 6: 6–10.

———, 1933b, Sahyncyna „babinecnin". – *Karaj Awazy* 6: 1–6.

———, 1933c, Sifcegi sałałarnyn. – *Karaj Awazy* 6: 22.

NÉMETH, M., 2009, Errors with and without purpose: A. Mardkowicz's transcription of Łuck-Karaim letters in Hebrew script. – *Studia Linguistica Universitatis Iagellonicae Cracoviensis* 126: 97–106.

PRIK, O.Ja., 1976, *Očerk grammatiki karaimskogo jazyka (krymskij dialekt)*, Machačkala.

PRITSAK, O., 1959, Das Karaimische. – Deny, J. et al. (eds.): *Philologiae Turcicae Fundamenta*, Wiesbaden: 318–340.

RADLOFF, V.V., 1911, *Opyt slovarja tjurkskich narečij. Versuch eines Wörterbuches der Türk-Dialecte*, 4, Sankt-Peterburg".

RS 1858 = Census record list (*Ревизская сказка*) conducted in Łuck in 1858 [in private ownership].

SGKP = CHLEBOWSKI, B. et al. (eds), 1902, *Słownik geograficzny Królestwa Polskiego i innych krajów słowiańskich*, 15/2, Warszawa.

SULIMOWICZ, J., 1972, Materiał leksykalny krymskokaraimskiego zabytku językowego (druk z 1734 r.). I–II. – *Rocznik Orientalistyczny* 35/1: 37–76; 36/1: 47–107.

STACHOWSKI, M., 2007, Die Etymologie von ttü. *şimdi* 'jetzt' und *işte* 'voilà' vor gemeintürkischem Hintergrund. – *Studia Etymologica Cracoviensia* 12: 171–176.

TIRIJAKI, V., 2004, Nekotorye osobennosti karaimskogo perevoda Dekaloga v izdanii TaNaHa 1841 g. – Abkowicz, M. / Jankowski, H. (eds.): *Karaj kiuńlari. Dziedzictwo narodu karaimskiego we współczesnej Europie*, Wrocław: 253–257.

YARDENI, A., 1997, *The Book of Hebrew Script. History, Palaeography, Script Styles, Calligraphy & Design*, Jerusalem.

ZAJĄCZKOWSKI, A., 1931–1932, Przekłady Trenów Jeremiasza w narzeczu trocko-karaimskiem. – *Rocznik Orjentalistyczny* 8: 181–192.

———, 1932, *Sufiksy imienne i czasownikowe w języku zachodniokaraimskim (przyczynek do morfologji języków tureckich)* (= *Prace Komisji Orjentalistycznej Polskiej Akademji Umiejetności* 15), Kraków.

———, 1968, Materiał kolokwialny arabsko-kipczacki w Słowniku « ad-Durra^{t} al-muḍīʾa fī-l-luġat at-turkīya ». – *Rocznik Orientalistyczny* 31/1: 71–115.

[11] [12] [13] [14] [15] [16] [17] [18] [19] [20] [21] [22] [23] [24]

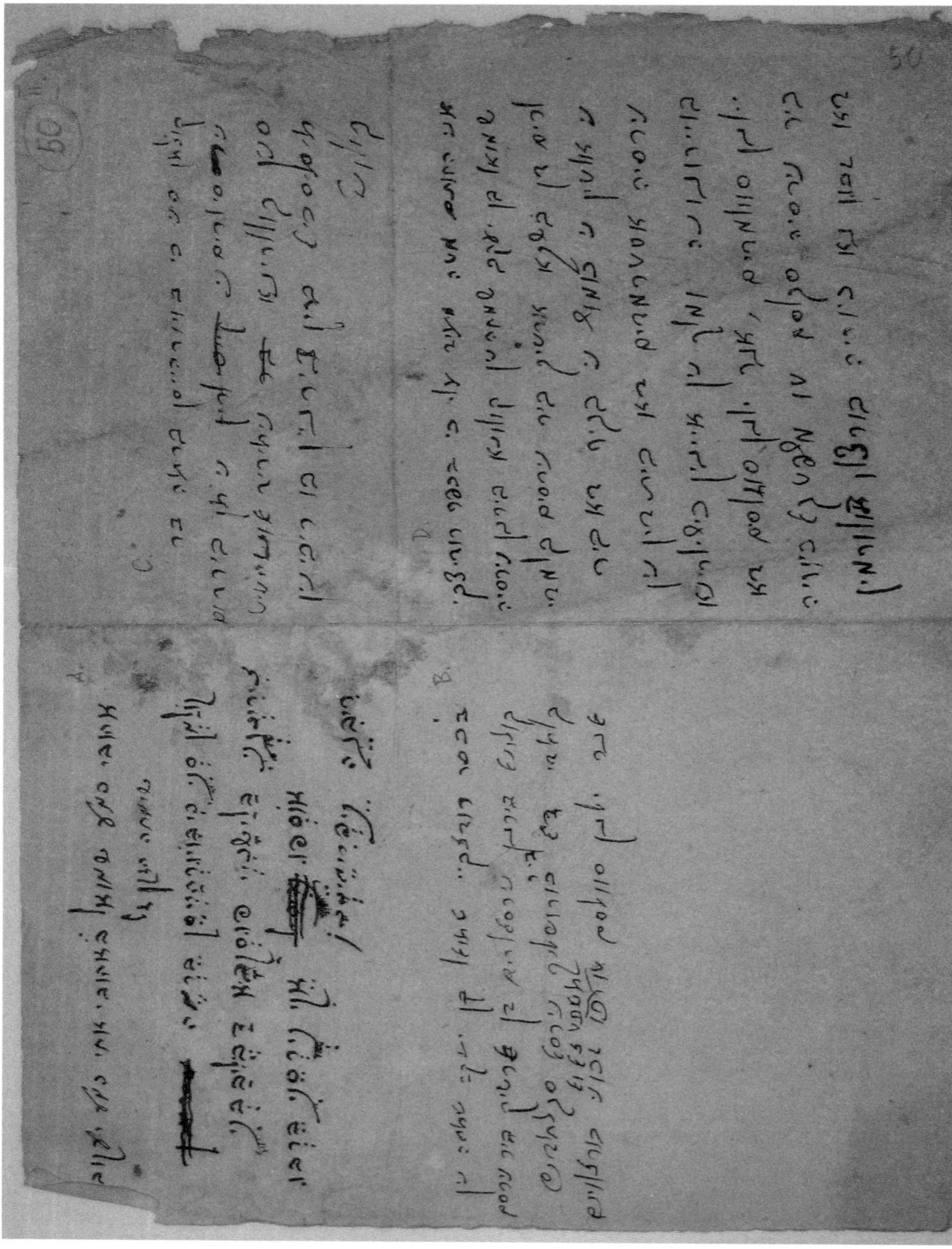

[1] [2] [3] [4] [5] [6] [7] [8] [9] [10]

Studies on the Turkic World
A Festschrift for Professor St. Stachowski on the Occasion of His 80th Birthday
edited by E. Mańczak-Wohlfeld and B. Podolak, Kraków 2010: 95–105

Luciano Rocchi (Trieste)

The Importance of Bernardino Pianzola's Work for Turkish Lexicography

1. Bernardino Pianzola (1721–1803) was an Italian missionary who stayed in countries of the Eastern Mediterranean for twelve years, in particular in Istanbul from 1771 to 1775, being appointed as Provincial Minister and Apostolic Prefect of the Orient Missions of the Conventual Minorites. After returning to Italy he wrote a grammatical-lexicographical work entitled *Dizionario, Grammatiche e Dialoghi per apprendere le lingue italiana, latina, greca-volgare, e turca (...),* which was published in two volumes in Padua in 1781. This work was reprinted twice, with various changes and corrections by the author and with slightly different titles: the second edition came out in Padua in 1789 in three volumes, the third one in Venice in 1801, this latter enlarged by the addition of a fourth volume containing a Turkish-Italian vocabulary *(Vocabolario turco, e italiano).* Pianzola (henceforth P.) states in the preface to his *Dizionario* (1st ed.) that, as far as the Turkish language is concerned, he consulted the '*Onomastico* del Ch. *Mininski*', i.e. Meninski's *Complementum thesauri linguarum orientalum seu Onomasticum latino-turcico-arabico-persicum* (Vienna 1687), 'con l'assistenza (...) di alcuni miei Correligiosi Orientali'.[1] These may be P.'s informants or collaborators in writing the work or gathering the material, but it is also possible that he refers to revisers of the work, whose names are known.[2]

[1] Another source used by P. for a part of his *Dialoghi* was J. B. Holdermann, *Grammaire turque* (Constantinople 1730), referred to as 'Grammatica francese-turca'. Besides, it is thought that P. took a number of words from Molino's dictionary (1641).

[2] In fact, a note signed by some Franciscan friars of the monastery of Castelfidardo is found at the end of the second volume of the *Dizionario* (1st ed.), where one

In any case, it is clear that P.'s Turkish lexicon is based not only on Meninski or other previous lexicographers, but also, to a large extent, on data by informants and/or revisers coming from different regions of the Ottoman Empire (Anatolia, Rumelia, Armenia), each of them contributing their own linguistic habits. Thus, besides well-known dialect features such as the change *ı* > *i* in word final position[3] (f. ex. *aci* 'bitter', *fuçi* 'cask', *mazi* 'oak gall'[4] [but not in all the cases, cf. *darı* 'millet', *karı* 'woman']) or the loss of /h/ in initial position[5] (in some instances like *hafta/afta*[6] 'week', *hısab (hısap, hisab)/ısab (ızab)* 'calculation', *ovarda* 'vagabond' for *hovarda*), P.'s Turkish text is very rich in features belonging to the most genuine popular speech, which are rare to be found in (old) written sources. Here just some of them are mentioned:

consonant droppings before another consonant, mostly of /k/, especially before /l/: *açıklık* 'brightness'/*açılık* 'opening', *arıklık*/*arılık* 'slenderness', *doğmaklık*/*doğmalık* 'birth', etc.; more rarely of other consonants, f. ex. *hızmetkâr*/*hızmekâr* 'servant', *kalbur*/*kabur* 'sieve', *kalıbağa* 'turtle; turtoise' for *kaplubağa* (Meninski 1680: 3619);

can read that 'accurate perlustravimus, ad incudem revocavimus, & ubi opus erat, emendavimus opus'. Signers who presumably dealed with the Turkish text are 'Franciscus Sperco Constantinopolitanus (...) Romeliae olim Provincialis, Missionarius, & Praefectus Apostolicus', 'Diodatus Caroglù Constantinopolitanus Natione Armenus' and 'Joannes Testa Constantinopolitanus'. As to the second edition, the printer publishes in an introductory note a letter of a certain Niccolò Dottori from Smirne (İzmir), who praises P.'s corrections and adds: 'E benchè non vi fosse grande necessità, non ho mancato di farvi le mie vieppiù esatte ed opportune correzioni ed aggiunte in ciò, che spetta alle Lingue Orientali'.

3 It is the first criterion used by Németh (1956: 12) for classifying West Rumelian dialects. In P.'s text, instead, the final *u* remains unchanged, cf. *boru, doğru, koşu, koyu*, etc. (while in West Rumelian *-u* > *-i*). P.'s interesting form *küprü* 'bridge' shows the change *ö* > *ü* as in West Rumelian, but preservation of the final *ü* as in East Rumelian.

4 P.'s data are from Rocchi 2009. The Turkish words are quoted in a normalized transcription based on the modern Turkish alphabet; as to P.'s original writing note: <y> = [ɨ], <s̄> = [ʃ], <c̄> = [ʧ], <ḡ> = [ʤ]. The meanings are translations of one of the Italian equivalents of the Turkish words given by P.

5 For the areal diffusion of this phenomenon see Kappler 2000: 165–167.

6 A large number of words in P.'s work occurs both in standard Ottoman-Turkish and in 'anomalous' forms, according to the various entries and/or editions and owing to different (oral/written) sources. These variants are separated by a slash (/) in this paper.

e p e n t h e s i s , frequently of /n/: *çadir/çandir* 'tent, pavilion', *lisan/linzan* 'language', *macar/mancar* 'German',[7] etc.; occasionally of other consonants, f. ex. *çivri* 'wedge' for *çivi, iskemle/iskemble* 'chair', *temsil/tempsil* 'comparison';

m e t a t h e s i s , found in many instances: *bayrak/baykar* 'flag', *islah/ilsah olunmuş* 'corrected', *keravan/kevran* 'caravan', *mayasıl/yemasil* 'hemorrhoid', etc.;

c o n s o n a n t   c h a n g e s , f. ex. *dağın* 'mine' for *lağım, geçik* 'passage' for *geçit, tezyar* 'loom' for *tezgâh*;

a l l e g r o - f o r m s , f. ex. *kamçılık* 'scourging' for *kamçılamaklık, kaşlamak* 'to curry' for *kaşağılamak, taclamaklık/taclık* 'crowning';

a n a l o g i c a l   e x t e n s i o n   o f   t h e   v e r b a l   i n f i x *-lA-*, f. ex. *adalamak* 'to vow' for *adamak, istelenmiş* 'asked (for)', while, as to the infinite, only the canonical *istemek* is recorded by P., *kurutmak/kurutlamak* 'to dry';

r e d u n d a n t   n e g a t i v e   i n f i x *-mA-*, f. ex. *bilmemezlik* 'inexperience', *geçinilmemezlik* 'impenetrability', *uymazlık/uymamazlık* 'inequality'.[8]

As it is obvious, this material enriches our knowledge of 18th-century spoken Turkish considerably. The aim of this paper is, however, to examine in particular the words of P.'s corpus that are, in my opinion, the most interesting ones for their documentary value. At least as far as we know, they are not recorded by any other Ottoman-Turkish lexicographical work nor mentioned in modern studies.[9]

2. Firstly, European loanwords are dealt with (including one Kurdism), dividing them according to their origin.

2.1 Grecisms

biçilemek 'to pinch' (54).[10] In my view, metathesis of a **çibilemek* analogous to Anatolian Turkish *çimbilemek* 'ucu sivri değnekle hayvan dürtmek'

[7] As far as we know, this is the only instance of a popular use of the word for 'Hungarian' (cf. P.'s other data *Macar (vilayet)* 'Hungary', *macarlı* 'Hungarian') in the meaning of 'German'.

[8] For further examples of these (and other) phenomena see Rocchi 2009: 18–21, passim.

[9] P.'s data are very little known, as they are almost totally ignored by Ottoman-Turkish historical lexicography. Among the very few exceptions is Stachowski, St., *Historisches Wörterbuch der Bildungen auf* -ci//-ici *im Osmanisch-Türkischen*, Kraków 1996.

[10] Numbers between brackets refer to pages of Rocchi 2009.

(DS 1221) < Greek *τσιμπώ* 'to prick, to sting, to pinch' (Tietze 2002: 518). Cf. also the variant *çinbiklemek* 'pincer' (Letellier 1838: 176), with /k/ probably inserted by hypercorrection.

giros 'edge' (107) < *γύρος* id. Traces of the Greek word are found in modern Anatolian dialects in particular meanings (Tzitzilis 1987: 38). This data from P. may be owed to a bilingual (Greek-Turkish) informant (see below).

ili kseri 'tartar (of barrels)' (128) < *ούλη ξερή* 'tartaro' (Somavera 1709: 301). The Turkish form *ili* is obviously due to the vowel harmony.

kavur 'crab' (145) < *κάβουρας* id., possibly through the medium of Rumelian dialects, cf. Balkan borrowings like Bulgarian *кавур* and Arumanian *cavur* mentioned by Tzitzilis (1987: 50). The Anatolian variant *kavro* 'yengeç' is attested in Adana dialect (DS 2691).

kerezman 'cemetery' (147) looks like a variant, with a paragogic nasal, of *kirizme* (modern Turkish *kirizma*) 'a deep trenching of land by spade' (Redhouse 1890:1537), with a semantic development to 'place where graves are digged'. The word is surely of Greek origin, but Tzitzilis (1987: 38) is uncertain whether it derives from *γύρισμα* 'turn; (dial.) ploughing' (this etymon is shared by Nişanyan 2007: 262) or *κύλισμα* 'deep ploughing'.

kiste 'basket' (152) < *κίστη* id., which at P.'s time could not have been used any longer in spoken Greek, as in the *Dizionario* the only Greek translation of 'canestro' is *panèri* (= *πανέρι*) < Italian *paniere.*

koskin 'sieve' (155) < *κόσκινο* id.

mardiros 'martyr' (168) < *μάρτυρας* id. P. records the derivative *mardirosluk* 'martyrdom' and the verbal phrase *mardiros etmek* 'to martyr' too.

mufl/müfl 'mouldy smell' (176), possibly from *μούχλα* 'mould' (in P. also 'mouldy smell') crossed with *küfl,* which is a Turkish equivalent of 'muffa' in the *Dizionario* (161).

patera 'Father' (= priest) (197) < *πατέρα*, vocative of *πατέρας* 'father'.

porfir 'porphyry' (200) < *πόρφυρον* 'porfido' (Somavera 1709: 340; in P. the variant *porfirion*). The word from P. has clearly to be separated from its modern homonym-synonym *porfir,* which is supposed to be a late borrowing from the French *porphyre* (TS 1620).

radiki/radık 'chicory' (201) < *ραδίκι* id. The other Ottoman forms *radik(i)ya, radik(i)e* (Meyer 1893: 34) are variants coming from the Greek plural *ραδίκια.*

skolopaksa 'woodcock' (216) < *σκολόπαξ* id.

sparan 'asparagus' (218) < *σπαράγγι* id. The final vowel of the Greek word was dropped by Turkish-speaking people because it was very likely interpreted as a grammatical morph. The subsequent passages **sparang* > **sparaŋ* > *sparan* do not present any difficulties.

zizi 'cicada' (269) < *τζιτζίκι* id. The Turkish word may have stemmed from an intermediate stage **ziziyi.*

It has to be added that some Grecisms that belong to common Ottoman-Turkish show in P.'s text forms definitely nearer to their Greek sources than those usually attested. They may be attributed to informants/revisers who were native speakers of Greek and had taught Turkish as a second language. The following examples are mentioned:

angınar 'artichoke' (39) < *αγκινάρα* id. The standard Turkish form is *enginar* (in Meninski [1680: 469] the variant *inginar*). An instance of the word with the initial *a-* preserved is found in Filippo Argenti, whose writing is ‹aggináras›[11] (Rocchi 2007: 26).

astakos 'crayfish' (42) < *αστακός* id. The other Ottoman-Turkish forms *istakos, ıstakos* (modern standard *ıstakoz*) come from the Greek variant *στακός* (Meyer 1893: 22).

dafne 'laurel' (75) < *δάφνη* id. The common Turkish *defne* shows the usual change owing to the vowel harmony.

makaronya 'macaroon' (167) < *μακαρόνια*, plural of *μακαρόνι* id. Commonly attested in Ottoman-Turkish is the syncopated form *makarna.* The earlier *makarun* from Molino (1641: 238) is probably a direct borrowing from Italian dial. *macaron(e).*

2.2 Latinisms

The Turkish names of the last four months of the Western calendar appear in the *Dizionario* as *september* (211), *oktember* (188), *noember* (185), *dekember/dektember* (78). They look like half-learned Latinisms which, however, must have been used in everyday language, as indicated by the process of contamination that originated the forms *oktember* and *dektember.* The names of these months from the other Ottoman dictionaries are of secondary Latin origin, as they entered Turkish through Greek dialects: *sitevris, süturis* < *σετέβρις*, *ahteris, ahterios* < *οχτώβρις*, *nuvaris* < *νοέβρις*, *dekevris* < *δεκέβρις* (Meyer 1893: 68).

[11] According to Kappler (ZDMG 159/1 [2009], p. 219) it is the reproduction of a Greek writing *αγγινάρας*.

2.3 Italianisms

busula 'compass' (61) < *bussola* id. This Turkish form is not recorded by Kahane–Tietze (1958: 127), where only the variants *busola, pusola, pusula, pusla* are listed.

butarika 'roe, fish eggs' (61) < *butarica* (obsolete, the form usually attested is *bottarga*) id. The Ottoman variant *butarġa,* which comes from the quoted standard Italian form, was found in Ciadyrgy (1832: 98).

fragol 'strawberries' (101) < *fragola* (plural *fragole*) id., possibly through Greek *φϱάγουλα* (spelt *fragola* in P.). For the dropping of the final vowel in the loanword cf. Ottoman *pistol* (P. gives an instance with the voiced bilabial: *bistol* [55]) 'pistol' < Italian *pistola* id.

kardinal/*kardenal* 'cardinal' (142) < *cardinale* id. The word is missing in Meyer (1893). The modern Turkish *kardinal* is in all probability a reborrowing from the French *cardinal* (Nişanyan 2007: 244, who dates the word from the sixties of the 19th century).

karneval 'carnival' (142) < *carnevale* id. The later form *karnaval* was very likely borrowed from the French *carnaval* (Nişanyan 2007: 246); for Meyer (1893: 67) it is an Italianism too.

konsol/*konsul* 'consul' (154) < *console* id. The standard Ottoman-Turkish form is *konsolos,* obviously mediated by the Greek *κόνσολος* (Somavera 1709: 195, with several variants).

ney 'mole (on the skin)' (184) < *nei,* plural of *neo* id.

onza 'ounce' (189) < Venetian *onza* (standard Italian *oncia*) id. The phonetic look of P.'s word is rather surprising, as in loanwords of Italian origin the original unvoiced alveolar affricate is usually pronounced as /ʧ/ by Turkish-speaking people; in fact, the variant *onça* recorded by Kerestedjian (1912: 54) may have been borrowed from the same abovementioned Venetian word rather than standard Italian. It is possible that P.'s *onza* reproduces an Italian dialectal pronounciation /ondza/. The widely diffused Anatolian Turkish *önge* (with many variants) reflects the Greek form *ουγγία* < Latin *uncia* (Tietze 1955: 234).

temiz 'sifter, sieve' (234) < Venetian *tamiso* id., with the derivative *temizlemek* 'to sift, to sieve'. It cannot be excluded that the Turkish word has undergone the folk-etymological influence of the adjective *temiz* 'clean'.

2.4 Slavisms

kılıçlamak 'to close, to shut' (149). It is my opinion that the base of this verb is of Balkan Slavic origin, cf. Serbian, Croatian *ključ,* Bulgarian *ключ*, dial. also *клич* (BER 2: 460), 'key'. For a parallel formation cf. *kilitlemek* 'to lock' from *kilit* 'lock'.[12]

okol 'pen (for cattle)' (188) < Croatian (dial.) *okôl* 'obor, tor' (AkRj 8: 827), perhaps not directly, but through Rumanian *ocol* 'cercado, encerradero, corral' (Cioranescu 1958–61: 576).

2.5 Kurdisms

dağışmak 'to fill up' (75) < Kurdish *dagirtin* id. (Chyet 2003: 119). The Turkish adaption of this word presents a regular morphological substitution of the infinitive suffix *-mak* for the Kurdish equivalent *-tin* and a change /r/ > /ʃ/ not clearly explicable. Perhaps a popular extension of the verbal infix *-(I)ş-* should be taken into account, cf. a case like Anatolian Turkish *gerişmek* for standard *gerinmek* (DS 2005).

3. As it is well known, onomatopeia is one of the most important devices in the creation of new words. P. gives some instances of it that seem not to be attested elsewhere:

gargamak '(for a crow) to caw' (103). Cf. standard Ottoman-Turkish *gaklamak* id., from *gak,* imitating the crow's cry. P.'s verb has very probably undergone a folk-etymological change under the influence of the noun *karga* 'crow', dialectally also *garga*[13] ('Ağızlarda *garga* olarak geçer', Eren 1999: 212).

nyavlamak 'to miaow' (186). The onomatopoeic base is the same as Italian *gnaulare* (in P.'s spelling *gnavolare*) and Greek *νιαούρίζω* id. The standard Ottoman-Turkish verb is *miyavlamak.*

topmak 'to burst, to explode' (238), with the derivative *topu* 'burst'. The root *top-* can be compared with *pat* 'a blow with a flat thing, that makes a loud, sharp noise; also, the noise from such a blow' (Redhouse 1890: 430), from which *patlamak* 'to burst' derives. The assonance with the noun *top* 'ball; cannon' (cf. also P.'s data *büyük top* 'bomb') may have contributed to form the onomatopoeic *top-*. The absence of the usual infix *-lA-* in the verb recorded by P. is noteworthy.

[12] Another Slavism of the same semantic field was quoted by L. Bassano in his work *I costumi, et i modi particolari de la vita de Turchi* (Roma 1545) in the following passage: 'Nessuna [bottega] se ne serra con chiaue; ma tutte con Luchetti, i quali loro [scil. the Turks] chiamano Catthanaz' (16r). It is a self-evident borrowing from Serbian, Croatian *kàtanac*, Bulgarian *катанац* 'lock'.

[13] This dialect variant was borrowed by Standard Bulgarian *гарга* too (Grannes et al. 2002: 46).

4. From the point of view of Turkology, it is important to point out the occurrence of a couple of Turkic verbs that are not entered in other Ottoman lexicographical works to our knowledge:

sızgırmak 'to whistle' (214). P. records the noun *sızgır* 'whistle' too, probably a backformation from the verb. This is already found in the Codex Cumanicus in the forms *syzġyr-, syzġur-* 'siuorare' (= Classical Latin 'sibilare') (Grønbech 1942: 230) and later in Kazan Tatar *syzgyr-* 'pfeifen' (Radloff 1893–1911: 4, 666). The variant *sızgımak* 'sibilare' appears in Meninski (1680: 2661) as a 'Tartar' word.

tırnamak 'to scrape' (237). The verb is well recorded both in medieval times, f. ex. Kipchak *tırna-* 'tırmalamak' (Toparlı et al. 2007: 274) and in modern Turkic languages, f. ex. Kirghiz *tırna-* 'jucken, kratzen, harken' (Radloff 1893–1911: 3, 1326), Uzbek *tirna-* 'to scratch' (Waterson 1980: 115).

5. Lastly, a very interesting feature of P.'s vocabulary has to be mentioned: the presence of some entries that anticipate strategies of word/phrase formation that can be found again just at the time of the 20th-century Turkish language reform *(dil devrimi)* promoted by Atatürk:

asılmamışlık 'independence' (42). Abstract of *asılmamış,* negative past participle of *asılmak* 'to hang, to be hung'. The idea of 'independence' is normally expressed by the Arabic loanword *istiklal* in Ottoman. If the *Öztürkçeciler* of the 20th century had known the word recorded by P., they would very likely have resorted to this instead of concocting the questionable neologism *bağımsızlık.*[14]

görmeye kudret '(the sense of) sight' (108). This phrase represents a first attempt of substituting a more Turkish form for the usual Ottoman (< Arabic-Persian) *kuvvet-i bāsıre* 'virtus, potentia *seu* facultas visiva' (Meninski 1680: 3781), recorded also by P. in the spelling *kuvet-i basire* (160) as equivalent of *görmeye kudret.* For the meaning of 'sight', phrases such as *görme duyusu* and *görme yetisi* '(il senso della) vista' have been introduced in modern Turkish (İBS 1351).

kokuyan kudreti '(the sense of) smell' (153). In my view, this phrase stemmed from the Turkicization of a **kudret-i şāmme* = Standard Ottoman *kuvvet-i şāmme* 'virtus, *seu* potentia odorativa, odoratus'

[14] '*Bağımsızlık* is the established replacement for *istiklâl* 'independence'. *Cep Kılavuzu* (1935), in the second part, from Turkish to Ottoman, has *bağınsız* for 'independent' (...). It is not clear who changed the *n* in *m*, and when, but it had happened by 1955. *-ım* is a deverbal suffix, but there is no verb *bağ-*, so the root has to be the noun *bağ* 'tie, bond, impediment'. That is not its only fault (...)' (Lewis 1999: 113).

(Meninski 1680: 2754) through two stages: **1)** the replacement of the Arabic participle *şāmme* 'odorans' with its Turkish equivalent *kokuyan;* **2)** the anteposition of the determiner to the determinant according to the syntactic regressive structure typical of Turkish. Phrases with this meaning found in modern Turkish are *koklama duyusu* 'fiuto, olfatto' and *koku alma duyusu* 'naso, odorato' (İBS 1495).

Literature

AkRj = *Rječnik hrvatskoga ili srpskoha jezika. Na svijet izdaje Jugoslavenska Akademija Znanosti i Umjetnosti,* 1–23, Zagreb 1881–1976.
BER = *Български етимологичен речник,* 1–, Sofia, 1971–.
DS = *Türkiye'de halk ağzından derleme sözlüğü,* 1–12, Ankara 1963–1982.
İBS = *İtalyanca Büyük Sözlük – İtalyanca-Türkçe, Türkçe-İtalyanca,* İstanbul 2005.
TS = *Türkçe Sözlük,* 10th impression, Ankara 2005.

Chyet, M. L.
2003 *Kurdish-English Dictionary. Ferhenga Kurmancî-Inglîzî,* New Haven–London.
Ciadyrgy, A.
1832 *Dizionario turco, arabo e persiano ridotto sul lessico del celebre Meninski in ordine alfabetico latino,* Milano.
Cioranescu, A.
1958–1961 *Diccionario etimológico rumano,* Tenerife–Madrid.
Eren, H.
1999 *Türk Dilinin Etimolojik Sözlüğü,* Ankara.
Grannes, A. – Hauge, Kj. Rå – Süleymanoğlu, H.
2002 *A Dictionary of Turkisms in Bulgarian,* Oslo.
Grønbech, K.
1942 *Komanisches Wörterbuch. Türkischer Wortindex zu Codex Cumanicus,* København.
Kahane, H. and R. – Tietze, A.
1958 *The Lingua Franca in the Levant,* Urbana.
Kappler, M.
2000 Verso un nuovo *Thesaurus* dei turcismi balcanici: la dimensione dialettale e materiale sui turcismi greco-epiroti dei se-

coli XVIII–XIX. – F. Fusco – V. Orioles (eds.), *Processi di convergenza e differenziazione nelle lingue dell'Europa medievale e moderna,* Udine: 157–194

Kerestedjian, B.

1912 *Quelques Matériaux pour un Dictionnaire Étymologique de la Langue Turque,* Londres.

Letellier, L.-V.

1838 *Vocabulaire oriental, français-italien, arabe, turc et grec,* Paris.

Lewis, G.

1999 *The Turkish Language Reform – A Catastrophic Success,* Oxford.

Meninski, Fr. à Mesgnien

1680 *Thesaurus linguarum orientalium turcicæ-arabicæ-persicæ. Lexicon turcico-arabico-persicum,* 1–3, Vienna [reprint İstanbul 2000].

Meyer, G.

1893 *Türkische Studien,* I: *Die griechischen und romanischen Bestandtheile im Wortschatze des Osmanisch-Türkischen,* Wien.

Molino, G.

1641 *Dittionario della lingua Italiana, Turchesca,* Roma.

Németh, J.

1956 *Zur Einteilung der türkischen Mundarten Bulgariens,* Sofia.

Nişanyan, S.

2007 *Sözlerin Soyağacı. Çağdaş Türkçenin Etimolojik Sözlüğü,* 3rd impression, İstanbul.

Radloff, W.

1893–1911 *Versuch eines Wörterbuches der Türk-Dialecte,* 1–4, Sankt-Peterburg.

Redhouse, J. W.

1890 *A Turkish and English Lexicon,* Constantinople.

Rocchi, L.

2007 *Ricerche sulla lingua osmanlı del XVI secolo – Il corpus lessicale turco del manoscritto fiorentino di Filippo Argenti (1533),* Wiesbaden.

2009 *Il lessico turco nell'opera di Bernardino Pianzola. Materiali per la conoscenza del turco parlato di fine Settecento,* Trieste.

Somavera, A. da
1709 *Tesoro della lingua italiana e greca-volgare, cioe ricchissimo Dizzionario italiano e greco-volgare,* Parigi.

Tietze, A.
1955 Griechische Lehnwörter im anatolischen Türkisch. – *Oriens* 8/2: 204–257.
2002 *Tarihi ve Etimolojik Türkiye Türkçesi Lugatı – Sprachgeschichtliches und etymologisches Wörterbuch des Türkei-Türkischen,* I: *A–E*, İstanbul–Wien.

Toparlı, R. – Vural, H. – Karaatlı, R.
2007 *Kıpçak Türkçesi Sözlüğü,* Ankara.

Tzitzilis, Chr.
1987 *Griechische Lehnwörter im Türkischen (mit besonderer Berücksichtigung der anatolischen Dialekte),* Wien.

Waterson, N.
1980 *Uzbek-English Dictionary,* Oxford.

Studies on the Turkic World
A Festschrift for Professor St. Stachowski on the Occasion of His 80th Birthday
edited by E. Mańczak-Wohlfeld and B. Podolak, Kraków 2010: 107–119

Claus Schönig (Berlin)

Osmanische Einflüsse auf das Krim-Areal

In dieser kleinen Arbeit sollen die Einflüsse des Osmanischen auf die Türksprachen der Krim aufgezeigt werden, auf das Krimtatarische, das Krimtschakische (soweit verfügbar) und das Krim-Karaimische. Gemeinsam mit dem Trakai- und Halitsch-Karaimischen (und möglicherweise einigen westlichen tatarischen „Dialekten" und anderen kleinen Sprachen am Schwarzen Meer) bilden diese Idiome das Fernwestlich-Kiptschakische.

Auf phonetischen Gebiet ist zu berücksichtigen, dass dieses Areal konservativ ist und beispielsweise bei Lautgruppen wie (-)*äv*(-) den typisch kiptschakischen Lautwandel zu *üy* nicht oder nur unvollständig vollzogen hat. So könnten die Entsprechungen von alttürkisch *tävä*(*y*) 'Kamel' (siehe CLAUSON 447f.) in Halitsch-Karaimisch (*tävä*, KARRPS 560), Trakai-Karaimisch (*t́äv́a*, KARRPS 520)[1] und Mischärisch (*tävä*, siehe MAXMUTOVA 58) einheimische Entwicklungen sein – oder sie sind Entlehnungen aus dem Osmanischen, vielleicht aufgrund von Handel, der die beteiligten Sprecher der ferwestlich-kiptschakischen Idiome in Kontakt mit der osmanischen Form dieser Tierbezeichnung brachte (da das betreffende Tier dort wohl nicht vorkommt); auch Standard-Tatarisch kennt übrigens ein *tävä* 'Kamel' (TATRS 566). Dafür, dass es sich bei *tävä* um eine osmanisch inspirierte Form handelt, spricht – neben den Entwicklung anderer *äv*-haltiger Wörter –, dass wir im Tatarischen auch eine typisch kiptschakische Form *döyä* finden (TATRS 143); allerdings sind hier noch weitergehende Untersuchungen notwendig. In Krim-Karaimisch mit *dävä* (KARRPS 183) ~ *tüyä* (553) und Krimtatarisch *dävä* (USEINOV 61) ~ *tüä* (DOERFER 378 = Azav 112)

[1] Zu Fragen der Lautharmonie in diesem Idiom siehe etwa STACHOWSKI.

sind die *-v*-haltigen Formen identisch mit den osmanischen, so dass sich hier wie auch im Fall des krimtschakischen *dävä* (Rebi 61) wie auch aus sprachgeographischen Gründen Entlehnung als Quelle aufdrängt.

Als Entsprechung von alttürkischem *äv* 'Haus(-halt)' finden wir in Halitsch-Karaimisch *iv* (KarRPS 192) ~ *yiv* (244) und in Trakai-Karaimisch *yuv́* (KarRPS 254) ~ *yüv* (260) ~ *üv́* (588), d.h. Formen, die nur wenig auf dem Weg zum kiptschakischen *üy* (in Tatarisch und Baschkirisch graphisch *öy*) vorangekommen sind. Krim-Karaimisch dagegen zeigt mit *äv* (KarRPS 653) ~ *üy* (589) ein anderes, extremes Bild: eine osmanische neben einer voll entwickelten kiptschakischen Form; auch im Krimtatarischen finden wir *äv* (Useinov 327, Doerfer 378; auch bei Radloff nur (I 940) *äv*) ~ *üy* (Doerfer 378). Die Belegsituation im Krimtatarischen spiegelt die politisch-kulturelle Situation der Krim deutlich wider: zwar aus dem Zusammenbruch der Goldenen Horde und der damit verbundenen lokalen Differenzierung des Kiptschakischen entstanden geriet es sei dem 15. Jahrhundert immer stärker unter osmanischen Einfluss, so dass die kiptschakischen Formen heute eher marginal sind (wie schon bei 'Kamel'); beide Formen konnten dann ins Krim-Karaimische dringen, während Krimtschakisch offenbar nur *äv* (214) zeigt. Ähnlich ist die Lage bei Entsprechungen zu alttürkisch *säv-* 'lieben': Halitsch-Karaimisch mit *siv-* (KarRPS 472) und Trakai-Karaimisch mit *śuv-* (KarRPS 500) zeigen wenig in Richtung Kiptschakisch entwickelte Formen, Krimtatarisch zeigt modernes standardsprachliches *säv-* (Useinov 219) neben älteren dialektalen *söy-* und *süy*-Formen (siehe Doerfer 378), Krim-Karaimisch zeigt mit *süv-* (KarRPS 485) ~ *säv-* (496) ~ *süy-* (486) alle drei Formen; Krimtschakisch hat altertümliches *süv-* (Rebi 174) neben der Ableitung *sävĕn-* 'radovat́sja' (Rebi 170).[2]

Die Lautgruppe *-aġ* zeigt weniger vielfältige Repräsentationen. Während alle karaimischen Dialekte für alttürkisch *taġ* 'Berg' und *aġïz* 'Mund' wie im Kiptschakischen (mehr oder minder) zu erwarten *taw* (KarRPS 503) und *awuz* (KarRPS 42) zeigen, hat Krim-Karaimisch zusätzlich noch *daġ* (KarRPS 168) ~ *taġ* (505; osmanisch inspiriert) und *aġïz* (KarRPS 44; neben *awïz*, 42). Osmanische *-ġ*-Formen erscheinen auch im Krimtatarischen *daġ* 'Berg, Wald' (Useinov 90) und im Krimtschakischen *daġ* 'Berg,

[2] Wie wir sehen, hat Halitsch-Karaimisch *äv* > *(y)iv* (näherungsweise), d.h. die Eigenschaft *Labialität* ist noch nicht vom Konsonanten auf den Vokal übergegangen, der aber bereits erhöht ist; im Trakai-Karaimischen mit *äv* > *(y)Uv* (näherungsweise) ist der Konsonant zwar noch Labial, aber auch der (erhöhte) Vokal ist bereits labial. Insgesamt widerspricht dieser Befund demjenigen bei den Wörtern für 'Kamel'.

Wald' (REBI 90).[3] Auch für altes *bäg* '(ein Titel)' findet sich die kiptschakische Form *biy* in allen karaimischen Dialekten (KARRPS 115), während Krim-Karaimisch zusätzlich das osmanische *bäy* (KARRPS 148) neben altertümlichem *bäg* (KARRPS 146) zeigt. Es zeigt damit dasselbe Verhalten wie Krimtatarisch, das *bäy* ~ *bäk* zeigt (USEINOV, 41); Krimtschakisch hat *bäy* 'praviteĺ, gospodin' (d.h. im offiziellen Bereich) (REBI, 77f.), die kiptschakische Form hat in krimtschakisch *biyaġa* 'brat muža' (d.h. im familiären Bereich) überlebt (REBI, 77f.).

Für 'Horn' setze ich für die proto- und alttürkische Periode **büŋiz* (? >) ~ **büńiz* an, das im westoghusischen Osmanisch mit *boynuz* das Merkmal *Nasalität* des intervokalischen Konsonanten bewahrt hat. Im Kiptschakischen ist dieses Merkmal weitgehend getilgt, so etwa in krimtatarisch *muyuz* (USEINOV 165; neben entlehntem *boynuz* (48), siehe unten), trakai-karaimisch *ḿuyuš* (KARRPS 417) ~ *miyuš* (407) und den weiteren karaimischen Formen (**büŋiz* > *müŋiz* > *mügiz* >) (Krim) *müwüš* (412), (Halitsch) *müwüs* (412) ~ *miwiz* (407) und (Trakai) *ḿuẃuz* ~ *ḿuẃuź* ~ *ḿuẃuš* (416).[4] Daneben zeigt Krim-Karaimisch noch *müŋüz* (412) ~ *muŋuz* (411), Krimtschakisch hat *muŋuz* (148). Sollten diese Nasale unter dem Einfluss des Osmanischen bewahrt worden sein?[5]

Für 'Schiff' zeigen alle uns interessierenden Sprachen Formen des Typs **kämi* (wie osmanisch *gämi*), so älteres Krimtatarisch *gämi* (RADLOFF II 1583; nicht in USEINOV), Krimtschakisch *gämĕ* (REBI 87), Krim-Karaimisch *gämi* (KARRPS 166) und sogar halitsch-karaimisch *ǵämi* (KARRPS 159), letzteres vielleicht deshalb, weil für die Halitsch-Karaimen die Osmanen diejenigen schiffsbenutzenden Türken waren, die ihnen am nächsten waren. Das im Kiptschakischen übliche **kemä* ist übrigens im Mischärischen belegt (*kämä* ~ *kimä*, MAXMUTOVA 43).

Für alttürkisch *sïġïr* 'Kuh' finden wir das altertümliche (und auch osmanische) *sïġïr* im gesamten Fernwestlich-Kiptschakischen (Krimtschakisch, REBI 176; Krimtatarisch, USEINOV 232; alle karaimischen

[3] Bemerkenswert sind hier die zusätzlichen Bedeutungen 'Wald', die auch im Krim-Karaimischen *taw* (503) vorliegen; diese Bedeutungen verbinden diese Sprachen mit (zumindest) Gagausisch (*daa* 'les', GAGRMS 127) und Jakutisch (*tïa* 'les, tajga', JAKRS 417).

[4] Diese Entwicklung liegt auch den Entsprechungen von **süŋ(g)ök* 'Knochen' in Halitsch-Karaimisch (*sivăk*, KARRPS 472), Trakai-Karaimisch (*śuv́ak*, 501) und Krim-Karaimisch (*süväk*, 485; neben *suyaq*, 483; letzteres wie krimtatarisch *süyäk*, USEINOV 175).

[5] Und was ist mit der krimtatarischen Form *mäŋ* 'Gehirn' bei RADLOFF (IV 2079)? Heute liegt proto- und alttürkisches **bäńi* ~ (? <) **bäŋi* 'Gehirn' in allen uns interessierenden Sprachen als *miy* vor (Krimtatarisch, USEINOV 155; alle karaimischen Dialekte, KARRPS 406; Krimtschakisch, REBI 147).

Dialekte, KarRPS 488), jedoch zeigen die nicht-krimischen Dialekte von Trakai and Halitsch daneben auch das ansonsten im Kiptschak verbreitete *sïyïr* (490). Auch die Wörter für 'Fuchs' liegen im Krim-Areal nicht in der für das Kiptschakische ansonsten typischen regressiv labialisierten Form *tilkü* > *tülkü* vor, sondern in der für etwa das Osmanisch-Türkeitürkische typischen delabialisierten Form vor, siehe krimtschakisch *tĕĺkĕ* (Rebi 188), krimtatarisch *tiĺki* (Useinov 262) und krim-karaimisch *tiĺki* (KarRPS 528); Trakai-Karaimisch dagegen hat *t́uĺḱu* (570), Halitsch-Karaimisch hat zwar ebenfalls delabialisiertes *tilki* (528), jedoch ist in diesem Dialekt die Delabialisierung ein charakteristischer Zug.[6] Weitere typisch osmanische anstelle von oder gemeinsam mit (westlich-)kiptschakischen Wortformen in Sprachen des Krim-Areals finden sich etwa auch bei den Wörtern für 'Blei',[7] 'Ei',[8] 'Gott',[9] 'groß',[10] 'Stern',[11] 'tausend',[12] 'weinen',[13]

[6] Siehe etwa *ätkär-* < *ötkär-* 'passieren lassen' (KarRPS 671), *dert* < *tö:rt* 'vier' (184), *giyä* (160) ~ *givä* < *küyä* 'Motte' (160), *iw* (192) ~ *yiw* < *äv* 'Haus(-halt)' (244), *ḱergiz-* < *körgüz-* 'zeigen' (306), *miwiz* < *mügüz* 'Horn' (407), *siv-* < *säv-* 'lieben' (472), *siväk* < *süŋäk* 'Knochen' (472), *yiri-* 'gehen; leben' (245) ~ *iri-* 'gehen' (205) < *yürü-*.

[7] Osmanisch *quršun*, kiptschakisch *qorġašïn*: krimtatarisch *quršun* (Useinov 132), krimtschakisch *quršun* (Rebi 136), krim-karaimisch *q"uršun*, *quršïn* (KarRPS 375); dagegen trakai-karaimisch *qorġašïn*, halitsch-karaimisch *qorġasïn* (333).

[8] Osmanisch *yumurta*, kiptschakisch **yumurtqa*: krimtatarisch (Useinov 92), krimtschakisch (Rebi 113) *yïmïrta*, krim-karaimisch *yumurta* (KarRPS 258) ~ *yumïrta* (259) ~ *yïmïrta* (266) ~ *ïmïrtqa* (650, die einzige kiptschakische Form); dagegen halitsch-karaimisch *yïmïrtqa* (266) ~ *yïmärtqa* (267) ~ *yämärtqa* (271), trakai-karaimisch *yumurtxa* (258) ~ *yïmïrtxa* (266f.) ~ *imïrtxa* (200) ~ Radloff I 1406 *ïmïrtqa* (T.) ~ III 500 *yïmïrtxa* (T.).

[9] Osmanisch: hintervokalisch; Kiptschakisch: vordervokalisch. Krimtatarisch, krimtschakisch *taŋrï* (Useinov 243; Rebi 181), krim-karaimisch *täŋri* (KarRPS 565) ~ *tanri* (511) ~ *taŋrï* (512); dagegen halitsch-karaimisch *tänri* 'Gott' ~ *tändri* (564), trakai-karaimisch *t́eńri* (521).

[10] Osmanisch *büyük*, kiptschakisch *biyik*: krimtschakisch (Rebi 81), krimtatarisch *buyuk* (Useinov 52), krim-karaimisch *büyük* (KarRPS 144) ~ *biyik* (alle karaimischen Dialekte, 115).

[11] Osmanisch *yïldïz*, kiptschakisch **yuldïz*: krim-karaimisch (KarRPS 264), krimtatarisch *yïldïz* (Radloff III 491f; Useinov 92); dagegen halitsch-karaimisch *yulduz* (KarRPS 256), *yuldus* (256), *yolduz* (248), trakai-karaimisch *yulduz* (256).

[12] Osmanisch *bin*, kiptschakisch *biŋ* ~ *bïŋ*: krimtschakisch *bin* (Rebi 78), krimtatarisch *biŋ* (Radloff III 491f; Useinov, 45), krim-karaimisch *bin* (KarRPS 119) ~ *min* (407); dagegen halitsch-karaimisch *min* (407), trakai-karaimisch *mińń* (407).

[13] Osmanisch *aġla-*, kiptschakisch *yïla-*: krimtschakisch (Rebi 54), krimtatarisch (Useinov 9), krim-karaimisch *aġla-* (KarRPS 44), *yïla-* (alle Dialekte, 264; zusätzlich in Trakai-Karaimisch *ila-*, 197).

und 'zeigen'.[14] Möglicherweise ist auch der Gebrauch von Formen des Typs **otur-* 'sich hinsetzen; sitzen' (krim-karaimisch *otur-* ~ *otïr-* (KARRPS 435), krimtschakisch *otïr-* (REBI 159), krimtatarisch *otur-* (USEINOV 190)) osmanischem Einfluss zuzuschreiben (aber auch Tatarisch hat *utïr-)*; Halitsch- und Trakai-Karaimisch haben dagegen *oltur-* (KARRPS 427; wie beispielsweise Kaukasus-Kiptschakisch, Baschkirisch und Nogaisch).[15]

Die Sprachen des südlich-türkischen Areals (etwa Oghusisch) haben die Struktur *s-...-č/ǯ* von türkischen Erb- und Lehnwörtern bewahrt, während die Sprachen des nördlich-türkischen Areals wie etwa die Kiptschaksprachen diese Struktur zu *č-...-č* verschoben haben (siehe SCHÖNIG); die Kiptschaksprachen des Krim-Areals allerdings haben unter osmanischem Einfluss die Struktur *s-...-č/ǯ* bewahrt. So finden wir *sač* 'Haar' in Krimtatarisch (USEINOV 216), Krimtschakisch (REBI 170) und Krim-Karaimisch (KARRPS 470; neben *säč*, 500); allerdings weist Krim-Karaimisch auch nördliches *čač* auf (KARRPS 625),[16] *sač* 'listovoj metall; žestjanoj, iz listovogo metalla' in Krimtatarisch (USEINOV 217; osmanisch 'Backblech'), *sač-* 'ausstreuen etc.' in Krimtatarisch (USEINOV 217), Krimtschakisch (REBI 170) und Krim-Karaimisch (LEVI 93, *sub*: sejať; XAFUZ 190 *säč-*; KARRPS 470 *sač-*, 500 *säč-*),[17] *sïčra-*'springen' in Krimtschakisch (REBI 178), Krimtatarisch (USEINOV 236; RADLOFF IV 658

[14] Osmanisch *göstär-*, kiptschakisch *körgüz-*: krimtatarisch *kośtär-* (USEINOV 109), krimtschakisch (REBI 119), krim-karaimisch *köstär-* (KARRPS 340) ~ *körgüz-* ~ *körgiz-* (339); dagegen halitsch-karaimisch *ḱergiz-* (306), trakai-karaimisch *ḱorǵuz-* (314); ein angebliches *x"örgiz-* (siehe etwa 339) kann ich in KARRPS nicht belegen.

[15] Auch das Überleben von Formen von **tabïšǵan* 'Hase; Kaninchen' neben Formen von **qodan* 'id.' ist vielleicht durch Osmanisch inspiriert, mag aber auch ein Merkmal der Ost-West-Ränder der türkischen Welt sein, das auch in sonstigem Oghusisch, in Jakutisch, Chakassisch, Südkirgisisch und Usbekisch erscheint; siehe krim-karaimisch *tawšan* (KARRPS 505) (*-f-*, 518) 'zajac' ~ *q"oyan* (368) 'zajac', trakai-karaimisch *qoyan* (329) 'zajac', halitsch-karaimisch *qoyan* (133) 'zajac' ~ *dawsan* 'zajac' (168) ~ *dafsan* 'krolik' (170), krimtatarisch *qoyan* 'krolik' (USEINOV 128) ~ *tavšan* 'zajac' (239), krimtschakisch *qoyan* (REBI 133) 'zajac' ~ *tavšan* 'krolik' (179). Auch die krim-karaimische Form *özäŋü* (KARRPS 438) 'Steigbügel' mag auf osmanischen Einfluss zurückgehen (wobei das anlautende *ö-* den Formen des Kaukasus-Kiptschakischen gleicht); Halitsch-Karaimisch zeigt *äziŋä* (655), für Trakai-Karaimisch, aber auch für Krimtschakisch und Krimtatarisch, habe ich leider keine Belege.

[16] Trakai-Karaimisch hat ebenfalls *čač* (KARRPS 625; siehe auch RADLOFF III 1905), Halitsch-Karaimisch *ćać* (KARRPS 613; RADLOFF IV 195).

[17] Dagegen sind für Halitsch- und Luzk-Karaimisch mit *ćać-* (KARRPS 613; RADLOFF IV 195 karL. 'säen, ausstreuen') und für Trakai-Karaimisch mit *čač-* (KARRPS 625) nur nördlich-türkische Formen belegt.

sïčïra-) und Krim-Karaimisch (LEVI 94; KARRPS 496),[18] *säč-* '(aus-)wählen' in Krimtatarisch ('zamečať, različať, primečať', selten 'vybirať', USEINOV 224), Krimtschakisch ('zamečať', REBI 172) und Krim-Karaimisch ('različať', KARRPS 500),[19] *sïč-* 'scheißen' in Krimtatarisch (siehe auch RADLOFF IV 657 *sïč-* osm., krm. 'Nothdurft verrichten, scheißen') und Krimtschakisch ('ispražnjaťsja, gadiť', REBI 178), *sïčan* 'Maus' in Krimtatarisch (USEINOV 326), Krimtschakisch (REBI 178, 'Ratte') und Krim-Karaimisch (*sïčqan* ~ *sïčan*, LEVI 52 u. KARRPS 495; *sïčan*, XAFUZ 141),[20] *suč* '(moralische) Schuld' in Krimtatarisch (USEINOV 231), Krimtschakisch (REBI 176) und Krim-Karaimisch (LEVI 52; KARRPS 485) und *sužuq* 'Wurst' in Krimtschakisch (*sužuq* 'kolbasa iz baraniny', REBI 176) und Krim-Karaimisch (*sužuq* 'kolbasa', KARRPS 483; LEVI 42, unter 'kolbasa: vjalenaja ploska k. iz syroj baraniny'). Hierher gehören auch Entsprechungen zu *sanč-* 'durchbohren' in Krimtatarisch (USEINOV 214), *zïnǯïr* 'Kette' in Krimtatarisch (USEINOV 76), Krimtschakisch (REBI 98) und Krim-Karaimisch (*zinǯir, zinǯil, zïnǯïr, zïnǯïl* 'cep̍', *zïnǯïla* 'okovy', KARRPS 189f., *sïnǯïĺ*, 492),[21] sowie *šaš-* in Krimtatarisch ('udivljaťsja,

[18] Bei krim-karaimisch *sïčïr-* (KARRPS 496) könnte es sich um eine formale Kontamination *sïčra-* und *säkir-* handeln. Dagegen zeigt Trakai-Karaimisch *čačrat-* 'rassejať' (KARRPS 625) (< *sačra-* + Kausativ, im Sinn von „die Saatkörner springen lassen"), vielleicht (zusätzlich) inspiriert von *sač-* 'ausstreuen; säen'.

[19] Krimtatarisch und Krimtschakisch sowie Krim-, Halitsch- und Trakai-Karaimisch zeigen aber auch ein Verb *sayla-* (KARRPS 460; USEINOV 211; REBI 167), das im gesamten Kiptschakischen dominiert.

[20] In Trakai-Karaimisch haben die assimilativen Tendenzen des Nördlich-Türkischen den Anlaut nicht in *č* sondern in *š* verwandelt (KARRPS 649 *šïčan*, 646 *šičan*; RADLOFF IV karT. 1059 *šïčan*), ein Effekt, der nicht auf Assimilation sondern auf Palatalisierung durch den folgenden hohen Vokal zurückgeht; Halitsch-Karaimisch zeigt mit *śćïčan* (KARRPS 487) eine Form mit Affrikate, die allerdings ebenfalls vom üblichen Schema abweicht. Im Karaimischen ist der Süd-Nord-Übergang auch am Suffix feststellbar: neben südlichen (oghusischen) *-an*-Formen erscheinen nördliche (kiptschakische) *-qan*(< *-ġan*)-Formen, und zwar mit sowohl südlich-unassimilierten als auch nördlich-assimiliertem Anlautkonsonanten.

[21] Von persisch *zanǯi:r* 'Kette'; osmanisch-türkeitürkisch *zinǯir* (RADLOFF IV 913; STEUERWALD 1053f.), türkmenisch *zïnǯïr* (TKMRS 342), Die *sïnǯïĺ*-Form in Krim-Karaimisch zeigt bereits die für die meisten Kiptschaksprachen typische Entstimmung des Anlauts sowie den Übergang in die hintere Reihe, jedoch ist die Zischlaut-Struktur noch durch oghusischen Einfluss bestimmt. Ähnliche Zwischenformen zeigt auch Halitsch-Karaimisch mit *sinǯir* ~ *sïndzïr* (KARRPS 474 bzw. 493); ebenfalls zwischen Oghusisch und Kiptschakisch steht die Form *sïnǯïr* des Trakai-Karaimischen (KARRPS 493), das mit *ǯïnǯïr* (KARRPS 174) auch eine nördlich-assimilierte Form (allerdings stimmhaft anlautend) mit hinterem Vokalismus aufweist.

poražaťsja, opešiť', USEINOV 321),[22] Krimtschakisch ('udivljaťsja, poražaťsja', REBI 211; 'to be surprised', ERDAL; IANBAY 134) und Krim-Karaimisch ('id.', KARRPS 645; XAFUZ 204). Unter osmanischem Einfluss hat Krim-Karaimisch ein *čïz-* 'Linien ziehen, zeichnen' (KARRPS 743; XAFUZ 211) bewahrt, das (anders als osmanisch-türkeitürkisch *čiz-*, vielleicht unter dem Einfluss von *sïz-*) hintervokalisch ist; Krimtatarisch zeigt hier die aus dem Osmanischen entlehnte Nominalform *čizgi* 'čerta, svojstvo, kačestvo' (USEINOV 304). Weiterhin ist eine west-oghusische Form *čöz-* ins ältere Krimtatarische gedrungen, siehe RADLOFF III 2045; daneben zeigen Krimtatarisch, Krimtschakisch und Krim-Karaimisch ein *čäz-* (USEINOV 301; REBI 203 und ERDAL; IANBAY 109; KARRPS 639; RADLOFF III 1991 krm. 'aufbinden, öffnen').[23]

Mitunter finden sich osmanische Wortformen nur vereinzelt. Bei den Entsprechungen von **yaŋV* 'neu' finden wir ein vordervokalisches *yäŋi* (wie osmanisch *yäni*) in Krimtschakisch (*yängĕ*, REBI 108), in RADLOFFs Karaimisch und älteres Krimtatarisch (RADLOFF III 323 *yäŋi* 'neu'); modernes Krimtatarisch (USEINOV 354) und Karaimisch zeigen dagegen die alte Form *yaŋï*.[24] Die meisten Kiptschaksprachen zeigen Formen des Typs *bar* 'existiert', *bar-* '(hin-)gehen', *ber-* 'geben', *bol-* 'werden; sein' und *tur-* '(auf-) stehen'; dagegen zeigen die Sprachen des Krim-Areals teilweise osmanisch beeinflusste Formen (*var*, *var-*, *vär-*, *ol-* und *dur-*), so Krimtschakisch (*var* (REBI 85), *var-* (85), *vär-* (86), *ol-* (156)), Krimtatarisch (*ol-*, USEINOV 184; *dur-*, RADLOFF III 1787) und Krim-Karaimisch (*bar* (KARRPS 102) ~ *var* (156), *bär-* (151) ~ *vär-* (158), *dur-* (181) ~ *tur-* (547).[25]

Bei den bisher besprochenen Formen von osmanischer Einwirkung handelte es sich (abgesehen wohl von den Ausdrücken für 'Kamel') entweder um phonetischen Einfluss oder um die Durchsetzung von osmanischen oder zumindest dem osmanischen ähnelnden Formen, die im Oghusischen und Kiptschakischen auf ein gemeinsames Etymon oder zumindest auf eine

[22] RADLOFF (III 1912) bezeugt eine tschagataisch aussehende Form *čaš-* für Krimtatarisch.

[23] Diese Form ist durch Kreuzung von *čöz-* und Entsprechungen von *säš-* > *šäš-* ~ *čäš-* entstanden; zu letzterem siehe CLAUSON (857) Verb *säš-* 'to loosen, untie, and the like', 'more or less syn. w. *čöž-*'; *säš-* existiert heute überall außer in Oghusisch und seinen kiptschakischen Satelliten.

[24] Karaimisch (alle Dialekte) *yaŋġï*, *yanġï* (KARRPS 225); RADLOFF III 89 *yanġï* Trakai-Karaimisch.

[25] Dagegen finden wir in Trakai-Karaimisch *bar* (KARRPS 102), *bar-* (102), *b́är-* (112f.), *bol-* (128), *tur-* (547), in Halitsch-Karaimisch *bar* (102), *bar-* (102), *bär-* (151), *bol-* (128), *tur-* (547).

gemeinsame Grundform (wie *_o(l)tur-_ ‘sich setzen; sitzen’ (analogisch aus _olur-_ < _olor-_ gebildet), *_yaŋV_ ‘neu’) zurückgehen. Daneben existiert eine ganze Reihe von osmanischen Lehnwörtern in Krimtschakisch, Krimtatarisch und Krim-Karaimisch, die auf ein im Kiptschakischen nicht nachweisbares Etymon zurückgehen und die in Halitsch und Trakai-Karaimisch fehlen; diese osmanischen Lehnwörter erscheinen in den Sprachen des Krim-Areals manchmal gemeinsam mit ihren kiptschakischen Entsprechungen. Zu nennen sind hier die Wörter für ‘Ameise’,[26] ‘gleichen’,[27] ‘Hilfe’,[28] ‘Insel’[29], ‘Knochen’,[30] ‘Nabel’.[31] Hinzu kommen Entsprechungen von *_bïraq-_,[32] Demonstrativa des

[26] Osmanisch _qarïnǰa_, Kiptschakisch *_qï(r)mïsqa_: krimtatarisch _qarïnǰa_ (Useinov 122) ~ (_qïmïrsqa_ ~ _qïrmïsqa_ (135)), Krim-Karaimisch _q”arïnǰa_ (KarRPS 365); Krimtschakisch, Trakai- und Halitsch-Karaimisch zeigen nur _qïmïrsqa_: krimtschakisch _qïrmïsqa_ (Rebi 139), trakai- und halitsch-karaimisch _qumurstqa_ (KarRPS 346), trakai-karaimisch _qumurstxu_ (374); Karaimisch (L.T.) _qumurstqa_ (Radloff II 1049).

[27] Osmanisch _bänzä-_ < _bäŋzä-_, kiptschakisch *_W(q)ša-_: krimtschakisch (Rebi 76), krimtatarisch _bäŋzä-_ (Useinov 42), krim-karaimisch _bänza-_ ~ _bänzä-_ ~ _bäŋzä-_ (KarRPS 150), in allen Sprachen neben Formen von _W(q)ša-_: krimtschakisch (Rebi 159), krim-karaimisch _oxša-_ (KarRPS 436), krimtatarisch _oša-_ (Useinov 191). Dagegen in Halitsch-Karaimisch _uqsa-_ (KarRPS 576) ~ _uša-_ (587), in Trakai-Karaimisch _uqša-_ (576) ~ _uxša-_ (585) ~ _uša-_ (587). Trakai- und Krim-Karaimisch zeigen dabei dieselbe Frikativisierung $K > x$ wie Tatarisch bei _oxša-_. Formen mit anlautendem _o-_ wie in Krim-Karaimisch, Krimtschakisch und Krimtatarisch finden sich auch in Kumükisch, Kirgis-Kiptschakisch, Südosttürkisch und Aseri, während die Formen mit _u-_ in Wolga-Ural-Kiptschakisch, Nogaisch, Karakalpakisch, Tara-Tatarisch und Küärik erscheinen.

[28] Osmanisch _yardïm_; Kiptschakisch hat auch Formen von *_boluš(luq)_. Krimtschakisch _yardïm_ (Rebi 106), krimtatarisch _yardïm_ (Useinov 356), krim-karaimisch _yardïm_ (KarRPS 232) ~ _bolušlïq_ (130); halitsch-karaimisch _bolus(luq)_ (129), trakai-karaimisch _bolušluq_ (130), _bolušlux_ (130).

[29] Osmanisch _ada_ < *_ata:ġ_, Kiptschakisch hat auch Formen von _otruġ_ > (*_o(l)t(ï)raġ_ > *_otIrVš_: krimtatarisch _ada_ (Useinov 10), krimtschakisch _ada_ (Rebi 54), krimkaraimisch _ada_ ‘Insel’ (KarRPS 44) ~ _oturïš_ ~ _otraš_ (435). Halitsch-Karaimisch hat _otlać_ ~ _otrać_ (434), Trakai-Karaimisch zeigt _otrač_ (434).

[30] Osmanisch _kämik_, kiptschakisch *_söŋök_: krimtschakisch _käměk_ (Rebi 114) ~ _süyäk_ (175), krimtatarisch _kämik_ (Useinov 96; Radloff II 1208), krim-karaimisch _kämik_ (KarRPS 391) ~ _suyaq_ (483) ~ _süväk_ (485); halitsch-karaimisch _siväk_ (472), trakai-karaimisch _śuv́ak_ (501).

[31] Osmanisch _göbäk_ < *_kö:bäk_, kiptschakisch _kindik_: krimtschakisch _göbäk_ (Rebi 87), krimtatarisch _kobäk_ (Useinov 102), krim-karaimisch _köbäk_ (KarRPS 336) ~ _kindik_ (alle Dialekte, KarRPS 320). Es fällt auf, dass das Krim-Karaimische kiptschakischen _k_-Anlaut anstelle von osmanischem _g-_ hat.

[32] Osmanisch _bïraq-_, kiptschakisch _tašla-_: krimtschakisch _bïraq-_ (84) ~ _tašla-_ (182), krimtatarisch _bïraq-_ (Radloff IV 1728) ~ _buraq-_ (1818) ~ _braq-_ (1904), krim-

Typs *šW* > *šu* und wohl auch Abwesenheit von Entsprechungen zu *töbän* 'unterer Teil'. In Krim-Karaimisch und Krimtatarisch findet sich auch das Verb *istä-* 'wollen' (krim-karaimisch (KarRPS 208), krimtatarisch (Useinov 84) *istä-*).[33] Entsprechungen des westoghusischen Verbs *čalïš-* finden wir in Krimtatarisch, Krimtschakisch und Krim-Karaimisch,[34] wobei ich Entsprechungen zu *čalïšqan* 'fleißig' nur in Krimtatarisch und Krim-Karaimisch nachweisen kann.[35] Schließlich weisen Krimtatarisch und Krim-Karaimisch, aber auch Halitsch-Karaimisch, die typisch osmanische (westlich-westoghusische) Form des Wortes *domuz* < *toŋġuz* für 'Schwein' mit labialisiertem Nasal auf; Krim-Karaimisch hat alternativ noch *domïz*. Krimtschakisch zeigt mit *dombuz* (Rebi 92) eine Form, in der das *-ġ-* der Ausgangsform bewahrt aber ebenfalls labialisiert ist.[36]

---

karaimisch (KarRPS 145) ~ *tašla-* (519); trakai-karaimisch *tašla-* (519), halitsch-karaimisch *tasla-* (517).

[33] Außer im Türkeitürkischen findet sich das Verb auch noch in Aseri (AzrRS 176); Türkmenisch hat *isle-* (TkmRS 361). Diese Formen scheinen ansonsten in Kiptschakisch zu fehlen, wo wir stattdessen Formen wie tatarisch *tilä-* (TatRS 531) finden.

[34] Krim-karaimisch 'staraťsja; trudiťsja, rabotať' (KarRPS 623), so auch in krimtatarisch (Useinov 298), krimtschakisch (Rebi 201) und auch in Azeri (AzrRS 388); Türkmenisch hat 'tauschen; sich bemühen' (TkmRS 721).

[35] Krim-karaimisch 'trudoljubivyj' (KarRPS 623), krimtatarisch 'rabotajuščij' (Useinov 298).

[36] Krimtatarisch *domuz* (Useinov 67), halitsch- und krim-karaimisch (KarRPS 179), krim-karaimisch *domïz* (179); dagegen halitsch- und trakai-karaimisch *tonġuz* (538), trakai-karaimisch *donġuz* (179), *toŋġuz* (538). So auch kumükisch *toŋġuz* (KmkRS 128), tatarisch *duŋġïz* (TatRS 138). Karatschaisch-Balkarisch hat vereinfachtes *toŋuz* (KrčRS 645), ebenso Nogaisch und Karakalpakisch mit *doŋïz* (NogRS 101 bzw. KkpRS 176) und Kirgisisch mit *doŋuz* 'Wildschwein' (KrgRS 197). Hierzu passt türkmenisch *doŋuz* (TkmRS 279); Aseri hat mit *donuz* (AzrRS 137) eine für Oghusisch zu erwartende Form, allerdings ohne den labialisierten Nasal wie in *sümük* < *süŋök* 'Knochen', den wir in türkeitürkisch *domuz* finden. Altertümlich ist die salarische Form *toŋġïz* (Tenišev 1976a, 514), ebenso wie gelbuigurisch *toŋġïs* ~ *tovys* (Tenišev 1976b, 213f.) oder im Chaladsch *doŋġuz* (XlǰWB 107). Im Südosttürkischen schließlich finden wir Formen wie usbekisch *tŭnġiz* '(Wild-)Schwein' (UzbRS 465) und neuuigurisch *toŋġuz* 'id.' (UigRS 320); schließlich finden wir im marginalen Zentraltürkisch des Altai-Gebiets noch tschalkanisch *tonġus* 'Wildschwein' (Baskakov 207). Siehe weiterhin die Angaben bei Radloff III für Altai Kizhi-Dialekt, Teleutisch *toŋïs* (1171), Tarantschi *toŋïs*, Tschagataisch, Komanisch *toŋuz* (1172), Kasachisch *doŋuz* (1709), Aseri *donuz* (1712), Osmanisch *domuz* (1726) und Tatarisch *duŋġïz* (1785). Für türkeitürkische Dialekte siehe DS IV 1562 *doŋuz* in den Provinzen (*il*) Isparta, Denizli, Bolu (~ *doġuz*), Amasya, Tokat, Ankara, Konya und İçel sowie die zahlreichen dort angegebenen Bildungen mit *donuz*.

Manche dieser Lehnwörter scheinen im Karaimischen zu fehlen. Für 'Lippe' finden wir in Krimtschakisch *dudax* (REBI 93) (wie in Osmanisch), in Krimtatarisch *dudaq* ~ *läb* ~ *ärin* (USEINOV 67, letzteres ist die typischerweise im Kiptschakischen verwendete Form), Karaimisch hat nur *ärin*;[37] Weiterhin finden wir für 'Hand' krimtatarisch (USEINOV 332) und krimtschakisch (REBI 215) *äĺ* (< alttürkisch *älig*), für 'zurückkehren' krimtatarisch *d́on-* (USEINOV 64) und krimtschakisch (REBI 92) *dön-* (neben **qadït-* > krimtschakisch (REBI 126), krimtatarisch (USEINOV 117) *qayt-*. Modernes Krimtatarisch zeigt *torġay* für 'Sperling' (USEINOV 266; d.h. ein in vielen Kiptschaksprachen belegtes Wort, siehe etwa krim- und trakai-karaimisch *torġay* (KARRPS 539), halitsch-karaimisch *turġay* (547)), während RADLOFF noch das oghusische *särčä* belegt (IV 470). Osmanischer Einfluss ist auch für den Gebrauch von *käči* für 'Ziege' in RADLOFFs Krimtatarisch verantwortlich, wo modernes Krimtatarisch *äčki* (USEINOV 340) zeigt; für 'Stirn' hat es *alïn* (USEINOV 21; wie Osmanisch) neben dem mongolischen Lehnwort *maŋlay* (USEINOV 146).

Auch auf morphologischem Gebiet finden sich osmanische Einflüsse im Krim-Areal. So existiert in Krimtatarisch, Krimtschakisch und KATANOVs Karaimisch (695) ein negativer Aorist auf *-mAz* (wie im Osmanischen) anstatt auf *-mAs* (wie im Kiptschakischen außer im Karatschaisch-Balkarischen, das ebenfalls *-mAz* hat); modernes Karaimisch hat jedoch *-mAs* (siehe etwa MUSAEV 271). Das osmanische Gerundium auf *-(y)ArAK* and das negative Gerundium auf *-mAdAn* wurde ins Krimtatarische entlehnt, was schon KATANOV belegt (700; *varmayïp*/*varmay*, *bilmäyip*/*bilmäy* etc., Mariupol. *almayïp*, *värmäyip*); er gibt auch karaimische Beispiele, allerdings unklarer Herkunft (*olmayïp*/*olmaya* (*olmay*), *görmäyip*/*görmäyä* (*görmäy*) etc.). Für 'anfangen zu X-en' gebraucht Krimtschakisch in *bašladïlar bĕrĺĕktä čalïšma* 'sie begannen, zusammen zu arbeiten' (REBI 32) eine Form, die dem osmanischen *-mAGA bašla-* nahe steht. Krimtschakisch hat eine Präsensform *-(I)y* (REBI 16), die wohl eine stark kontrahierte Form von **-A yorïr*, d.h. eine typisch oghusische und damit auch osmanische Präsensform ist. Krimtatarisch hat die südlich-türkische Präsensform *-mAK* + *Lokativ* entlehnt, die es neben der kiptschakischen Form *-UwdA* verwendet. Das Täternomen des Krimtatarischen wird, wie im Osmanischen, mit *-(y)IǰI* gebildet (osmanische Herkunft verrät auch der Hilfskonsonant *y*) (statt mit *-(U)wčI* wie im Kiptschakischen). Die (Un-)möglichkeitsform des Krimtatarischen

[37] Alle Dialekte *ärin* (KARRPS 665), Trakai-Karaimisch *äriń* (666); RADLOFF (I 766f.) karLT. *ärin*.

ist *-A bil-* (wie im Osmanischen), die negativen Formen lauten *-p olma-* (kiptschakisches Muster mit osmanisch geformtem Verb), *-A alma-* (kiptschakisch) und *-Ama-* (letzteres aus Osmanisch; zu den Formen siehe DOERFER (389) und SEVORTJAN (244)). Das Futur auf *-AǰAK* ist keine exklusiv osmanische (oder auch nur westoghusische) Form, aber es sei and dieser Stelle angemerkt, dass es im Krimtatarischen (neg. *-mAyǰAK* (!)) und Krimtschakischen, nicht aber in Karaimisch erscheint.[38] Neben den nördlichen Akkusativ-Formen des Possessivsuffixes der dritten Person auf *+(s)In* zeigt Krimtatarisch auch die südliche Form *+(s)InI* (SEVORTJAN (240) und DOERFER (382)), die die normale Form in Krimtschakisch zu sein scheint (REBI 13f.).

Was Pronominalformen angeht, finden wir in Krimtschakisch ein *nas* ('kak, kakoj', REBI 23), das auf Osmanisch *nasïl* zurückgehen dürfte. Auch auf dem Gebiet der Postpositionen finden wir Osmanisches im Krim-Areal. Für 'mit' zeigen Karaimisch und Krimtatarisch Formen von **bi(r) lä(n)* (karaimisch *bïla*, krimtatarisch *bilän*). Daneben hat Krimtatarisch aber auch *+lä*, *+ilä(n)* und *+lAn*, die auf osmanischen Einfluss zurückgehen dürften; ein entsprechendes *ilän* existiert auch in Krimtschakisch. Osmanischer Einfluss dürfte auch für die Verwendung von *alt* 'unterer Teil' (RADLOFF I 400; XAFUZ 149, *sub* 'niz') in Krimtatarisch und Krim-Karaimisch verantwortlich sein.

Wie wir sehen, finden sich auf dem Krim-Areal, d.h. in den eigentlich kiptschakischen Sprachen Krimtschakisch, Krimtatarisch und Krim-Karaimisch, zahlreiche sprachliche Einflüsse aus dem Osmanischen. Mitunter sind in den betroffenen Sprachen alternativ kiptschakische Formen erhalten geblieben, vor allem im Krim-Karaimischen. Natürlich bleiben bei einer solchen kurzen Präsentation viele Elemente unberücksichtigt und viele Fragen unbeantwortet: Wie wurden die Merkmale vermittelt? Hat das Osmanische die betroffenen Sprachen alle direkt beeinflusst oder gibt es unter den Sprachen des Krim-Areals eine (zumindest in vielen Fällen wirksame) interne Weitervermittlung (etwa vom Krimtatarischen ins Krim-Karaimische)? Sind die osmanisch-"krimischen" Gemeinsamkeiten allesamt vom Osmanischen vermittelt oder sind zumindest einige der altertümlichen Gemeinsamkeiten einfach unabhängig voneinander erhaltene, am Westrand der türksprachigen Welt erhaltene Archaismen? Und wie sind die (wenn auch wenigen)

[38] Als *-AǰA(K)* oder *-(A)ǰA(K)*? Nach REBI (18) bezeichnet es eine Art Nezessitativ, etwa *käläǰäk* 'on dolžen prijti'. Außer in Oghusisch erscheint dieses Partizip in Wolga-Ural-Kiptschakisch, Kumükisch, Karakalpakisch, Usbekisch und sporadisch in Karatschaisch-Balkarisch; Nogaisch hat *-AyAK*.

osmanisch aussehenden Elemente im Halitsch-Karaimischen zu bewerten? All diese Fragen müssen hier unbeantwortet bleiben, versprechen aber bei zukünftiger Bearbeitung neue Einblicke in die Mechanismen gegenseitiger Beeinflussungen der Türksprachen.

Literaturverzeichnis

AzrRS = *Azerbajdžansko-russkij slovaŕ.* Ed. Abdullaev, B.T.; Tagieva, Z.R. Baku 1985.

Baskakov, N.A., 1985, *Dialekt lebedinskich tatar-čalkancev* (*Kuu-kiži*). Moskva.

Clauson, G., 1972, *An etymological dictionary of pre-Thirteenth-Century Turkish.* Oxford.

Doerfer, G., 1959, Das Krimtatarische. – *Philologiae Turcicae Fundamenta.* I. Ed. Deny, J. e.a. Wiesbaden, 369–390.

DS = *Derleme Sözlüğü.* I–XII. Ankara 1963–82.

Erdal, M.; Ianbay, I., 2000, The Krimchak book of miracles and wonders. – *Mediterranean Language Review* 12, 39–141.

GagRMS = *Gagauzskogo-russko-moldavskij slovaŕ.* Ed. Baskakov, N.A. Moskva 1973.

JakRS = *Jakutsko-russkij slovaŕ.* Ed. Slepcov, P.A. Moskva 1972.

KarRPS = *Karaimsko-russko-polśkij slovaŕ.* Ed. Baskakov, N.A.; Zajončkovskij, A.; Šapšal, S.M. Moskva 1974.

Katanov, N.O., 1903, *Opyt" izslědovanija urjanchajskago jazyka.* Kazań.

KkpRS = *Karakalpaksko-russkij slovaŕ.* Ed. Baskakov, N.A. Moskva 1958.

KmkRS = *Kumyksko-russkij slovaŕ.* Ed. Bammatov, Z.Z. Moskva 1969.

KrčRS = *Karačaevo-balkarsko-russkij slovaŕ.* Ed. Tenišev, Ė.R; Sujunčev, Ch.I. Moskva 1989.

KrgRS = *Kirgizsko-russkij slovaŕ.* Ed. Judachin, K.K. Moskva 1965.

Levi = Levi, B.Z., 2005, *Russko-karaimskij slovaŕ. Krymskij dialekt.* Simferopol.

Maxmutova, L.T., 1978, *Opyt issledovanija tjurkskich dialektov.* Moskva.

Musaev, K.M., 1966, Karaimskij jazyk. – *Jazyki Narodov SSSR.* II. *Tjurkskie jazyki.* Ed. Baskakov, N.A. Moskva, 260–279.

NogRS = *Nogajsko-ruskij slovaŕ.* Ed. Baskakov, N.A. Moskva 1963.

Radloff, W., 1893–1911 *Versuch eines Wörterbuches der Türk-Dialekte.* I–IV. St. Petersburg.

Rebi, D., 2004, *Krymčaksko-russkij slovaŕ.* Simferopol.

SCHÖNIG, C., 2009, Zischen will gelernt sein. – *Acta Orientalia Academiae Scientiarum Hungaricae* 62 (2), 131–184.

SEVORTJAN, Ė.V., 1966, Krymsko-tatarskij jazyk. – *Jazyki Narodov SSSR. II. Tjurkskie jazyki.* Ed. BASKAKOV, N.A. Moskva, 234–259.

STACHOWSKI, K., 2009, The discussion on consonant harmony in North-western Karaim. – *Türkbilig* 18, 158–193.

STEUERWALD, K., 1972, *Türkisch-deutsches Wörterbuch.* Wiesbaden.

TATRS = *Tatarsko-russkij slovaŕ.* Ed. GOLOVKIN, O.V. Moskva 1966.

TENIŠEV, Ė.R., 1976a, *Stroj salarskogo jazyka.* Moskva.

———, 1976b, *Stroj saryg-jugurskogo jazyka.* Moskva.

TKMRS = *Turkmensko-russkij slovaŕ.* Ed. BASKAKOV, N.A.; KARRYEV, B.A.; CHAMZAEV, M.JA. Moskva 1968.

UIGRS = *Ujgursko-russkij slovaŕ.* Ed. RACHIMOV, T.R. Moskva 1968.

USEINOV, S.M., 2005, *Krymskotatarsko-russkij slovaŕ.* Simferopoĺ.

UZBRS = *Uzbeksko-russkij slovaŕ.* Ed. BOROVKOV, A.K. e.a. Moskva 1959.

XAFUZ, M.Ė, 1995, *Russko-karaimskij slovaŕ. Krymskij dialekt.* Moskva.

XLǰWB = DOERFER, G.; TEZCAN, S., 1980, *Wörterbuch des Chaladsch (Dialekt von Xarrab).* Budapest.

Studies on the Turkic World
A Festschrift for Professor St. Stachowski on the Occasion of His 80th Birthday
edited by E. Mańczak-Wohlfeld and B. Podolak, Kraków 2010: 121–129

Ewa Siemieniec-Gołaś (Kraków)

Turkish Proverbs in *A Grammar of the Turkish Language* by Thomas Vaughan (1709)

As Erika Hitzigrath Gilson writes:

> ... There are (...) sources for Ottoman-Turkish without which the study of historical Turkish linguistics – phonology and dialectology in particular – will be quite restricted. These are recordings of the Turkish language by foreigners, represented in their own respective writing system as they perceived and interpreted the acoustical shape of the utterances. Such "Transkriptiostexte" supply invaluable data for Ottoman-Turkish of the fifteenth to the nineteenth centuries (Gilson 1987: 1).

One of the such "Transkripionstexte" is *A Grammar of the Turkish Language* written by an Englishman – Thomas Vaughan – and published in London 1709.

A few words about the author and the content of its work follow.

The author mentions his profession on the front page of his *Grammar* where we can read "Thomas Vaughan, Late of Smyrna, Merchant".[1] From the second page we find out that the book was dedicated to George Boddington Esq. of whom Thomas Vaughan was a nephew. Gilson writes in her book that very little is known about Vaughan's life, but she adds that he was associated

[1] The original copy of the *Grammar* is not available due to numerous ticks and reading-marks, both in the margin and the body of the text. However, the facsimile of the *Grammar* is available, published by The Scolar Press Limited in Menston, England 1968 under the title: *Thomas Vaughan. A Grammar of the Turkish Language 1709.*

with the Levant Company and it is quite probable that he could have stayed in Turkish-speaking territory for 12 years from 1697 to 1709. She also pays attention to comments included in the *Preface* to his *Grammar* which allows us to deduce that he was well-educated, knew several foreign languages, and the field of his various interests was very broad (Gilson 1987: 3).

Vaughan's work consists of the following parts: *The Preface* (v–xxiii), *Turkish alphabet (Arabic script)*, seventeen grammatical chapters including some general remarks on the language and the parts of speech (pp. 1–53), *Turkish Dialogues* (pp. 54–71), *Esop's Fables* (p. 71), *Proverbs* (pp. 71–76) and *Turkish Words* (pp. 76–103). The text of the *Grammar* ends with *Errata*, which is on a separate unnumbered page.

Vaughan's *Grammar*, with all grammatical problems described by the author, together with the lexical contents, was presented in Gilson's publication. However, Gilson did not include in her book the texts which together with other parts of Vaughan's work constitute the whole content of the *Grammar*. On several pages (71–76), Vaughan presented 53 Turkish proverbs together with their translation into English.

Here are the proverbs collected by Vaughan in his *Grammar*:

1. *Atalerdan kalme söz dür, bu gün ki yumurte yarınki ta(v)ukdan yek dür* (Atalerdan kalme suz dur, by gyun ky yumurte yarinky taukdan yec dur) 'This an old Saying, that an Egg to Day is better than a Hen to Morrow'[2]
2. *Azı bilme(y)in çoğı hiç bilmez* (Azy bilmein choghy hich bilmez) 'He who knows not a little, will never know much'.
3. *Er ölür adı kalur; at ölür meydanı kalur* (Ar ulur ady kalur; at ulur meidany kalur) 'When a Man dies, his Name remains; when a Horse dies, the Racing-Place remains';
4. *Oglan ağlama(y)ince meme vermizler* (Oglan aglamainge meme virmezler) 'Till the Child cries, they will not give it suck';
5. *Ac ayu oynamaz* (Adg ayu oinamaz) 'A hungry Bear will not play';
6. *Ucuz etiŋ çorbası tatsız olur* (Ojuz etting churbasy tatsiz olur) 'The Broath of cheap Flesh is tastless';

[2] For Turkish proverbs collected by Vaughan I propose my own transcription (in italics), however, both the Turkish words (in parentheses) and their English translations (in citation marks) are presented in original orthography used by the author. It should be added that as far as the English translation of the Turkish proverbs is concerned we quote them as they were written by Vaughan not trying to propose their modern version in terms of both vocabulary and orthography.

7. *İş işi gösterer* (Ish ishy gyusterer) 'One Bargain begets another';
8. *Eski dost düşman olmaz* (Esky dost dushman olmaz) 'An old Friend will not be an Enemy';
9. *Eşek maymunler arasınde ne işler?* (Eshec maimunler arasinde ne ishler?) 'An Ass amongst Monkeys, what Work will they make';
10. *Alma ağacdan ayrak düşmez* (Alma agadgdan airak dushmez) 'An Apple falls not far from the Tree';
11. *Eyü kılıç yaramaz demirdan olmaz* (Eyu kilich yaramaz demirdan olmaz) 'Bad Iron will not make a good Sword';
12. *Adamden adame fark var* (Adamden Adame fark var) 'There's Difference between Man and Man';
13. *Eski dost, eski hamam* (Esky Dost, esky hamam) 'An old Friend and an old Bagno';
14. *Eyü güni görmeyen, kem güni bayram sanur* (Eyu gyuny gurmeyen, kem gyuny Bairam sanur) 'He who never sees a good Day, takes a bad one for a Festival, or holy Day';
15. *El eli yur, iki el yüzi yur* (El elly yur, iky el yuzy yur) 'One Hand washeth the other, and both the Face';
16. *Eşek dağde ölür, zararı eve gelür* (Eshec dagde ulur, zarary evve ghelur) 'The Ass dies on the Hill, but the Loss comes home';
17. *Ayneye bakan kendi görür* (Auineye[3] bakan kendy gurur) 'He who looks a Looking-Glass, sees Himself';
18. *Eyülike eyülik, kemlike kemlik bulunur* (Eyulike eyulic, kemlike kemlik bulunur) 'A Man meets with Good for Good, and Evil for Evil);
19. *Ölmiş arslanıŋ sakalını yolarsın* (Ulmish Arslaning sakaliny yolarsin) 'You may pluck the Beard of a dead Lyon';
20. *Burun yüzdan düşmez* (Burun yuzdan dushmez) 'The Nose drops not from the Face';
21. *Büyük başın, büyük agrısı olur* (Buyuc bashin, buyuc agrisy olur) 'The Pain of a great Head is great';
22. *Bakşış atıŋ dişine bakılmaz* (Bakshish atting dishine bakilmaz) 'No Body looks a Gift-Horse in the Mouth';
23. *Baluk başdan kokar* (Baluk bashdan kokar) 'A Fish stinks from the Head';
24. *Bugün bize yarın size* (Bugyun bize, yarin size) 'To Day for us, to Morrow for you';

[3] The form of this word (*Auineye*) seems to be incorrect. We cannot exclude typographical error in reference to the grapheme "u".

25. *Bir ok ile iki kuş (v)urulmaz* (Bir ok ile iky kush orulmaz) 'Two Birds are not to be shot with one Arrow';
26. *Tez viren iki kere virir* (Tez viren, iky kerre virir) 'He who gives soon, gives twice';
27. *Çok viren göŋülsiz virer; az viren candan virir* (Chok viren gyungulsiz virer; az viren jandan virir) 'He who giveth much, gives not cordially; who gives little, doth it from it soul;
28. *Hesabsız ne sakalıŋ var köse?* (Hyssabsiz ne sakaling var kyuse?) 'What makes your Beard so thin without an Account, (or Reckoning). Which if large, is enough to make a Turk pluck up his Beard by the Roots';
29. *Hastaye döşegimi sorarsın?* (Hastaye dusheghimy sorarsin?) 'Do you ask my Bed for the sick (Man?);
30. *Kırsız hırsıze yoldaş dur* (Kirsiz khirsize yoldash dur) 'One Rouge, or Robber, is Companion for another';
31. *Dostum ağladır, düşman güldürür* (Dostum agladir, dushman guldurur) 'My Friend mourns, and my Enemy laughs';
32. *Dost ileyi iç, alış viriş ayleme* (Dost ileyi ich, alish virish aileme) 'Drink with a Friend, but don't deal with him (in Buying and Selling);
33. *Dostler arasınde teklif yok dur* (Dostler arasinde teklif yok dur) 'Among Friends there's no Ceremony';
34. *Delüye her gün Bayram* (Delluye her gyun Bairam) 'Every Day is holy Day to a mad Man';
35. *Seveniŋ kulıyuz, sevme(y)iŋ Sultanı* (Sevening kulijuz, sevmeining Sultany) 'He who is Lord over them that love him, is the Slave of such as do';
36. *Söz söylemek avretleriŋ dur, işlemek Erleriŋ dur* (Suz suilemec avretlering dur, ishlemec Arlering dur) 'Tis Womens Business to talk, Mens to act';
37. *Sakale gülen, yüze güler* (Sakale gyulen, yuze gyuler) 'He that laughs at your Beard, laughs at or to your Face';
38. *Soŋ pişmanlık fayde virmez* (Sung pishmanlik faide virmez) 'Repentance profiteth not when the Matter is at an End';
39. *Acemi Nalbend Cehud Eşekinde ögrenür* (Agemy Nalbend Gehud Esheckinde ugrenur) 'The Persian learns to be a Farrier by the Jew's Ass';
40. *Gerib kuşuŋ yuvasın taŋrı yapar* (Gherib kushung yuvasyn tangry yapar) 'God makes the Nest of a Bird that's a Stranger';

41. *Fakiriŋ oğlı olmakdan Düvletlüniŋ kulı olmak yek dir.* (Fakiring ogly olmakdan Duvletluning kully olmak yec dir) 'It's better to be the Slave of the Rich, than Son of the poor Man';
42. *Kapu ki pek kapadı Allahe ısmarla* (Kapu ke pec kapade Allahe ismarla) 'Bid adieu to a Door that's close shut';
43. *Gişi sevmedügi şeydan faide gelür* (Ghishy sevmedughy sheidan faide ghelur) 'We often are profited by what we despise';
44. *Göz görme(y)ince göŋül kalanur* (Gyuz gurmeinge gyung-ul kalanur) 'So long as the Eye sees not, the Heart's secure';
45. *Gözdan ayrak olan, göŋüldan dahı ayrak olur* (Gyuzdan airac olan, gyunguldan dahy airac olur) 'He who is far out of Sight, is farther out of Mind';
46. *Göŋüldan göŋüle yol var dur* (Gyunguldan gyungule yol var dur) 'There's a Path from Heart to Heart';
47. *Göŋül kimi severse güzel o dur* (Gyungul kimy severse guzel o dur) 'He is handsome who is beloved';
48. *Görünen küye, kulağız ne lazım?* (Gurunen cuiye, kolaghiz ne lazim?) 'Having shewn our selves, or been seen at the Bath, what need hale we of Ears (that is, of other Ears);
49. *Gömlek koftandan yakın dur* (Gumlec coftandan yakin dur) 'The Shirt is nearer than the Under-vest or Cassock);
50. *Münasıb yoldaş yolde binit yerinde dür* (Munasib yoldash yolde binit yerinde dur) 'Comes facundus in via pro vehiculo est';
51. *Viresi şerab içen, iki kere serhoş olur* (Viresy sherab ichen, iky kerre serhosh olur) 'He who drinks Wine free-cost, will be twice drunk';
52. *Ya Devi öle, ya Devici Dimişler* (Ya Devy ule, ya Devigy Dimishler) 'The Camel dy'd, and they said 'twas the Camel-Driver';
53. *Yazıcı kendüye kem yazmaz* (Yazigy kenduye kem yazmaz) 'The Scrivener writes not badly for himself'.

What can we say about the presented above collection of proverbs? First of all, if we confront this material with contemporary dictionaries or collections of Turkish proverbs we can state that many of the analysed proverbs are well known in contemporary Turkish.[4] However, in some cases, the eighteenth-century versions differ from their contemporary counterparts

[4] There are many collections or dictionaries of Turkish proverbs and idioms. For the purpose of our analysis we used *Atasözleri ve Deyimler Sözlüğü* by Ömer Asım Aksoy, I–II, Istanbul 1988.

lexically, but rather not semantically, e. g.: the proverb: *Oġlan aġlama(y)ince meme virmezler*[5] has its modern counterpart which is: *Ağlamayan çocuğa meme vermezler.*[6]

In some cases both historical and modern versions of a particular proverb are the same, excluding obvious phonetic differences e. g.: *Baluk başdan kokar* 'A Fish stinks from Head' – cf.: *Balık baştan kokar* id.

While analysing the proverbs we can try to ascertain the sources from which Vaughan collected his material. We cannot exclude that he excerpted some of the proverbs from the collection of proverbs included in Hieronymus Megiser's *Institutionum linguæ turcicæ libri* IV, Leipzig 1612.[7] Such supposition can be supported by the fact that among proverbs collected by Vaughan we find one which is translated into Latin: *Münasıb yoldaş yolde binit yerinde dur* 'Comes facundus in via provehiculo est'. We find the same proverb in Megiser's *Institutionum...* written, of course, in German orthography and translated into Latin with the same words that we find in Vaughan's *Grammar* (Stein 1984: 75).

When comparing Vaughan's proverbs with their modern counterparts we cannot exclude that some of his proverbs have dialectal forms, so Vaughan could have heard them from someone speaking in a dialect not in a literary language. He only sketchily mentioned some sources he used when preparing his *Grammar*, however we do not know whether these were grammars by Meninski, Seaman or someone else.[8] He stated that in the following words:

> But there is some Variation in the Grammar it self; and the Dialogues, Proverbs and Words, are a collection from other Books, and my own Observation.[9]

[5] However, it seems that in this case Vaughan did not translate this proverb correctly. He translated: "Till the Child cries, they will not give it suck", whereas the meaning of the proverb is quite opposite, what results from the negative form of the gerund *aġlama(y)ince* 'until sb does not cry'. Thus the translation of this proverb should be as follows: "Until child does not cry they do not give him suck".

[6] The examples of contemporary Turkish proverbs are cited from the above mentioned dictionary.

[7] See: Stein H. (1984): *Eine Türkische Sprichwortsammlung des 17. Jahrhunderts.* "Acta Orientalia Academiae Scientiarum Hung.", XXXVIII (1–2), pp. 55–104.

[8] Meniński à Mesgnien F. (1680): *Linguarum Orientalium Turcicæ, Arabicæ, Persicæ Institutiones seu Grammatica Turcica, in qua Orthographia, etymologia, syntaxis, prosodia,* Viennæ; Seaman W. (1670): *Grammatica Linguæ Turcicæ,* Oxoniæ.

[9] This information we can find in *The Preface* to his *Grammar*, p. XVI.

Surprisingly, in proverbs collected by Vaughan, there are some old phonetic features of the Turkish language typical of the period of old Ottoman-Turkish, where labial vowels dominated in stems and in suffixes.[10] We find these features in such instances as: *baluk*, *ayu*, *kalur* and others. However, in the seventeenth century the words presented above had either forms with illabial vowels or parallel forms with labial and illabial. This phenomenon showed that the vowel harmony was still in the process of developing.[11] Generally, in the eighteenth century the so-called labial harmony was already consolidated in reference to words both with illabial and labial sequences. Since in Vaughan's *Grammar*, published in 1709, we still meet forms with sequences as is shown in the above examples, therefore we may assume that these forms come rather from dialects and not from literary Turkish. It is obvious that dialects preserve some obsolete forms which are no longer in use in the literary language.

The matter which we should also mention here is the orthography Vaughan used when transcribing Turkish words. Judging by the form of some Turkish words we notice that the author was not consistent in the transcription he used. Admittedly, Gilson in her work explains the transcription methods and rules used by Vaughan but from many examples we see that not all Turkish words are written by him with compliance to the rules mentioned (Gilson 1987: 10–27). This remark generally refers to his recording of vowels. Trying to explain his own methodology with reference to recording vowels he wrote in Chapter I (*Of Orthography*) the following statement:

> The formes of the Alphabets gives the Names of the Letters; and they are to be pronounc'd after the *English* way of sounding the Vowels (Vaughan 1709: 1).

Nevertheless, such a statement can only, to some extent, explain his method of transcription.

In the examples given below we see that, in some cases, the grapheme "a" represents the /a/ phoneme as in: *ayu* 'bear', in some other, /e/ phoneme as in: *er* (*ar*)[12] 'man', *elma* (*alma*)[13] 'apple', etc. The grapheme "e" is

[10] This problem is widely discussed by Räsänen M. (1949): *Beiträge zur Frage der türkischen Vokalharmonie*, "Journal de la Société Finno-Ougrienne", XLV, p. 3.

[11] See: *baluk, balık* in Meniński à Mesgnien F. (1680): *Thesaurus Linguarum Orientalium Turcicæ, Arabicæ, Persicæ*, Viennæ, I, p. 687.

[12] Vaughan's transcription is given in parenthesis, unless it is the same as ours.

[13] In this case we cannot exclude that this is a dialectal form *alma*, since such a form still exists in modern Anatolian dialects.

sometimes used for /e/ as in *perde* 'a curtain', sometimes for /i/ as in *cihan* (*gehan*) 'world'. The English author uses for /i/ once "i" and once "y", e. g.: *kemlik* 'evil', *iki* (*iky)* 'two'. In some cases he also uses "u" both for /ü/, /u/, or even /ö/, e. g.: *ölür* (*ulur*) 'he dies', *kalur* 'he remains'.

It is obvious that the transcription system Vaughan used for Turkish words is based upon English orthography, but still, as it has already been ascertained, Vaughan was inconsistent. We cannot exclude that he followed some orthographic changes introduced to the English language, trying to apply them to Turkish transcription (Gilson 1987: 10–27). Besides, Vaughan could have also followed transcription systems used by such other European authors as Meniński, Molino or Megiser. Some features of his transcription (Italian "gi" for Turkish /c/ or Italian "ch" for Turkish /k/) may confirm this thesis.[14]

Last but not least, when trying to evaluate the transcription system used by Vaughan one can again quote Gilson: "Certain Common Turkic phonemes involving mainly the vowels /ö/, /ü/ and /ı/ are very often not represented in the "Transkriptionstexts". In the literature pertaining to transcribed material, lack of a clearly defined grapheme for a Turkish phoneme has been rather consistently attributed to the fact that the Latin graphs at the transcriber's disposal were deficient, forcing him to conscious underrepresentation" (Gilson 1987: 24).

The above-presented collection of Turkish proverbs can perfectly contribute not only to the studies on the history of Turkish proverbs but also, in a wider aspect, to the scientific research on the culture of the Turkish world. After Aksoy we can repeat that:

> Her ulusun atasözleri, kendi varliğının ve benliğinin aynasıdır.
> [= The proverbs of each nation constitute the mirror of its existence and personality.] (Aksoy 1988: 27).

Bibliography

Aksoy Ö. A. (1988): *Atasözleri ve deyimler sözlüğü*, I–II, İstanbul.

Gilson E. H. (1987): *The Turkish Grammar of Thomas Vaughan. Ottoman-Turkish at the End of the XVIIth Century According to an English "Transkriptionstext"*, Wiesbaden.

[14] In the text of *Proverbs* there are no examples of such features, but one can find some in the whole Turkish material included in Vaughan's *Grammar*.

Megiser H. (1612): *Institutionum linguæ turcicæ libri IV,* Leipzig.

Meniński à Mesgnien F. (1680): *Thesaurus Linguarum Orientalium Turcicæ, Arabicæ, Persicæ,* I–III, Viennæ.

Meniński à Mesgnien F. (1680): *Linguarum Orientalium Turcicæ, Arabicæ, Persicæ Institutiones seu Grammatica Turcica, in qua Orthographia, etymologia, syntaxis, prosodia,* Viennæ.

Räsänen M. (1949): *Beiträge zur Frage der türkischen Vokalharmonie,* "Journal de la Société Finno-Ougrienne", XLV, p. 3.

Seaman W. (1670): *Grammatica Linguæ Turcicæ, In Quinque partes distribute,* Oxoniæ.

Stein H. (1984): *Eine Türkische Sprichwortsammlung des 17. Jahrhunderts.* "Acta Orientalia Academiae Scientiarum Hung.", XXXVIII (1–2), pp. 55–104.

Vaughan Th. (1709): *A Grammar of the Turkish Language,* London (facsimile reproduced by The Scolar Press Limited, Menston, Yorkshire, 1968).

Studies on the Turkic World
A Festschrift for Professor St. Stachowski on the Occasion of His 80th Birthday
edited by E. Mańczak-Wohlfeld and B. Podolak, Kraków 2010: 131–138

Hatice Şirin User (İzmir)

Türk Dillerinde *çilek* ve *yilek*

Türk dillerinde böğürtlen (*Rubus caesus*), çilek (*Fragaria vesca*), ahududu (*Rubus idaeus*), yabanmersini (*Vaccinium myrtillus*) gibi üzümsü meyvelerin (İng. *berry*, Alm. *Beere*) – alıntı ögeler ve kimi zaman *böğürtlen* hariç tutulduğunda – üç sözcükle adlandırıldığını görmekteyiz: *kat*, *çilek* ve *yilek*. Kaşgarlı Mahmut tarafından "mugaylan dikeni meyvesi; Yemek, Kıpçak, Kay, Tatar, Çomul dillerinde herhangi bir ağacın meyvesi" olarak tanımlanan (III: 146–147) *kat*, günümüzde Alt., Tuv., Tof. *kat*, Hak. *hat* "yemiş" olarak varlığını sürdürür (Tenişev 1997: 121).

Çoğu gülgiller (*Rosaceae*) ailesinden çalı formundaki bitkilerin meyveleri olan *çilek* ve *yilek*in fonetik benzerliklerinin yanı sıra, Türkçenin tarihsel ve modern alanlarında bazı topluluklarca tek bir meyveyi, çoğunlukla da yabani türleriyle birlikte çileği adlandırmak üzere kullanılmaları, yani anlam açısından birleşmiş olmaları, etimoloji sözlüklerinde bu sözcüklerin tek bir maddede toplanmasına neden olmuştur.

Opıt slovarya Tyurkskih Nareçiy'de Nog. *çiglek*, Ttü. *çilek*, Altayca ve ağızlarındaki (Tel., Kmd. vb.) *yīlek* "der Erdbeere ähnliche Beeren" sözcükleri birleştirilmiş (OSTN III: 511, 2115); böylece Radloff birbirinden bağımsız bu iki ayrı biçimi aynı öbekte toplayarak, kendisinden sonraki araştırmacıları yanılgıya düşürmüştür (Ramstedt 1914–1915: 143; Poppe 1960: 28; Egorov 1964: 226; Musayev 1975: 252–253).

Räsänen, *gl* ~ *δl* (*-gd*) nöbetleşmesi bağlamında Nog. *čigläk*, Çağ., Osm. *čiläk*, Tkm. *čigäläk* biçimlerini Kzk. *jidäk*, Oyr., Tel. Kmd. *jīläk* "Erdbeere", Tel. *d'iläk*, Leb. *jigläk*, Çağ., Tob. Tar. *jiläk* "Heidelbeere, Erdbeere", Koyb. *t'estäk*, *t'istäk*, *d'istäk*, Çuv. *śirla* "Gartenerdbeer" sözcüklerini aynı ailede değerlendirmiştir (1949: 226–227). Räsänen'in bu birleştirmeyi yapma nedeni, Radloff verilerini kabul etmesinden çok, Türkçede *y-* ~ *ç-* ses nöbetleşmesini benimsemesidir (1949: 188).

Poppe, Moğ. *jigde* "Brustbeere" = Evnk. *jikte* "Beere" = Çuv. *śirla* biçimlerini eşitleyerek, kökenleri için **yigdläk* "Beere" sözcüğünü tasarlamış ve bunları Altayca ve ağızlarındaki biçimlerle birleştirmiştir (1960: 28). Daha önce Ramstedt (1914–1915: 143) tarafından yapılan bu birleştirmedeki Moğolca ve Evenkice verilerin, *çilek* ve *yilek* değil, Eski Türkçe *yigde* "iğde" ile ilişkili olduğu açıktır.

Tenişev *yagoda* "yemiş" başlığı altında **kat*, **čistek* ve **yigellek* biçimlerini tasarlamış; Alt. *d'istek;* Hak. *čistek* ve Şor. *čestek* biçimlerini **čistek* ile; Ttü., Gag. *çilek*, Tkm. *çigelek*, Krç.Blk. *cilek*, Kmk. *ciyelek*, Tat. *cilek*, Tat. ağızları, Bşk. *yilek*, Nog. *yelek*, Kzk. *jide* ~ *jidek*, Alt. *d'ilek* biçimlerini ise **yigellek* ile ilişkilendirmiştir. Tenişev, *zemlyanika* "yaban çileği" ve *klubnika* "çilek" başlıkları altında Ttü. Gag. *çilek*, Az., Tkm. *çigelek*, Krç.Blk. *cilek*, Kzk. *jidek*, Tat. *cir cilegé* ve Alt. *d'er d'ilek* ögeleri için **jegelek* biçimini tasarlamıştır (1997: 121–122, 140–141).

İlk kez 1967'de Doerfer, *çilek* (**çiyelek* < **çigelek*) sözcüğünün ses bakımından *yilek* biçimiyle birleştirilemeyeceğini belirtmiş (TMEN III: 1110); Eren de, *Türk Dilinin Etimolojik Sözlüğü*'de, *çilek* maddesi altında sözcükle ilgili literatürü özetledikten sonra, Doerfer'in bu düşüncesinin haklılığını dile getirmiştir (1999: 92–93). Ancak bu bilim adamlarının hiç biri, *çilek* ve *yilek* sözcüklerinin alt anlam katmanlarını da içeren etimolojilerine değinmemiştir.

Bu iki sözcüğün köken bilgilerinin aydınlatılmasında Çuvaşça *śirla* ve Türk dillerindeki diğer biçimler kilit roller oynamaktadır:

I. *yilek* sözcüğünün Çuvaşçadaki şekli (*śirla*), Macarcaya *szőlő* "üzüm" olarak geçmiştir. Fedetov, Macarca *szőllő* < **szödlő* < Eski Çuv. **śidläg* aşamalarını kaydettikten sonra, Çuv. *śirla*'nın etimolojisinin hâlâ karanlık kaldığını belirtmiş (1996:156); Macar dilinin etimoloji sözlüğü ise, Türkçe **yid+lek* olarak tasarladığı bu ögenin kök biçimi **yid*'e herhangi bir anlam yüklememiştir (MNES: 794). Ancak bu tasarlamada açık olan nokta, *śirla*'nın *ç-* ön sesli değil, *y-* ön sesli bir sözcükten gelişmiş olması ve ilk hecedeki son ünsüzün Eski Türkçe *-d-* ünsüzüne denk gelmesidir.[1]

II. Kazakçadaki *j-*'li biçim, Eski Türkçe sedalı ön damak yarı ünlüsü *y-*'ye gittiği için, modern Türk dillerinden Ttü., Nog., Az. ve Tkm.

[1] Bu ses gelişmeleri için bkz. Ceylan 1997.

ye, sırasıyla *çilek*, *çiglek*, *çiyeley* ve *çiğelek* olarak yansıyan biçimle birleşemez.

III. Alt., Tel. ve Koyb.daki *t'*- ve *d'*-'li biçimler, ön sesi *y*'li olan bir biçime gider.

IV. Bşk. *yilek*, **çigelek*'ten gelişmiş olsaydı, *yilek* değil, *silek* biçiminde yansıma gösterirdi. Dolayısıyla Başkurtçadaki biçimde önses korunmuştur.

V. Tat. ve Krç.Blk. *cilek* biçimi ön sesi *y*'li olan bir biçime gider.

VI. Tuv. *çestek-kat*, Şor. *çestek,* Hak. *çistek* "yemiş", *çazı çistegi, çir çistegi* biçimleri de ön sesi *y*'li olan bir biçime gider.

VII. Oyr., Tel. Kmd. *jīläk* biçimindeki uzun ünlünün *-iy* (< *-id-*)'den geldiği Eren tarafından belirtilmiştir (1999: 93).

Türkçenin tarihsel ses gelişimi ve değişimleri temelinde ortaya çıkan yukarıdaki tabloya göre, karşımızda **1.** Önsesi *y-*, ilk hecesinin sonsesi *-d-*; **2.** Önsesi *ç-*, ilk hecesinin ikinci ünsüzü *-g-* olan iki ayrı sözcük vardır. Bir başka ifadeyle tarihsel ve modern Türk dillerinde **çigelek* ve **yıdlak* biçiminde tasarlanabilecek iki ayrı meyve adı vardır.

Bu sözcüklerin eski Türkçede hayvan adlarının, özellikle kuş türlerinin adlarının yapımında görev alan *+lAk* ekiyle (OTWF: 89–90) teşekkül etmiş sözcükler olduğunu ileri sürmenin hatalı bir yargı taşımadığını öngörmekteyiz. Bu bağlamda *-lAk* ekinin, OTWF'de bitki ve hayvan adları yapımındaki işlevselliği vurgulanan *+gAç*, *+gA* ve *+gAn* ekiyle görevdaş olduğunu düşünüyoruz. Bu ek, *kumlak* "şerbetçiotu" (ED: 628a), *kozalak* "kozalaklıların, genellikle dibi yuvarlak, tepesi koni biçiminde ve odunsu dokulu meyvesi", *burçalak* "yerelması biçiminde, yumru gövdeli, kara kabuklu bir çeşit yaban bitkisi; söğüt yaprağına benzer yapraklı bir çeşit bitki", *bürçelek* "kökünde patates gibi yumruları bulunan ve yenilebilen bir bitki", *ebelek* "yaprakları yenilebilen, tohumlarından da çay yapılan ıspanağa benzeyen bir çeşit ot, labada", *gögelek* "kışın yapraklarını dökmeyen asalak bir bitki" (TS; Baytop 2007: 54, 120) gibi bitki adlarının yapımında da yer almış görünüyor. **çigelek, kozalak, burçalak, bürçelek, gögelek* sözcüklerinin, sırasıyla *çig* "çiğ", *koz* "kabuklu meyve, ceviz" ", *burç* "filiz; ökse otu; karabiber" (< *bur-ı-ç*) ve *kök* "yeşil" sözcüklerine *+gA+lAk* biçimbirimlerinin eklenmesiyle teşekkül ettikleri anlaşılmaktadır.

çilek < *çigelek* < *çig+gA+lAk* gelişimindeki *çige* (< *çig+gA*) sözcüğünün varyantları, Türk dillerinde "vişne" ve "kabuklu meyvelerin içi" anlamlarıyla tespit edilir: Kırg., *çiye*, Özb. *çiya*, Tat. *çiye* "vişne", Bşk. *séye* "vişne", Nog., Kklp., Kzk. *şiye* "vişne", Ttü. ağızları *çiğe* "ceviz ve badem içi", *çiye* "kabuklu meyvelerin içi; fasulyenin içi; çam kozalağının tohumu". Bu sözcük Moğolcada *çiy* "bozkır kirazı" biçimindedir (MTS: 289).

* * *

Bitki adlandırmalarındaki temel kavramlar niteleme (özellikle renk) adlarından başka "vurmak, dövmek", "gömmek"[2], "büyümek, olgunlaşmak" (*ösüm*, *erik* vb.), "kalkmak" (*turma*; *turp* vb.) anlamlı eylemlerdir. Türkçede *yemek*, *yaş* ve *kök* kavramları ise, genel olarak meyve ve sebzeyi adlandırmakta kullanılmışlardır. Bu sözlerden *yaş* ve *kök*, "taze, yaş olma" ve "renk" bilgilerinin alt anlam katmanından üst katmana taşınmasıyla "meyve; sebze" anlamına ulaşmışlardır: Krg. *caşılşa* "sebze", Tat. *yeşilçe* "sebze", Bşk. *yeşilse* "sebze", Ttü. *yeşillik*, Kzk. *kök, kökönis* "sebze", Krç-Blk. *köger* "meyve", *köget* "sebze", Kmk. *yaşıllık* "sebze", Tkm. *gȫk*, *gȫkönüm* "sebze", Uyg. *köktat* "sebze", Özb. *köket* "sebze", Hak. *kök özim, kök ot* "sebze", Tuv. *kök* "sebze" vb.

Bitki adlarına kaynak olabilen niteleleyiciler, hiç kuşkusuz yalnızca renk adları değildir. *Yaşlık*, *ıslaklık*, *nem* ve *koku* kavramları da bitki adlarının kaynakları olabilmektedir. Bu bağlamda, *çilek* < *çigelek* < *çig+gA+lAk* bitki adının, *çig* "nemli, ıslak" sözcüğünden geldiğini ileri sürüyoruz. Bu sözcük (*çig*), olgunlaşma sürecini güz ve ilkbahar yağmurlarından sonra ıslak toprakta tamamlayan ve bazıları çiğ yenilen bitki türlerinin adına kaynaklık etmiş görülüyor:

çigdem "crocus sativus" bitki adının kökeni de, *çig* sözcüğüyle ilişkilendirilerek açıklanabilir. Sözcüğün *çig*'den türeme ve "çiğ, nemli" anlamı taşıması ihtimali Clauson tarafından belirtilmiştir (ED: 414b). Ancak Erdal, Clauson'un *çigdem* sözcüğü için örnek verdiği TT V'te kayıtlı *özlerdeki özeklerdeki yava çigidem suvlardakı ögenlerdeki sargan otı* cümlesindeki *çigidem* ile Osmanlıca *çiğdem*'in eşbiçimler olmayabileceğini söyleyerek, bu açıklamaya şüpheyle yaklaşır. Ona göre, *yava* ve *sargan otı* sözlerinin bitki adı olmasına karşın, *çigidem* sözcüğü, *suvlar ve ögen*'i niteleyen bir sıfat olabilir (1991: 84.d.n.).

Oysa, söz konusu cümle incelendiğinde, 13'lü hece ölçüsüyle manzum tarzda yazılmış bir beyitle karşılaşmaktayız.[3] Bu da *çigidem* değil, *çigdem* biçimini doğrular. Erdal'ı bu cümleyle ilgili kuşkuya düşüren nokta,

[2] Bu kategorizasyon için bkz. K. Stachowski 2008: 104.

[3] *özlerdeki özeklerdeki yava çigdem / suvlardakı ögenlerdeki sargan otı.* Burada 4+5+4 şeklinde bir hece vezni vardır. Ayrıca, Uygur şiirinde genel olarak dikkati çeken kıtalar başındaki düzenli ses tekrarını, çokluk, bulunma ve aitlik ekleri ara-

-dAm ekinin niteleme adlarının yapımındaki etkin rolüdür. Oysa, özellikle bitki ve hayvan adlarının alt anlam katmanları incelendiğinde, bu sözcüklerden bir kısmının sıfat tamlaması aşamasından sonra elipsleşmeler yaşayarak üst anlam katmanları kazandıkları görülebilir: *ısırgan otu* > *ısırgan*; *küstüm çiçeği* > *küstüm*; *madımak otu* > *madımak* veya *üzüm asması*, *yaban asması* vb. bitki türlerinin genel olarak *asma* adıyla yaygınlaşması gibi.

Dolayısıyla burada "çiğ olan, yaş olan, taze" vb. anlamlı *çigdem* sözcüğünün, muhtemelen *çigdem çiçeği* / *yemişi* vb. bir tamlama yapısından kısalarak özel bir bitkinin adı haline gelmesi söz konusudur.

Çilek de, tıpkı çiğdem gibi bahar aylarında yağan yağmurun nemlendirdiği toprakta yetişen bir bitki olduğundan *çig* sözcüğüyle bağlantısının makul olduğunu düşünüyoruz. Sözcük, yukarıda da vurgulandığı gibi, **çig+gA* > **çigge* > **çige* "vişne" > Kırg., *çiye*, Özb. *çiya*, Tat. *çiye* "vişne", Bşk. *séye* "vişne", Nog., Kklp.,Kzk. *şiye* "vişne", Ttü. ağızları *çiğe* "ceviz ve badem içi", *çiye* "kabuklu meyvelerin içi; fasulyenin içi; çam kozalağının tohumu" gelişimi yaşamış; bu gelişimin yanı sıra *+lAk* ekiyle genişleyerek *çigelek* biçimini teşkil etmiş olmalıdır.

* * *

Bitki adlarına kaynak olabilen niteleyicilerin *koku* kavramından da gelişebildiğini yukarıda belirtmiştik. Kaşgarlı Mahmut, *yıd* "koku"dan geliştiği açık olan *yıḍıg ot* bitkisini "Kaşgar dilince 'üzerlik otu' anlamınadır. Uç ve Barsgan dillerinde *eldrük*, Oğuzcada *yüzerlik*tir" olarak tanımlamaktadır (III: 12). XV. yüzyıldan itibaren bir çok Eski Anadolu Türkçesi metninde ve sözlüğünde[4] geçen *yıylankuç* "limon büyüklüğünde ve kavun gibi güzel kokan bir meyve, şamama", bu sözcüklerden biridir. Tarama Sözlüğü'nde *yıylagaç* ~ *yıylagıç* ~ *yıylagaç* ~ *yıylakaç* ~ *yiğlengeç* biçimleri kayıtlı olan bu sözcüğün, güzel ve keskin kokulu olduğu özellikle vurgulanır ki, bu da *yıd* "koku" sözcüğünden geliştiğini net biçimde ortaya koyar. Sözcüğün morfolojisi de açıktır: *yıd-lA(-n)-GAç (/-Gıç)*. Bu eylem, Eski Anadolu

---

cılığıyla (*-lardakı, -lerdeki*) burada da görürüz. Uygur şiirindeki paralel beyitler üzerine kurulu, simetrik tekrar düzenlemeleri için bkz. Kortantamer 1993.

[4] Bu metin ve sözlükler şunlardır: *Miftâhü'l-Cenne* (XV. yy.), *Ahmed Paşa Divânı* (XVI. yy.), *Şâmilü'l-Lûga* (XVI. yy.), *Et-Tuhfetü's-Seniyye* (XVI. yy), *Lûgat-i Ni'metullah* (XVI. yy.), *Câmiü'l-Fâris* (XVII. yy.), *Bürhân-ı Katı Tercümesi* (XVIII–XIX. yy.), *Kâmûs-ı Osmânî* (XIX. yy.)

Türkçesinde hem kalın hem de ince ünlülü biçimiyle (*yıyla-/yiyle-/yiyile-/yile-* "koklamak") kayıtlıdır (YTS: 4624).

yıd "koku" sözcüğünden gelişen bir başka bitki adı da *yiyircik*'tir. Bir çalı türü olan bu bitki, bitki adları sözlüğünde "*Anagrys foetida* (*Leguminosae*) 1–3 metre yüksekliğine çalı görünüşünde kuvvetli kokulu bir ağaççık" olarak tanımlanır (Baytop 2007: 293–294). Ttü. ağızlarına has olan *yiyircik* bitki adının, standart Türkçedeki adı *kokar çalı*dır (Yaltırık 1972). Sözcüğün morfolojisi, *yıylanguç*'ta olduğu gibi rahatlıkla çözülebilir. Zira Batı Türkçesinde *yiyir* "koku, pis koku" (< *yıd-I-* "kokmak" + *r* "kokar, kokan") sözcüğünü, XIV. yüzyıl metinlerinden itibaren izlemekteyiz (YTS: 4623). Aynı sözcüğün, *yiyirce göcen* söz öbeğinde yer almış biçimiyle, *kokarca* adlı hayvanı adlandırmak üzere kullanıldığı, Eski Anadolu Türkçesi metinlerinden *Ahmed Paşa Divânı*'nda (XVI. yy.) belgelenmiştir (YTS: 4624).

Ttü.de *buram buram* "koku etkili bir biçimde yayılarak", *burcu burcu* aynı söz öbeklerinde köküne rastladığımız *bur-* "kokmak" eyleminin de (ED: 355a) bir dizi türevi, çeşitli bitki adlarının yapımında yer almaktadır. Clauson tarafından Sans. *marica*dan alıntı olabileceği bildirilen *burç ~ murç* "karabiber" (ED: 771b) bitkisine Çağatay alanında verilen *isti ot* "fülfül, siyah biber" (Kúnos 1902: 92) adı, bu bitkinin Türklerce "koku" ile ilişkilendirildiğinin açık göstergesidir.[5] Çeşitli bakliyat türlerinin genel bir adı olan *burçak* sözcüğünün, "koku" ilişkisiyle *bur-* eyleminden gelebileceği, Clauson tarafından bildirilmiştir (ED: 357b). Eski Türkçe *yıpar* "koku" sözcüğünün Farsçaya *yıpar/ipar/cigar* biçimlerinde "kekik", Macarcaya *gyopár* biçiminde "sarı renkli dağ çileği" anlamında geçmesi de oldukça önemlidir (TMEN 411; Karaağaç 2008: 928)

Sonuç: Modern Türk dillerindeki *çilek* ve *yilek* sözcüklerinin biçimsel açıdan **I.** Ana Tü. **yıdlak* > Çuv. *śirla*; Kzk. *jidek*, Tat., Krç.Blk. *cilek*, Bşk. *yilek*; Tuv. *çestek-kat*, Hak. *çistek* "yemiş"; Oyr., Tel. Kmd. *jīläk*; Koyb. *t'estäk*, *t'istäk*, *d'istäk*; Tel. *d'iläk*, Koyb. *t'estäk*, *t'istäk*, *d'istäk* **II.** Ana Tü. *çigelek* > Nog. *čigläk*; Çağ., Osm. *čiläk*; Tkm. *čigäläk* olarak; anlamsal açıdansa **I.**in *yıd* "koku" ve **II.**nin *çig* "nemli, ıslak" ile ilişkilendirilerek açıklanması gerektiğini düşünüyoruz.

[5] Ttü. ve ağızlarında "acı biber" karşılığında kullanılan *isot* sözcüğü, yaygın inanışın (< *ıssı ot* "sıcak ot") aksine *ıstı ot* "kokulu ot" < *ıssı ot* < *ısot* < *isot* gelişmesiyle Eski Türkçenin "koku" anlamlı sözcüklerinden biri olan **ıys*'tan gelişmesi daha olası görünmektedir (*is* "koku" için bkz. Sevortyan 1974: 380–381; Egorov 1964: 76, Tenişev 1997: 370–371).

Kaynaklar

BAYTOP, T. (2007), *Türkçe Bitki Adları Sözlüğü*, Ankara: Türk Dil Kurumu Yayınları, 3. baskı.

CEYLAN, E. (1997), *Çuvaşça Çok Zamanlı Ses Bilgisi*, Ankara: Türk Dil Kurumu Yayınları.

DLT: *Divanü Lûgat-it-Türk Tercümesi* (Çev. B. ATALAY) (1999), 4 cilt, Ankara: Türk Dil Kurumu Yayınları.

Türkiye'de Halk Ağzından Derleme Sözlüğü (1993), 12 cilt, Ankara: Türk Dil Kurumu Yayınları.

ED: CLAUSON, G. (1972), *An Etymological Dictionary of Pre-Thirteenth-Century Turkish*, Oxford: Clarendon Press.

EGOROV, V. G. (1964), *Étimologiçeskiy slovar' çuvaşskogo yazıka,* Çeboksarı: Çuvaşskoye knijnoye izdatel'stvo.

EREN, H. (1999), *Türk Dilinin Etimoloji Sözlüğü*. Ankara: Bulak Neşriyat.

FEDETOV, M. R. (1996), *Étimologiçeskiy slovar' çuvaşskogo yazıka,* I–II, Çeboksarı: Çuvaşskiy gosudarstvennıy institut gumanitarnıh nauk.

KARAAĞAÇ, G. (2008), *Türkçe Verintiler Sözlüğü*, Ankara: Türk Dil Kurumu Yayınları.

KORTANTAMER, T. (1993), "Türk Şiirinde Ses Konusu ve Ses Gelişmesinin Devamlılığı Üzerine Genel Bazı Düşünceler": *Makaleler I*, Ankara: Akçağ Yayınları

KÚNOS, I. (1902), *Šejχ Sulejman Efendi's Čagataj-Osmanisches Wörterbuch*, Budapest: Publications de la Section Orientale de la Société Ethnographique Hongroise.

MNES: *A magyar nyelv történeti-etimológiai szótára Ö–Zs* (1976), Budapest: Akadémiai Kiadó, 2. edition.

MTS: LESSING, F. D. (2003), *Moğolca-Türkçe Sözlük* (Çev. KARAAĞAÇ, G.), 2 cilt, Ankara: Türk Dil Kurumu Yayınları.

MUSAYEV, K. (1975), *Leksika tyurkskih yazıkov v sravnitel'nom osvetsenii (zapadno kıpçakskaya gruppa)*, Moskva: Izdatel'stvo Nauka.

OSTN: RADLOV, V. V. (1893–1911), *Opıt slovarya Tyurkskih Nareçiy,* VIII, Sanktpeterburg': Prodletsya u komisionerob' imperatorskoy akademii nauk.

OTWF: ERDAL, M. (1991), *Old Turkic Word Formation, A Functional Approach to the Lexicon*, I–II, Wiesbaden: Harrassowitz.

POPPE, N. (1960), *Vergleichende Grammatik der altaischen Sprachen,* 1: *Vergleichende Lautlehre*, Wiesbaden: Otto Harrassowitz.

RAMSTEDT, G. J. (1914–15), "Zur mongolisch-türkischen Lautgeschichte", *Keleti Szemle* XV, 134–150.

RÄSÄNEN, M. (1949), *Materialien zur Lautgeschichte der türkischen Sprachen*, Helsinki: Societas Orientalis Fennica.

SEVORTYAN, E. V. (ed.) (1974), *Étimologiçeskiy slovar' tyurkskih yazıkov. Obşçetyurkskie i mejtyurkskie osnovı na glasnıe*, Moskva: İzdatel'stvo "Nauka".

STACHOWSKI, K. (2008), *Names of Cereals in the Turkic Languages*, Studia Turcologica Cracoviensia 11, Edited by Stanisław Stachowski, Kraków: Jagiellonian University Institute of Oriental Philology.

TENİŞEV, E. R. (1997), *Sravnitel'no-istoriçeskaya grammatika tyurkskih yazıkov—Leksika*, Moskva: Nauka.

TMEN: DOERFER, G. (1963–1975), *Türkische und mongolische Elemente im Neupersischen*, Wiesbaden: Franz Steiner Verlag.

TS: *Türkçe Sözlük*, 2 cilt, Ankara: Türk Dil Kurumu Yayınları, 1998.

YALTIRIK, F. (1972), "Türkiye'de Yazın Yaprak Döken Odunsu Bir Bitki: Kokar Çalı *Anagysis Foetida* L.) ve Ormancılık Pratiğinde Taşıdığı Önem": *İstanbul Üniversitesi Orman Fakültesi Dergisi*, 22, 1, İstanbul: İstanbul Üniversitesi Basım ve Yayınevi Müdürlüğü, 295–296.

YTS: *Yeni Tarama Sözlüğü*, Ankara: Türk Dil Kurumu Yayınları, 1983.

Kısaltmalar

Alt. Altayca
Az. Azerice
Bşk. Başkurtça
Çağ. Çağatayca
Çuv. Çuvaşça
Evnk. Evenkice
Gag. Gagavuzca
Hak. Hakasça
Kmd. Kumandıca
Kmk. Kumukça
Koyb. Koybalca
Krç.Blk. Karaçay-Balkarca
Kklp. Karakalpakça
Krg. Kırgızca
Kzk. Kazakça
Leb. Lebetçe
Moğ. Moğolca
Nog. Nogayca
Osm. Osmanlıca
Oyr. Oyrotça
Özb. Özbekçe
Sans. Sanskritçe
Şor. Şorca
Tar. Tarançice
Tat. Tatarca
Tel. Teleütçe
Tkm. Türkmence
Tob. Tobolca
Tof. Tofalarca
Ttü. Türkiye Türkçesi
Tuv. Tuvaca
Uyg. Uygurca

Studies on the Turkic World
A Festschrift for Professor St. Stachowski on the Occasion of His 80th Birthday
edited by E. Mańczak-Wohlfeld and B. Podolak, Kraków 2010: 139–156

Kamil Stachowski (Kraków)

On First Syllable Reduplications in Karaim

0. Introductory notes

Among the many types of reduplication in the Tkc. languages, at least four are essentially a reduplication of the first syllable. One of them, the reduplication of the first syllable with an appended closing consonant,[1] vastly outnumbers the others. It also appears to be the type usually meant when using the term first syllable reduplication in everyday speech. (Cf. 2.1.) In general, the phenomenon is poorly investigated. In particular, there does not seem to be any works devoted to its manifestation in Kar.

I decided to split the material presented here into two groups: **1.** Reduplication with a closing consonant (**1.1.** Material, and **1.2.** The closing consonant issue), and **2.** other reduplications of the first syllable, i.e. taking into account the number of examples, Special cases (**2.1.** Actual first syllable reduplication; **2.2.** Reduplication with an inserted vowel; **2.3.** Reduplication with *-ma-* / *-ta-*, and **2.4.** Apparent reduplications).

Notes on the presentation of the material:

– When reading the literature on Kar., one finds it difficult to escape the impression that introducing a new transcription every now and then

[1] Or to put it more precisely, reduplication of the initial (consonant and) vowel, to which an extra closing consonant is appended. This applies to all the uses in this paper of the term *syllable* in this context.

seems to be considered good practice in the millieu of researchers in Kar. I have chosen to follow this tradition. I will use a mostly phonological notation which treats each dialect separately. The decision not to use the original transcriptions will allow me to avoid unnecessary repetitions (such as e.g. *бэдава* → *бэс-бэдава* (KRPS), *бэдава* → *бэс-бедава* (RKS-X), *бедава* → *бэс-бэдава* (RKS-L)), and enable a sensible alphabetical ordering of the entries. Forms from languages other than Kar. are kept in the original orthography.

- Because the semantics of reduplication is clear, I do not quote the meanings where they are either a simple intensification of the base word, or they have been left unchanged (such as e.g. *ak* 'white' → *apak* 'snow-white' (Zajączkowski 1931), 'white' (KSB, KRPS)).
- For reasons of brevity, I do not quote the base word in all the attestations for all the dialects, and I reduce the meanings to an approximate Engl. translation (unless they are non-standard, see above).
- Where dialect specification was missing, I made a decision on the basis of the place of the attestation or the phonetics.
- Entries are ordered alphabetically, and chronologically with regard to the places of attestation.

1. Reduplication with a closing consonant

1.1. Material

ačyk 'open' ♦ E_1 ***apačyk*** (KRPS, RKS-X s.v. *открытый настеж* and *распахнуть*, RKS-L); ***apačmak***[2] 'to break open, to throw open' (RKS-X) ♦ E_2 ***appačyk***[3] (KRPS, RKS-L)

ak[4] 'white' ♦ E_1 ***apak*** (KRPS, RKS-L) ♦ E_2 ***appak***[3] (RKS-X s.v. *белоснежный*) ♦ NW ***apax*** (Józefowicz 2008 s.v. *białuteńki* and *bieluteńki*) ♦ SW_1 ***apak*** (Zajączkowski 1931, KSB, Musaev 1964: 183, KRPS) ♦ SW_2 ***appak***[3] (KRPS)

[2] The only example of a reduplicated verb. However, because there is only one example of such a phenomenon, it seems more probable that it had been secondarily derived from the adjective per analogy to the *ačmak* : *ačyk* pair, than that it had been reduplicated as a verb. Cf. also a parallel example from AKipch. *çop çovralan-* 'otaczać dokoła | entourer tout autour' (DAK).

[3] [Ad: Kar.E *appačyk*, Kar.E and SW *appak*] The only two examples with a doubled closing consonant and no inserted vowel. It is possible that a vowel had originally been present there (**appa.ačyk* and **appa.ak*) and only *-aa-* merged into *-a-*; cf. 2.2. Whether these forms were created before the Kar. split, or whether the Kar.SW *appak* is a borrowing from Kar.E, is impossible to determine at present.

[4] Cf. *ak* in 2.2.

al 'red' ♦ E ***apal*** (KRPS, RKS-L)

ansyz(yn|dan) 'sudden(ly), unawares' ♦ E_1 ***afaŋsyz***[5] (KRPS) ♦ E_2 ***apansyz*** (KRPS s.v. *ансыз* and *ап*(-)*ансыз*, RKS-X, RKS-L); ***apansyzdan***[6] (KRPS, RKS-X s.v. *от внезапности,* RKS-L); ***apansyzyn*** (RKS-L)

aryk 'thin, lean' ♦ E ***aparyk*** (KRPS, RKS-L) ♦ NW ***aparyx*** (Józefowicz 2008)

baška 'other' ♦ E ***bambaška*** (KRPS, RKS-L)

bedava 'free of charge' ♦ E ***besbedava*** (KRPS, RKS-X s.v. *совершенно даром*, RKS-L)

belli 'clear, obvious' ♦ E ***besbelli*** 'probably' (KRPS, RKS-L)

beter 'worse' ♦ E ***besbeter*** (KRPS, RKS-L)

bijaz 'white' ♦ E ***bimbijaz*** (KRPS, RKS-X s.v. *белоснежный*, RKS-L)

boš 'empty' ♦ E ***bomboš*** (KRPS, Prik 1976, Musaev 1977: 7, RKS-X s.v. *совершенно пустой*) ♦ NW_1 ***bomboš*** (KRPS, Józefowicz 2008) ♦ NW_2 ***bopboš***[7] (Musaev 1964: 183; Musaev 1977: 7) ♦ SW ***bopbos***[7] (Musaev 1977: 7)

bošyna 'in vain' ♦ E ***bombošyna***[8] (RKS-X, RKS-L)

[5] The base **aŋsyz* is not attested. If *f* is original here, this is the only example with *f* as a closing consonant. It seems more probable then that it is just a spirantized version of *p*. This, and the archaic *ŋ* indicate the old age of this form.
A borrowing is not likely since a reduplicated form with *f* does not seem to exist in AKipch., CTat., Ott. or Urum. However, a contamination with Urum *аңсыз* 'несподівано, раптово' (UrumS) is not impossible. There does not seem to be any reason to assume a borrowing of either the base word or its reduplication with *p*, even though such forms exist in the neighbouring languages.

[6] The base **ansyzdan* is not attested.

[7] [Ad: Kar.SW *bopbos* and NW *bopboš*] These two forms are surprising. In Tksh., where reduplications have been investigated far more thoroughly than in any other Tkc. language, it is not allowed that the difference between the closing consonant of the reduplicated syllable and the initial consonant of the base word, be voice alone. Had it not been for these two forms, the situation in Kar. would be the same.
The Kar.NW form is attested twice; the Kar.SW form is only attested once. All attestations are by the same author. In both cases, the context leaves no room for doubt as to the eventuality of a misprint.
Parallel forms do not seem to exist in AKipch., CTat., Ott. and Urum. Moreover, should these forms be true, they would be the only ones in Kar., where the closing consonant varies between dialects.
It seems that an immediate solution of this riddle can only be provided by some linguistic conspiracy theory. As to a more conventional answer, it is not yet clear to me whether some revision of alleged rules for the closing consonant is necessary, or rather an errata. Cf. *bombošyna* in 1.1. and *bošbošu|yna* in 2.1.

[8] Cf. *bošbošuna* in 2.1.

bütün 'whole' ♦ E ***büsbütün*** (KRPS, RKS-L)

čebik 'quick(ly)' ♦ E_1 ***čarčebik***[9] (KRPS, RKS-L) ♦ E_2 ***čerčebik*** (KRPS, RKS-X, RKS-L) ♦ E_3 ***čyrčebik***[10] (RKS-X)

čevre[11] 'around' ♦ E_1 ***čepčevre*** (KRPS) ♦ E_2 ***čöpčövre***[12] (KRPS, RKS-L); ***čöpčüvre*** (KRPS, RKS-L) ♦ E_3 ***čüpčüvre*** (KRPS, RKS-L) ♦ SW ***ćipćivre*** (KSB: 71, KRPS)

čevretin[13] 'from around' ♦ E_1 ***čöpčevirtin***[14] (KRPS, RKS-L); ***čöpčövretin***[15] (KRPS, RKS-L) ♦ E_2 ***čüpčüvretin***[16] 'from all around' (KRPS, RKS-L); 'around' (RKS-L)

čyplak 'naked' ♦ E ***čyrčyplak*** (KRPS, Prik 1976, RKS-X s.v. *догола*, *нагишом* and *совершенно голый*, RKS-L)

9 Lack of vowel harmony in this form is surprising (cf. also footnote 33). I can see at least two possible explanations for this form: **1.** by a contamination with CTat. *çar-çabik* id. (AiM) or maybe Ott. *çar çabuk* (LiO) (a reduplicated form appears to be missing from AKipch. and Urum.), and **2.** by assuming that the reduplication had gone out of use and had become incomprehensible before a harmony shift took place in **čabyk* (VEWT proposes *čap-* 'to hit' as the etymon, but with a question mark; at any rate, back harmony is more likely to be original here because of the initial *č-*). Unfortunately, I am unable to deploy any conclusive arguments.

10 This form is not clear. It seems most probable that it should be attributed to the Kar.E manner of pronouncing /e/ in the first syllable: higher and more in the back than in non-first syllables, and more than is usual in most Tkc. languages (cf. Prik 1976: 25n. and Jankowski 1997: 7n.). Cf. *jymješly* and also footnotes 44 and 52 on *bokbaklavat* and **kiryšyk* respectively.

11 In **Kar.E**, only *čevre* and *čüvre* are attested. *Čövre* is not, but it is attested in CC—where its reduplicated form is also noted, *čöp čövre*. Knowing this, and the Tkc. languages' general dislike of the *ö* in the first syllable, it should be safe to explain *čepčevre*, *čöpčövre* and *čüpčüvre* by assuming that in Kar. **čövre* > *čevre*, *čüvre* in both the non-reduplicated and reduplicated versions, and has remained fossilized only in the reduplicated form. What is left to be explained is the perhaps interesting form *čöpčüvre*, which might suggest that reduplication was already unproductive and incomprehensible when this change happened.

An external influence does not seem likely: AKipch. only has *čovra* (DAK, Schültz 1968), CTat., Ott. and Urum only have *čevre* (AiM, LiO, Meninski 2000, UrumS).

In **Kar.SW**, *ćivre* (< **čüvre*) is attested, and does not seem to raise any doubts. Cf. also footnote 12.

12 The base **čövre* is not attested but cf. footnote 11. The form *čöpčovre* (RKS-X s.v. *вокруг*) is most probably a misprint for *-*ö*-.

13 On vowels, cf. footnote 11. The un-Kar. Abl. in *-tin* requires further investigation.

14 The base **čevirtin* is not attested, and neither **čevir* alone but cf. *čevirme* 'окружение | otoczenie' (KRPS).

15 The base **čövretin* is not attested but cf. footnote 13.

16 The base **čüvretin* is not attested but cf. footnote 13.

čyrt*[17] 'silence' ♦ E ***čymčyrt* 'полная тишина, безмолвие | niezmącona, zupełna cisza, milczenie' (KRPS); 'полная тишина' (RKS-X s.v. *полная тишина*); 'безмолвие, полная тишина' (RKS-L)

incke 'thin' ♦ NW_1 ***ińińčke*** (Musaev 1964: 183); ***ińińčka*** (KRPS, Musaev 1977: 36, Józefowicz 2008) ♦ SW ***ipińćke*** (KSB, KRPS)

****jaban*** 'alien, foreign' ♦ E ***jat-jaban*** (KRPS, RKS-X, RKS-L): probably an apparent reduplication; see 2.4.

jalyŋyz 'lone' ♦ E ***japjalyŋyz*** (RKS-L)

jaxšy 'good' ♦ NW ***japjaxši***[18] (Musaev 1977: 36); ***japjaxšy*** (Musaev 1964: 183, Berta 1998, Józefowicz 2008 s.v. *dobry-przedobry*) ♦ SW ***jap-jaksy*** (Musaev 1977: 36)

ješil 'green' ♦ E_1 ***jemješil*** (Prik 1976); ***jemješil*** (RKS-L) ♦ E_2 ***jymješly***[19] (RKS-X s.v. *совершенно зеленый*) ♦ NW ***jem̓ješil*** (Józefowicz 2008 s.v. *zieloniutki*) ♦ SW ***jemješił*** (Zajączkowski 1931)

juvarlak 'round' ♦ E ***jusjuvarlak***[20] (RKS-L)

juv́uš́ 'wet' ♦ NW ***öṕjuv́uš́***[21] (Józefowicz 2008)

kara 'black' ♦ E ***kapkara*** (KRPS, Prik 1976, RKS-X s.v. *до черна, совершенно черный* and *черный-пречерный*, RKS-L) ♦ NW ***kapkara*** (KTDT s.v. *kara*, Józefowicz 2008 s.v. *czarniusieńki*) ♦ SW ***kapkara*** (Zajączkowski 1931)

karavlyk 'darkness' ♦ E ***kapkaravlyk***[22] '**1.** темным-темно, черным-черно | bardzo ciemno; **2.** темнота, чернота | ciemność, czerń' (KRPS); '**1.** темным-темно, черным-черно; **2.** чернота' (RKS-L)

[17] One of two examples of a reduplicated noun (the other being *kapkaravlyk* but cf. footnote 22). The base word is not attested, which serves to add to its conspicuousness. Despite the meaning, perhaps an onomatopoeia?

[18] Most probably a typo caused by Russ. orthography, pro **jaxšy*. Cf. ‹йахшы› on pp. 33, 35 &c.

[19] Cf. footnote 10 on *čyrčebik*.

[20] Cf. *jumjumarlak* in 2.1.

[21] This form is completely unclear. ***Juv́uš́*** is fairly common in the Tkc. languages (see Zajączkowski 1932: 60, VEWT s.v. *jibi*, and others), always with *-i-i-* or its reasonably understandable derivatives (see Zajączkowski 1932: 154 for more details on labialization in Kar. and elsewhere). ****Öṕ***, on the other hand, is completely opaque to me. A reduplication is conceivable here as follows: **juṕ.juv́uš́* > **üṕ-* > *öṕ-*. Alternation of the initial *ü-* ~ *ju-* is a well-known phenomenon in Kar.NW. A shift from *ü-* to *ö-*, however, is at best extraordinary. The probability of a simple composition is not very high since **öp* does not seem to be attested as a separate word with a compatible meaning in Kar. or any of the neighbouring languages.

[22] One of two examples of a reduplicated noun (the other being *čymčyrt* but cf. footnote 17). It needs to be noted that while the base word has only a nominal meaning, its reduplicated form has both, a nominal and an adjectival one—despite its seem-

kat*[23] 'hard' ♦ E ***kaskat 'остолбенение' (RKS-L)

kenete[24] 'sudden(ly)' ♦ E ***kepkenete*** (Sulimowicz 1973[25], KRPS, RKS-L, RKS-L) ♦ NW ***ḱepḱeńaťa*** (KTDT, KRPS, Józefowicz 2008); ***ḱepḱeńeťa*** (KTDT, KRPS, KKS, Józefowicz 2008) ♦ SW ***ḱepḱenete*** (Sulimowicz 1973)

****koǯa***[26] 'huge' ♦ E ***koskoǯa*** 'неимоверно' (RKS-X); 'неимоверный, огромный' (RKS-L)

****kos***[27] 'stupid' ♦ E ***komkos*** (RKS-X s.v. *совершенно глупый*)

kök 'blue' ♦ E ***kömkök*** (KRPS, RKS-X s.v. *темно-голубой*, RKS-L)

kuru 'dry' ♦ E ***kupkuru*** (RKS-X, RKS-L)

kyzyl 'red' ♦ NW ***kypkyzył*** (Musaev 1964: 183, Józefowicz 2008 s.v. *czerwony-czerwoniutki*) ♦ SW ***kypkyzył*** (Zajączkowski 1931, Musaev 1964: 183)

---

ingly clearly nominal suffix. However, as it is the only example of such a type, it is impossible to decide at present whether this difference in meaning results in any way from reduplication or rather, from the nature of the Tkc. languages as a whole.

[23] The base **kat* is not attested in a similar meaning in Kar. and neighbouring languages, and this form is not clear. Apart from the separate attestation in the meaning 'остолбенение', it appears in two idioms: ~ *kalmak* 'опешить (досл. в остолбенении остаться)' and ~ *külmek* 'громко смеяться; хохотать' (RKS-L). In Ott. and other Tkc. languages, *kat* has, among others, the meaning '(to be) hard' and appears with these two verbs in similar meanings. A combination of these three features in one language, however, appears to be much more difficult, if even possible, to find.
The origin of this form and its usage in Kar.E might be explained in different ways. It could be that *kaskat* is a native Kar.E reduplication, and only its base had gone out of use, as it appears, without attestation. (I omit here the attestation in the meaning of 'layer' (KRPS, RKS-L).) But it might also be that it is a loanword in Kar.E. If this is the case, the meanings would suggest that it was borrowed as a part of the phrase ~ *kalmak*, from which *kaskat* was extracted. The source of the borrowing and the usage in ~ *külmek*, however, would remain unclear. A comprehensive examination for the etymology of *kaskat* goes beyond the scope of this paper.

[24] The base **kenete* is not attested but cf. *kenete* 'plötzlich | gelich' (CC).

[25] Transcribed as ‹kepkenátá› but cf. Jankowski 1994.

[26] The base **koǯa* is not attested. The reduplication might have also readily been native in Kar., even if the base word has not been preserved. It is, however, at least equally probable that it was borrowed in the reduplicated form from Ott. *koskoca* 'huge' (LiO and others). The word is also present in CTat. (only in a non-reduplicated form and in the meaning of 'муж') but seems to be missing from AKipch. and Urum. Cf. footnote 29 on **sijax* and 30 on *syrsyklam*.

[27] The base **kos* is not attested in a similar meaning in Kar. and neighbouring languages. The form and meaning of *komkos* resemble strongly a reduplication but are unclear.

mavy 'blue' ♦ E ***masmavu*** (KRPS s.v. *маву*, RKS-L); ***masmavy*** (Prik 1976, RKS-L)

mor 'violet' ♦ E ***mosmor*** (RKS-X s.v. *темно-лиловый*, RKS-L) 'dark violet'

saglam '1. healthy; 2. whole' ♦ E ***sapsaglam***[28] (KRPS s.v. *сагълам*, RKS-X s.v. *совершенно здоробый*, RKS-L)

sary 'yellow' ♦ E ***sapsary*** (RKS-X s.v. *совершенно желтый* and *желтый-прежелтый*) ♦ NW ***sapsary*** (Musaev 1964: 183 , KRPS) ♦ SW ***sapsary*** (Zajączkowski 1931, Musaev 1964: 183)

****sijax***[29] 'black' ♦ E ***simsijak*** 'coal-black' (KRPS, RKS-L); 'совершенно синий' (RKS-X s.v. *совершенно синий*); simsijax (KRPS, RKS-L)

****syklam***[30] 'wet' ♦ E ***syrsyklam*** (KRPS); **<сыр-сыклам>**[31] (RKS-L after KRPS)

sylak 'wet' ♦ E_1 ***symsylak*** (KRPS s.v. *кӧт*); **<сым>-сылак**[31] (RKS-L after KRPS) ♦ E_2 ***sypslax***[32] (RKS-X s.v. *насквозь промокший*) ♦ E_3 ***syrsylak*** (KRPS s.v. *сылакъ*); **<сыр>-сылак**[31] (RKS-L after KRPS)

[28] Cf. 2.4. on *sav-saglam*.

[29] Probably borrowed in the reduplicated form from Ott. *simsiyah* id. (LiO s.v. *sim* and *siyah*, and others). The word appears to be missing from AKipch. It is present in CTat., only without the final consonant: *siya*. In Urum, the word itself is attested as *сийа*, *сийаh* and *сийах* but in a reduplicated form only as *сим-сийа*.
As the word originates from Pers. (Ott. *sijax*, CTat., Kzk. *sija* < Pers. *siyāh* (Stachowski 1977, 1998)), it is unlikely that it was inherited from an earlier stage of Kar., but only in its reduplicated form.
Cf. footnote 26 on *koskoǯa*.
The final *-k* can probably be attributed to a hypercorrection, as the word had originally had *-x*. Spirantization of final *-k* is a common phenomenon in Kar.NW and numerous Tksh. and Tkc. dialects, whence it is often regarded as non-literal and rustic. Cf. footnote 32 on **slax*.

[30] The base **syklam* is not attested. It is most probably borrowed in the reduplicated form from Ott. *sır sıklam* id. (LiO and others). In AKipch., CTat. and Urum, neither *sıqlam* and *sır-sıqlam* nor similar forms seem to exist. The origin of the word is not clear. It is not impossible then, that it is inherited in Kar. but has only survived in the reduplicated form. Cf. footnote 26 on *koskoǯa*.

[31] [Ad: *<сым>-сылак*, *<сыр>-сылак* and *<сыр-сыклам>*] Angle brackets are used in RKS-L to mark *начало и конец перевода, правильность которого по первоисточнику вызывает сомнение*. Unfortunately, the reason for doubt is not specified.

[32] The base **slax* is not attested. It is probably a slovenly (dialectal? rustic?) pronunciation of *sylak*. Cf. Kar.E *slak* 'мокро' (RKS-X) and footnote 29 on *simsijak*. The preservation of *syp-* probably means that such pronunciation came into being only after reduplication as the method became unproductive.

tamam 'whole, wholly' ♦ E_1 ***tastamam*** (KRPS s.v. *тамам,* RKS-L); ***testaman***[33] 'как раз' (RKS-X)

tek*[34] 'stupid; sloven' ♦ E ***tentek* (KRPS, RKS-X s.v *раздильдяй*, RKS-L s.v. *нерадивый*, *разгильдяй* and *рассеянный*) ♦ NW ***ťeńťak*** (KRPS, Józefowicz 2008) ♦ SW ***tentek*** (KSB, KRPS)

temiz 'clean' ♦ E_1 ***teptemiz*** (RKS-X) ♦ E_2 ***tertemiz*** (KRPS s.v. *тэр* II and *тэр-тэмиз*, RKS-X s.v. *совершенно чистый*)

tez 'quick(ly)' ♦ E ***teptez*** (KRPS s.v. *тэз,* RKS-L)

tok 'full, satiated' ♦ E_1 ***tomtok*** (RKS-L) ♦ E_2 ***toptok*** (KRPS, RKS-L)

tokal 'blunt' ♦ E ***tostokal*** (Kakuk 1991)

tolu[35] 'full' ♦ E ***toptolu***[36] (RKS-X s.v. *битком набито* and *полным-полно*); ***toptoly*** (KRPS, RKS-L) ♦ NW ***toptołu*** (KRPS, Musaev 1964: 183, Musaev 1977: 36, Józefowicz 2008 s.v. *pełniutki* and *przepełniony*) ♦ SW ***toptołu*** (Zajączkowski 1931, KSB, KRPS, Musaev 1964: 183, Musaev 1977: 36)

tomalak 'round' ♦ E ***tostomalak*** (KRPS, RKS-L)

tögerek 'round' ♦ E ***tömtögerek*** (KRPS, RKS-L)

tüz[37] 'straight' ♦ E_1 ***tümtüz*** (KRPS, Kakuk 1991 s.v. *tïmqara* after KRPS, RKS-X s.v. *совершенно ровный,* RKS-L) ♦ E_2 ***tüptüz*** (RKS-L)

tyk[38] 'vertical, upright' ♦ E ***tymtyk*** (RKS-X)

uzun 'long' ♦ E ***upuzun*** (Prik 1976)

[33] This form is unclear. Another form with a destroyed vowel harmony is *čarčebik* (cf. footnote 9). In this case, however, a pair needed for contamination (**testemem* or *temem*) appears to be missing. **Taman* with *-n* does not seem to be attested except in this word, either. The form might have resulted from even two dissimilations: *-a-a-a-* > *-e-a-a-* and *-m-m* > *-m-n*. While the latter appears to be considerably more credible (for it does not assume a destruction of vowel harmony), I can offer no proof for either, or in fact, any other more plausible explanation.

[34] The base **tek* is not attested in Kar. and neighbouring languages. The form and meaning of *tentek* resemble strongly a reduplication (perhaps < **tem.tek*) but are unclear.

[35] Cf. *tolu* in 2.3.

[36] The base **tolu* is not attested but cf. Kar.SW and NW *tolu* id.

[37] It is possible that one more form belongs here: *tüztümüz* 'straight' (RKS-X). Its structure, however, is unclear.

[38] The spelling with ‹ы› is probably only meant to mark a non-palatalized pronunciation of *t*, or a somewhat velar pronunciation of *i* (though not the actual /y/ yet). KRPS spells the word *тик*. AKipch., CTat., Ott. and Urum all only have the palatal variant, too.

Altogether, 104 forms are listed. The following ones deserve perhaps a particular attention:

- unclear (fourteen cases): *appačyk* and *appak* (footnote 3), *bopbos* and *bopboš* (7), *čöpčevirtin*, *čöpčövretin* and *čüpčüvretin* (13), *čymčyrt* (17), *kaskat* (23), *komkos* (27), *öṕ.juv́uš́* (21), *tentek* (34), *testaman* (33) and *tüztümüz* (37),
- base not attested (nine cases): *čöpčevirtin*, *čöpčövretin* and *čüpčüvretin* (13 and 14), *čöpčövre* (12), *kaskat* (23), *komkos* (27), *sypslax* (32), *tentek* (34) and *tüztümüz* (37),
- probably (also) reduplicated in a different way (seven cases): *bošyna* (cf. 2.1.), *jaban* (2.4.) *juvarlak* (2.1.), *saglam* (2.4.), *tolu* (2.3.) and probably *ačyk* and *ak* (2.2.),
- the reduplicated and initial base syllables not matching (four cases): *čöpčüvre* (footnote 11), *čyrčebik* and *jymješly* (10), and *sypslax* (32),
- borrowed (all < Ott.; three cases): *simsijax* (29), *syrsyklam* (30) and perhaps *koskoǯa* (26),
- non-Kar. formation (three cases): *čöpčevirtin*, *čöpčövretin* and *čüpčüvretin* (13),
- closing consonant doubled (two cases): *appačyk* and *appak* (3),
- closing consonant only differing with voice from the initial consonant of the base (two cases): *bopbos* and *bopboš* (7),
- non-harmonic (two cases): *čarčebik* (9) and *testaman* (33),
- nouns (two cases): *čymčyrt* (17) and *kapkaravlyk* (22),
- closing consonant spirantized (one case): *afaŋsyz* (5),
- verb (one case): *apačmak* (2).

1.2. The closing consonant issue

Below is a summary of the closing consonants of the reduplicated syllable (unclear and borrowed forms, nouns and the verb are excluded).

base	E	SW	NW	base	E	SW	NW
ačyk	*p*	–	–	*bijaz*	*m*	–	–
ak	*p*	*p*	*p*	*boš*	*m*	–	*m*
al	*p*	–	–	*bošyna*	*m*	–	–
ansyz(...)	*p*	–	–	*bütün*	*s*	–	–
aryk	*p*	–	*p*	*čebik*	*r*	–	–
baška	*m*	–	–	*čevre*	*p*	*p*	–
bedava	*s*	–	–	*čevretin*	*p*	–	–
belli	*s*	–	–	*čyplak*	*r*	–	–
beter	*s*	–	–	*incke*	–	*p*	*p*

base	E	SW	NW	base	E	SW	NW
jalyŋyz	*p*	–	–	*sary*	*p*	*p*	*p*
jaxšy	–	*p*	*p*	*sylak*	*m, p, r*	–	–
ješil	*m*	*m*	*m*	*tamam*	*s*	–	–
juvarlak	*s*	–	–	*temiz*	*p, r*	–	–
kara	*p*	*p*	*p*	*tez*	*p*	–	–
karavlyk	*p*	–	–	*tok*	*m, p*	–	–
kenete	*p*	*p*	*p*	*tokal*	*s*	–	–
kök	*m*	–	–	*tolu*	*p*	*p*	*p*
kuru	*p*	–	–	*tomalak*	*s*	–	–
kyzyl	–	*p*	*p*	*tögerek*	*m*	–	–
mavy	*s*	–	–	*tüz*	*m, p*	–	–
mor	*s*	–	–	*tyk*	*m*	–	–
saglam	*p*	–	–	*uzun*	*p*	–	–

To the best of my knowledge, there have been four, reasonably similar, attempts to describe the situation in Kar.: Zajączkowski 1931 (Kar.SW), Musaev 1964: 183 (Kar.NW and SW), Prik 1976 (Kar.E) and Musaev 1977: 36 (Kar.NW and SW). They all note that *p* is the most common closing consonant; some mention *ješil* as an exception, and Prik 1976 is the only one to enumerate all the possibilities: *m*, *p*, *r* and *s*. None, however, goes so far as to produce a distribution rule.

This is not very surprising. I know of no other study devoted to reduplication in Karaim. In Tksh., the quality of the closing consonant has been subject to intensive study in recent years; see Müller 2004 for a comprehensive summary and commentary. But despite the considerable effort of those involved, this research did not yield anything close to a straight-forward and definite answer. There does not seem to be any sound historical explanation for reduplication in Kar., Tksh., or Tkc. in general, and neither is there any effectual correlation with the phonetic shape of the base word, its meaning or anything else.

It is my belief that the answer can only be obtained through a much broader study that encompasses diachronically the entire family. Despite their preliminary and supplementary character, I will discuss below some of the conclusions drawn from the Kar. material.

As early as 1931 Zajączkowski observed that *p* is the most common closing consonant: out of the 49 forms[39], it occurs in 24 (including seven beginning

[39] I only count forms with different closing consonants. Forms from different dialects are counted as one, since in all the cases where one word has a reduplication in more than one dialect, the closing consonant is always the same.

with a vowel, where it seems to be obligatory[40]); it is followed by *m* that occurs in eleven forms, *s* in ten, and *r* occurs in four forms only. There are four words with more than one possible reduplication: *sylak*, *temiz*, *tok* and *tüz*. *P* can be the closing consonant in all of them, *m* in three, *r* in two and *s* in none. This is almost inversely proportional to the total number of appearances, except in the case of *p* and *s*, which are swapped with one another.

There is surely more than one way of interpreting the above data. Below I present those that I believe to be the most plausible:

- *P* is most widely used (in half of the examples); it seems to be exclusive to the words that begin with a vowel; it appears in all the undecided words (i.e. those which have more than one possible closing consonant), and in the apparently archaic *afaŋsyz* (cf. footnote 5).[41] This points to the conclusion that *p* is the oldest of all the closing consonants.
  However, none of these facts seems actually to exclude the possibility of *p* being, conversely, the youngest and the most expansive.
- On the other hand, *r* has a very limited usage and a half of its occurrences are in undecided forms. It seems reasonable to assume that it was introduced not very long before the mechanism of reduplication became unproductive.
  But again, the opposite could also be suspected: *r* could be the oldest closing consonant and might have become unproductive sufficiently long ago that it was displaced from all but four of the forms that it had previously been present in.
- *M* and *s* are in the middle of the field. They appear eleven and ten times respectively, but *m* is just one of the possible options in a fourth of the forms while *s* is always the only one. This may suggest the following explanation: both *m* and *s* appeared as closing consonants at approximately the same time. *M*, however, became unproductive quite early on, and was displaced by *p* (*p* and *r* in one case: *sylak*), while *s* remained productive as long as, or nearly as long as reduplication itself.
  Why it was *p*, and not *s* or *r*, that displaced *m* can possibly be explained by the fact that *p* appeared earlier than *s* and *r*, and became much more common (i.e. more frequent in everyday speech) by the time of the termination of *m*.

[40] Seven examples are, in my opinion, not enough to allow us to say with certainty that this rule derived from Tksh., is also valid in Kar.

[41] Also, in two seemingly impossible and indeed unclear forms, *bopboš* and *bopbos* (cf. footnote 7) and the typologically unclear *appačyk* and *appak* (cf. footnote 3).

To summarize, on a relative time scale the following scheme seems to be the most plausible: **1.** appearance of *p*; **2.** appearance of *m* and *s*; **3.** termination of *m*; **4.** appearance of *r*.

2. Special cases

2.1. Actual first syllable reduplication

It could be considered a little surprising that the actual first syllable reduplication is considered a special case here. In everyday speech, first syllable reduplication in reference to a Tkc. language is usually understood as first syllable reduplication with an appended or modified closing consonant. This is the result of the ratio of the number of examples: in Kar., reduplication with a closing consonant outnumbers actual first syllable reduplication more than twelve times.

It is noteworthy that two of the four forms listed below can also be reduplicated with a modification of the closing consonant: *bošbošuna* : *bombošyna* and *jumjumarlak* : *jusjuvarlak*.

birlej 'only, sole, single' ♦ E ***birbirlej***[42] (KRPS, RKS-X, RKS-L) ♦ SW ***birbirłej*** (KRPS s.v. *бир-бирлэй* and *бирлэй*)

****boklavat***[43] 'meanness, baseness, villainy' ♦ E ***bokbaklavat***[44] (RKS-X); ***bokboklavat*** (KRPS)

bošuna[45] 'in vain' ♦ E ***bošbošuna*** (RKS-X); ***bošbošyna*** (KRPS, RKS-L)

jumarlak[46] 'round' ♦ E ***jumjumalak*** (KRPS, RKS-L); ***jumjumarlak*** (KRPS, RKS-L)

2.2. Reduplication with an inserted vowel

This type of reduplication is built as follows: first syllable of the base word + a closing consonant (see below) + *a*/*e* + the base word.

It appears that in Kar. there are only two (or perhaps four? see below) examples of this type of reduplication. I decided however, to separate it into another group because there are more in Tksh. (*çep.*(*e.*)-

[42] The base **birlej* is not attested but cf. Kar.SW *birłej* id.

[43] The base **boklavat* is not attested. Its connection with *bok* 'faeces' (KRPS) seems to be apparent but the form itself is not clear.

[44] The base **baklavat* is not attested. Probably a reduction similar to that in *čyrčebik* and *jymješly* (cf. footnotes 10 and 19 respectively).

[45] Cf. *bombošyna* in 1.1.

[46] Cf. *jusjuvarlak* in 1.1.

çevre, *düp.(e.)düz*, *gep.(e.)genç*, *sap.(a.)sağlam*, *tıp.a.tıp*, *yap.(a.)yalnız* (Stachowski 2009: 119n), also *güpegündüz*), and therefore it can be expected that from the point of view of the entire family, it is not such an uncommon type.

In both Kar. examples, the closing consonant of the first syllable is doubled. In the whole material, there are in total four forms with such a doubling. This suggests that the remaining two, *appačyk* and *appak* (cf. footnote 3), might in fact originate from **appa.ačyk* and **appa.ak* with a repaired hiatus, and should therefore be counted among this group rather than in 1.1. The Tksh. examples above make it clear that doubling is not obligatory from the general Tkc. perspective. The two (four?) Kar. examples do not form a basis that is solid enough to draw final conclusions on the rules in Kar.

ak 'white' ♦ NW ***appa.ax*** (Józefowicz 2008 s.v. *bialuteńki* and *bieluteńki*)

kündüz(ün) 'at daytime' ♦ E ***küppe.gündüz***[47] (Jankowski 2005); ***küppe.kündüz(ün)*** (KRPS, RKS-L s.v. *середъ*)

2.3. Reduplication with *-ma-* / *-ta-*

This type or reduplication is constructed as follows: first syllable of the base word (see below) + *-ma-* / *-ta-* + the base word.

It might be interesting to observe that reduplication with *-ma-* / *-ta-* can, but does not have to be combined with a reduplication with a closing consonant: in five out of nine cases, the consonant was changed (*basta.barabar*, *darma.dagy-* and *topma.tolu*), and in the rest it was left unmodified. The case of tolu is especially interesting as it is the only one with both an attested combined and a non-combined form. It is perhaps not coincidental that *tolu* is one of just three words whose reduplications exist in all the dialects (always with *p* as the closing consonant; the other two are *kara* and *sary*), and is the only one that also has a form reduplicated with *-ma* / *-ta*.

-Ta appears only once, in *bas.ta.barabar*. The other five forms all have *-ma*. This might suggest that this type is in fact a reduplication with *-ma*, and *bas.ta.barabar* is just accidentally phonetically similar (cf. also 2.4. Apparent reduplications)

[47] The base **gündüz* is not attested; probably a simple intervocalic sonorization.

barabar 'together' ♦ E ***bas.ta.barabar*** (KRPS, RKS-X)
dagy-*[48] 'scatter(ed)' ♦ E ***dar.ma.dagylgan*[49] (RKS-X); ***dar.ma.dagan***[50] 'разбросанность' (RKS-L s.v. *разбросанностъ*); ***dar.ma.dagyn***[51] (KRPS, RKS-L)
karyšyk 'mixed' ♦ E ***kar.ma.karyšyk*** (KRPS, RKS-X); ***kar.ma.-kiryšyk***[52] (RKS-X)
syk '**1.** often; **2.** thick' ♦ E ***syk.ma.syk*** 'full; overfilled' (KRPS, RKS-X, RKS-L)
tolu[53] 'full' ♦ E ***tol.ma.tolu*** (RKS-X s.v. *книжный шкаф*); ***top.ma.tolu*** (RKS-X s.v. *переполненный*)

2.4. Apparent reduplications

There are five cases which could be described as reduplicational will-o'-the-wisps.[54] It appears to be rather more probable that they are all semantic juxtapositions (such as e.g. Kar.E *ǯan-ǯyger* 'closest, dearest, beloved' < *ǯan* '1. soul; 2. life' + *ǯyger* '1. liver 2. kidneys' (KRPS)) even though their shape so strongly resembles the first syllable reduplications. I believe, nevertheless, that they might turn out to be actually quite interesting for the study of reduplication in that their existence raises some stimulating suppositions as to the origin of the phenomenon as a whole.

48 It is uncertain whether *dyrma-dorgan* 'disorder, mess' (RKS-X) belongs here, too. It seems to give the impression of an echo-word rather than a reduplication but its structure is not clear.
49 The base **dagylgan* is not attested but cf. *dagylmak* 'to scatter' and *dagylyk* 'scattered' (KRPS, RKS-X, RKS-L).
50 The only example of a noun.
51 The base **dagyn* is not attested except for in the meaning 'ещё' (KRPS, RKS-L), but cf. *dagynyk* 'scattered' (KRPS).
52 The base **kiryšyk* is not attested. Cf. footnote 10 on *čyrčebik*.
53 Cf. *tolu* in 1.1.
54 I only include here words which give the impression of reduplication. I omit forms whose alleged base does not exist separately (e.g. *sersem* 'oafish, gawky' (KRPS and others) < probably via Ott. *sersām*, *sersem* 'betäubt, erstaunt, erstarrt' < MPers. *sarsām* 'Fieberwahn, Delirium; Gehirnhautentzündung' < *sar* 'Kopf' + *sām* 'Entzündung' (Stachowski S. 1976, republished 1998)), or whose closing consonant is neither *m*, *p*, *r* or *s*, nor the same as the second consonant of the supposed base word (e.g. Kar.E *kuč-kuvat* 'very strong' < *küč* 'power' + *kuvat* 'power' (on backward harmonization cf. e.g. *subašy* in Majtczak 2011) or Kar.E *bašbat(u)ra* '1. completely; 2. forever', probably an ancient composition of *baš* 'head' + *bat.ur.a* 'drowning (*transitive*)').

jaban* 'alien, foreign' ♦ E ***jat-jaban* (KRPS, RKS-X, RKS-L)

Probably borrowed in this form from Urum *йат-йабан* 'зовсім чужий' (UrumS): *jat* is present in AKipch., CTat., Kar.E, and Urum.; *jaban* 'foreign' is present in AKipch., CTat. and Urum, and *jat-jaban* is present in Kar.E and Urum. This points quite clearly to a borrowing Urum > Kar.E. Cf. **selamet* below.

To the best of my knowledge, there is no study on the quality of the closing consonant in the reduplicated first syllable in Urum. It is therefore not possible to exclude a reduplication in this case, and especially so, as *t* apparently can be used in this function in CTat. (cf. Jankowski 1992: 129; e.g. *чет-чешит* 'very diverse, varied' < *чешит* 'diverse').

A semantic juxtaposition seems to be at least equally probable.

jasnavuk 'lightning' ♦ NW ***jas-jasnamax*** (KTDT, KRPS, Józefowicz 2008); ***jas-jasnavux*** (KTDT, KRPS, Józefowicz 2008) ♦ SW ***jas-jasnavuk*** (KRPS s.v. *йас*)

Jas 'lightning' (KRPS and others) exists in both Kar.NW and SW; *jasnavuk* is attested for Kar.SW; *jasnavux* and *jasnamax* are not attested for Kar.NW but they seem to be possible derivatives from Kar. NW and SW *jasna-* 'to flash, to shine, to glitter'. It appears therefore that the composed forms here are juxtapositions rather than actual first syllable reduplications.

mal 'property' ♦ E ***mal-malal*** (KRPS); ***mal-meľal'*** (KRPS, RKS-L s.v. *имущество* and *состояние*)

Most probably borrowed in this form from Ott. مال ملال *mâl melâl* 'Hab und Gut' (Zenker 1866 s.v. ملال *melâl*). Neither *ma|elal* nor *mal-ma|elal* seem to exist in AKipch., CTat. or Urum. *Melal* itself is an Ott. distortion of منال *menâl* (< Ar.) which can also be used in a composition with *mal*, but not without a *ve*: مال و منال *mâl ve menâl* (Zenker 1866 s.v. منال *menâl*).

In the light of the above data, it would seem to be highly unlikely that this form is a reduplication rather than a trivial semantic juxtaposition.

The Kar.E form with *-a-* appears to be a simple secondary harmonization.

saglam '1. healthy; 2. whole' ♦ E ***sav-saglamym*** [pro: *sav-saglam*] (RKS-L)

While the possibility of *v* as a closing consonant, or that of *p* being spirantized cannot be definitively excluded (cf. *afaŋsyz* and *saglam* in 1.1. and **selamet* below), it seems considerably more probable that this form is a composition of the well-attested *sav* 'healthy' with the equally well-attested *saglam*.

selamet* 'well-being, prosperity, health' ♦ E ***sav-selamet* (KRPS, RKS-L, RKS-X)

Probably borrowed in this form from Urum *сав-селамет* 'здоровый, щасливий, благополучний' (UrumS): *sav* is present in Kar.E and Urum[55]; *selamet* is present in CTat. and Urum, and *sav-selamet* is present in Kar.E This quite clearly points to a borrowing Urum > Kar.E. Cf. **jaban* above.

To the best of my knowledge, there is no study on the quality of the closing consonant in the reduplicated first syllable in Urum. It is therefore not possible to exclude a reduplication in this case. It is also not possible to exclude a spirantization; cf. *sahlam* above. But it also needs to be noted, that *sav* appears in other compositions, too; cf. *sav-esen* 'very healthy' (KRPS and others) and *saglam* above. In this light, a semantic juxtaposition seems to be more probable.

Abbreviations

AKipch. = Armeno-Kipchak | **CTat.** = Crimean Tatar | **E** = Kar.E. | **Engl.** = English | **Kar.** = Karaim | **Kar.E** = Karaim, Eastern (Crimean) dialect | **Kar.NW** = Karaim, northwestern (Trakai) dialect | **Kar.SW** = Karaim, southwestern (Halych) dialect | **Kzk.** = Kazakh | **MPers.** = Middle Persian | **NW** = Kar.NW | **Pers.** = Persian | **Russ.** = Russian | **Ott.** = Ottoman | **SW** = Kar.SW. | **Tkc.** = Turkic | **Tksh.** = Turkish

References

AiM = *Alem-i Medeniye*, 2009.09.27, http://medeniye.org/lugat.

Berta Á. 1998, West Kipchak Languages. – Johanson L. / Csató É.Á., ed., *The Turkic Languages*, London–New York, 301–17, 306.

CC = Grønbech K. 1942, *Komanisches Wörterbuch. Türkischer Wortindex zu* Codex Cumanicus (= *Monumenta Linguarum Asiæ Maioris. Subsidia* I), København.

DAK = Tryjarski E. 1968–72, *Dictionnaire Arméno-kiptchak d'après trois manuscrits des collections viennoises*, 1, Warszawa.

ÈSTJa = Levitskaja A.S. / Dybo A.V. / Rassadin V.I. 1997, *Ètimologičeskij slovaŕ tjurkskix jazykov. Obščetjurkskie i mežtjurkskie leksičeskie osnovy na bukvy «k», «q»*, Moskva.

Jankowski H. 1992, *Gramatyka języka krymskotatarskiego*, Poznań.

[55] The CTat. shape is *sağ*, not **sav* (AiM).

Jankowski H. 1994, Jak krymscy Karaimowie czytali *pataḥ* i co z tego wynika? – Górska E. / Ostafin B., ed., *Studia Orientalia Thaddaeo Lewicki Oblata*, Kraków, 107–13.

Jankowski H. 1997, A Bible Translation Into the Northern Crimean Dialect of Karaim – *Studia Orientalia* 82, 1–84.

Jankowski H. 2005, Reading Loose Sheets of Paper Found among the Pages of Crimean Karaim *Mejumas* – *Mediterranean Language Review* 16, 145–65.

Józefowicz G. 2008, *Słownik polsko-karaimski w dialekcie trockim*, Troki–Wilno–Warszawa–Wrocław–Gdańsk–Nashville.

Kakuk Zs. 1991, Ein krimkaraimisches Wörterverzeichnis – *Acta Orientalia Academiae Scientiarum Hungaricae* XLV (2–3), 347–401.

KKS = Çulha T. 2006, *Karaycanın Kısa Sözvarlığı. Karayca-Türkçe Kısa Sözlük* (= *Dil ve Edebiyat Dizisi* 6), İstanbul.

KTDT = Kowalski T. 1929, *Karaimische Texte im Dialekt von Troki. Eingeleitet, erläutert und mit einem karaimisch-polnisch-deutschen Glossar versehen* (= *Prace Komisji Orjentalistycznej Polskiej Akademji Umiejętności* 11), Kraków.

KRPS = Baskakov N.A. / Zajončkovskij A. / Šapšal S.M. 1974, *Karaimsko-russko-poĺskij slovaŕ*, Moskva.

KSB = Mardkowicz A. 1935, *Karaj sez-bitigi. Słownik karaimski. Karaimisches Wörterbuch*, Łuck.

LiO = Ahmet Vefik Paşa 2000, *Lehce-i Osmânî* [hazırlayan: R. Toparlı], Ankara.

Majtczak T. 2011, Old Turkic *sü* 'army' – its form, meaning and etymology – [to appear in] *Studia Etymologica Cracoviensia* 16.

Meninski à Mesgnien F. [1]1680, [2]2000, ed. Ölmez M. / Stachowski S., *Thesaurus Linguarum Orientalium Turcicæ-Arabicæ-Persicæ*, [1]Vienna, [2]İstanbul.

Musaev K.M. 1964, *Grammatika karaimskogo jazyka. Fonetika i morfologija*, Moskva.

Musaev K.M. 1977, *Kratkij grammatičeskij očerk karaimskogo jazyka*, Moskva.

Müller H.G. 2004, *Reduplikationen im Türkischen. Morphophonologische Untersuchungen* (= *Turcologica* 56), Wiesbaden.

Prik O.Ja. 1976, *Očerk grammatiki karaimskogo jazyka (krymskij dialekt)*, Maxačkala, 85.

Rad = Radloff W. 1893–1911, *Opyt slovarja tjurkskix narečij. Versuch eines Wörterbuchs der Türk-Dialecte*, Sanktpeterburgъ.

RKS-L = Levi B.Z. 1996, *Russko-karaimskij slovaŕ. Krymskij dialekt. Urus-Karaj sözlük*, Odessa.

RKS-X = Xafuz M.È. 1995, *Russko-karaimskij slovaŕ. Krymskij dialekt*, Moskva.

Schültz E. 1968, *An Armeno-Kipchak Chronicle on the Polish-Turkish Wars in 1620–1621*, Budapest.

Stachowski M. ²2009, *Gramatyka języka tureckiego w zarysie*, Kraków.

Stachowski S. 1977, Studien über die neupersischen Lehnwörter im Osmanisch-Türkischen. V, *Folia Orientalia* XVIII, 87–118.

Stachowski S. 1998, ed. Ölmez M., *Osmanlı Türkçesinde Yeni Farsça Alıntılar Sözlüğü*, İstanbul.

Sulimowicz J. 1973, Materiał leksykalny krymskokaraimskiego zabytku językowego (druk z 1734 r.). II: Słownik – Dictionnaire – *Rocznik Orientalistyczny* XXXVI/1, 47–107.

UrumS = Garkaveć O. 2000, *Urumśkij slovnyk*, Alma-Ata.

VEWT = Räsänen M. 1969, *Versuch eines etymologisches Wörterbuchs der Türksprachen* (= *Lexica Societatis Fenno-Ugricae* XVII/1), Helsinki.

Zajączkowski A. 1931, *Krótki wykład gramatyki języka zachodnio-karaimskiego (narzecze łucko-halickie)*, Łuck, 17 (§22).

Zajączkowski A. 1932, *Sufiksy imienne i czasownikowe w języku zachodniokaraimskim* (= *Prace Komisji Orjentalistycznej Polskiej Akademji Umiejętności* 15), Kraków.

Zenker J.Th. 1866, *Türkisch-arabisch-persisches Handwörterbuch. Dictionnaire turc-arabe-persan*, Lepizig.

Studies on the Turkic World
A Festschrift for Professor St. Stachowski on the Occasion of His 80th Birthday
edited by E. Mańczak-Wohlfeld and B. Podolak, Kraków 2010: 157–167

Edward Tryjarski (Warszawa)

Names of Animals in Armeno-Kipchak: A New List Brought to Light

Names of animals among the Turkic peoples belong to those chapters of the Turkic vocabulary which had been studied very early and rather carefully. In fact, they were object of interest both of various peoples who contacted the Turks throughout the ages and of several generations of researchers, anthropologists and linguists. Suffice it to remind of the lists of zoological terms and special studies of such scholars publishing in the nineteenth and at the beginning of the twentieth century as J. von Hammer-Purgstall, *Falkenklee, bestehend in drey ungedruckten Werken über die Falknerey. 1. Bāznāme das ist: das Falkenbuch*, Pesth 1840, J. Scully, "Turki names of birds", in: R.B. Shaw, *A sketch of the Turki language as spoken in Eastern Turkistan*, Calcutta 1878, *Journal of the Asiatic Society of Bengal*, 47, pp. 209–215. The twentieth century brought new methods of research both on the part of zoologists and professional Turkologists in many world centers in Turkey itself and in Turcophonic republics of the Soviet Union. At that time the question was both of largening the list of terms and deepening the knowledge of the etymology of a zoological term, its geographical range, a research of cultural and linguistic aspects of the matter. Those studies brought explicitness of etymology of many zoological terms, established their internal and external relations and emphazised their ethnical and religious meanings. To give some examples let us adduce the following: W. Bang, "Über die türkischen Namen einiger Grosskatzen", *Keleti Szemle*, 17, 1916–1917, pp. 112–146. A. v. Le Coq, "Bemerkungen über türkische Falknerei", *Baessler-Archiv*, 4, 1914, pp. 1–13.

The second half of the twentieth century brought a considerable number of works of a similar character: L. Bazin, "Noms de la 'chèvre' en turc et en mongols", in: *Studia Altaica*, Wiesbaden 1957, pp. 28–32; the same, "Les noms du 'yak' chez les peuples turcs et mongols", in: *Beiträge zur Alten Geschichte und deren Nachleben*, 2, Berlin 1970, pp. 213–221; the same, "Note sur **aŋγïrt*, nom turco-mongol d'une variété de 'canard' ", in: *Studia Turcica*, 1971, pp. 35–59; the same, "Les noms turcs de l''aigle' ", *Turcica*, 3, 1971, pp. 128–132; the same, "Les noms turcs et mongols de l''ours' ", in: *Quand le crible était dans la paille. Hommage à Pertev Naili Boratav*, ed. by R. Dor and M. Nicolas, Paris 1978, pp. 83–93; the same, "Note sur le turc *suġur* (*soġur*?) 'marmotte' ", *Journal Asiatique*, 272, 1984, pp. 339–341; A. Zajączkowski, "Staropolska nazwa 'żyrafy' – *sarnapa*", *Język Polski*, XXVI, styczeń–luty 1946, pp. 19–23; J.-P. Roux, "Le chameau en Asie Centrale. Son nom, son élevage, sa place dans la mythologie", *Central Asiatic Journal*, 5, 1959, pp. 35–76; I. Hauenschild, "Türksprachige Benennungen für den Maulwurf", *Orientalia Suecana*, 45–46, 1996–1997, pp. 63–80; the same, "Türksprachige Benennungen für Eidechsen", *Acta Orientalia Academiae Scientiarum Hungaricae*, 51, 1998, pp. 131–158; the same "Krimtatarische Tierbezeichnungen", *Orientalia Suecana*, 47, 1998, pp. 29–54; E. Tryjarski, "The dog in the Turkic area: An Ethnolinguistic Study", *Central Asiatic Journal*, 23, 1979, pp. 279–319. The appearance of a study by A.M. Ščerbak entitled "Nazvanija domašnih i dikih životnyh v tjurkskih jazykah", in: *Istoričeskoe razvitie leksiki tjurkskih jazykov*, Moskva 1961, pp. 82–172, Izdatel'stvo Akademii Nauk SSSR was of special importance. A vast mythological and religious background of the animal world among the Turks and Mongols has been shown in precious monographs by J.-P. Roux, especially in his *Faune et flore sacrées dans les sociétés altaïques*, Paris 1966, Adrien Maisonneuve. A cultural and historical character has a paper by E. Tryjarski, "Pigeons on the Turkish Roof. Some Historical and Linguistic Remarks", in: *Altaica Osloensia. Proceedings from the 32nd Meeting of the Permanent International Altaistic Conference. Oslo, June 12–16,* 1989, ed. by B. Brendemoen [Oslo 1991], pp. 361–370, Universitetsforlaget; its Turkish translation: "Türk çatılarında güvercinler. Bazı tarihsel ve dilbilimsel notlar", *Toplumsal tarih*, 25, 5, Ocak 1996, pp. 39–45.

The beginning of the present century brought a couple of works of substantial importance for the problem in question, viz. *The King's Dictionary The Rasûlid Hexaglot: Fourteenth Century Vocabularies in Arabic, Persian, Turkic, Greek, Armenian and Mongol*, translated by T. Halasi-Kun,

P.B. Golden, L. Ligeti and E. Schütz with introductory essays by P.B. Golden and Thomas T. Allsen, Brill, Leiden–Boston–Köln 2000. *Handbuch der Orientalistik.* Achte Abteilung. *Zentralasien*, vierter Band, containing many Turkic zoological terms in Arabic script in transliteration and translation. The second is I. Hauenschild, *Die Tierbezeichnungen bei Mahmud al-Kaschgari. Eine Untersuchung aus sprach- und kulturhistorischer Sicht*, Wiesbaden 2003, Harrassowitz Verlag a competent and detailed study of zoological names appearing in *Dīvān luγāt at-turk*, quite indispensible for every interested person. The third has been recently published by the last author: I. Hauenschild, *Lexicon jakutischer Tierbezeichnungen*, *Turcologica*, 77, 2008, Harrassowitz Verlag. Here also a paper by E. Tryjarski, "Fish, animals and herbs of Dauria as described by Rev. Father Faustyn Ciecierski", *Studia Turcologica Cracoviensia,* 10, 2005, pp. 473–479, can be mentioned.

It goes without saying that most of zoological terms can be found in general and specialized dictionaries or glossaries embracing particular Turkic languages.

Last but not least, it should be added that also the celebrator of the present Jubilee, Professor Dr. S. Stachowski himself, made many precious contributions to the origin and etymology of zoological terms, mainly those wandering on the Turkic-Slavic linguistic border (for instance such rare items as: *alabalïq* 'perch, bass', *aqqu* 'swan', *bostorγay* 'skylark', *duduquš* 'parrot', *išan* 'mouse', *ôpôp* 'hoopoe', *qarsïγa* 'goshawk', *šïğavïl* 'vulture' and others in the language of the Dobrudja Tatars. See his rich bibliography).

As far as Armeno-Kipchak zoological terms are concerned, they have not been an object of any special attention mainly on account of the incompleteness of the necessary material. In fact, the terms in question appeared only sporadically in the published texts. So, for instance, in *L'arméno-coman et les « ephémérides » de Kamieniec (1604–1613)*, published by J. Deny, Wiesbaden 1957, we can find such common words as: *at* 'cheval', *buğay* 'taureau; juvencus', *çulu* 'abeille', *d̮žanavar* 'animal', *ḫoy* 'mouton', *ḫozu* 'agneau', *inak* 'vache', *it* 'chien', *oguz* 'boeuf', *sarança* 'sauterelles', *tonğuz* 'porc'. In judicial acts contained in: *Dokumenty na polovetskom jazyke XVI v. (Sudebnye akty kamenets-podol'skoj armjanskoj obščiny)* published by T.I. Grunin (ed. by Ė.V. Sevortjan, Stat´ja J.R. Daškevič, Moskva 1967) we find such names as: *at* 'kon´, lošad´', *bajtal* 'kobyla', *gaç̣i* (*gäç̣i*) 'koza, kozij', *inak* 'korova', *tulku* 'lis´ja škurka', *xoj* 'baran, ovtsa'. A few names of common animals (*χoy* 'sheep, ram', *oguz* 'ox', *aslan* 'lion', *χïsγač* 'crab', *balïχ* 'fish', *ėç̣kʿi (munguzi)* 'unicorn' and *i̯ašç̣eriçay* 'lizard' have been mentioned in a paper by E. Tryjarski, "Une liste arméno-kiptchak des signes du zodiaque", *XI. Türk Dil Kurultayında Okunan Bilimsel Bildiriler*, Ankara 1968, pp. 140–152.

The first detailed dictionary of Armeno-Kipchak (E. Tryjarski, *Dictionnaire arméno-kipchak d'après trois manuscits des collections viennoises* I, 1–4, Warszawa 1968–1972) contains a considerable number of zoological terms: *ad͜ždaχa* 'dragon', *ankγ, angγ,* 'vautour', *at* 'cheval', *ayuv* 'ours', *baγa, baha* 'grenouille', *baran* 'bélier, mouton', *baytal* 'jument', *bazilišėkʿ* 'basilic, crocodile?', *bėdana, bi̯edana* 'caille, râle des genêts', *bit* 'pou', *bïzov* 'veau', *boçan* 'cigogne', *boru* '1. loup. 2. ours?', *buγa* 'taureau', *burça, barça* 'puce', *buyvol* 'buffle', *çapla* 'héron, aigrette', *çibin* 'mouche', *çïpçïχ* '(petit) oiseau, moineau', *dana* 'veau; génisse', *dėva* 'chameau', *dėva χušu* 'autruche', *dudokʿ* 'huppe', *d͜žanavar* 'bête (féroce)', *d͜žand͜žiŕn* 'mouche', *ėçkʿi, ėkʿçi* 'chèvre, bouc', *ėšakʿ* 'âne', *grïf* 'griffon', *hayvan, hayman* 'animal, bête (de trait)', *hnida* 'lente', *horliçkʿa* 'tourterelle', *humri* 'tourterelle', *inakʿ* 'vache', *it, itʿ* 'chien', *iž* 'hérisson', *i̯aloviça* 'génisse', *i̯astrėmb* 'autour', *i̯ašçurkʿa* 'lézard', *i̯ėdnorožėç, i̯ėndorožėç* '(animal) unicorne', *i̯ėlėn* 'cerf', *i̯ėlėniça* 'biche, famelle du cerf', *i̯ïlan* 'serpent', *kʿani̯a* 'milan', *suv-kʿani̯asï* 'eau-milan?', *kʿarkʿardan* 'animal unicorne, rhinoceros', *kʿawkʿa* 'choucas', *kazan* 'bête féroce', *kʿėkʿlikʿ* 'caille', *kʿiyikʿ* '2. bête féroce, cerf?', *kʿobalakʿ* 'papillon', *kʿomar* 'cousin, moustique', *kʿoza* 'chèvre', *kʿrėt* 'taupe', *kʿrokʿödil* 'crocodile', *kʿruhlikʿ* 'lapin', *kʿugurçin* 'pigeon', *χara χuš* 'aigle', *χaz* 'oie', *χïmïrsïχa* 'fourmi', *χoroz* 'coq', *χoy* 'mouton, agneau', *χoyan* 'lièvre', *χoyun* 'brebis, mouton', *χoyungina* 'petite brebis, ouaille, agneau', *χozu* 'agneau, agnelet', *χrušç* 'hanneton', *χurt* 'ver', *χurtkʿina* 'petit ver, vermisseau', *χuš* 'oiseau', *laglag* 'cigogne', *lani̯a* 'biche', *lasiça, lašiça* 'belette', *lastuvkʿa* 'hirondelle', *lėbėd* 'cygne', *los* 'élan', *maçi, maši* 'chat', *maymud* 'singe', *mïnd͜ži̯eγ* 'moustique, cousin', *mol* 'mite', *ni̯ėdopïr* 'chauve-souris', *ni̯ed͜žvi̯adėkʿ, ni̯ed͜žvi̯adokʿ* 'ourson; Scorpion (astr.)', *norokʿ* 'oiseau, représentant de la famille *Podicipedidae*', *oguz* 'boeuf', *osa* 'guêpe', *osėniça* 'chenille', *ovi̯eçkʿa, ovėçkʿa* 'brebis, ouaille', *pawukʿ* 'araignée', *pçola, pïçola* 'abeille', *pėlikʿan* 'pélican', *pi̯awkʿa* 'sangsue', *pokʿlunkʿa* 'huppe (nom d'oiseau)', *puhaç* 'grand-duc', *rarog* 'lanaret', *rïs* 'lynx', *sçurokʿ* 'raton, petit rat', *sėmp, si̯emp* 'vautour', *sėnakʿ* 'vespe, frelon', *sėrna* 'chevreuil', *sinakʿ* 'espèce de mouche', *sivri sini̯ag* 'moustique, cousin', *sïçχan, çïçkʿan* 'souris', *sïγïr* 'boeuf', *skʿop* 'mouton (châtré)', *smod,* instead of *smokʿ* 'dragon', *sova* 'hibou', *soykʿa* 'geai, *Garrulus glandarius* L.', *strus* 'autruche', *suv aslanï* 'lion marin, phoque?', *suv kʿani̯asï* 'foulque (*Fulica atra*), milan marin?', *suv χara χušu* 'aigle marin?', *suv sïγïrï* 'buffle?', *šadi* 'espèce de singe', *tavuχ* 'poule, coq', *tχor* 'belette, putois', *tulkʿu* 'renard', *tuvar* '[...] taureau [...]', *vi̯ėlorïb* 'baleine', *vorobiy* 'moineau', *zayi̯eç̣* 'lièvre', *žaba* 'grenouille', *žėrėbi̯a* 'poulain, poulichon', *žuraw* 'grue'.

One could suppose that the above relatively detailed list has been closed for researchers, or can eventually be supplemented by bringing to light an atlas of animals, a zoological school-book or the like. Much to our surprise, a considerable number of zoological names has been lately detected in a text of a... religious and philosophical character.

In the impressive volume of Armeno-Kipchak texts published by A. Garkavets (*Qypchaq Written Heritage*, II: *Monuments of spiritual culture*, Almaty 2007, pp. 895–901) we find an interesting text in Armenian and in Armeno-Kipchak entitled: "Dialogi iz posobija Avedika po grammatike, teologii, filosofii i sistematike". It is a manuscript written in Lviv in 1634 and kept in Erevan (Matenadaran Ms. No. 3522). The basic Armenian text is followed by a Kipchak one being its careful translation. The work is composed of questions and answers. One could distinguish two layers of the whole: the first presents an elementary catechism of Christian faith while the second is directed to give the reader some elements of Greek classical philosophy, namely of theology, essence and construction of the nature, and before all others, of systematics and taxonomy. As a main source of all those considerations elements of the Platonic and, in the first place, Aristotelian ideas are used.

It seems pretty sure that they origin mainly from the famous treatises of the latter philosopher entitled: *Generation of animals*, *Parts of animals* or *Movement of animals*. Just in this connection the names of various animals, both in Armenian and in Kipchak, appear in Avedik's text as examples of living creatures being elements of philosophical categorizing of the universe.

It would be interesting to know more precisely in which way the creation of philosophical and zoological terms in Armeno-Kipchak[1] was performed. At any case, it should be remembered that the interest of Aristotle and his works can be observed in Armenia very early and that it manifested itself in translation of his main treatises. The first known translations of his works, namely those made by Jacob from Edessa, appeared in the 7th century. In 10–11th centuries, Gregory Magistros did some translations of Plato's

[1] It seems pretty sure than some Armeno-Kipchak philosophical terms used by Rev. Avedik were coined by himself.

works.[2] Philosophical ideas of both philosophers became an object through ages of scholarly discussions and teaching. Awedik, author of the dialogues, most probably a clergyman who still remains a person little known to us, must have been a well instructed man who presumably was fulfilling his educational mission.

It seems evident that his main intention was not only to deliver to his pupils a body of information of religious and philosophical character along with fundamental principles of ancient logic and taxonomy but also to teach them the Armeno-Kipchak terminology concerning those domains.[3]

As far as the zoological terms used in the manuscript are concerned,[4] they refer both to wild, domesticated and, ocassionally, also half-mythical animals.[5] No sensible conclusions can be drawn concerning their linguistic distribution. On the other hand, their immediate derivation seems to be

[2] "Ce furent les Syriens d'en deça de l'Euphrate qui subirent les premiers l'ascendant de la Grèce" [...] Les livres de liturgie, les décrets des conciles furent également traduits du grec en syriaque, par des foncionnaires de l'Église affectés spécialement à ces traductions, et qui furent désignés sous le titre d'« interprètes ou traducteurs ». On cite parmi eux [...] Jacques d'Édesse, au septième siècle, qui, outre ouvrages des Pères, traduisit plusieurs livres d'Aristote, notamment les Catégories, les Interprétations, les Analitiques, et le Compendium de la philosophie aristotélique de Nicolas [...]", Victor Langlois, *Collection des historiens anciens et modernes de l'Arménie publiée en français sous les auspices de Son Excellence Nubar-Pacha* [...], tome premier, Paris MDCCCLXXX. Librairie de Firmin-Didot et Cie, pp. XVIII and XIX–XX.

[3] The whole manuscript should be made easier accessible to a larger circle of readers.

[4] To avoid any misreading, the Armeno-Kipchak zoological terms presented by A. Garkavets in his new transcription, have been, as far as possible, reshaped in accordance with my old system, used in my *Dictionnaire arméno-kiptchak*, see above.

[5] Abbreviations:

CCG – K. Grønbech, *Komanisches Wörterbuch Türkischer Wortindex zu Codex Cumanicus*, Kopenhagen 1942. *Monumenta Linguarum Asiae Maioris.*

HauMK – I. Hauenschild, *Die Tierbezeichnungen bei Mahmud al-Kaschgari. Eine Untersuchung aus sprach- und kulturhistorischer Sicht*, Wiesbaden 2003. *Turcologica* 53.

HexaGol – *The King's Dictionary. The Rasûlid Hexaglot: Fourteenth Century Vocabularies in Arabic, Persian, Turkic, Greek, Armenian and Mongol.* Translated by Tibor Halasi-Kun, Peter B. Golden, Louis Ligeti and Edmond Schütz with introductory essays by Peter B. Golden. Ed. with notes and commentary by Peter B. Golden, Leiden–Boston–Köln 2000. *Handbuch der Orientalistik.*

KłhM – A. Mardkowicz, *Karaj sez-bitigi. Słownik karaimski. Karaimisches Wörterbuch*, Łuck 1935.

OttRed – *New Redhouse Turkish-English Dictionary*, İstanbul 1968. ☞

evident: they either present the original Kipchak stock or descend from Ottoman, Armenian, or Polish (a few also from Old Ukrainian). I group the whole material as follows: Mammalia, Birds, Reptiles, Amphibians, Fish, Crustacea, Insects, Half-Mythical animals.

Mammalia

aslan 'lion' KłhM *arsłān* 'Löwe'; HauMK *arslān* 'Löwe (*al-asad*)'.

aslangina 'a small lion' or 'lion's cub'.

at 'horse' KłhM *at* 'Pferd'; CCG *at* 'Pferd – equus'; HauMK *at* 'Pferd (*al-faras*)'.

ayuv 'Bär' KłhM *ajuw* 'Bär'; CCG *aju* 'Bär – ursus'.

borsukʿ 'badger' HauMK *borsmuq* ~ *borsuq* 'der Dachs *Meles meles'*.

boru 'wolf' KłhM *beri* 'Wolf'; CCG *böri, börüʿ* Wolf – lupus'; HauMK *böri* 'Wolf (*aḏ-ḏiʾb*)'.

ça̧χal 'jackal' HexGol *čağal* 'jackal'.

ça̧ravurt 'grazing (animal)'? Cf. OttRed *çerahar, çerahur* 'grazing (animal), herbivorous'.

dėva 'camel' KłhM *tewe* 'Kamel'; CCG *töve* 'Kamel – gamellus'; HauMK *tewe(y), tävä, dävä* 'Kamel (*al-ibil*)'.

ėçkʿi, ėkʿçi 'goat' KłhM *ećki* 'Ziege'; CCG *ečki* 'Bock – betus'; *tiši ečki* 'Ziege – capra'; HauMK *äčkü* 'Ziege (*al-anzʿ*) [...] das bei den Oγuz durch Metathese zu [...] *käči* umgeformt ist [...]'.

ėšėkʿ 'ass, donkey' CCG *ešek* 'Esel – asinus'; HauMK *äšgäk* 'Esel (*al-ḥimār*); eine von zwei Dialektvarianten, die andere ist *äšyāk*'.

fil 'elephant' KłhM *fil* 'Elephant'; CCG *fil* 'Elefant; *pil* (p.) 'Elefant – alofans'.

it 'dog' KłhM *it, jit* 'Hund'; CCG *it* 'Hund – canis'; HauM *it* 'Hund (*al-kalb*).

kʿirpi 'hedgehog' KłhM *kyrpy* 'Igel'; HauMK *kirpi* 'Igel (*al-qunfuḏ*)'; OttRed *kirpi* '1. hedgehog *zool. Erinaceus europaeus.* 2. porcupine *zool. Erethizon dorsatum.*

kʿrėt 'tap' < Pol. *kret* id.

χaplan 'tiger, panther' KłhM *kapłan* 'Tiger'.

χatïr 'mule' CCG *qatyr* 'Maultier – mulus'; HauMK *qatir* 'Maultier (*al-bağl*)'.

χatïrgina 'small mule' or 'mule's cub'.

PoissonsN – M. Nicolas, *Poissons et pêche en Turquie, Langues et Civilisations Orientales*, Paris 1974, Editions du Centre National de la Recherche Scientifique.

χoyan 'hare' KłhM *kojan* 'Hase'; CCG *qojan* 'Hase – lepus'.

χoyïn 'sheep' HauMK *qōy* 'Schaf (*al-ġanam*)... Im Krimtatarischen findet sich neben *qoy* auch [...] *qoyun*'; HexaGol *qoyın, qoyun* 'sheep, ewe or lamb'.

mač̣i 'cat' KłhM *maci* 'Kater'; HauMK *mūš* 'Katze (*al-hirra*), Čigil-Dialekt [...] Eine weitere Benennung für die Katze ist der seit dem 13. Jahrhundert bezeugte Terminus *mačï*, den Clauson zu *mūšük* und *pišik* stellt'.

sïč̣χan 'mouse'; HexaGol *sıčan, sıčqan* 'mouse; rat'; OttRed *sıčan* 'rat, mouse'.

sïč̣χangina 'small mouse or small rat'.

sïγïr 'ox, steer' KłhM *syhyr* Kuh, Ochs'; CCG *syγyr* 'Ochs – bos'; HauMK *siγir* 'Rind *(al-baqar)*'.

sïrna 'roe-deer' < Pol. *sarna, sarn* id, Ukr. *sarna* id.

suv sïγïr 'water buffalo?' CCG *su-syγyr* 'Büffel – bufarus'; HauMK *sūw siγiri* 'Büffel (*al-ǧāmūs*); das ist das Wasserrind'.

toχlu 'yearling lamb'; HauMK *toqli* 'ein junges Schaf (*al-ǧaḏaʿ mina ḏ-ḏaʾnʾ),* das sechs Monate alt ist'.

tulkʿu 'fox' KłhM *tiłki* 'Fuchs'; CCG *tülkü* 'Fuchs; Fuchsfell – (pellis) vulpe'; HauMK *tilkü* 'Fuchs (*aṭ-ṯaʿlab*)'.

vi̯elorïb 'whale' < Pol. *wieloryb* id.

vėvurkʿa 'squirrel' < Pol. *wiewiórka,* err. *wewiórka* id < Lat. *viverra.*

yunuzbalïχï 'porpoise' OttRed *Yunus balığı* 'porpoise *Phocaena phocaena*; common dolphin; grampus, *Delphinus delphis'.*

zurafay 'giraffe' OttRed. *zürafa, zürafe* 'A giraffe *zool. Giraffa camelopardalis*'.

Birds

ankʿ ? HauMK *aŋ* 'Name eines Vogels, dessen Fett als Medizin gebraucht wird [...] mit *aŋ* eventuell die Wasseramsel gemeint ist'.

bėdana 'quail' KłhM *bedene* 'Wachtel'. Cf. OttRed *bedenos* G[ree]k 'kind of grouse'; HauMK 'Bei einigen Türkvölkern wird die Wachtel mit dem mongolischen Lehnwort *bödüna* benannt [...]'.

d͜žalam 'wren' Cf. Ar. *ǧallam*^{un} 'strigal´, strigal´ščik' and Pol. *strzyżyk* 'wren', from *strzyc* 'cut, shear'.

gakʿarož? A bird with a straight beak.

hrivač̣ 'kind of pigeon' < Pol. *(gołąb-)grzywacz* through Ukr.

indikʿ 'turkey' < Pol. *indyk* < Lat. *Gallus indicus.*

kʿaz 'goose' KłhM *kaz* 'Gans'; CCG *qaz* 'Gans – ocha'; HauMK *qāz* 'Gans (*al-baṭṭ*), eigentlich Ente'.

kʿėkʿlikʿ 'partridge' HauMK *käklik* 'Steinhuhn (*al-qabǧ*)'; OttRed *keklik* 'partridge *Perdix perdix*'.
kʿugurč̣i[n?] 'pigeon, dove' KłhM *kigircin* 'Taube, Taubin'; CCG *kügürčin* 'Taube'; HauMK *kökörčgūn* 'Taube (*al-ḥamām*)'.
χaraχuš 'eagle' KłhM *karakus* 'Adler'; CCG *qara-quš* 'Adler – aquila'; HauMK *qara quš* 'Adler (*al-ʿuqāb)*'.
χoruz 'cock, rooster' CCG *χoroz* (p.) 'Hahn – galum'; OttRed *horoz* 'cock, rooster'.
χumri 'turtledove' OttRed. *kumru* (Arabic *kumri*) 'turtledove *zool. Streptopelia turtur*; ringdove *zool. Columba palumbus*'.
laglag 'stork' OttRed *lâklâk* 'stork'; cf. *lâklâk* 'clucking noise made by storks'.
ordakʿ 'duck' KłhM *erdek* 'Ente'; HauMK *ördök* 'Ente (*al-iwazz*, eigentlich 'Gans')'.
pava 'pea-cock' < Old Pol. *pava* id. < Lat. *pavo* id.
pʿunig? A bird with a straight beak.
salam 'snipe, long-bill'? Maybe translated from Pol. *słomka* (properly *słonka* '*Scolopas rusticola*') 'snipe'. Pol. *słomka* 'small straw' is different, but cf. CCG (r) *salam* 'Stroh – palia'.
salam kʿėkʿlikʿ 'straw-partridge'? cf. CCG (r.) *salam* 'Stroh – palia' + *kʿėkʿlikʿ* 'partridge'? Or names of two birds?
turad͡ž 'francolin' OttRed. *turaç* 'francolin *zool. Francolinus francolinus*'.
turna 'crane' KłhM *turna* 'Kranich'; CCG *turna* 'Kranich – grua'; HauMK *turna* 'Kranich (*al-kurkī*)'.

Fish

χïlïč̣balïχï 'swordfish' OttRed *kılıč balığı* 'swordfish *zool. Xiphias gladius*; PoissonsN *kılıç balığı* 'L'Espadon (*Xiphias gladius* L., *Xiphiidés*) est le plus majestueux des poissons migrateurs. Il porte le nom populaire de *kılıç balığı* "poisson-épée" [...] à cause du rostre, en forme d'épée, qu'il possède à la mâchoire supérieure et qui est généralement aussi long que les deux tiers de son corps'.
χïzïlalad͡žabalïχ? *χïzïl* 'red' + *alad͡ža* 'motley, particoloured' (CCG *alača* 'scheckig, gestrift') + *balïχ* 'fish'.
sarïkʿobakʿbalıχ 'a yellow shark'? *sarï* 'yellow'; 'Squales et requins sont considérés comme des "poissons-chiens" (*köpek*) [...] pour les zoologists, le *köpek balığı* proprement dit est l'Emissole (*Mustelus mustelus* L.), tachetée ou lisse' PoissoinsN, p. 34.

tėk^cirbalïχï 'striped goatfish' OttRed *tekirbalığı* 'striped goatfish *Mullus surmuletus*'; PoissonsN *tekir balığı* 'le Surmulet *Mullus surmuletus* L. [...] du grec *τίγρις* tigre'.
yïlanbalïχï 'eel' OttRed *yılanbalığı* 'eel *zool. Anguilla anguilla* L.'.
usgumbru 'mackerel' OttRed *uskumru* Gk 'mackerel '*zool. Scomber scomber*; PoissonsN *uskumru balığı* 'Le Maquereau (*Scomber scomber* L.) a en turc un nom d'origine qrecque: *σκόμβρος*'.
zėyrak^c ulu-balïχlar? 'intelligent great fish? whales?'.

Reptilia

tozbaγa 'tortoise; turtle?' OttRed *tosbağa* 'tortoise'. Cf. TłhM *baha* 'Frosch'
yaščėriça see *yaščurk^ca*
yaščurk^ca, yaščėriça 'lizard' < Pol. *jaszczurka*, Old Pol., also *jaszczerzyca*
yïlan 'snake, serpent; viper?' KłhM *jiłan* 'Schlange'; CCG *jylan, ylan* 'Schlange – serpens', 'Natter – bixia'; HauMK *yilān* 'Schlange (*al-ḥayya*)'

Amphibians

χurbaχa, γurbaγa 'frog' HauMK *qūrbaqa* 'der Frosch des Landes (*aḍ-ḍifda^c al-barrī*)'; OttRed *kurbağa* '1. frog. 2. stargazer, *Uranoscopus scaber'*

Crustacea

χïsχač 'crab' HauMK *qisγāč* 'ein schwarzes kleines Tier, das die Menschen beißt; Dialekt der Oγuz'; HexaGol *qiṣqač* 'crayfish'

Insects

χarïndža 'ant' HauMK *qarinča* 'Ameise (*an-naml*); Dialekt der Oγuz'; OttRed *karınca* 'ant, *zool. Formica'*
pawuk^c 'spider' < Ukr. *pawuk* id.
sarïnčχa 'locust' CCG *sarynčqa* 'Heuschrecke – hoyšrekke'; HauMK *saričγa* 'Heuschrecke (*al-ǧarād*)

Half-Mythical animals

adždaha 'dragon' KłhM *acdaha* 'Drache, Schlange'[6]
lowiat^can 'leviathan, legendary monster in the Bible like a snake, crocodile or whale'; KłhM *liwjatan* 'Wallfisch'

[6] According to some researchers, a Greek term *drako* 'dragon' with Aristotle did not mean a legendary creature but a fish or a snake.

It is difficult to identify the names ended with the suffix *-gina/-kʿina* indicating a diminutive form like: *aslangina, χatīrgina, sičχangina*. In fact, it is rather hard to know whether the question is of a young, immature person ('lion's cub', 'mule's foal', 'mouse's cub') or a full-grown animal of a particular kind, unprecisely defined.

Studies on the Turkic World
A Festschrift for Professor St. Stachowski on the Occasion of His 80th Birthday
edited by E. Mańczak-Wohlfeld and B. Podolak, Kraków 2010: 169–189

Heinrich Werner (Bonn)

Zum historisch-kulturellen Hintergrund der jenissejisch-türkischen Wortparallelen

Mit der Verbreitung der türkischen Welt in Eurasien kamen gravierende kulturelle Veränderungen ins Leben der einheimischen Völker der entsprechenden eroberten Regionen. Vielerorts übernahmen diese Völker die Sprache und die Wirtschaftsweise, vor allem die Viehzucht, der Eingewanderten, auch wenn sich mancherorts spürbare Spuren der traditionellen örtlichen Kultur oder auch die einheimische Sprache erhalten konnten. Im folgenden versuche ich, auf die entsprechende Situation in der historischen jenissejisch-türkischen Kontaktzone einzugehen, vorwiegend aufgrund von mythologischen und sprachlichen Daten und eines Vergleiches der jenissejischen und südsibirischen türkischen traditionellen kulturellen Besonderheiten.

Es hat sich durch die türkische Expansion in West- und Mittelsibirien so zugetragen, dass die einheimische Bevölkerung ihre Sprache und traditionelle Kultur nur in den Breiten der sibirischen Taiga erhalten hat, während in der südsibirischen Steppenzone das Türkische vorherrschte. Auch wenn in dieser Region die Viehzucht zur dominierenden Wirtschaftsweise wurde, die bestimmte Innovationen in die Lebensart der einheimischen Bevölkerung mit sich brachte, weist die geistige Kultur dieser Bevölkerung weitgehende Züge der traditionellen Vorstellungen auf. Diese Überbleibsel in der geistigen Kultur zeugen eindeutig davon, dass man es bei der südsibirischen türkischen Bevölkerung mit einem älteren nichttürkischen ethno-kulturellen Substratum zu tun hat, und eine Reihe von Übereinstimmungen mit der jenissejischen Protokultur bekräftigen es.

Die Vorstellungen der südsibirischen türkischen Völker über den Weltaufbau kamen nicht von anderswoher (ganz bestimmt nicht von Völkern iranischer Abstammung, wie in Gogolev 1993:20 vermutet), sondern sie stellen die ursprüngliche traditionelle Weltsicht der ursprünglichen einheimischen südsibirischen Bevölkerung von Jägern, Fischern und Sammlern aus der vortürkischen Zeit dar, die sich in der geistigen Kultur, auch wenn mit bestimmten späteren Innovationen, erhalten konnte. Es handelt sich hier z.B. um Glaubensvorstellungen, die für die traditionellen Kulturen Nordeurasiens und Nordamerikas kennzeichnend sind (Werner 2007:98–102).

Je nach dem Charakter der wirtschaftlichen Tätigkeit und der Lebensweise unterscheiden sich die südsibirischen türkischen Völker voneinander, jedoch dominieren in ihrer geistigen Kultur ähnliche oder identische Züge im Rahmen einer einheitlichen Tradition; je älter die Kulturschichten sind, desto näher stehen diese Völker zueinander in kultureller Hinsicht und desto mehr Übereinstimmungen weisen sie mit der traditionellen Kultur der Jenissejer auf.

Hier sei vor allem auf die wie bei den Jenissejern bestehende holistische Vorstellung von der Welt als Ganzheit hinzuweisen, eine Welt ohne Gegenüberstellung von *Sein* vs. *Nichtsein* oder *natürlich* vs. *übernatürlich*. Das allgemeine Weltbild ist so dreistufig strukturiert (irdische, himmlische und unterirdische Welten), dass das Universum überschaulich ist: Dabei sind die obere und untere Welten Kopien von der mittleren irdischen Welt, jedoch mit verabsolutierten positiven Eigenschaften im Falle der himmlischen und negativen Eigenschaften im Falle der unterirdischen Welt. Genauso wie in den Vorstellungen der Jenissejer (Findeisen 1929:36–37) geht man auch in den Vorstellungen der südsibirischen Türken (L'vova u.a. 1988:92–97[1]) davon aus, dass es in der himmlischen wie unterirdischen Welten Flüsse, Berge und Wälder gibt, dass dort auch Menschen leben, die auf die Jagd gehen, Fische fangen und Behausungen mit allen notwendigen Sachen haben. Die Menschen der himmlischen Welt sind aber nur als Sterne sichtbar und wohnen in gläsernen Jurten.[2]

Oft ist die unterirdische Welt als spiegelbildlich und „verdreht" und derer Gestalten als bleich und hesslich dargestellt. So ist z.B. die in einem unterirdischen schwarzen Meer lebende *Xuu Inej* des chakassischen Pantheons (auch als „Bleiche Mutter" übersetzt) als hessliche Greisin mit

[1] Bei der hier folgenden Beschreibung der jenissejisch-türkischen kulturellen Parallelen stützte ich mich hauptsächlich auf diese wertvolle Arbeit aus Novosibirsk.

[2] Vgl. die Bemerkung in Anučin 1914:3, dass der himmlische Hauptgott der Jenissejer mit seiner Frau im östlichen Teil des Himmels in einem grossen gläsernen Zelt wohnt.

Hanfhaaren dargestellt und erinnert sehr an die ketische Herrscherin der Unterwelt *Hosedam* (auch als „Weib des Meeres“ bekannt), die zerzaustes Haar, triefende Augen hat, und in derer Gegend nur einige weiße (bleiche) Grashalme und knorrige Sträucher wachsen.

Bei den jenissejischen wie südsibirischen türkischen Völkern ist die Entstehung der Welt als die Entstehung der irdischen Welt aus den ewigen Gewässern dargestellt. Es geschah in unbestimmter mythologischen Zeit, und die nun entstandene (geschaffene) irdische Welt ist durch die Linearzeit gekennzeichnet, wobei es sich auch um eine zyklische Zeit handelt, da die Welt immer wieder durch Sintfluten verschwindet und neu entsteht.

Nun kommt nach den traditionellen kosmogonischen Vorstellungen mit der Entstehung der irdischen Welt Ordnung ins Universum, und zwar durch die Gegenüberstellung von *Zentrum* und *Peripherie*. Eigentlich ist der Weltaufbau in der traditionellen Weltsicht der Jenissejer und der südsibirischen Türken völlig identisch: Nach der vertikalen Gliederung unterscheidet man, wie schon erwähnt, die himmlische, irdische und unterirdische Welten, die durch den Weltenbaum (die Weltachse) miteinander verbunden sind. Auf allen Ebenen ist die Weltachse das Zentrum; auf Erden handelt es sich dabei um das Zentrum der irdischen Welt, das bei diesen Völkern auch als Nabel der Erde (ket. *baŋtul*) bezeichnet wird, und dem in der himmlischen Welt der Polarstern entspricht, der auch als Eingang in die obere Welt gilt (vgl. ket. *Esdə diōxt* ‘Öffnung am Himmel’, Ivanov & Toporov 1969:152). Die obere Welt symbolisieren der Himmel, die Himmelskörper (vor allem die Sonne und der Mond), die Baumkrone (die Krone des Weltenbaumes), die Flussquelle und die Vögel; die unterirdische Welt symbolisieren dagegen der Eingang in diese Welt, ihre „düstere“ Sonne, die Wurzeln eines Baumes (des Weltenbaumes), der Unterlauf eines Flusses sowie die „unterirdischen“ (in Höhlen lebenden) Tiere. Bei den Jenissejern handelt es sich dabei z.B. um den Maulwurf (ket. *uja*) und die Fledermaus (ket. *hʌlataŋ-keŋs*, imb. *sakdoos*, kot. ass. *tagala*). Als Zeichen der „mittleren“ (irdischen) Welt dienen die Tiere der realen Welt und der Mensch oder seine Behausung (s. Werner 2007:79).

Identisch ist auch in den traditionellen Vorstellungen der südsibirischen Türken und der Jenissejer der besonders ausführlich dargestellte Aufbau der irdischen Welt. Hier leben die Menschen der realen Welt, chak. *künniŋ kizi* ‘Sonnenmenschen (Menschen des Sonnenlichtes)’, ket. *kʌndeŋ*, jug. *kʌndʲeŋ* ‘Menschen der Helle, des Tageslichtes’ und die Tiere der realen Welt, aber auch Wesen der übernatürlichen Welt, vor allem die Herrinnen und Herren der Berge, Flüsse, Ufer, Wälder sowie der Tierwelt, die man ständig durch rituelle Vorgänge begütigen muss, um den Erfolg z.B. auf der Jagd oder beim Fischfang zu sichern.

Das Leben der Menschen dieser Welt war immer durch eine enge Verbundenheit mit dem Raum ringsum und dem gesamten Universum gekennzeichnet; ihr Wohnort mit der Behausung war zwischen den vier Haupthimmelsrichtungen, den vier Zwischenhimmelsrichtungen und den sechs Weltrichtungen, d.h. den vier Himmelsrichtungen, dem Oben (Himmel) und dem Unten (Unterwelt) verankert und nach dem Osten (dem Sonnenaufgang, dem Morgen, dem Wohnort des himmlischen Hauptgottes) orientiert.

Während der Osten als Hauptorientierungspunkt, als Haupt- oder Vorderseite wahrgenommen wurde, galt der Westen als Hinterseite (Seite des Sonnenuntergangs, des Abends), als Land der Toten. Entsprechend galt dabei der Süden als die rechte Seite, die Seite des hellen Tages, und der Norden als die linke Seite, die Seite der Nacht und Dunkelheit. Von besonderer sakraler Bedeutung war hier die Linie *West–Ost*, denn während rituellen Vorgängen und Gebeten wandte man das Gesicht dem Osten, der vorderen Seite zu, der Seite des beginnenden neuen Tages und neuen Lebens, und die rituellen Bewegungen nach dem Gang der Sonne symbolisierten den Kreislauf des Lebens.

Diese Solarorientirung bestimmte auch die Topographie und Einrichtung der Behausung, egal ob es sich dabei um ein Zelt, eine Jurte oder ein Haus handelte. Die Behausung war vor allem nach der erwähnten Linie *West–Ost* orientiert. Hier gab es nur einen Unterschied nach der Orientierung des Einganges: bei den Jenissejern befand er sich im Westen und bei den südsibirischen türkischen Völkern umgekehrt im Osten. Alle anderen Details der Einrichtung der Behausung waren so gut wie identisch. Die Haupt- oder die Vorderseite befand sich dem Eingang gegenüber. Diesen Bereich durften die Frauen nicht betreten, hier hielten sich in der Regel nur das Haupt der Familie und die Ehrengäste auf. Die nördliche (linke) Hälfte der Behausung war für die Frauen und die südliche (rechte) für die Männer bestimmt. Die Kultgegenstände der Jenissejer (*allalɯŋ*) und der südsibirischen Türken (die *Tösfigürchen*) stellten die beschützenden Geister der Behausung dar und konnten deshalb nur auf der vorderen (heiligen) Seite aufbewahrt werden.

Das sakrale Zentrum der Behausung war die Feuerstelle; aber auch die Eingangstür und das Rauchloch hatten sakrale Bedeutung, denn durch sie war der Innenraum mit der Aussenwelt verbunden. In den Vorstellungen der Chakassen wurde der Innenraum der Behausung in ein Verhältnis mit dem Himmelszelt gebracht, und der Polarstern galt als Rauchloch dieses

Zeltes. Die Eingangstür wurde bei den Jenissejern wie den südsibirischen Türken mit einer Art Ornamentierung versehen, wodurch man die Behausung in Einklang mit dem Universum brachte. Ausserhalb der Behausung war bei den südsibirischen Türken der Pikettphahl von sakraler Bedeutung, eine Innovation, die mit der Viehzucht (Pferdezucht) kam.

Die Errichtung der Behausung, auch wenn es dabei bloß darum ging, ein Birkenrindezelt aufzuschlagen, war schon immer mit bestimmten rituellen Vorgängen, Regeln und Vorschriften verbunden, denn seit uralter Zeiten war es eine sakrale Aktion von Raumdomestizierung. Wichtig waren vor allem die Zeit und der Ort, an dem die Bahausung errichtet werden sollte. Ein Zelt konnte nur am Vormittag und nur von Frauen aufgeschlagen werden; dabei musste sich der Bestattungsort der Toten flussabwärts von der Behausung befinden. Handelte es sich um die Erbauung eines Hauses bei den südsibirischen Türken, so konnte damit nur bei Vollmond und in der Regel nur im Frühling begonnen werden.

Ausserdem begann die Errichtung einer beliebigen Behausung immer mit der Bestimmung der Stelle für die *Mutter Feuer* (ket. *bokam* < *bɔˀk* 'Feuer' + *a·m* 'Mutter' oder auch *boqqɯm* 'Feuerweib' < *bɔˀk* 'Feuer' + *qi·m* 'Frau', 'Weib'; vgl. chak. *ot inezi* 'Mutter Feuer'), d.h. des Platzes für die Feuerstelle (den Herd), das sakrale Zentrum der Bahausung. Dabei war die Zeremonie des ersten Tees (des ersten Teetrinkens) von besonderer Bedeutung: Erst nach dem ersten Feuer an der Feuerstelle und dem ersten hier gekochten Tee konnte bei den Jenissejern das Birkenrindezelt und bei den südsibirischen Türken die Jurte bedeckt werden.

Das lässt sich dadurch erklären, dass bei diesen wie anderen sibirischen Völkern das Feuer als ein grosses Heiligtum, ein weblicher Geist, verehrt wurde. Diese Verehrung war mit einer Reihe von Verboten und Vorschriften verbunden: Das Feuer durfte nicht ausgehen, und für die Nacht ließ man auf der Feuerstelle einen grösseren verkohlten glühenden Birkenholzscheit liegen; man durfte die Holzscheite nicht quer ins Feuer legen (damit es sich daran nicht 'verschluckte' wie z.B. ein Lebewesen an einem Knochen), nichts Unreines ins Feuer werfen oder ins Feuer urinieren; man durfte das Feuer mit keinem spitzen Gegenstand berühren, um ihm nicht weh zu tun, und durfte nicht übers Feuer schreiten. Beim Umzug nahm man die Glut in einem mit frischem Moos gefüllten Birkenrindetrog mit. Weitergeben durfte man das Feuer nur an Verwandte (Anučin 1914:16; Alekseenko 1967:179–180).

Eben deshalb begann man die Errichtung einer Behausung mit der Einrichtung der Feuerstelle. Sie befand sich am Schnittpunkt der vier Himmelsrichtungen, wurde vom übrigen Wohnraum durch vier Hölzer oder auch durch Steine getrennt und war nach der Linie *West–Ost* orientiert. Das vordere Querholz an der vorderen Seite der Behausung (bei den Jenissejern war es die östliche, bei den südsibirischen Türken die westliche Seite) galt als „Kopf" und das hintere Querholz als Hinterteil der Feuerstelle. So war auch mit dem Begriff der Feuerstelle das Zuhause, die Familie und der eigene Klan verbunden. Darin lag eigentlich der Sinn der Raumdomestikation: Ein Teil des „wilden" und „fremden" Raumes wurde durch die Begütigung des übernatürlichen Herrn des Ortes während der Zeremonie des ersten Teetrinkens und nach der „Zustimmung" dieses Herrn zum Zuhause der Familie. Die Behausung war also nicht nur eine Unterkunft, sondern auch eine Stätte mit sakraler Bedeutung: Sie wurde im Einklang mit dem Universum eingerichtet und war als domestizierter Raum unter dem Schutz der guten Hausgeister, während im „wilden" Raum ringsum die Besitzergeister herrschten.

Auch im Pantheon der Jenissejer und der südsibirischen Türken lassen sich weitgehende Übereinstimmungen beobachten. Den jenissejischen Hauptkraftzentren in der übernatürlichen Welt, dem Vater Himmel *Es* und der Mutter Erde *Baŋam*, entsprechen im Pantheon der südsibirischen türkischen Völker der himmlische Hauptgott *Ülgän* (die männliche Urquelle des Lebens) und die Urmutter *Umaj* oder *Ymaj*. Eine Identität der himmlischen Hauptgötter *Es* und *Ülgän* in beiden Traditionen mit dem zentralasiatischen *Tengri (Tengere)* der altaischen Völker ist kaum zu leugnen. Sie leben oberhalb des höchsten Himmels im Osten und werden beide als Höchste Wesen dargestellt, die sich in die irdischen Angelegenheiten nicht direkt einmischen, überlassen es den zweit- und drittrangigen Gottheiten. Beide nehmen auch an der Schöpfung teil, erschaffen die Menschen und Tiere (in der jenissejischen Version schickt sie *Es* auf die Erde), obwohl auch übernatürliche Wesen geringerer Würde daran beteiligt sind, z.B. der ketische *Dotet* und der südsibirische türkische *Erlik*: Während aber *Es* und *Ülgän* alles Gute, Schöne und Nützliche schaffen, entstehen durch die Tätigkeit von *Dotet* und *Erlik* nur unbrauchbare, bergige Landschaften; ausserdem liessen diese zwei Wesen die Insekten frei, die für die Lebewesen auf Erden lästig sind.

Eine weitere Ähnlichkeit zwischen *Es* und *Ülgän* besteht darin, dass sie wegen ihrer Universalität im Umgang mit anderen übernatürlichen Wesen und mit Menschen in ihren unterschiedlichen Manifestationen auftreten, wodurch sie zuweilen auch unterschiedliche Namen haben. Dies betrifft übrigens auch *Tengri*, der je nach späteren nationalen Traditionen unter verschiedenen, manchmal auch entlehnten, Namen auftritt (vgl. chak. *Qodaj*, *Tura*, tel. *Tatai*, orchon. *Yduk jer-sub*, jak. *Aar Ajyy tojon*, mong. *Chormusta-tengri* < soghd. *Churmazda* / *Churmuzta*, burj. *Chörmos-tengri*, tuv. *Kurbustu*, alt. *Uč-Kurbustan* / *Kubustan-aakai* u.a.).

Die später eingetretenen Veränderungen im Pantheon der betreffenden Völker konnten aber die Verehrung der ursprünglichen Hauptgeistmächte, des himmlischen Hauptgottes und der Mutter Erde nicht völlig verdrängen. Davon zeugt das ihnen gewidmete Sommersonnenwendefest bei den Jenissejern und den südsibirischen Türken (vgl. auch das inhaltlich identische Sonnenfest *Ysyach* der Jakuten, das am 21.–22. Juni, dem Tag der Sommersonnenwende stattfand und zugleich auch ein Neujahrsfest, ein Fest der Wiedergeburt von Natur und Menschen sowie des Dankes an die übernatürlichen Hauptgeistmächte war, Gogolev 1993:27). Bei den Jenissejern war das Sommersonnenwendefest am 21.–22. Juni ein rituelles Jahresfest, das ebenso als Neujahrsfest galt und den Menschen eine neue Zuversicht im Leben, eine Erneuerung des Lebens im Einklang mit dem Jahreszyklus in der Natur gab, ja auch mit der Verehrung der Hauptgeistmächte der übernatürlichen Welt, dem himmlischen *Es*-Gott und der Mutter Erde *Baŋam* verbunden war. Die Verehrung dieser Gottheiten erfolgte in zeremoniellen Vorgängen mit Opfergaben. An den heiligen Stätten brachte man ihnen folgende Opfer: an Opferbäume (ket. *qɔq-soks*, pl. *qɔqsaq*) gebundene weiße Stoffstreifen wurden dem *Es*-Gott, und an junge Zedernbäume (ket. *hajgit*, pl. *hajgat*) gebundene schwarze Stoffstreifen der Mutter Erde *Baŋam* geopfert. Früher wurden außerdem der Mutter Erde schwarze und dem *Es*-Gott weiße Rentiere geopfert (man ließ diese Opferrentiere (ket. *qɔqssen*) einfach frei, und so „opferte" man sie den Göttern).

Bei den südsibirischen Türken mit weit verbreiteter Viehzucht gehörte zu dem *yzyach* 'Opfertier' vor allem das Pferd, obwohl zuweilen auch andere Tiere (Schafe oder Rinder) geopfert wurden. Ausserdem gab es hier Opfertiere, die als „den Geistern gewidmete Tiere" galten; sie befanden sich in den Herden unter anderen Tieren, wurden aber nicht geschlachtet, nicht geschlagen und nicht als Zugtiere gebraucht; fremde Frauen durften sie nicht anrühren.

Mit den Opfertieren ist auch der Kult der heiligen Tiere verbunden, und eben aus dieser Sicht lässt sich das Phänomen der „Pferde mit Geweih" z.B. in der Pazyryk-Kultur erklären. Der Hirschkult der ursprünglichen einheimischen Bevölkerung der Region wurde allmählich durch den Kult Pferdes der nomadischen Viehzüchter iranischer und alttürkischer Abstammung verdrängt, und das „Pferd mit Geweih" war ganz bestimmt nur eine Übergangserscheinung (Altheim 1969: 308–309).

Man fragt sich, wie diese kulturellen Übereinstimmungen bei den jenissejischen und südsibirischen türkischen Völkern zu deuten sind – als gemeinsame Urquelle, wenn man vom jenissejischen oder jenissejisch-samojedischen ethnischen Substratum der südsibirischen türkischen Völker ausgeht, oder als eine Anpassung der nach Südsibirien gekommenen Türken an die dort lebende jenissejische oder samojedische Bevölkerung? Da sich die alttürkische Welt nomadischer Viehzüchter und die jenissejische Welt von Jägern, Fischern und Sammlern voneinander zu sehr unterschieden, ist kaum denkbar, dass die türkischen Völker ihre produzierende Viehzüchterkultur dabei aufgegeben und zur primitiven aneignenden Kultur der einheimischen Urbevölkerung Südsibiriens gewechselt haben. Glaubwürdig ist deshalb die Vermutung über das jenissejisch-samojedische ethnische Substratum der südsibirischen türkischen Welt.

Die Übereinstimmungen in den Glaubensvorstellungen lassen sich in diesem Fall am besten erklären, wenn man vom primären (ursprünglichen) und sekundären (späteren) Tengrismus ausgeht (s. Werner 2007:51–59). Der primäre Tengrismus basiert auf uralten animistischen Vorstellungen bei der einheimischen Urbevölkerung Zentralasiens, Nordeurasiens und Nordamerikas, wonach das Universum von unzählbaren Geistwesen auf allen Ebenen bewohnt ist; das mächtigste von ihnen wurde mit dem Himmel, dem riesigen blauen Himmelszelt identifiziert, und es beherrschte durch seine Grösse und Universalität das ganze Universum: Es war überall und es war alles, es war die Ursache aller Dinge der Welt. Dabei handelte es sich um eine begriffliche Ganzheit _Himmel / Gott_ und um keine semantische Entwicklung _Himmel > Gott;_ dies beweisen Beispiele wie idg. *_t'i̯eu̯-_, alt. *_tengri_, jenis. *_es_, samojed.-ugr. _num_ usw. Dagegen sollte man unter dem sekundären Tengrismus, der in Róna-Tas 1987:44 auch als „hochentwickelter" bezeichnet ist, eine Art Religion der Völker der Steppenzone im Mittelalter verstehen, welche aufs engste mit der Herrscherschicht verbunden war und allmählich durch solche Hochreligionen wie den Buddismus, Islam, Zoroastrismus, Manichäismus, Nestorianismus oder das Judentum abgelöst wurde.

Durch das identische Weltbild und gleiche Glaubensvorstellungen lässt sich auch eine Reihe weiterer kultureller Ähnlichkeiten zwischen den jenissejischen und südsibirischen türkischen Völkern beobachten. Hier wäre vor allem der Schamanismus zu erwähnen, der bei diesen Völkern ausser einigen Abweichungen identisch ist, da er hier ein Teilsystem des primären (ursprünglichen) Tengrismus darstellt.

Bei diesem Schamanismus handelt es sich um Vermittler zwischen den Welten.

> Der Schamane ist ein Mensch, der aufgrund einer besonderen Begabung in der Lage ist, in Trance zu geraten und in diesem Zustand in einen direkten Kontakt zu nichtmenschlichen Wesen, 'Göttern', zu treten, um dadurch seiner Gemeinschaft zu nützen... Er benutzt für seine Reise in der Regel eine Trommel und einen Stock, die ihm als Transportmittel dienen, wobei er bestimmte Bewegungen vollzieht, die auch die Form eines Tanzes haben können. Ihm zur Seite stehen Hilfsgeister. (Sagaster 1998:74).

Eine der wichtigsten Aufgaben solch eines Schamanen war die Heilbehandlung der Kranken, die Rettung ihrer Seelen. Eigentlich war seine Tätigkeit immer aufs engste mit seiner Gens verbunden, er war gleichzeitig so gut wie Priester, Seher, Verkündiger, Berater und Wahrsager. Außer diesen Hauptfunktionen kam der Schamane den Menschen in mehreren alltäglichen Situationen zur Hilfe. Und er tritt auch als Tänzer, Sänger, Erzähler von Märchen und Geschichten und Hüter der Tradition auf. Nach seinen Vermittlungsfunktionen ist er jedoch kein Priester wie es ihn in einer Hochreligion gibt, denn er ist kein Diener eines bestimmten Kultes. Von üblicher Priestertätigkeit unterscheiden sich auch seine Techniken, seine besondere Begabung, in Trance zu geraten. Hier handelt es sich ums „Hinaustreten" der Geistseele des Schamanen, das als konstitutive schamanistische Technik betrachtet wird. Im späteren Tengrismus wird diese Technik immer öfter durch die „Besessenheit" ersetzt, wobei sich der Schamane auf keine Reisen ins Jenseits begibt (Sagaster, ebd.).

Die weitere Evolution führte dazu, daß der Schamane allmählich zum Priester eines bestimmten Kultes wurde, zu einer Figur, die sich auch einer Hochreligion anpassen konnte:

> Das sogenannte Staatsorakel von Tibet, der 'Orakelpriester' von Nätschung, ist nichts anders als ein Schamane höchster Ordnung; die gesamte, weitverbreitete Institution der Orakelpriester des tibetisch-mongolischen Buddhismus ist in die Hoch-religion integrierter Schamanismus. (Sagaster 1998:73).

Bei den jenissejischen wie südsibirischen türkischen Völkern handelte es sich eben um Schamanen der Trance-Technik, d.h. um Schamanismus des primären Tengrismus. Während sich in den nomadischen staatlichen

Gebilden der Steppenzone, incl. der alttürkischen, der Schamanismus des „hochentwickelten“ Tengrismus beobachten lässt, bewahrt sich bei den südsibirischen Türken der traditionelle ursprüngliche Schamanismus. Auch in diesem Fall sollte man nicht von einem „kulturellen Verfall“ im Vergleich zu der klassischen alttürkischen Zeit ausgehen, wo es sich um eine ganz andere Welt handelte (vgl. Kljaštornyj 1964; Gumiljov 1967), sondern eben von der Bewahrung der ursprünglichen Tradition bei den eroberten und türkisierten Völkern Südsibiriens, die auf eine Kultur mesolithischen Charakters zurückgeht.

Interessant sind auch einige Übereinstimmungen bei den Jenissejern und südsibirischen Türken in der Symbolik und in Bräuchen, die durch bestimmte „Ritualisierung“ geprägt sind. So erinnert z.B. an die graue Vergangenheit, an die Zeit, als die Jagd in beiden Traditionen die wichtigste Quelle des Lebensunterhalts war, das weit verbreitete Symbol von Bogen und Pfeil. Es war ein Zeichen des Wohlergehens und zugleich der Sicherheit der Familie, konnte bei den Jenissejern auch oft unter den Familientamgas erscheinen und wies auf den Besitzer eines Gebrauchsgegenstandes oder einer Jagdwaffe hin. Ausserdem wurde das Zeichen oft auf Unterlagen anstatt einer Unterschrift gezeichnet (Alekseenko 1967:73).

Eine besondere Bedeutung wurde in beiden Traditionen der „Ritualisierung“ verschiedener Tätigkeiten beigemessen. Oben wurde bereits auf zeremonielle Vorgänge, Regeln und Vorschriften bei der Errichtung einer Behausung hingewiesen. Ähnliche Vorgänge begleiteten auch die Jagd, den Fischfang, das Handwerk und bei den Viehzüchtern Südsibiriens auch bestimmte Umstände, die mit der Viehzucht verbunden waren. So glaubte man z.B., dass der Erfolg auf der Jagd oder beim Fischfang nicht nur von der Geschicklichkeit oder Findigkeit der Jäger und Fischer abhängt, sondern auch von der Stimmung (Zuneigung) der Herren der Gewässer, des Waldes und der Tierwelt sowie von der sakralen Reinheit der Jagdwaffen und der Fischereigeräte. Eben deshalb wurden Kleidung und Waffen vor der Jagd durch Räucherung gereinigt. Verbunden damit waren auch verschiedene Verbote und Vorschriften, die auf die sakrale „Unreinheit“ der Frauen zurückgeführt wurden. Bei den Keten und Jugen mussten die Frauen z.B. ihre Kleider und Bettsachen durch Räucherung sorgfältig „reinigen“, sie durften nicht über die Fischfanggeräte und Jagdwaffen ihrer Manner schreiten, ihre Sachen nicht auf den Polarschlitten der Manner legen usw. (Alekseenko 1967:174).

Aus der gemeinsamen Vergangenheit der einheimischen Bevölkerung stammt auch bei den Jenissejern und südsibirischen Türken eine Reihe von ähnlichen Besonderheiten bei der Bestattung der Verstorbenen. Hier sei vor allem darauf hingewiesen, dass das Land der Toten mit dem Westen verbunden war. Deswegen war das Grab in der Regel an der Linie *West–Ost* orientiert, und zwar wurde der Tote mit dem Kopf nach Osten beigesetzt; und das Grabmal symbolisierte den Weltenbaum (Gogolev 1993:18): Bei den Jenissejern ist der Weltenbaum auch als Schamanenbaum bekannt, entspricht in den wichtigsten Details dem Schamanenstab und tritt in vereinfachter Form eines Dreizacks auch als Grabmal anstatt eines Kreuzes auf; im letzteren Fall besteht er aus einem entrindeten Erlenbaum mit sieben Ringen (Anučin 1914:71). Als man den Ort der Bestattung verliess, „versperrte" man hinter sich den Weg mit einem Querstock oder gekreuzten Zeigen, damit der Verstorbene nicht zurückkehrte. Kleine Kinder wurden oft in einem ausgehöhlten Baum beigesetzt. Beisetzungen mit einem Pferd waren bei den türkischen Völkern eine von Nomaden iranischer Abstammung übernommene Innovation (Gogolev 1993:34).

Auch in der Folklore der Jenissejer und der südsibirischen Türken gibt es eine ganze Reihe von ähnlichen Motiven (Nikolaev 1985:102–109). Von besonderem Interesse ist das chakassische Epos „Abynži" (Kadyšev 1951), welches inhaltlich an die ketisch-jugischen *Alba*-Mythen erinnert und nach R. V. Nikolaev zusammen mit diesen Mythen auf eine gemeinsame Quelle zurückgeführt werden kann. Auszuschliessen ist es nicht, obwohl es sich dabei auch um Wandermotive handeln könnte.

Eine viel zuverlässigere Quelle, um uralte interethnische Kontakte, Urverwandschaft oder auch ursprüngliches ethnisches Substratum zu ermitteln, stellt jedenfalls der Wortschatz dar. Im gegebenen Fall sind jene Wortparallelen in den jenissejischen und südsibirischen türkischen Sprachen von Interesse, die auf ältere Zeiten zurückgehen und in der Regel den Grundwortschatz betreffen, als uralte Bezeichnungen auf dem Gebiet des mesolithischen geistigen und materiellen Kulturgutes betrachtet werden können.[3] So zeugen vielleicht von einem jenissejischen Substratum in der südsibirischen türkischen Welt einige jenissejisch-türkische Parallelen in Butanaev 1992 und 2004. Dabei handelt es sich vor allem um Bezeichnungen von Objekten der geographisch-klimatischen Umgebung und Bezeichnungen auf dem Gebiet der Flora und Fauna, die bei der einheimischen Bevölkerung Südsibiriens seit jeher im Gebrauch waren und sich in der Sprache erhalten konnten:

[3] Wie bekannt, lässt sich für die protojenissejische Zeit eine mesolithische Kultur von Jägern, Fischern und Sammlern rekonstruieren (Werner 2006).

jenis. **qaˀj* 'steiles Ufer', 'Berg', ket. *qaˀj*, jug. *χaˀj* id.; ass. *ena-haj* 'Wald' < *ena* 'Fichten' + *haj*, das an ket. *qaˀj*, jug. *χaˀj* erinnert; in Kostjakov 1985:84 werden dazu folgende türk. Parallelen vermutet: atü. *qaja*, tof. *haja*, alt. *kaja*, tuv. chak. jak. *xaja*, azer. *gaja*, ttü. *kaγa*, tat. *kɨja*, bašk. *qaja*, uzb. *qoja*, turkm. *gaja* 'Felsen', 'Klippe'; da die türkischen Wörter nur geringen Unterschied voneinander aufweisen, könnte es sich um eine alte Entlehnung aus den Jenissej-Sprachen handeln;

jenis. **tʰoqpɯl*, ket. *tɔqpɯl* / *tɔqpul*, jug. *tɔχpɯl* 'Schnee auf einem Baumzweig' (ein Kompositum < **tʰoq* ? + **pʰɯl* 'Anhäufung'); chak. *tikper* id.;

jenis. **dakəj*, kot. (C) *takai* / *tagai*, ass. (M, W, VW) *tagaj* / *takaj* 'Kopf', ar. (H) *kedake* id. (< *ke* ? + *dake* 'Kopf'); chak. *tigej*, alt. *tegej*, tuv. *tej* 'Gipfel', 'Kuppe';

jenis. **seˀs* / **čeˀt* 'Lärche'; ket. *sɛˀs*, jug. *sɛˀs*, ar. (M, W, Kl) *tʲšit* / *čit*, ass. (M, W, Kl) *šet* / *čet* (Kl), kot. (M, W, Kl) *šet*, kot. (C) *šêt* (pl. *šat*) id.; chak. *čet* / *sit*, alt. tuv. *šet* 'kleine Lärche';

jenis. **sulpʰi* 'eine Art von Beeren'; kot. (C) *šulpi* 'Beere', ar. (M, W, H) *šulpʲa* 'Beere', 'Erdbeere', ar. *šulbe* 'Ebereschenbeere', *konšulbe* 'Preiselbeere'; chak. *sobe* 'Eberesche';

jenis. **suj-oksə* / **sujəŋ-oksə* 'Erle' < **suj-* (pl. **sujəŋ-* ?) + **oksə* 'Baum'; ket. *sujiŋoks*, jug. *sujiŋoksɯ* id. (vgl. *suj-* in ket. *sujd* 'Kopftuch' < *suj-* + *dɯˀ* 'Mütze'; ket *sujat* 'Hemd, Kleid' < *suj-* + *qaˀt* 'Oberbekleidung'; jug. *suŋgulap* 'Lappen' < *suiŋ* + *gu* + *laˀp* 'Stück'); imb. (M) *sujuŋ*, ket. (Tret'jakov) *soiga*, ar. (H) *šujg[i]n* 'Erle'; chak. *sug agazɨ* id.;

jenis. **im*, ket. *i·m*, jug. *im*, kot. (C) *îm*, ar. (H) *im* 'Zedernnüsse'; ket. *emdɔ:*, jug. *emdʲou* 'Vorräte an Nüssen anlegen'; jug. *ɛmgou* 'Nusskern'; chak. dial. *ɛmin* 'Nusskern';

kot. (C) *topâk* / *topâx* 'Baummoos'; chak. dial. *tabɨj* id.;

ket. *taγɯnna ɛ:lʲ*, jug. *tagɯnna sammɯ* 'Moosbeeren', wörtl. 'Beeren der Kraniche'; vgl. die chakassische Lehnübersetzung *turna azɨ* 'Moosbeeren', wörtl. 'Beeren der Kraniche';

jenis. **qalʲəŋ*, ket. *qalʲeŋ*, jug. *χalʲiŋ* 'Möwe'; chak. dial. *xajlax* id.;

ket. *togdulʲta* / *togdulʲt* 'eine Art kleiner Waldvögel'; chak. dial. *toŋdolbus* 'kleiner Schlammläufer';

jug. *čičik*, kot. (C) *čičipa* 'Bachstelze', kot. (H) *čičiba* 'Meise'; chak. *čičigej* 'Meise' (vgl. auch selk. *čičik* 'Vöglein' (< jug.);

Wie bekannt, widerspiegelt der jenissejische Volkskalender (die Monatsnamen) eine sesonal organisierte Wirtschaftsweise von Jägern, Fischern und Sammlern. Solch einen Volkskalender gab es vermutlich auch bei der einheimischen Bevölkerung Südsibiriens vor der türkischen Expansion, und manche traditionellen Monatsbezeichnungen trifft man immer noch in den südsibirischen Türksprachen als Lehnübersetzungen aus dem Jenissejischen, obwohl die Bevölkerung hier meist die Viehzucht und den Ackerbau betreibt, vgl.:

jenis. *_diˀqip_, ket. _di·ɤɯp_, jug. _di·χep_ 'März', wörtl. 'Adlermonat' < _diˀ_ 'Adler' + ket. _qi·p_, jug. _χep_ 'Monat'; chak. dial. _xuzurγul ajɨ_ 'Februar', wörtl. 'Adlermonat';

jenis. *_kopʰənqip_, ket. _kɔ:nɯp_, jug. _kɔfɯnp_ / _kʌfɯnχep_ 'April', wörtl. 'Monat der Erdeichhörnchen' < _kɔˀp_, pl. ket. _kɔ:n_, jug. _kɔfɯn_ 'Erdeichhörnchen' + ket. _qi·p_, jug. _χep_ 'Monat'; chak. dial. _köpik ajɨ_ 'März', wörtl. 'Monat des Erdeichhörnchens'.

Auch Bezeichnungen einiger Fortbewegungsmittel, Werkzeuge und Jagdwaffen, die an die Zeit der traditionellen Wirtschaftsweise der uralten einheimischen Bevölkerung Südsibiriens erinnern, haben sich in den Sprachen der südsibirischen Türken erhalten:

jenis. *_sogəm_, ket. jug. _sɔ:m_, pl. _sɔ:mɯŋ_, imb. (M) _sogomoŋ_ (pl.) 'Pfeil mit stumpfer Spitze' (russ. _томáр_); chak. _sogam_ 'Pfeil';

jenis. *_sogəʎ_ / *_čogəʎ_ 'Polarschlitten'; ket. _su:l_, jug. _soul_, kot. (C) _čugar_ / _čukar_, ass. (M, W, Kl) _čegar_ / _čogar_, ar. (M, W, Kl) _šal_, pump. (W) _cel_ id.; chak. _soor_, tof. _šɛger_, čul.-türk. _cuur_ / _čoor_ 'Schlitten';

jenis. *_a:jpʰʌŋ_ 'Schleppnetz', jug. _ajfʌŋ_ id. < _aʰ:j_ 'Sack (mittlerer Teil eines Fischernetzes)' + _fʌˀŋ_ 'Fischernetz'; ket. _ajeŋ_ id. < _aj_ 'Sack' + _hʌˀŋ_ 'Fischernetz'; chak. dial. _ajbuŋ_ id.;

jenis. *_daˀʎ_ 'Sehne', ket. _daˀl_, jug. _daˀr_, kot. (C) _tal_ 'Sehne', 'Faden'; vgl. tü. _täl_ 'Faser', 'Faden', 'Draht';

ket. _abɯl_ 'Stock (mit spitzem Ende für Ausgrabung von Wurzelwerk?)' < _a_ (?) + _bu·l_ 'Fuss' (vgl. eine analoge jenis. Bildung: ket. _atis_, jug. _ačis_, kot. C _ašiš_ 'Feile' < _a_ ? + ket. _tɯˀs_, jug. _čɯˀs_, kot. (C) _šiš_ 'Stein'); chak. _abɨl_ 'Werkzeug (eine Art Hacke) für die Bearbeitung (Auflockerung) der Erde';

jenis. *_quˀs_ 'Birkenrindezelt', ket. _quˀs_, jug. _χuˀs_, kot. (Castrén) _hûš_ id.; ar. (Kl) _hu_ / _kus_ (Str), ass. (M, Kl, W, VW) _huš_ / _xɯš_ (Kl), kot. (M, Kl, W, VW, H) _guš_ / _xuš_, pump. _hu-kút_ 'Haus', ar. (H) _ajbikʲus_ 'mein Haus' (< _aj_ + _bi_ 'mein' + _kʲus_ < *_quˀs_ 'Zelt'); atürk. *_koš_ / *_kuš_ 'Zeltlager'; diese Parallele könnte zu derselben Wortgruppe gerechnet werden, da sich das Zelt auf das jenissejische mesolithische materielle Kulturgut bezieht, wenn man in diesem Fall tatsächlich von Kognaten ausgehen kann (s. Stachowski 1997/2:231).

Obwohl die einheimische Urbevölkerung ihre Muttersprache (das Jenissejische) aufgegeben und zum Türkischen übergegangen war, blieben viele Flussnamen in ihrer ursprünglichen jenissejischen Form im Gebrauch, und zwar die Toponyme auf *-ses*, *-sas*, *-zes*, *-zas* (vgl. ket. *se·s*, jug. *ses* 'Fluss') und *-tet*, *-tat*, *-det*, *-dat* (vgl. pump. *tet*, *tat* 'Fluss'), z.B. *Tojzas*, *Torzas*, *Olbynzas*, *Kezes*, *Kajzas*, *Kandat*, *Tüchtet*, *Altat*, *Turtat*, *Bogdat* u.a. Dies gilt auch für Ethnonyme wie chak. *Ara* / *Aara* (vgl. jenis. *Arin*), chak. *Xajdɨŋ* < jenis. *χaˀj* 'steiles Flussufer', 'Berg' + *deˀŋ* 'Menschen', 'Leute' > 'Volk', vgl. altjug. *χajbaŋ*[*dʲɛˀŋ*] 'Volk vom Dupčes-Fluss', wörtl. 'Volk (*dʲɛˀŋ*) vom Ort (*baˀŋ*) des steilen Flussufers (*χaˀj*). Jenissejischer Herkunft könnte auch das Ethnonym kirg. *želdeŋ*, chak. *čildeg* sein (*-deŋ*, *-deg* erinnern eindeutig an ket. *dɛˀŋ*, jug. *dʲɛˀŋ* 'Leute', 'Volk'). Ausserdem will man den Namen der Göttin des Südens ket. *Tɔmam* < *Tɔm* / *Tɔma* + *am* 'Mutter' mit *Tuma* / *Tuba* in der Region des Sajan-Altai-Gebirges verbinden.

In Werner 2007:160 habe ich darauf hingewiesen, dass die Entlehnungsrichtung (jenissejisch > türkisch oder türkisch > jenissejisch) nicht immer leicht festzustellen sei, insbesondere, wenn sich für die entsprechenden jenissejischen Wörter eine protojenissejische Form rekonstruieren lässt. Wie nun bekannt, ist in der Regel der meiste Kulturwortschatz in den Jenissej-Sprachen der späteren Zeit türkischer Herkunft. Dabei handelt es sich auch um einige sozial-politische Termini wie z.B. jenis. **qan* 'Khan'; ket. *qa·n* (pl. *qanáŋ* / *qana:ŋ*), jug. *χan* (pl. *χane:ŋ*) id.; kot. (Castrén 1858:205) *kan* (pl. *kânáŋ*) 'Fürst' < türk. *qân*, *qan* 'Fürst' (vgl. alt. *kaan*, tuv. *xaan*, chak. *xan*, kirg. *kan* 'Khan', 'Kaiser'. Eine hybride Form stellt dagegen höchstwahrscheinlich der allgemein bekannte türk.-mong. Terminus *qaγan* 'Khan', 'Kaiser', wörtl. 'Grosser Khan' dar < **qaˀ-qan* / **qeˀ-qan* < jenis. **qaˀ* / **qɛˀ* 'gross' + **qan* (< türk. *qan*) 'Khan'.[4] Dass hier das erste Kompositionsglied tatsächlich ein jenissejisches Wort ist, beweist die semantische Vielfalt des jenis. Wortes **qa* / **qe* (sket. *qœ̀*, mket. *qɛˀ*, jug. *χɛˀ*) 'gross', vgl.:

1) mket. *qɛˀ*, jug. *χɛˀ* 'gross' > 'allgemein': SK *qœren* (pl. *qœrenaŋ*) 'Fest' < *qœ* 'gross' + *den* / *ren* 'Tag' / 'Tagesanbruch' (vgl. *inden* / *indin* 'es wird Tag'); mket. *qœden* / *q́ɛden* (pl. *qœdeneŋ* / *q́ɛdeneŋ*), jug. *χɛ́dʲi·n* / *χɛdʲi:n* (pl. *χɛ́dʲi·nɯŋ*) id. < *χɛˀ* 'gross' + *di:n* 'Tag' / 'Taganbruch';

[4] S. Vovin 2007:184: „qaγan can be traced back to Xiongnu and Yeniseian".

2) mket. *qεˀ*, jug. *χεˀ* 'gross' > 'universell': sket. *qæ̀ e·s* 'Welt', 'Universum', wörtl. 'grosser Himmel (Gott)'; jug. *χεˀ es* id.;
3) mket. *qεˀ*, jug. *χεˀ* 'gross' > 'sehr': sket. *qæ̀ ɔnaŋ* 'sehr viele', sket. *qæ̀ sulam*, jug. *χεˀ surbε*^{h}*:s* 'purpurrot', wörtl. 'sehr rot';
4) mket. *qεˀ*, jug. *χεˀ* 'gross' > 'der ältere / der älteste': sket. *qæ̀ bisep* 'der älteste Bruder / die älteste Schwester', sket. *qæ̀ hɨˀp*, Yugh *χεˀ fɨˀp* 'der älteste Sohn';
5) mket. *qεˀ*, jug. *χεˀ* 'gross' > 'alt': ket. *qœʁim* 'alte Frau', *qœγet* 'alter Mann', *qœŋdεŋ* 'alte Leute'; jug. *χa*^{h}*:m* 'alte Frau' / 'Grossmutter' < *χεˀ* 'gross' (> 'alt') + *χem* 'Frau' oder *am* 'Mutter'; jug. *χačet* / *χačit* 'alter Ehemann' < *χεˀ* 'gross' (> 'alt') + *čet* 'Ehemann';
6) mket. *qεˀ*, jug. *χεˀ* 'gross' > 'Gross-': sket. *qæ̀ a·m* 'Grossmutter', *qæ̀ qima* 'Urgrossmutter', *qæ̀ qi·p* 'Urgrossvater';
7) mket. *qεˀ*, jug. *χεˀ* 'gross' > 'Haupt / Vorgesetzter / Chef': sket. *qæ̀s*, jug. *χε*^{h}*:si* 'Chef' < sket. *qæ̀*, jug. *χεˀ* 'gross' + *-s* / *-si* (suff.);
8) mket. *qεˀ*, jug. *χεˀ* 'gross' > 'Haupt' / 'Herrscher': dem sket. *qæ̀s*, jug. *χε*^{h}*:si* entspricht also **qaˀ-qan* 'grosser / grösster Khan' > *qaγan* id. (Vovin 2007:184);

und türk. *qapγan* 'grosser Khan' kann ebenfalls auf jenis. (ket.) *qip-* / *qep-* 'Grossvater' oder 'ältester Verwandter väterlicherseits' (s. die *qip*-Gruppe von Verwandten in Werner 2006:78–81) + *qan* 'Khan' zurückgeführt werden (über andere Deutungen dieses Terminus von D. Sinor und H.H. Schraeder als Intensivum oder eine Entlehnung des parthischen *kav* 'König' s. Altheim 1969:207–212).

Vielleicht können auch weitere jenissejische Entlehnungen dieser Art in den türkischen Sprachen vorkommen; man denke z.B. an

atürk. *tengrí* / *tengerí* 'Himmel' / 'Gott', azer. *tanri* id., jak. *tanger* / *tangara* 'Himmel' / 'Gott' oder auch 'guter Geist', 'Ikone'; chak. (kač.) *tegír* / *tigír* / *ter* 'Himmel', *tigir-taux* 'Opfer dem Himmel', chak. (kyz.) *tɨgɨr* 'Himmel', šor. *tegri* 'Himmel', čul.-türk. *tengri* 'Himmel', tom.-türk. *tengri* 'Gott', kirg. *tengri* 'Gott', kkal. *tengri* 'Gott', ttü. *tangrɨ* 'Gott', karaim. *ten'ri* / *tanrɨ*, *tandri*, *tεnri* / *tan'ri* 'Gott', savir. *tengri* 'Gott des Himmels' und amo. *tengri* 'Himmel' / 'Gott', mo. *tεngεr* / *tanger* 'Himmel' / 'Wetter', burj. *tεngεri* / *tεngri*, kalm. *tεngεr* 'Himmel', ewenk. *taŋara*, lamut. *taŋara* 'Gott', 'Ikone', sol. *teŋer* 'Himmel' < jenis. **tiŋgʌλ* / **tiŋgʌl*^{j} 'hoch', ket. *tiŋgal*, jug. *tɨŋgɨl*, pump. *tokar-du* id. (Georg 2001:83–100);

atürk. (Starostin u.a. 2003:501)**ēl* 'peace, people, country' (?), (Sevortjan 1974:339–343) tü. *êl* / *el*, *īl* / *il* < *e̥l* / **ē̥l* 1. 'Volk', 2. 'Leute' (allgemeiner Begriff), 3. 'Gesellschaft', 4. 'Stamm' (später > 'Stammesverband'), 5. 'Staat' (auch 'Gouvernement', 'Siedlung', 'Dorf'), 6. 'Macht', 'Herrschaft', 7. 'Land' (auch 'Heimat', 'Seite', 'Welt'), 8. '(Bienen)-Schwarm', 9. 'Dorfgesellschft' (russ. > *мир*), 10. 'Heer'; vgl. jenis. **el-* / **il-* 'zur irdischen Welt gehörig': ket. *ilʲ-baŋ* 1. 'Universum' > 2. 'Welt' > 3. 'irdische Welt'; *ilʲ-dʌq* 'Leben als Daseinsform' (auf Erden oder einem anderen Planeten); ar. *ilʲ-qoj* / *ilʲ-koj* 'Stern' (vgl. ket. *qʌˀ* 'Stern'); ket. *ilʲ-get* 'Mensch der irdischen Welt' (vgl. ket. jug. *kɛˀt* 'Mensch'), *ilʲlʲam* 'Frau der irdischen Welt' (< *ilʲ-* + *qi·m* 'Frau'), *ilʲ-deŋ* 'Menschen der irdischen Welt' (vgl. ket. *dɛˀŋ* 'Menschen', 'Leute'), *ilʲ-asselʲ* 'Tier der irdischen Welt' (vgl. ket. *asselʲ* 'wildes Tier'); ar. *il-čep* 'Hund' (vgl. ket. *ti·p*, jug. *či·p* 'Hund');[5]

atürk. *qut* 1. 'Seele', 2. 'Lebenskraft', 3. 'Geist', 4. 'Glück, Wonne'; *qut qolun-* 'ein Gebet verrichten', 'flehentlich um glückliches Wiederaufleben, Wonne und Würde bitten' (über den sakralen Charakter und die Bedeutung dieses türk. Wortes sieh insbesondere Róna-Tas 1987:40 ff.); vgl. jenis. **quˀədʲ(ə)* / **quˀəd(ə)*, ket. (Donner 1955:70) *qût* 1. 'der erste „grosse" Mensch', 2. der wichtigste Hilfsgeist eines Schamanen'; ket. *qutn*, jug. *χutn* (mit der *n*-Erweiterung) 'Brustlatz eines Schamanen'; ket. *qutqat*, jug. *χutʲχat* 'Schamanenmantel' (< ket. *qut-* + *qaˀt* 'Pelzmantel', jug. *χutʲ-* + *χaˀt* 'Pelzmantel'); sket. *qut*, nket. *qu·t* / *qu:t*, jug. *χuʰ:tʲ* 'Schamanieren', ket. *sɛnaŋda qu:t* 'Schamanieren des Schamanen'; ket. *dije-ʁut* / *dij-ʁut* 'ich schamaniere', *da-qut-qirit* 'sie lässt mich schamanieren'; jug. *χudʲ-ɛsaŋ* 'um zu schamanieren';

atürk. *kün* 1. 'Sonne', 2. 'Tag': ttü. kum. *gün*, chal. *kin*, *kün*, tat. *kön*, tuv. tof. *xün*, čuv. *kon* usw., nach Starostin u.a. 2003:553 < atürk. **gün(el)* / **gü-ńal* 'sun', 'day' mit weiteren Parallelen; vgl. jenis. **kʌˀn* 'hell', ket. jug. *kʌˀn* 'hell'; kot. *han-* in *hannačeen* 'Arinen', wörtl. 'helle Menschen'; kot. *-kan-* in *tɨ-kan-a* 'es ist hell', ass. *-gan-* / *-kan-* in *tɨ-kan-tu* 'er ist hell', *tɨ-gan-a* 'es ist hell'; vgl. auch ket. jug. *kə·n*, kot. (C) *kinig* / *kinîx* 'Morgenröte' < ket. *kʌˀn* 'hell' + *iˀ* 'Tag', kot. *kin-* 'hell' + *îg* / *îx* 'Tag'; ket. *kʌn-ej* 'leuchten'.

Aus dieser Sicht scheinen einige vermutliche türkische Entlehnungen in den Jenissej-Sprachen in Timonina 1986:74–77 umstritten zu bleiben:

[5] Zur Begründung der jenissejischen Urquelle siehe die Erläuterung in Werner 2007:161.

jenis. **kɯˀt* ‘Fett’, ket., jug. *kɯˀt* id., imb. *kɯ:t* ‘Butter’, ‘Fett’ (ob kot. *ki:r* ‘Fett’ damit verbunden ist, bleibt fraglich) < alt. tuv. *xir*, chak. jak. kirg. *Kir* ‘Schmutz’;

jenis. **al* / **a·l* / **a:l*, ket. *a·l* / *a:l* ‘Fleischbrühe’, ‘Fischsuppe’ < ket. *a·* (Yugh *a·p*) ‘heiss’ + *u·l* ‘Wasser’ < türk. (alt. schor. koib. *ül*, ujg. *jel*, jak. *γөl* ‘feucht’, ‘nass’; vgl.mong. kalm. *öl* ‘Nahrung’;

jenis. **saˀλ* ‘Schneide’, ket. *saˀl*, jug. *saˀr*, kot. (Castrén) *šal* id. < atürk. aujg. *čal-* ‘schlagen’, kirg. *čal-* ‘schlachten’ (vgl. mong. *čali* ‘Schneide’);

jenis. **qam* ‘Pfeil’, ket. *qa·m*, jug. *χam*, kot. (Castrén) *xem* / *qem* id. < kirg. *kɯma* ‘Speerspitze’;

jenis. **qap*^{h} / **qep*^{h} ‘Boot aus Birkenrinde’, ket. *qap* / *qaˀp*, jug. *χap* / *χaˀp* id., kot. (Castrén) *xep* / *xêp* / *qep*, ‘Boot’, ass. (M) *xaip* id., ass. (W, F, Kl) *xaip* / *kep*, ar. (VW) *l*^{j}*ulap* (< *l*^{j}*ul-χap*) ‘Schiff’ < türk. (alt. *keme*, tuv. *xeme*, kumand. *kebe*, *keve*, *keme*, *kibe*) ‘Boot’.

Dagegen hat man es, wie erwähnt, in den Jenissej-Sprachen im Falle fast aller späteren Innovationen auf dem Gebiet der materiellen Kultur, insbesondere auf dem Gebiet der Landwirtschaft, Viehzucht, Hüttenkunde mit türkischen Entlehnungen zu tun (Timonina 1978; 1986; Stachowski 1996; 1997; 2004; vgl. auch Bouda 1957:75–78). Es handelt sich vor allem um die Sprachen jener Jenissejer, die im unmittelbaren Kontakt mit den südsibirischen türkischen Völkern waren, und zwar um die Arinen, Assanen, Kotten und Pumpokoler.

Auf dem Gebiet der Landwirtschaft handelt es sich um Bezeichnungen von einigen Getreidearten, von Mehl und Brot:

ar. *arba* ‘Gerste’, ass. *arpá*, kot. *arba* / *áriš* id.; vgl. ar. *čarba* ‘Getreide’, ‘Roggen’ (vgl. alt., kumand. *arba*, kirg. *arpa* ‘Gerste’);

ar. *sulu* ‘Hafer’, ass. *šulí*, kot. (Castrén) *šuli* / *šul*^{j}*e* / *šul*^{j}*i*, pl. *šulaŋ*, kojb. (Castrén) *šulu* id. (vgl. chak. *sula*, tuv. *sula*, kumand. *suli* / *sula* id.);

kot. (Castrén) *âreš* (pl. *âretn*) ‘Roggen’, ass. *aríš* id., kot. (18. Jh.) *aríš* ‘Weizen’, pump. *oros*^{j}, koib. (Castrén) *âreš* ‘Roggen’ (vgl. alt. *ariš*, chak. *aris*, kumand. *ariš* id.);

ket., jug. *tállin* / *tàlín* ‘Mehl’, kot. *tálgan* / *talkan*, ass. *talkán*, imb. (18. Jh.) *tálan* / *tálgat*, jenis. **talkən* id.; vgl atürk. *talqan* ‘Mehl’, tof. *dalhan*, tuv. *dalgan*, alt. *talkan*, chak. *talγan* ‘Hafermehl’, kumand. *talgan* ‘Gerstenmehl’ (Timonina 1978);

neben ket. *naˀn* ‘Brot’, jug. *n*^{j}*εˀn*^{j}, imb. (18. Jh.) *na:n* / *nän* / *nan*^{j} id., ein Iranismus, der über die uralischen Sprachen in die jenissejischen kam (Stachowski 1997/2:237), gibt es auch eine Entlehnung aus den türkischen Sprachen: kot. (Castrén) *itpak* / *iptak*, pl. *itpakŋ* / *iptakŋ* ‘Brot’, kojb. (Castrén) *ippäk*, ar. *itp'ák* / *itpák* / *itpek*, ass. *itpák* id., vgl. schor. *itpak*, alt. *ötpök*, kumand. *ɛtpek* id. (Timonina 1978);

auch ket. *saban*, kot. *šaban* ‘Pflug’, kot. *šabančaŋ* ‘ackern’, *šabančaŋâkŋ* / *šabančanthâkŋ* ‘ich ackere’, prät. *šabančaŋolôkŋ* ist eine türk. Entlehnung (vgl. atürk. *saban* ‘ploughing ox-team’, ‘ploughing’).

Während die Terminologie der Pferdezucht in den Jenissej-Sprachen türkischer Herkunft ist (Timonina 1978), scheint das Wort für „Pferd“ eine sehr frühe Entlehnung aus einer vortürkischen Quelle zu sein (jenis. **kuˀs* / **kuˀt* ‘Pferd’, jug. *kuˀs*, kot. *huš*, ar. *qus* / *kus*, ass. *huš* / *hɨš*, pump. *kut* id.), und idg. **ek̂(ʰ)u̯os* (lat. *equus*) ‘Pferd’ ist nach Gamkrelidse / Ivanov 1984/2:561 als Quelle nicht auszuschliessen. Dies betrifft auch das jenis. Wort für „Kuh“ (jenis. **tʰigə*, kot. *tʰigä* / *tʰiˀä*, ar. *t'u:ja*, ass. *tɨg* / *tɨk*, kot. in Helimski 1986 *tɨg* id.), das zwar an atürk. *tekä* ‘Ziegenbock’, mong. *tex* ‘Bergbock’ erinnert, aber vielleicht doch, wie in Gamkrelidze / Ivanov 1984/II: 586 vermutet, als alter Migrationsterminus betrachtet werden kann. Zweifellose türkische Entlehnungen sind dagegen folgende Bezeichnungen von Haustieren:

kot. (Castrén) *askar*, ar. (M, W, Kl) *askɨr*, ass. (M, W, Kl) *askir* / *askɨr* (Kl), kot. (M, W, Kl) *askɨ́r*, kot. (H) *askɨr* ‘Hengst’; vgl. kam. (Castrén) *askár;* nach Timonina 1978/3:8 < atürk. *aδγïr*, *adγïr*, *ajγïr* (kumand. *ajgɨr*, tuv. *askɨr*, chak. *asxɨr*, tat. *asqɨr*) id.;

kot. (Castrén) *boga*, ar. (M, Kl, W) *bugá*, ass. (M, Kl, W) *šar* / *boka* (Kl) ‘Stier’; nach Timonina 1978/3 < atürk. *buqa*, alt. *buka*, tuv., tat., turkm. *buga*, kumand. *buga*, *puga* id.;

kot. (M, W, Kl) *tabat*, ass. (M, Kl, W) *tabát* / *tapat* (Kl), ar. (M, Kl, W) *tebé* ‘Kamel’; nach Timonina 1978/3:9 und Stachowski 1996/1:107 < tuv. *tävä*, chak. *tibä*, tof. *tɛbé*, jak. *taba* id.;

kot. (Castrén) *koi*, koib. (Castrén) *koi*, kot. (M, W, Kl, H) *koj*, ass. (M, W, Kl) *koj* / *kaj* (Kl) ‘Schaf’; vgl. kot. (Castrén) *ig koi* ‘Widder’, ass. (M, Kl, W) *koj* / *ukkoj* (Kl), kot. (H) *koaskir* ‘Schafbock’ (< *koj* ‘Schaf’ + *askir* ‘Hengst’), kot. (Castrén) *pʰeŋe koi* / *feŋe koi* ‘Schaf (Weibchen)‘; nach Timonina 1978/3:8 < atürk. *qoj*, chak., tub. *xoj*, alt., kirg. *koj*, kas. *qoj* id.;

kot. (Castrén) *šoška*, salb. (Castrén) *šoška*, koib. (Castrén) *soska*, ar. (H) *šoška;* ‘Schwein’; nach Timonina 1978/3:8 < türk. *čočuq*, chak. *sosxa*, kumand. *čočka* id.

Auch alle Bezeichnungen von Metallen sind in den Jenissej-Sprachen türkische Entlehnungen (Werner 2006: 166–167) mit nur einer Ausnahme – der Bezeichnung für „Eisen“:

1) jenis. **egə*, ket. *e·*, jug. *e;* imb. (M) *e* / *eg* (W), ost. (M) *ej*, pump. (W) *ag*, eed-šeš (Mes) *ɨg* ‘Eisen’, vgl. auch ket. *eγ* / *eγa*, jug. *ega* ‘eisern’;
2) jenis. **tʰep*, kot. (Castrén) *tʰip*, ar. (M, W, H) *tep* / *ten* (Str), ass. (M, W) *tip*, kot. (M, W, H) *tip*, koib. (Castrén) *tîmir* ‘Eisen’, vgl. ket., jug. *atəp* ‘Zange’ < *a* < *e* ‘Eisen’ + *təp* ‘Eisen’, kot. (Castrén) *ištʰip* 1. ‘eiserner Nagel’, 2. ‘Schmiedezange’ < *iš* + *tʰip*.

Nach einer ketischen Überlieferung war der erste ketische Schmied ein Fremdling; nachdem er den Einheimischen sein Handwerk beibrachte, ging er nach Süden (Anučin 1914:16). Hier könnte es sich um eine idg. Quelle handeln.

Literatur

Alekseenko, Evgenija A. (1967): *Kety. Istoriko-etnografičeskie očerki.* Nauka, Leningrad.

Altheim, Franz (1969): *Geschichte der Hunnen*, Bd. 1, 2. Aufl., Berlin (1. Aufl. 1959).

Anučin, Vasilij I. (1914): Očerk šamanstva u enisejskich ostjakov. – *Sbornik muzeja antropologii i etnografii*, 2/2. Sankt-Peterburg.

Bouda, Karl (1957): Die Sprache der Jenissejer: Genealogische und morphologische Untersuchungen. – *Anthropos* 52/1–2:65–134.

Butanaev, Viktor Ja. (1992): Chakassko-ketskie leksičeskie paralleli. – *Journal de la Société Finno-Ougrienne* 84; Helsinki 1992:21–29.

Butanaev, Viktor Ja. (2004): Linguistic Reflections of Xakas Ethnohistory. – *Languages and Prehistory of Central Siberia.* John Benjamins Publishing Company. Amsterdam–Philadelphia: 215–233.

Castrén, Matthias A. (1858): *Versuch einer jenissei-ostjakischen und kottischen Sprachlehre nebst Wörterverzeichnissen aus den genannten Sprachen.* Sankt Petersburg.

Donner, Kai (1955): *Ketica. Materialien aus dem Ketischen oder Jenissei-Ostjakischen* (hrsg. von A. J. Joki). = *Mémoires de la Société Finno-ougrienne* 108. Helsinki.

Findeisen, Hans (1929): *Reisen und Forschungen in Nordsibirien 1927–1928.* Berlin.

Gamkrelidze, Tamaz V. / Ivanov, Vjačeslav Vs. (1984): *Indoevropejskij jazyk i indoevropejcy*, I–II, Izdatel'stvo Tbilisskogo universiteta, Tbilisi.

Georg, Stefan (2001): Türkisch / mongolisch *tengri* 'Himmel, Gott' und seine Herkunft. – *Studia Etymologica Cracoviensia* 6. Kraków:83–100.

Gogolev, A. I. (1993): *Jakuty. Problemy etnogeneza i formirovanija kul'tury*. Jakutsk.

Gumiljov, Lev N. (1967): *Drevnie tjurki*. Moskva.

Helimski, Eugen A. (1986): Archivnye materialy XVIII v. po enisejskim jazykam. – *Paleo-aziatskie jazyki*. Nauka, Leningrad:179–212.

Ivanov, Vjačeslav Vs. / Toporov, V. N. (1969): Kommentarij k opisaniju ketskoj mifologii. – *Ketskij sbornik: Mifologija, ėtnografija, teksty*. Nauka, Moskva:148–166.

Kadyšev, S. P. (1951). *Albynži*, Chakgiz, Abakan.

Kljaštornyj, S. G. (1964): *Drevnetjurkskie runičeskie pamjatniki kak istočnik po istorii Srednej Azii*. Moskva.

Kostjakov, Michail M. (1985): Leksika, oboznačajuščaja geografičeskie objekty i absoljutnye orientiry v enisejskich jazykach. – *Leksika i grammatika jazykov Sibiri*. Barnaul 1985:80–87.

L'vova, Eleonora L. / Oktjabrskaja, Irina V. / Sagalaev, Andrej M. / Usmanova, Mar'jam S. (1988): *Tradicionnoe mirovozzrenie tjurkov Južnoj Sibiri. Prostranstvo i vremja. Veščnoj mir*. Nauka, Novosibirsk.

Nikolaev, Roman V. (1985): *Fol'klor i voprosy etničeskoj istorii ketov*. Izdatel'stvo Krasnojarskogo universiteta, Krasnojarsk.

Róna-Tas, András (1987): Materialien zur alten Religion der Türken. – *Synkretismus in den Religionen Zentralasiens. Studies in Oriental Religions* 13. Otto Harrassowitz Verlag, Wiesbaden:33–45.

Sagaster, Klaus (1998): Schamanismus. – *Theologische Realenzyklopädie (TRE)*, XXX, 1:72–76.

Sevortjan, Ervand B. (1974): *Etimologičeskij slovar' tjurkskich jazykov (obščetjurkskie i mežtjurkskie osnovy na glasnye)*. Nauka, Moskva.

Stachowski, Marek (1996): Über einige altaische Lehnwörter in den Jenissej-Sprachen. – *Studia Etymologica Cracoviensia* 1. Kraków:91–115.

Stachowski, Marek (1997): Altaistische Anmerkungen zum „Vergleichenden Wörterbuch der Jenissej-Sprachen". – *Studia Etymologica Cracoviensia* 2. Kraków:227–239.

Stachowski, Marek (2004): Anmerkungen zu einem neuen vergleichenden Wörterbuch der Jenissej-Sprachen. – *Studia Etymologica Cracoviensia* 9. Kraków:189–204.

Starostin, Sergei / Dybo, Anna / Mudrak, Oleg (2003): *Etymological Dictionary of the Altaic Languages*, 1–3. Brill, Leiden & Boston.

Timonina, Ljudmila G. (1978): Tjurkskie zaimstvovanija v kottskom jazyke. – *Sovetskaja tjurkologija*, 1978/3:7–13, Baku.

Timonina, Ljudmila G. (1986): Enisejskaja kul'turnaja leksika tjurkskogo proischoždenija. – *Issledovanija po grammatike i leksike enisejskich jazykov*. Nauka, Novosibirsk:69–79.

Vovin, Alexander (2007): Once again on the etymology of the title *qaγan*. – *Studia Etymologica Cracoviensia* 12, Kraków:177–187.

Werner, Heinrich (2006): *Die Welt der Jenissejer im Lichte des Wortschatzes (Zur Rekonstruktion der jenissejischen Protokultur)*. = *Veröffentlichungen der Societas Uralo-Altaica* 69. Harrassowitz Verlag, Wiesbaden.

Werner, Heinrich (2007): *Die Glaubensvorstellungen der Jenissejer aus der Sicht des Tengrismus*. = *Veröffentlichungen der Societas Uralo-Altaica* 73. Harrassowitz Verlag, Wiesbaden.

Studies on the Turkic World
A Festschrift for Professor St. Stachowski on the Occasion of His 80th Birthday
edited by E. Mańczak-Wohlfeld and B. Podolak, Kraków 2010: 191–197

Abdurishid Yakup (Berlin)

A New Fragment of the *Mañjuśrīnāmasaṃgīti* in Old Uyghur

0. Introduction

Mañjuśrīnāmasaṃgīti is one of the most popular and important texts of Tantric Buddhism. The text is relatively short and consists of 160 verses and a prose section. The verse part of the text, according to the Sanskrit text, starts with sixteen verses on requesting instruction and continues with six verses in reply, ten verses, plus a quarter, on the mirror-like gnosis, fourty-two verses on the gnosis of individual inspection, twenty four verses on the gnosis of equality, and ends with five verses on the gnosis of the five Tathāgatas; the next part of the text comprises various observations from the first to the sixth rounds of (discussion on) benefits, including also a mantra and an epilogue consisting of five verses; see Davidson 1981.

Altogether 44 block-printed fragments originating from a folded block-printed book present the Old Uyghur translation of the *Mañjuśrīnāmasaṃgīti*. With the exception of one fragment published in the *Uigurische Sprachdenkmäler* (Nr. 59, henceforth *Usp*) by W. Radloff, the remaining fragments are from the Berlin Turfan Collection. 39 fragments, including the fragment published in the *Usp* was edited by G. Kara and P. Zieme as Text B in BT VIII. Further 4 fragments, which were identified after the publication of BT VIII, have been investigated by G. Kara; see Kara 1981. In the course of cataloguing the woodblock-printed Old Uyghur texts in the Berlin Turfan-Collection I identified U 4286b (T III M 200) originating from the same woodblock as a parallel to the first page of the block-printed fragment

U 4713 (T III M 198) comprising two pages. A description of all fragments of the *Mañjuśrīnāmasaṃgīti* from the Berlin Turfan Collection is now available in Yakup/Knüppel 2007 (Catalogue numbers 235–272).

Besides the block-printed fragments mentioned above, some Chinese fragments of the text written in Old Uyghur script were also discovered among the fragments kept in the St. Petersburg and Berlin collections. M. Shōgaito edited six fragments housed at the Institute of Oriental Manuscripts in St. Petersburg and P. Zieme published a one leaf belonging to the Berlin Turfan collection; see Shōgaito 1995, Zieme 1996 and Elverskog 1997: 114–116. This shows that the text was read by Old Uyghur Buddhists both in the Old Uyghur translation and in the transcription of the Chinese text.

This paper presents an edition of the Berlin fragment U 4286b (T III M 200), the only known Old Uyghur fragment of the *Mañjuśrīnāmasaṃgīti* which remained unedited. As I have mentioned above, the fragment is a parallel to the first page of the block-printed fragment U 4713 (T III M 198) published in BT VIII as part of Text B. Since it contains some important elements missing on U 4713, it allows us to improve some readings of related parts of edition as Text B in BT VIII; this is especially true of several reconstructed phrases.

1. The Berliner fragment U 4286b (T III M 200)

Judging from the siglum denoting the find-site, the Berlin fragment U 4286b must have been obtained in Murtuq in the Turfan basin within the present Xinjiang Uyghur Autonomous Region of China during the Third German Turfan Expedition, which was carried out between 1906 and 1907. The fragment is badly damaged: from the first line no word fully survived, in lines 2–3 only some words that survived. The other fragments of the same block-printed text it has six lines of text. The page-width of this fragment is 12 cm, page-height is 17.2 cm, the line-spacing is 1.8 cm. Originally, the fragment must have belonged to a block-printed folded book as the other block-printed fragments of the *Mañjuśrīnāmasaṃgīti*. In the Digital Turfan Archive (DTA) it occurs as part of one image together with U 4286a, the other block-printed fragment in Old Uyghur, which actually belongs to the *Ārya-aparamitāyur-jñāna-nāma-mahāyāna-sūtra*.[1] Below is the transliteration, transcription and translation of U 4286b.

[1] See Yakup/Knüppel 2007: 184, fn. 298; A description of U 4286a is given in Yakup/Knüppel 2007: 103 (Catalogue number 111).

Transliteration

1. [ ]y' :
2. [ ]*t*ynk' : ''nt' 'wytrw
3. [ ] twrwldwrqwlwq l'r[ ]dwr
4. [ ]qws yyrtyncwk '//mys vcyr 'wyz
5. [ ] : ''cylmys ywrwnk lynqw ' q' 'wqs'ty
6. [ ]*q* lynqw' q' 'wqs'ty ywwzlwk : 'wyz

Transcription

1. [namo budaya : namo d(a)rmaya : nama sangga]ya[2] :
2. [yükünürm(ä)n urı bolmıš mančusiri bodis(a)t(a)v ku]*t*ınga : anta ötrü
3. [čoglug yalınlıg v(a)čiratari : alp][3] turuldurguluklar[ıg turul]dur-
4. [tačılarta yegi alp üč u]guš yertinčüg *u*[t]mıš(?)v(a)čir üz-
5. [ä ärklig kizläg eligi] : ačılmıš yürüng linhuaka ohšatı
6. [közlüg : ačılmıš padumlu]*g*(?) linhuaka ohšatı yüüzlüg : öz

Translation

[Namo Buddhāya! Namo dharmāya! Namo saṃghā]ya!
[I homage to the] majesty of [*Mañjuśrī* Bodhisattva who has become son:][4]
Then [the splendid resplendent Vajradhara, superb and hero] among [those who] tame those [difficult] to tame, having succeeded the [triple] world, a secret ruler[5] [possessing] a vajra, [having eyes] as opened white lotuses, having a face like [opened] lotus [of *padma*], self [...]

Notes to the text

4. [üč u]guš yertinčüg *u*[t]mıš(?): As far as I know, in Old Uyghur texts *ut-* is usually used as part of the biverb *ut- yegäd-*, which means 'to defeat' or 'to succeed', see for instance Zieme/Kara 1978, l. 875: *nizvanılıg šmnug utup yegädip* 'Man besiegt (Hend.) den Leidenschafts-Māra''; BT VII A 489: *bo buyan üzä al[ku] tınl(ı)glar šumnunı utmakları yegädmäkläri bolzun* 'Durch dieses Verdienst mögen alle Lebewesen Māra besiegen (Hend.)!'; for further examples see Erdal 1991: 490. Therefore, the reconstruction here is not secured. It should be noted,

[2] The reconstruction follows U 4713 and the readings in BT VIII, p. 91.

[3] The reconstruction follows U 4713 and the readings in BT VIII, p. 91.

[4] The text (U 4713) has *urı bolmıš*, G. Kara and P. Zieme translate it 'jung geworden'; as a parallel we find *kumārabhūtāya* 'true prince'; see Davidson 1981: 49.

[5] The text has *kizläg eligi*, this might also be translated as 'an esoteric ruler'; see Davidson 1981: 18.

however, that in *Irq Bitig* and the Karakhanid Turkic *ut-* is also used alone, governing the direct object, e.g. *yana tookuz on boš kony utmıš* 'he yet won ninety loose sheep' (Irq Bitig 29), *andag erig kim utar* 'who can beat a man like that'; see Tekin 1993: 16, Clauson 1972: 38b–39a. Although *y[egäd]miš* might also be a possible candidate, there is enough space for it.

4–5. *v(a)čir üz[ä ärklig]*: This phrase means here 'possessing a vajra' and is associated with the weapon of Vajradhara, the *vajra*; see Davidson 1981: 19, fn. 54. BT VIII B 4–5 has the reconstructed form ***včira*** *ärklig*. However, as U 4286b has *'wyz* after *v(a)čir*, we regard that the *alif* ‹'› that occurs at the beginning of the next line on U 4713 is a part of the word *üzä*, but not of *v(a)čir*, as was regarded in BT VIII B 4–5. For examples for ... *üzä ärklig* used in the meaning 'possessing ...' see Röhrborn 1977ff, 438b.

5. *ačılmıš yürüng linhuaka ohšatı*: This phrase is missing on U 4713. G. Kara and P. Zieme fill the gap with [*ačılmıš ak linhuaka ohšatı*]. The only difference is that our fragment has *yürüng* but the reconstructed text has *ak*. Note, however, that both *yürüng* and *ak* mean 'white'.

6. [*ačılmıš padumlu*]*g(?) linhuaka ohšatı yüüzlüg*: This phrase might be translated as 'having a face like [opened] lotus [of *padma*]' or 'having a face like [opened lotus], (which is) [*padma*]. Clearly, our text differs here from the reconstruction in BT VIII, which has *ačılmıš padumlug olurur orunlug* 'der einen [Sitzplatz] auf geöffnetem Lotos hat'. Perhaps the base of this reconstruction in BT VIII is the Mongolian sentence *delge-renggüi linqu-a-yin sayurintur sayuysan* 'sitting place like a fully opened (lit. enlarged) lotus' (mong. 1592, 3b). However, the Tibetan source text and another Mongolian parallel sentence of this part of text quoted also in BT VIII clearly testify to the wording on U 4286b. Thus consider the parallel phrases in the Mongolian and Tibetan texts:

Mongolian:	*delgereg linqu-a metü niyur-du* (BD 2a) 'face like an opened lotos'
Tibetan:	*pad-ma rab-tu rgyas-pa'i žal* (tib. Kanjur, Rgyud Ka 1) 'face like a fully opened lotos'

The Sanskrit text has a slightly different *protphullakamalānanaḥ* 'his face like a pale red lotus in bloom'; see Davidson 1981: 19, 49.

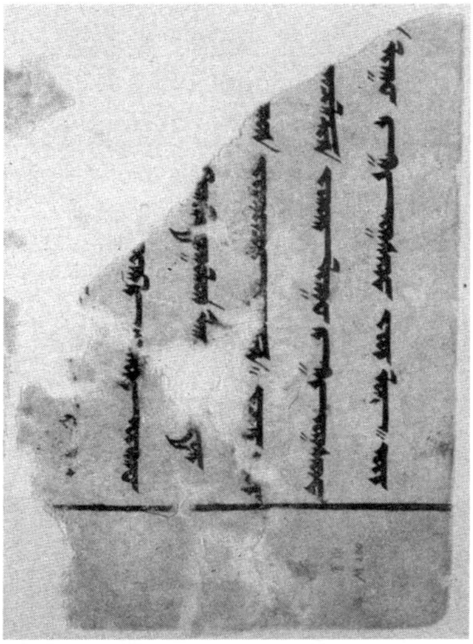

U 4286b (T III M 200): Depositum der BERLIN-BRANDENBURGISCHEN AKADEMIE DER WISSENSCHAFTEN in der STAATSBIBLIOTHEK ZU BERLIN – Preußischer Kulturbesitz Orientabteilung

2. Reconstructed parts of U 4713 (T III M 198) and U 4286b (T III M 200)

Many factors, e.g. the same number of lines of text, the same line spacing, the same page-width and the same marginal-lines etc. allows us to consider 4713 and U 4286b as prints from the same block, that is they contain the same text. Therefore, the damaged parts of both fragments might be reconstructed on the basis of both of them. The reconstructed parts of U 4286b in our transcription, as we have mentioned, are based upon the parallel lines of U 4713. This enabled us to reconstruct the missing parts of our fragment rather surely. The following table enables us to more clearly show some differences between the reconstructed parts of the two fragments.

U 4713	U 4286b
nama **sanggaya**	[nama sangga]ya
mančusiri bodis(a)t(a)v kut**ınga**	[mančusiri bodis(a)t(a)v ku]*t*ınga
alp **turuldurguluklarıg turuldur**	[alp] turuldurguluklar[ıg turul]dur

U 4713	U 4286b
ačılmıš ak linhuaka ohšatı közlüg	ačılmıš yürüng linhuaka ohšatı [közlüg]
ačılmıš padum**lug olurur orunlug**	[ačılmıš padumlu]*g*(?) linhuaka ohšatı yüüzlüg

Table 1: A comparison of the reconstructed parts of U 4713 and U 4286b6

3. References

Clauson, Gerard 1972. *An Etymological Dictionary of Pre-Thirteenth-Century Turkish.* Oxford: Clarendon Press.

Davidson, Ronald M. 1981. The Litany of Names of Mañjuśrī. Text and Translation of the *Mañjuśrīnāmasaṃgīti.* In: Strickmann, Michel (ed.), *Tantric and Taoist Studies in Honour of R. A. Stein.* Brüssel: Institut Belge des Hautes Études Chinoises, 1–69. (Mélanges Chinois et Bouddhiques XX.)

Elverskog, Johan 1997. *Uygur Buddhist Literature.* Turnhout: Brepols. (Silk Road Studies I.)

Erdal, Marcel 1991. *Old Turkic Word Formation. A functional approach to the lexicon.* Vols. I–II. Wiesbaden: Otto Harrassowitz. (Turcologica 7.)

Erdal, Marcel 2004. *A Grammar of Old Turkic.* Boston: Brill. (Handbook of Oriental Studies, Section 8: Uralic & Central Asian Studies 3.)

Kara, Georg 1981. Weiteres über die uigurische *Nāmasaṃgīti. Altorientalische Forschungen* 8: 227–236.

Kara, Georg and Peter Zieme 1976. *Fragmente tantrischer Werke in uigurischer Übersetzung.* Berlin: Akademie Verlag. (Schriften zur Geschichte und Kultur des alten Orients. Berliner Turfantexte VII.)

Kara, Georg and Peter Zieme 1977. *Die uigurischen Übersetzungen des Guruyogas „Tiefer Weg“ von Sa-skya Paṇḍita und der Mañjuśrīnāmasaṃgīti.* Berlin: Akademie Verlag. (Schriften zur Geschichte und Kultur des alten Orients. Berliner Turfantexte VIII).

Radloff, W. 1928. *Uigurische Sprachdenkmäler. Materialen nach dem Tode des Verfassers mit Ergänzungen von. S. Malov herausgegeben.* Leningrad: Verlag der Akademie der Wissenschaften der Union der Sozialistischen Soviet Repukliken.

[6] On U 4713 the letters in the bold type refer to the reconstructed parts.

Röhrborn, Klaus 1977ff. *Uigurisches Wörterbuch. Sprachmaterial der vorislamischen türkischen Texte aus Zentralasien.* 1–6. Wiesbaden 1977–1998.

Shōgaito, Masahiro 1995. ウイグル文字音写された漢語仏典断片について—ウイグル漢字音の研究 Uigurumoji onshasareta kango butten danpen ni tsuite—Uiguru kanjion no kenkyū [English subtitle: Chinese Buddhist texts in Uigur Script]. *Linguistic Research* 14: 65–153 + 9 plates.

Tekin, Talat 1993. *Irk Bitig, the Book of Omens.* Wiesbaden: Harrassowitz Verlag. (Turcologica 13.)

Yakup, Abdurishid and Knüppel, Michael 2007. *Alttürkische Handschriften.* 11: *Die Uigurischen Blockdrucke der Berliner Turfansammlung.* 1: *Tantrische Texte.* Stuttgart: Franz Steiner Verlag. (Verzeichnis der Orientalischen Handschriften in Deutschland 13,19.)

Zieme, Peter 1992. *Religion und Gesellschaft im Uigurischen Königreich von Qočo. Kolophone und Stifter des alttürkischen buddhistischen Schrifttums aus Zentralasien.* Opladen. (Abhandlungen der Rheinisch-Westfälischen Akademie der Wissenschaften 88.)

Zieme, Peter 1996. A fragment of the Chinese *Mañjuśrīnāmasaṃgīti* in Uigur Script from Turfan. *Studies on the Inner Asian Languages* 11: 1–14 + 2 plates.

Zieme, Peter and Kara, G. 1978: *Ein uigurisches Totenbuch. Nāropas Lehre in uigurischer Übersetzung von vier tibetischen Traktaten nach der Sammelhandschrift aus Dunhuang British Museum Or. 8212 (109).* Budapest: Akadémiai Kiadó. (Bibliotheca Orientalis Hungarica XXII.)

Studies on the Turkic World
A Festschrift for Professor St. Stachowski on the Occasion of His 80th Birthday
edited by E. Mańczak-Wohlfeld and B. Podolak, Kraków 2010: 199–210

Emine Yılmaz, Nurettin Demir (Ankara)

***Ḳıṣaṣ-ı Enbiyā*'dan. Eski Anadolu Türkçesinin Sözvarlığına Katkılar II**

Arap edebiyatının en önemli *Ḳıṣaṣ-ı Enbiyā* yazarlarından biri olan Ṣaʿlebī'nin *Kitābu ʿarāʾisiʾl-mecālis fī ḳıṣaṣiʾl-enbiyāʾ* adlı eseri değişik tarihlerde Türkçeye çevrilmiştir. Bunların en önemlilerinden biri, 14. yüzyılda, Aydınoğulları döneminde Türkçeye çevrilmiş ve Türk Dil Kurumu kütüphanesinde A 145 numara ile kayıtlı olan nüshadır. Yayına hazırlamış olduğumuz 954 sayfalık bu nüsha, Anadolu sahasındaki en eski ve en kapsamlı metinlerden biridir. Eser geniş hacmi sayesinde dönemin dilini bütün ayrıntılarıyla incelemeye imkân sağlamaktadır. Özellikle Türk Dil Kurumu ve Bursa nüshaları, *Tarama Sözlüğü*'nde ve şu ana kadar yayımlanmış Eski Anadolu Türkçesi metin ve sözlüklerinde yer almayan, çok az rastlanan veya bu yazmalardaki ses ve/veya biçim özellikleri ile ilk kez karşılaştığımız sözcükleriyle Türkçenin sözvarlığına da katkıda bulunabilecek en önemli eserler arasında yer alırlar.

Eser üzerindeki kimi araştırmalarımız daha önce bazı yazılara konu olmuştu (Yılmaz-Demir 2005, 2009a, 2009b, 2009c). Bunlardan biri de TDK nüshasının sözvarlığı üzerinde, Bursa, Manisa, Bağdadlı, Marmara ve İznīḳī nüshalarından da yararlanarak yaptığımız araştırma idi. *Talat Tekin Armağanı* içinde yayımlanmış olan *Ḳıṣaṣ-ı Enbiyā'dan Eski Anadolu Türkçesinin Sözvarlığına Katkılar I* (2009b) adlı bu yazıda *Tarama Sözlüğü* ve Eski Anadolu Türkçesine ait diğer sözlük ve metin yayınlarının da dikkate alınmasıyla, yedi ayrı grup oluşturulmuştu:

İlk grupta, bugünkü bilgilerimize göre, sadece *Ḳıṣaṣ-ı Enbiyā*'da bulunduğunu düşündüğümüz sözcük ve deyimler yer almaktaydı: *arur-* ~ *arır-*, *binür*, *biter*, *dir*, *üyer-*, *yaḳımraḳ*, *yinçi*; *güneş gözine*, *yil vir-*, *yir(üñ) yüzin yala-*.

İkinci grupta, TS'de bulunmamakla birlikte, çok nadir de olsa döneme ilişkin diğer kaynaklarda belirlenen sözcük ve deyimler bulunmaktaydı: *çög-*, *dügünük*, *dünlerek*, *emlü*, *oyru*, *şimşek doḳu-*, *yivil-*, *yivlimiş*, *yoġnal-*, *yoḳla-*; *siñer su*.

Ses yapıları mevcut verilerden farklı olanlar üçüncü grubu oluşturmaktaydı: *ḳulaḳ dozı (dözi, duzı, düzi?)*, *keẕ*, *oturġan*, *ölgen*, *yıvuḳ*.

Anlamsal farklılık gösterenler dördüncü grupta ele alınmıştı: *binü*, *ḥaḳḳına ḳo-*.

Sözkonusu yazıdaki son grupta, TS'de tek tanıklı görünen madde başları için metnimizde ikinci tanık durumunda olan sözcükler incelenmişti: *ḳuyḳa*, *siy*, *yaḫşur-*, *yatsun*.

Bu yazının konusunu ise *altıncı* ve *yedinci* grupta yer alan, yani sorunlu olduğunu düşündüğümüz Türkçe kökenli sözcükler ile ilk kez metnimizde belirlendiğini düşündüğümüz Arapça, Farsça alıntılar oluşturmaktadır.

VI. *Ḳıṣaṣ-ı Enbiyā*'nın TDK nüshasında, anlamları bağlamdan sezilen ancak çoğu durumda diğer nüshalarda, TS'de ve diğer kaynaklarda aynı veya benzer biçimlerini bulamadığımız için okunuş ve anlamlarından emin olamadığımız sözcükler de yer almaktadır. Ses ve biçimleri nedeniyle Türkçe olduklarını düşündüğümüz bu sözcükler, kopyalama yanlışı olasılığı da göz önünde bulundurularak, mevcut yazımın elverdiği ölçüde çözümlenmeye çalışılmıştır:

añsuz "deliksiz (?)"
Ḳıṣaṣ-ı Enbiyā'nın TDK nüshasında bir kez belgelenmiş olan *elif*, *kef*, *sin*, *ze* harf dizisi *añsuz* veya *eñsüz* biçimlerinde okunabilir:

> Süleymān eyitdi bunuñ içinde bir güher var delüksüz ve bir boncuḳ var delüklü yalavaç eyitdi gerçeksin imdi ol *añsuz incü*[*yi*] del ve ol egri delüklü boncuḳa iplik geçür (661–3).

Sözvarlığı açısından TDK nüshasına en yakın olan Bursa nüshasında bu cümlenin paraleli bulunmaz; Marmara'daki paralel cümlede ise *añsuz incü*'ye denk gelen bölümde *incü* herhangi bir sıfat almamıştır:

> Süleymān eyitdi bunuñ içinde bir şāhdāne incü ve egri deliklü bir boncuḳ var ilçi eyitdi ṣaḥīḥ söylediñ *incüyi delüp* ve ipligi boncuġa geçür (380–3-5).

Arapça metinde, *añsuz incü* çevirisine esas olan bölümde *dürrete s̱emīnete bilā s̱aḳb* "deliksiz kıymetli inci" (Ar. 319) ifadesi yer alır.

Özer'in *eñsüz* "dar" okuyuşu hem ses hem de anlam açısından uygun değildir (2008: 53). "Geniş" anlamındaki sözcük art damaksıl *ñ* değil, diş yuvasıl *n* iledir. Krş. Clauson 1972: *ēn*. Ayrıca metinde "dar inci"den değil, Marmara nüshasındaki *şāhdāne* sıfatının da gösterdiği gibi iri bir inciden söz edilmektedir.

añsuz okuyarak "deliksiz" anlamı verdiğimiz bu sözcük, bu biçimiyle başka kaynaklarda belgelenmemiştir. Bu yapı, Anadolu ağızlarında yaygın olarak kullanılan *an* ~ *añ* "iki tarla arasındaki sınır, set şeklindeki ayrıntı" kökünden geliyor olabilir. Bu durumda *añ* kelimesinin "ara" anlamı yanında "delik" anlamı da olmalıdır. Tezcan'a göre *añ*, Türkiye Türkçesi ağızlarında yaşayan, *Derleme Sözlüğü*'nde bulunan en eskicil sözcüklerden biridir ve *eñ* okunmalıdır (1994: 75). Biz ağızlarda art ünlülü biçimin daha yaygın olmasından hareketle *añ* okuyuşunu tercih ettik.

Bu kök TS'de de çok sayıda örnekle belgelenmiştir: *añ*, *añ yiri*, *eñ yiri*, *ek*, *ek yeri* "oynak yeri, büküm yeri, eklem, bitişik iki şey arasındaki çizgi". Ayrıca metnimizin TDK ve Bursa nüshalarında da kullanılmıştır:

> ḳapu *añ*ına aġzumı urdum (TDK 10–14),
> ḳapuyı yapa şöyle kim hīç *añ* yiv ḳalmaya (TDK 39–15),
> ḳapu *añ*ına aġzum urdum (Bursa 28–10)

añ kökü, Türk edebiyatının köyü konu alan ilk ürünlerinden olan *Kara Bibik*'te de (Nâbî-Zâde Nâzım 1944: 5) bir ağız sözü olarak geçmektedir.

ḳoca ḳorpı "yaşlı kadın veya erkek"
TDK nüshasında bir kez geçen bu ikilemenin anlamı bağlamdan sezilmektedir:

> soñ ḳalan *ḳoca ḳorpı* ve żaʿīfler İbrāhīm ḳatından geçdiler (TDK 146–11).

Diğer nüshaların tümünde *zayıf* kelimesinin bulunması da anlamda şüphe bırakmaz:

> żuaʿfālar (Marmara 98-21),
> żuaʿfā (Manisa 93b-2),
> şol żaʿīfleri ḳaldı (İznīḳī 178b–8).

Herhangi bir yazılı kaynakta rastlayamadığımız bu sözcük, sürmekte olan, TÜBİTAK destekli Ankara ağızlarının dokümantasyonu projesi çerçevesinde yapılan kayıtlar sırasında, Kocasar beldesinde *goca gorpı* "yaşlı erkek ya da kadın" olarak tespit edilmistir.

köklü "gür, çok (?)"
Metnimizde bir kez geçen, açıkça *köklü ~ göklü* okunacak biçimde yazılıp harekelenmiş olan bir sözcük de diğer nüshalarda ve herhangi bir kaynakta, bağlama uygun bir anlamla belirlenememiştir:

> *köklü* saḳallu ḥakīm ve bilüsi çoḳ eridi (TDK 249–14)

Diğer nüshalarda ve çeviriye esas olan Arapça metinde açıklayıcı bir veri yer almaz (Ar. 123). Eğer bu sözcük *görklü* yerine bir yazım yanlışı değilse, *kök* kökünden "gür, sağlam, köklü" anlamlarında bir türev olması mümkündür. *Derleme Sözlüğü*'nde *köklü* kelimesinin "büsbütün, çok, tüm" anlamlarına da gelmesi bu olasılığı güçlendirmektedir.

sarıncaḳ "düz; sarp (?)"
sin+re+nun+cim+kaf harfleriyle yazılan ve *sarıncaḳ* okunacak biçimde harekelenmiş olan bu sözcük de metnimizde bir kez belgelenmiştir:

> ṭağlar tañrı taʿālā Mūsāya tecellī ḳılmaḳdan öñ ḳatı ve *sarıncaḳ* idi (424–7).

Marmara nüshasındaki paralel cümlede ise dağların *tecellī*'den önce "gedik ve yarıḳ olmayup düpdüz" (250–17–18) olduğu yorumu yapılmıştır.

Özer'in *serin-caḳ* "serin" okuyuşu ses ve anlam açısından uygun değildir (2008: 15). Ön ünlülü *serin* sözcüğünün art ünlülü *-cAk* yanbiçimini aldığını düşünmek için bir neden yoktur. Ayrıca *sin* harfinin EAT'de yalnız ön ünlülerle kullanılmadığı da açıktır.

Tarama Dergisi'nde *sarın-* "sabretmek, tahammül etmek" eylemi varsa da anlamsal birleştirme mümkün değildir. Karşılaştırma için kullanılabilecek bir diğer veri TS'deki *ṣıyrıncaḳ* yapısıdır. Bu sözcüğün "kaygan" anlamı Marmara'da "gedik ve yarıḳ olmayup düpdüz idi" ifadesi ile karşılanmış olabilir. Bu durumda *sarıncaḳ*'ı *ṣıyrıncaḳ* yerine bir yazım yanlışı saymak gerekir.

DS'de bulduğumuz *sırpıncaḳ*'ın ikinci anlamı olarak verilen "sarp yer", TDK nüshasında *sarıncaḳ*'tan önce *ḳatı* sıfatı da kullanıldığı için dikkate değerdir. DS'de sözcüğün *sıypıncak* biçimi de bulunur.

Bu durumda *sarıncaḳ*'ın *sırpıncaḳ*, *sıypıncaḳ* "sarp yer" yerine bir yazım yanlışı olduğu düşünülebilir. Ya da bunlardan tümüyle farklı, Marmara'daki "gedik ve yarıḳ olmayup düpdüz idi" ifadesini karşılayan bir *sarıncaḳ* sıfatı ile karşı karşıyayız. Ancak *Derleme Sözlüğü*'nde "kaygan, düz, parlak" anlamında *zıypıncak* da geçmektedir. Eğer bu sözcükler arasında bir bağ varsa, "düz" anlamı metne uygun düşmektedir.

sesü "ses (?)"
TDK nüshasında iki yerde açıkça *sesü* okunacak biçiminde harekelenmiş bir yazım bulunur:

> pes *sesü* ve at gürüldüsin işitdiler (910–11)
> Yūnus ol balıḳ ḳarnı içindeken bir *sesü* işitdi (870–14)

Bağlam, anlamın da "ses" olmasını gerektiriyor ancak sözcük diğer nüshalarda bulunmaz. Marmara nüshasındaki paralel cümlede *āvāze* karşılığı bulunuyor (485–8).

Herhangi bir yerde tespit edemediğimiz bu sözcüğün yanlış yazılma olasılığı da bulunmakla birlikte, Türk Dil Kurumunun sanal *Büyük Türkçe Sözlük*'ünde *sesi* "ayak gürültüsü" verisine rastlanmıştır. Sanal sözlükte TS kaynaklı gösterilen sözcük, daha sonra TS verilerinin bu sözlükten kaldırılması nedeniyle artık erişilebilir durumda değildir. Basılı TS'de ise bu sözcük yer almaz.

Çuvaşçadaki iki heceli *sasĭ* "ses" biçimi karşılaştırma açısından ilginç olabilir (Çuvaşçada ayrıca *sas* da var). Söz sonunda ünlü türemesi Çuvaşçada uzun ünlülü köklerden sonra tipik bir gelişmedir: *var*, *varĭ* "öz" < *ȫz*; *vut*, *vutĭ* "ateş" < *ōt* vb. (Tekin 1995: 156–157). Fakat *ses*'te birincil uzun ünlü bulunmadığı için Çuvaşça biçimde söz sonu ünlü türemesi için bir neden yoktur. Sözvarlığı açısından Çuvaşça ve Oğuz grubu Türk dilleri arasındaki ilginç paralellikler daha önce de araştırma konusu olmuştu (Fedotov 1977, Levitskaya 1982). Örneğin *dudak* = *tutĭ*, *göbek* = *kĭvapa* vb.

setkünleri yillen- "öfkeden boyun damarları şişmek; çok öfkelenmek (?)"
Yūsuf'un, gördüğü bir rüyada on bir yıldızın, ayın ve güneşin kendisine secde ettiğini öğrenen on bir kardeşinin öfkesi, metnimizde "bularuñ *setkünleri yillen*di ve Yūsufa ḳaḳımaḳdan derileri ditrerdi" (226–8) ifadesiyle anlatılır. Diğer nüshalardaki paralel cümleler de *setkünleri yillen*di deyiminin anlamında şüphe bırakmaz:

ġażaba ve hiddete gelüp öfkelerinden gevdeleriniñ ḳılları ḳalḳup (Marmara 145–16)
ġażaba ve hiddete gelüp ol övkeden gevdeleriniñ ḳılları ḳalḳup (Manisa 131a-1)
şöyle ġażaba geldiler kim ṭamarları şişdi ḳılları ürperüp örü ṭurdı (İznīḳī 232a-10)

Metnimizde açıkça *setkün/setgün* okunacak biçimde yazılmış olan bu sözcük diğer nüshalarda ve herhangi bir kaynakta tanıklanamamıştır. Ancak yine de bunu TDK nüshasında okunuşu sorunlu bir başka sözcükle karşılaştırmak mümkündür. Öldürüldükten sonra dirilen ve katilinin kim olduğunu söyleyen birinin öyküsü anlatılırken kurulan "dirilüp duru geldi ve *sütügen*lerinden ḳan aḳarıdı" (TDK 486–14) cümlesi içinde geçen *sütügen/sütüken* sözcüğü Marmara nüshasında *ṭamar* ile karşılanmıştır:

pes öyle idicek maḳtūl *ṭamar*ından ḳanı aḳaraḳ ṭurup (283–15).

Ancak "damar" anlamında bir *sütügen* de herhangi bir kaynakta tespit edilememiştir. TDK nüshasındaki genel yazım ve hareke özensizliği dikkate alındığında belki her iki verinin, şimdilik ses yapısı kesin olmayan ve "damar" anlamına gelen aynı sözcüğü gösterdiği düşünülebilir. Bu durumda *setkünleri yillen-* deyimi de damarların şişmesi, yani mecazen öfkelenmek anlamına geliyor olmalıdır.

Yine 14. yüzyıla ait bir tıp metni olan *Ḫulāṣa*'da, bir damar türünü anlatan bir tamlama içinde geçen sözcük de *setkün* okunacak biçimde yazılmıstır:

bu renc ḳandan olduġınuñ nişanı *setkün ṭamarı* ṭolu olmaḳ ve yüz ḳızıl olmaḳdur (17b/3).[1]

Ayrıca, yine 14. yüzyıla ait olduğu tahmin edilen ve Hekim Bereket tarafından yazılmış olan *Tuhfe-i Mübarizi*[2] adlı tıp metninde setkün biçiminin anlamı şöyle açıklanmıştır:

şiryān ṭamarı iki baḫş olur... bir baḫşı yoḳaru boynına varur aña setkün derler (12b daire)

Yazım ve anlam açısından metnimizdeki veriyi destekleyen bu örnek, şu ana kadar TDK nüshası dışında belirleyebildiğimiz iki örnektir.

[1] Paris Bibliotheque National'de 171 numara ile kayıtlı bulunan bu yazma B. Erdağı-Doğuer tarafından yayıma hazırlanmaktadır.

[2] Bu yazma eser de B. Erdağı Doğuer tarafından yayıma hazırlanmıştır ve Türk Dil Kurumu'nda baskı aşamasındadır.

sütügen, bk. setkünleri yillen-

tonuḳluḳ (tonaḳluḳ?) "giyim, kuşam (?)"
Bu bölümde tartışılacak son sözcük, metnimizde *tonuḳluḳ* okunacak biçimde yazılıp harekelenmiştir. Sözcük, Şeddād'ın, İreme Ẕatüʾl-ʿİmād adlı şehri inşa ettirdikten sonra oraya çok sayıda insanı yerleştirerek her türlü ihtiyaçlarının karşılanması için emir verdiğini anlatan bir cümle içinde geçer:

> bulara yiyesi ve *ṭonuḳluḳ/ṭonaḳluḳ* tamām buyurdı (TDK 302–15).

Diğer nüshalar içinde sadece Marmara'da bu cümlenin paraleli bulunur ancak tümüyle farklı sözcüklerle:

> ḫadem ve ḥaşemden istedügi deñlü (Marmara 187–24)

Arapça metinde çeviriye esas olan bölüm *biʾl ʿıṭāʾ veʾl ʾerzāḳ*'tır (Ar. 148).

Bağlama uygun bir *ṭonuḳluḳ* biçimi herhangi bir kaynakta belirlenememiştir. İkinci hecenin harekesinin *üstün* yerine yanlışlıkla *ötre* olması mümkündür. Bu durumda sözcük, DS'deki *donaḳ* "gelin elbisesi, kadın elbisesi; çeyiz; süs, ziynet" (< *ton*) verisiyle karşılaştırılabilir. Ayrıca bk. Tietze 2002 *donaḳ* ay. Metnimizdeki veri, *tonaḳ* biçiminden *-lXk* ile türemiş "giyecek, giysi, giymeye yarar şey" anlamında bir sözcük olabilir ve bu anlamıyla bağlama da uygun düşer.

VII. Bu bölümdeki sözcükler, genel olarak metnimizde ilk kez geçtiğini düşündüğümüz Arapça, Farsça alıntılardır. Bunlardan *kenef*, *ḳunbar*, *mūl* ve *sayalan-* başka kaynaklarda tespit edilememiştir. *lubd* ve *nārincāt*'ın ses yapıları metnimize özgüdür. *Bürke* ise Türkçede çok eski bir alıntı olmakla birlikte TS'de tek tanıklıdır.

bürke "havuz, küçük su birikintisi"
TDK nüshasında sadece "gözi *bürke* ḳırañında bir ʿavrata şeş oldı" (582–12) cümlesi içinde tanıklanan bu sözcük diğer nüshaların hiçbirinde bulunmaz. Türkçede çok eski bir Arapça alıntı olan bu sözcük (bk. Tietze 1958: 265 *birka* "küçük göl", Devellioğlu 1970 *birke* "büyük havuz, küçük göl, gölcük") *Tarama Sözlüğü*'nde tek tanıklıdır: *birike* "hazine, mahzen, sarnıç". *Âşık Paşazade Tarihi*'nden alınmış olan bu tek tanığın (XVI. yy.: 208: "Yolda su *birikeleri* vardı, anları harap gördü") *birike* yazılışı, sözcüğün belki de Türkçe *birik-* fiiliyle ilişkilendirilmiş olduğunu düşündürüyor.

Âşık Paşazade Tarihi dışında, sözcüğü tespit ettiğimiz tek kaynak *Ḳıṣaṣ-ı Enbiyā*'nın TDK nüshası da değildir. Hazai-Tietze tarafından yeni yayımlanmış olan *Ferec baʿd eş-şidde* nüshasında da görülür: *birke* (91b: 3, 243b: 6). 2006 tarihli bu yayın, bilinen Türkçe *Ferec baʿd eş-şidde* nüshalarının en eskisi olan Budapeşte nüshasını ele alır (istinsah tarihi 1451[3]). Ayrıca Tietze'nin, bu nüshanın sözvarlığına da yer vermiş olduğu sözlüğünde *birke*, *birge*, *bürke* "havuz" madde başları bulunur (2002).

Bu üç kaynak dışında sözcük, Anadolu ağızlarında da *börke*, *bürke* "havuz" biçimlerinde tespit edilmiştir (DS).

kenef "ip, sicim"
Eski Anadolu Türkçesi sözvarlığı içinde tanıklayamadığımız bir başka alıntı da yine metnimizde bir kez geçen Farsça *kenef* "keten ip" sözcüğüdür:

> ol *kenef*ler kim anuñıla şuḳḳayı çekerler ḳurbān yüñinden ola (TDK 487–14).

Aynı sözcük için Marmara nüshasındaki paralel cümlede *ṭınāb* "çadır ipi" (284–7) bulunur.

Farsça *kenef* için bk. Kanar 2008 "kenevir", Steingass 2005 "keten ip".

ḳunbar, **ḳunbar ḳuş** "tarla kuşu"
Metnimizde dört kez geçen Arapça *ḳunbar* "tarla kuşu" alıntısı da diğer nüshalarda bulunmaz:

> ḳaçan *ḳunbar* ötse eydür iy çalabum Muḥammed ümmeti sevmeyene laʿnet ḳılġıl (TDK 614–5).
> daḫı rivāyetdür kim *ḳunbar* Süleymān yolında yumurtladı (TDK 614–15)
> *ḳunbar ḳuşı* öticek ne dir (TDK 879–12), *ḳunbar ḳuş* öticek ne dir (TDK 881–10)

Herhangi bir tarihi kaynakta ve Osmanlıca sözlüklerde bulamadığımız bu sözcük Arapça metinde ve Arapça sözlüklerde *ḳunbur* (Ar. 2004: 297) biçimindedir. Krş. Wehr 1976: *ḳunbur* "tarla kuşu, çayır kuşu".

lubd "akbaba"
Loḳmān peygambere yedi *kerkes kuşu* ("akbaba") ömrünce ömür verildiğini anlatan bölümde beş kez geçen Arapça kökenli *lubd* "akbaba" sözcüğü,

[3] Bu nüsha hakkında ayrıntılı bilgi için bk. Yılmaz 2010.

metnimizde *kerkes*'in sıfatı gibi kullanılmış, hatta anlamının "bularuñ dilince rūzigār" olduğu açıklaması yapılmıştır:

> işbu kerkes ʿömri *lubd*-durur ve *lubd* bularuñ dilince rūzigār-durur ḳaçan ol kerkesüñ daḫı ʿömri geçdi pes ḳamu kerkesler ṭağdan uçdı aşağa indi ve ol *lubd* kerkes inmedi ḳaçan Loḳmān gördi kim *lubd* ol kerkeslerle bile inmedi pes durdı ṭağa çıḳdı ol kerkesi göre gideriken gendü nefsinde süstlıḳ buldı kim ilerü eyle olduğı yoğıdı ḳaçan ṭağ üstine çıḳdı gördi kim *lubd* kerkesi anda düşmişdi pes bir ün geldi kim *lubd* kerkesi ḳaldur (TDK 124–5, 6, 7, 8, 9).

TDK dışındaki nüshalardan sadece Marmara'da bulunan sözcük, burada *labad* okunacak biçimde harekelenmiştir (86–10). TDK nüshasındaki yazılış ise sadece *lubd* okunmasına izin verir. Sözcük bu biçimiyle başka kaynaklarda bulunmaz.

Arapça metinde sözcüğün orijinal biçimi olan *lubad* bulunur (Ar. 2004: 67). Ayrıca krş. *lubed* "Lokman tarafından seçilmiş yedi akbabadan sonuncusunun adı" (Redhouse 2006).

mūl (bayramı) "bereket bayramı (?)"
TDK nüshasında "*mūl* bayramıñız içün geymeklige Firʿavndan ve ḳavmından dürlü bezek ve ṭonlar ʿāriyet dileñ" (407–13) cümlesi içinde geçen *mūl* sözcüğü de diğer nüshalarda ve Eski Anadolu sahası içinde başka bir kaynakta belirlenememiştir. Marmara nüshasındaki paralel cümlede sadece *ʿıyd* bulunur: "ve ol *ʿıyd* içün" (242–5).

Arapça sözlüklerdeki *mul* "zengin olmak (özellikle hayvan sürüsü açısından)" (krş. Wehr 1976) fiiliyle ilişkili olduğunu düşündüğümüz bu sözcük "bereket, bolluk vb. bayramı" anlamına geliyor olmalıdır.

nārincāt "büyüler, sihirler"
Yine sadece TDK nüshasında tespit ettiğimiz bir sözcük de *nārincāt*'tır:

> bayıḳ şeyṭānlar Süleymān taḫtından ırılduğı zamān içinde cāẕuluḳ ve *nārincāt* yazdılar (92–9)

Özer'in *nār-ı necāt* "Rettungsfeuerbuch" okuyuşu anlamsal nedenlerle kabul edilemez (2008: 60). Bağlam, "sihir, büyü" anlamında bir sözcük gerektiriyor. Ancak Osmanlıca-Türkçe, Farsça-Türkçe sözlüklerde bu anlamlara gelen sözcük *nārincāt* değil, genellikle *nīreng*, *neyrenc*, *nīrenc*, *neyrencāt* vb. (bk. Devellioğlu 1970, Kanar 2008 vb.) biçimlerindedir. Hem anlam hem de ses açısından aradığımız yapı Moʾin'in *Ferheng-e*

Fārsī'sinde yer alır. Bu sözlükte *nārenc* 2 madde başı altında, sözcüğün, Farsça *nīreng*'in ("büyü, sihir") Arapçalaşmış biçimi olduğu, *nārencāt* başlığı altında da *nārenc*'in çoğulu olduğu belirtilmiştir (1371: 4564–4565). Yani Anadolu sahasında sözcüğün Farsça biçimi yaygın olduğu halde, Arapçalaşmış *nārenc*, *nārinc* biçimi, şu anki bilgilerimize göre sadece *Ḳıṣaṣ-ı Enbiyā*'nın TDK nüshasında geçmektedir.

sayalan- "törpülenerek düzleşmek"
TDK nüshasında, "müşgden ve zaʿferāndan pınduḳlar"ı koklayarak hiç koku kalmadığını fark eden Muʿāviye, bunun nedenini "çoḳ zamān geçmekden *sayalan*mışdur ve daş yüzi[nd]e yıyı ḳalmamışdur" (TDK 298–11) biçiminde açıklar. Ses yapısı nedeniyle ilk bakışta Türkçe olduğunu düşündüren *sayalan-*, diğer nüshalarda bulunmaz. Bu cümlenin paraleli Marmara ve Manisa nüshalarında şöyledir:

> miski ḳoḳlayup anda rayiḥā bulmadı (Marmara 185–18)
> ḳoḳlayup anda rayiḥā bulmayup (Manisa 166a-8)

Eylemin Türkçe kökü olabilecek bir *saya* adı GTS'de varsa da anlamı "ayakkabının yumuşak olan üst bölümü"dür. Bağlama uygun bir *saya* adı veya *sayalan-* eylemi herhangi bir tarihi kaynakta belirlenememiştir.

Ancak *sayalan-* fiili madencilikte "törpülenmek, düzleştirilmek" anlamında kullanılmaktadır (Kulaksız vd. 2005). Kitabın hazırlayıcılarından S. Kulaksız ile yaptığımız görüşme sonucu, herhangi bir terim sözlüğünde de yer almayan bu sözcüğün maden işletmeciliğinde çok yaygın bir kullanımı olduğunu öğrendik.

Türkçe kökenini belirleyemediğimiz sözcük, büyük olasılıkla Farsça *sāyīden* "sürterek aşındırmak" eyleminden erken bir ödünçlemedir.

Kısaltmalar ve Kaynaklar

Ar.: *Ḳıṣaṣ-ı Enbiyāʾ el-Müsemmā ʿArāʾisüʾl-Mecālis* (2004). Beyrut–Lübnan: Dar el Fikr.

Bayraktar, Nesrin (2008). *Ebūʾl-Faẓl Mūsā bin Ḥacı Ḥüseyn İznīḳī Ḳaṣaṣüʾl-Enbiyā Tercümesi. Metin-Dizin.* Ankara: Ebabil Yayınları.

Bursa: bk. Ökten 2000.

Clauson, Sir Gerard (1972). *An Etymological Dictionary of Pre-Thirteenth-Century Turkish.* Oxford: Clarendon Press.

Devellioğlu, Ferit (1970). *Osmanlıca-Türkçe Ansiklopedik Lûgat.* Ankara: Aydın Kitabevi.

DS = *Derleme Sözlüğü*. (1963–1982). 12 c. Ankara: TDK Yayınları.

Fedotov, M. Romanoviç (1977). "O nekotorıx oguzskix çertax çuvaşskogo yazıka". *Sovetskaya Tyurkologiya* 1977-1: 25–32.

GTS = *Güncel Türkçe Sözlük*. www.tdk.gov.tr.

Hazai, György; Tietze, Andreas. (2006). *Ferec baᶜd eş-şidde „Freud nach Leid". (Ein frühosmanisches Geschichtenbuch)*. 1: *Text*. Berlin: Klaus Schwarz Verlag.

İznīḳī: bk. Bayraktar 2008.

Kanar, Mehmet (2008). *Farsça-Türkçe Sözlük*. İstanbul: Say Yayınları.

Koç, Mustafa (1998). *El-Ferecü Baᶜdeʾş-Şidde*. [Doktora tezi. İstanbul Üniversitesi Sosyal Bilimler Enstitüsü].

Kulaksız, Seyfi (2005). *Doğal Taş (Mermer) Maden İşletmeciliği ve İşleme Teknolojileri*. Ankara: TMMOB Maden Mühendisleri Odası.

Levitskaya, L. Sergeyevna (1982). "İmeyutsya li v çuvaşskom yazıke oguzskiye elementı?". *Chuvash Studies*. Wiesbaden: Otto Harrassowitz.

Marmara: *Ḳıṣaṣ-ı Enbiyā*'nın Marmara nüshası.

Moʾin, Mohammed (1371). *Ferheng-e Fārsī*. 4. Tehrān: Moessese-e Enteşārāt-e Kebīr.

Nâbî-Zâde, Nâzım (1944). *Kara Bibik. -Büyük Hikaye-*. İstanbul: Vakıt Matbaası.

Ökten, Meriç (2000). *Saᶜlebi'nin Kısasüʾl-Enbiyâ'sının XIV. Yüzyılda Türkçe Tercümesi. Metin-Sözlük*. İstanbul. [Doktora tezi. İstanbul Üniversitesi Sosyal Bilimler Enstitüsü.].

Özer, Şerife (2008). *Die nominale Wortbildung im Altosmanischen. Am Beispiel der Übersetzung von Ṭaᶜlabīs Qiṣaṣ al-Anbiyāʾ aus dem 14. Jahrhundert*. (Turcologica 73.). Wiesbaden: Otto Harrassowitz.

Redhouse, Sir James W. (2006). *A Turkish and English Lexicon*. İstanbul: Çağrı Yayınları.

Steingass, F. Joseph (2005). *A Comprehensive Persian-English Dictionary*. İstanbul: Çağrı Yayınları.

Tarama Dergisi = *Osmanlıcadan Türkçeye Söz Karşılıkları Tarama Dergisi*. I. (1934). Türk Dili Tetkik Cemiyeti. İstanbul: Maarif Vekaleti Yayınları.

Tarama Dergisi = *Osmanlıcadan Türkçeye Söz Karşılıkları Tarama Dergisi*. II. *Türkçeden Osmanlıcaya İndeks*. (1934). Türk Dili Tetkik Cemiyeti. İstanbul: Maarif Vekaleti Yayınları.

TDK: *Ḳıṣaṣ-ı Enbiyā*'nın Türk Dil Kurumu nüshası.

Tekin Talat (1995). *Türk Dillerinde Birincil Uzun Ünlüler*. Ankara: Simurg.

Tezcan, Semih (1994). *Süheyl ü Nev-bahār Üzerine Notlar.* TDA Dizisi 6. Ankara: Simurg.

Tietze, Andreas (1958). "Direkte arabische Entlehnungen im anatolischen Türkisch". *Jean Deny Armağanı. Mélanges Jean Deny*: 255–333. Hazırlayan Eckmann, J. vd. Ankara: TDK Yayınları.

Tietze, Andreas (2002). *Tarihi ve Etimolojik Türkiye Türkçesi Lugati.* 1: *A–E.* İstanbul-Wien: Simurg Yayınları.

TS = *Tarama Sözlüğü.* I–VIII. 2. baskı: 1996. Ankara: TDK Yayınları.

Wehr, Hans (1976). *Arabisches Wörterbuch für die Schriftsprache der Gegenwart.* Beirut, London: Librairie du Liban. Macdonald & Evans Ltd.

Yeni Tarama Sözlüğü (1983). Düzenleyen: Dilçin, Cem. Ankara: TDK Yayınları.

Yılmaz, Emine; Demir, Nurettin (2005). "Bir Saʿlebi Çevirisi: Kısas-ı Enbiya". *Mustafa Canpolat Armağanı. International Journal of Central Asian Studies.* 10-1: 1–8.

Yılmaz, Emine; Demir, Nurettin (2009a). "Şerife Özer (2008). *Die nominale Wortbildung im Altosmanischen. Am Beispiel der Übersetzung von Talabis Qisas al-Anbiya aus dem 14. Jahrhundert*". *bilig* 49. Bahar: 231–240.

Yılmaz, Emine; Demir, Nurettin (2009b). "Kısas-ı Enbiya'dan Eski Anadolu Türkçesinin Sözvarlığına Katkılar I". *Festschrift to Commemorate the 80th Anniversary of Prof. Dr. Talat Tekin's Birth.* Hazırlayan Yılmaz, Emine, Eker, Süer, Demir, Nurettin. *International Journal of Central Asian Studies.* 13: 495–517.

Yılmaz, Emine; Demir, Nurettin (2009c). "S̱aʿlebī'nin *Kitābu ʿarāʾisiʾl-mecālis fī ḳıṣaṣiʾl-enbiyā*'sının Anadolu Sahasında Yapılmış Çevirileri". *Festschrift in Honor of Cem Dilçin. Journal of Turkish Studies* 33/II: 357–370.

Yılmaz, Emine (2010) "György Hazai, Andreas Tietze, (2006), *Ferec baʿd eş-şidde (Ein frühosmanisches Geschichtenbuch)*, 1. Band, Text, Klaus Schwarz Verlag. Berlin, 650 s.", *bilig* 52: 243–248.

Studies on the Turkic World
A Festschrift for Professor St. Stachowski on the Occasion of His 80th Birthday
edited by E. Mańczak-Wohlfeld and B. Podolak, Kraków 2010: 211–222

Grażyna Zając (Kraków)

Gezi Edebiyatının Öneminde Ahmet İhsan ve Şerafeddin Mağmumi'nin Yeri

Giriş

Yakın tarihe dair araştırmacılar için en önemli kaynaklardan biri, hatıra türü eserlerdir. Son yıllarda bu türe ilişkin eserlerin hatıra severler tarafından büyük bir ilgi ve merakla okunduğu gerçeği de bilinmektedir. Bu ilgi ve merak Avrupa ülkelerinde olduğu gibi Türkiye'de de görülmekte ve her yıl Türkiye'de anı türünden onlarca kitap ya ilk baskılarıyla ya da farklı yayınevlerinden yeni baskılarıyla okurlarına sunulmaktadır.[1] Bu eserlerden kimileri ya Latin alfabesine geçişten önce eski gazetelerde tefrika olarak yer almış, ya da eski alfabe ile kitap şeklinde yayımlanmış eserler oldukları nedeniyle, sonuçta, gerçekten güzel bir kültürel hizmet verilerek hem unutuldukları kütüphane raflarından, hem eski gazete ve mecmuaların tozlu sayfaları arasından yavaş yavaş kurtarılarak yeniden günışığına çıkarılmakta ve günümüz okurlarının bilgisine sunulmaktadırlar. Unutmamak gerekir ki Türkiye'de hâlâ el yazması özgünlükleriyle muhafaza edilen anılar da var; özellikle onların büyük emekler ve özveriler sonucunda dünden bugüne aktarılmaları övgüye değer bir başka kazanımdır.

Şu gerçeğin altını çizmek gerekir ki, Türkiye'de eski anıların yeniden baskıya hazırlanmaları konusunda çok yararlı işler yapıldı, yapılmaktadır. Ancak son 20 yıl içerisinde yayınlanmış anı kitaplarına göz attığımız zaman

[1] Her yıl yayınlanmakta olan *Türkiye Kültür ve Sanat Yıllığı*'ndaki "Hatırat" bölümünden öğrenebildiğimiz gibi Türkiye'de yılda 40–50 civarında anı türü kitap bastırılmaktadır.

kimi kitapların çok iyi, kimilerinin çok kötü yöntemlerle bastırıldığını görüyor; kimi yayınevlerinin konuya yaklaşımlarının çok ciddî, kimilerinin alabildiğine sorumsuz olduğunu farkediyor; eski ve özgün metni yayına hazırlayanları ise kimi zaman dikkatli, titiz ve yaptığı kültürel hizmete saygılı, kimi zamansa gerekli saygıyı, duyarlılığı ve sorumluluğu hiç dikkate almamış umarsızlıklar içerisinde tespit edebiliyoruz. Bu yöndeki yanlışlara ilişkin geniş bilgi ve örneklemeler birçok eleştiri yazısında yer aldıkları nedeniyle[2] tekrarına gidilmeyecek, ancak sıkça tekrarlanan birkaç yanlış ve usulsüzlüğe de değinmeden geçemeyeceğim.

Kanımca, yayıncının ve yayına hazırlayanın en ciddî hatası, anı yazarının isminin, kitap kapağı üzerinde belirgin olarak yer almamasıdır. Dikkat edenler anımsayacaktır; kapakta yazarın isminin olması gereken yerde yayına hazırlayanın ismi bulunmakta, asıl yazarın ismi ise kitap başlığının içerisine taşınmaktadır. Böylece, ön plana çıkan yazar değil, editördür! Buna haksızlık adını vermezsek, ne ad vermeliyiz... Ali Birinci bu haksızlıklara ilişkin olarak oldukça sert bir söylemle şöyle yazar:

> Bu durumda kitaba bir isim koymayı bile beceremeyen bir yayıncılık ziyancılığı bahis mevzuudur (Birinci 2007: 585).

Bu haklı tepkiye en çarpıcı örnek olarak kapağında Metin Kayahan Özgül imzasının bulunduğu ve üzerinde de *Ali Ekrem Bolayır'ın Hatıraları* başlığını taşıyan, 1991 yılında yayınlanmış kitabı gösterebiliriz. Böyle bir kapak tasarımı okuru mutlaka yanıltabilir çünkü kapaktan ilk anda anlaşılan, kitap yazarının aslında M. K. Özgül olduğu ve bu yazarın (!) yayımladığı kitabının da türü itibariyle hatıraları ele alan bir araştırma ürünü olduğudur.

Kimi kitaplarda da bu tür usulsüzlüğü yazarın bir yakınının sergilediği görülmektedir. Örneğin İstiklal Savaşı kahramanlarından Şehidullah Fikri'nin hatıralarını damadı M. R. Serhadoğlu 2005 yılında yayına verirken, kapağa yalnızca kendi ismini yazmış, kitabın adını da öylece uydurarak, *Savaşçı Doktorun İzinde* demiştir. Bu şekliyle ortaya hatıraların sahibi kayınpeder, hatıraların yazarı ise sanki damatmış gibi tuhaf, tuhaf olmanın da ötesinde trajikomik bir durum çıkmıştır. Bu tür davranışlarla ilgili bir başka hataysa, eski metinlere yeni ve tamamen uydurulmuş bir başlık aranırken gereğinden fazla uzun ve dahası debdebeli bir başlık seçilir olmasıdır. Örneğin Orhan Kemal'in oğlu Işık Öğütçü dedesinin hatıralarını 2005 yılında yayına hazırlarken, oldukça gereksiz diyebileceğimiz

[2] Hatıratların baskıya hazırlanması çalışmaları sırasında yapılan kimi hatalarla usulsüzlüklere dair birkaç makale prof. Ali Birinci tarafından ele alındı; ör. Birinci 2005a, Birinci 2005b, Birinci 2007.

Orhan Kemal'in Babası Abdülkadir Kemali'nin Anıları başlığını kullanması gibi. Böylesi tutum ve davranışları "kitap kapaklarının reklâm panosu muamelesi görmesi" şeklinde değerlendiren Ali Birinci

> [bu] hatıra neşrinde baba ne kazandı bilinmez ama, bu arada, hiç de müstahak olmayan dede, her nedense, harcanmıştır. Sanki dedenin bütün hususiyeti Orhan Kemal'in babası olmaktan ibaretmiş gibi

yorumunu da getirir (Birinci 2007: 586). Bu örneklere benzer başka bir "suçu" da, ilk Türk kadın ressamlarından Naciye Neyyal Biren'in torunu olan Fatma R. Hürmen işler. Hürmen, anneannesinin hatıralarını 2000 yılında yayına hazırlarken kitaba *Münevver Bir Türk Hanımı Ressam Naciye Neyyal'ın Mutlakiyet, Meşrutiyet ve Cumhuriyet Hatıraları* diye görkemli bir ad bulmuş, ancak, her ne hikmetse (!) bu görkemliliğe karşın kitap kapağına gerçek anı sahibi yazarın soyadını koymayı bile ya uygun görmemiş ya da unutmuştur! Bu türden gelen yanlış tutum ve tavırları yalnızca akrabalarda değil, yazara tamamıyla yabancı olan editörlerde de görebiliriz. Akla gelen örneklerden ilki, Şerafeddin Mağmumi'nin *Seyahat Hatıraları. Anadolu ve Suriye'de* başlıklı gezi hatıralarının günümüzde *Bir Osmanlı Doktorun Anıları* başlığı altında yayınlanması, ikincisi ise Âli Bey'in *Seyahat Jurnali. İstanbul'dan Bağdad'a ve Hindistan'a. Min sene 1300 ilâ sene 1304* başlığını verdiği gezi kitabına yeni baskısında *Dicle'de Kelek İle Bir Yolculuk* adının verilmesidir.

Yeni yayınlanan kitaplarda görülen bir başka hatalı tutum ve davranışsa, hatıraların ve seyahat kitaplarının çok önemli ve vazgeçilmez parçalarından olan kişi ve coğrafya adları indeksinin verilmemesidir. Bu kitapların eski baskılarında – belki dönemin teknik olanaksızlarından – indekslere yer verilmemiş olsa bile, metni Latin harfleriyle yeniden baskıya hazırlayan redaktörlerin de indeksleri kitaba eklememeleri, doğrusu, günümüz yayıncılığı ve okurları adına affedilmez bir hatadır. Kişi dizini olmayan Hüseyin Cahit Yalçın'ın *Edebiyat Anıları* (yeni baskı: 1999), Ahmet İhsan Tokgöz'ün *Matbuat Hatıralarım* (1993) ile Celal Esat Arseven'in *Sanat ve Siyaset Hatıralarım* (1993) ve seyahat kitabı olup da coğrafya adları dizini olmayan Şerafeddin Mağmumi'nin *Bir Osmanlı Doktorun Anıları* (2002) ve Âli Bey'in *Dicle'de Kelek İle Bir Yolculuk* kitapları (2003), yukarıda sözünü ettiğim redaktör hatalarına örnek yayınlardandır. Osmanlı ve Cumhuriyet dönemlerinin ünlü cerrahı Cemil Paşa Topuzlu'nun hatıralarını 2002 yılında yeni baskıya hazırlayan ve en az Cemil Paşa kadar ünlü olan torunu, cerrah Cemalettin Topuzlu'ya gelince, o da dedesinin hatıralarının sonunda kişi dizini ve sözlük bulunmasına önem vermesine karşın, her nedense, bu çok kapsamlı hatıratı bir "İçindekiler" kısmı ile geliştirip zenginleştirmeyi uygun görmemiş...!

Hatıra kitaplarının yeni baskılarında yapılan bir başka büyük hata ise, özgün metine müdahalede bulunmaktır. Okul öğrencileri için ele alınarak hazırlanan metinlerin günümüz Türkçesine tercüme edilmelerini akılcı ve yararlı olarak kabul etsek bile, araştırmacılara hizmet edecek ciddî bir baskıyı hazırlayan ve özellikle eski metnin Latin alfabesinde ilk baskısını verecek olan yayınevi bu yöntemden kesinlikle kaçınmalıdır. Çünkü günümüz diline çevrilen hatırata müdahalede bulunulduğu zaman özgün dil tamamıyla değer kaybederken, yayınlanmış olan kitap da bilgi – belge aktarımı yönüyle çok daha az güvenilir bir duruma düşer. Daha da kötüsü, bazı hatırat kitaplarının dili tümden sadeleştirildiği halde, kitap içerisinde bu sadeleştirmeye dair tek kelimelik bir bilgi ve açıklamaya bile gerek duyulmamasıdır. Böyle bir davranış, aslında, okuru aldatmaktan başka bir şey değildir... Bazı kitapların önsözlerinde ise gerçek dışılığın fantastik karışımında bir itiraf buluruz, tıpkı Basiretçi Ali'nin hatıralarının 1976'da yapılmış yeni baskısında yer alan şu cümle gibi:

> Kitabın bu yeni baskısında, dili günümüze uygulanmakla birlikte yazarın üslûbundaki özelliklere dokunulmamış.

Basiretçi Ali'nin dilini günümüz Türkçesine çevirmek ve bu çeviriyi yaparken de üslûbuna dokunmamak nasıl mümkün olabilir, doğrusu bunu anlamak pek de kolay olmasa gerek.

Çok şükür ki eski anıları günümüz okurlarına sunma tutku ve çabasını kutsal bir görev sayan ve bu uğraşıyı ciddî bir yaklaşım ve sorumlulukla üstlenen yayınevleri de vardır. Bu makalemde, son üç yıl içerisinde övgüye lâyık bir titizlikle hazırlanmış ve yayınlanmış iki gezi hatırasına değinmek istiyorum. Bu hatıraların ikisi de, XIX. yüzyılın sonlarına doğru iki Türk tarafından gerçekleştirilmiş Avrupa gezilerine dair hatıralardır. Biri, Tarih Vakfı Yurt Yayınları'nın yayını olan Ahmet İhsan (Tokgöz)'ın *Avrupa'da Ne Gördüm. Tuna'da bir Hafta* başlıklı eseri (Ahmet 2007), diğeri Boyut Kitapları'nda çıkan Şerafeddin Mağmumi'nin *Avrupa Seyahat Hatıraları* kitaplarıdır (Şerafeddin 2008). Şimdi, bu iki değerli seyyahın yaşamöykülerine ve eserlerine birlikte bakalım...

Ahmet İhsan ve Şerafeddin Mağmumi – yaşamları ve seyahatları

Cumhuriyet döneminde Tokgöz soyadını alan Ahmet İhsan (1868–1942) Mekteb-i Mülkiye mezunu, Fransız edebiyatı tercümanı, yazar, gazeteci ve her şeyden önce bir yayıncı olarak Türk basın ve edebiyat tarihinde iz bırakan ünlü Servet-i Fünun gazetesinin de kurucusudur. Çocukluğundan beri seyahat etmeyi düşleyen Ahmet İhsan, bu düşünü 1891 yılında gerçekleştirir. O yıl, yayınlamaya yeni başladığı Servet-i Fünun dergisine modern matbaa teknikleriyle çinkografi ve fotoğraf bastırma yöntemlerini kazandırmak için, Batı Avrupa'daki matbaa çevreleriyle tanışmak ve bilgi edinmek amacıyla seyahate çıkar. Henüz 23 yaşında genç bir basın tutkunuydu. Üç ay boyunca sürdürdüğü bu seyahatinde bir yandan aradığı çağdaş baskı tekniklerini öğrenirken, öte yandan da büyük bir disiplin ve titizlikle gezi notlarını yazmayı sürdürmüştür. İzlenimlerini Avrupa dönüşünden hemen sonra önce tefrika halinde Servet-i Fünun'da, 1892'de de 588 sayfalık bir kitap olarak *Avrupa'da Ne Gördüm* başlığı altında yayınlamıştır. Sonraki yıllarda II. Abdülhamit'in uyguladığı ağır kurallar nedeniyle Türklerin yurtdışı yolculukları engellenmiş ve bu engeller ancak padişahın tahttan indirilişinden (1908) sonra ortadan kalkmış olduğundan Türklerin gezi olanakları yeniden sağlanmıştır. Bu gelişmelerle birlikte Ahmet İhsan ikinci kez Avrupa'ya giderek Paris'i ziyaret etmiş, üçüncü gezisini de 1911 yılında Almanya'ya yapmıştır. Tuna üzerinde yaptığı bir haftalık yolculuğunu *Tuna'da Bir Hafta* başlıklı makalesinde anlatır ve aynı yıl kendi matbaasında 35 sayfalık bir kitapçık şeklinde yayınlar. Ahmet İhsan'ın 1891 ve 1911 yıllarına ait gezi hatıralarını kapsayan yeni baskı kitabı Alain Servantie ile Fahriye Gündoğdu'nun ortak çalışmaları olarak yayına hazırlanır ve 2007'de *Avrupa'da Ne Gördüm. Tuna'da Bir Hafta* adıyla yayınlanır. (Ahmet 2007).

Şerafeddin Mağmumi (1869–1927) Gülhane Askerî Tıbbiyesi'nden mezun bir doktor ve aynı zamanda İttihat ve Terakki Cemiyeti'nin de kurucularından. O da Ahmet İhsan gibi çocukluğundan beri seyahat etmeyi düşlemiş ve bu düşünü ilk kez 1894'te gerçekleştirmiş. İlk seyahati Anadolu'da çıkan kolera salgınıyla ilgiliydi. Genç doktor karantina müfettişi olarak Bursa, Bandırma, Balıkesir, Edremit, Ayvalık gibi bölgeleri yalnızca gezmemiş, gezip gördüklerini de büyük bir titizlikle not etmiş. Bir yıl sonra aynı görevle bu kez Mersin, Tarsus, Adana, Halep, Beyrut ve Şam bölgelerini gezmiş ve seyahat gözlemlerini yine çok detaylı olarak kâğıtlara aktarmış.[3] 1896 yılında Paris'e kaçarak mülteci bir yaşam sürdürmüş, uzun yıllar boyunca önce Paris, ardından Kahire'de doktorluk ve siyasî yayıncılıkla uğraşmış. Mağmumi'nin 1897–98 yıllarında yazılmış ikinci gezi kitabı Brüksel ve

[3] Her iki seyahatı anlatan kitabın ilk baskısı Kahire'de 1909'da çıkmış: *Anadolu ve Suriye'de*, 312 sayfa.

Londra seyahatini, üçüncü gezi kitabı ise 1899 yılına ait Fransa, İtalya ve İsviçre gözlemlerini konu alır.[4] İkinci ve üçüncü gezilerini içeren *Avrupa Seyahat Hatıraları* kitabı ise Nazım H. Polat'la Harid Fedai işbirliğinde yayına hazırlanarak 2008 yılında yayınlandı.

Ahmet İhsan'ın *Avrupa'da Ne Gördüm. Tuna'da Bir Hafta* adıyla 2007'de yayınlanan gezi hatıraları oldukça titiz bir çalışmanın ürünü olarak dikkat çeker. Ancak bu gerçek şaşırtıcı değildir. Çünkü, Tarih Vakfı Yurt Yayınları'nın bütün yayınlarında üst seviyenin korunmasına önem verdiği bilinmektedir. Yazarın diline dokunulmamıştır; bugün için anlaşılmayan eski sözcükler kitaba eklenmiş 20 sayfalık bir "Sözlük"te açıklanmıştır. Kitabın olumsuz yanı, kişi ve coğrafya adları indekslerinin bulunmamasıdır. Kişi indeksinin kitaba eklenmemesinin nedeni belki kişi adlarının az anılmasıdır – yazarın seyahati sırasında görüştüğü, tanıştığı veya ismini duyduğu kişilere daha az dikkat etmesi bir gerçektir, kişilerden çok gezdiği yerleri merak ediyor; ancak bu değerli kaynağa yer adları dizininin neden eklenmediğini anlamak zordur. Gezi hatıratı gibi bir kitapta yer adları indeksinin bulunmaması büyük bir boşluktur. Yeni baskıda kullanılan yabancı coğrayfa ve kişi adlarının imlâsı da oldukça tartışmalı. XIX. yüzyıl sonlarında hatıralarını not eden bir yazar, doğal olarak Arap harflerini kullanmış ve yabancı sözcükleri de duyduğu gibi yazmak zorunda kalmıştır ama bunları Latin harflerine aktaran günümüz editörlerinin de örneğin 'Britiş Muzeum', 'Fontenblo', 'Pale dökristal', 'Per Laşez', 'Oksfort Strit, 'Trafalgar Skuvar', 'Ogüst Plaj' (Augustplatz!), 'Kuk' (Cook) diye fonetik olarak yazmalarına haklı bir neden bulamıyoruz. Transkripsiyon (çeviri yazı)'nun amacı bu değil ki... Kitapta düşündürücü olan bir başka anlamsızlık da, yayıncı tarafından kullanılan 'çevriyazı' sözcüğüdür. TDK'nın – mantıklı olarak – önerdiği imlâ 'çeviri yazı'[5] şeklindeyken, her nedense kitabın birkaç yerinde 'çevriyazı' diye tuhaf ve anlamsız bir kelimenin kullanımına gidilmiştir...

Şerafeddin Mağmumi'nin *Avrupa Seyahat Hatıraları* kitabı da aynen Ahmet İhsan'ın kitabında olduğu gibi yazarın diline hiç dokunulmadan ve aslı korunarak yayına hazırlandı. N. H. Polat ve H. Fedai bunu "Önsöz"lerinde açıklarlarken çok haklı olarak şöyle yazdılar:

> Eski metinlerin orijinal diliyle yayımlanmadan önce, değiştirilmiş bir dille yayımlanmasını uygun bulmuyoruz. Mağmumi'nin *Seyahat Hatıraları*

[4] Bu kitaplardan ilki 1908'de Kahire'de (*Brüksel ve Londra'da*, 239 sayfa), ikincisi de 1914'te ve yine Kahire'de bastırılmış (*Fransa ve İtalya ve İsviçre'de*, 303 sayfa).

[5] Bk. http://tdkterim.gov.tr/seslisozluk/

> Latin harfleriyle ilk defa yayımlanıyor. Onun için günümüz Türkçesine aktarmaya gerek görmüyoruz" (Şerafeddin 2008: 10).

Keşke eski edebiyat eserlerini yeni baskıya hazırlayan tüm editörlerde böyle bir yaklaşım olsa. Polat ve Fedai'nin yabancı özel isimlerin yazılışına dair tavırları da Ahmet İhsan'ın eserinde görülenden çok farklı; 'Strit', 'Britiş' gibi tuhaf yazılışa rastlamıyoruz. Bu konudaki açıklamaları çok mantıklı olup, eski metinleri Latin harfleriyle yayına hazırlayan bütün Türk yayıncılar tarafından benimsenmeli:

> Yazar, özel isimleri, genellikle orijinal diliyle fakat yazılışı değil, söylenişi gösterecek biçimde vermiştir: Mon Blan. Latin harfleriyle okunduğu gibi yazdığımız takdirde, herhangi bir müracaat eserinde, aynı imlâ ile söz konusu özel isimlere ulaşmak mümkün değildir. Onun için böylesi durumlarda okunuş değil, orijinal imlâ kullanılmıştır: Mont Blanc (Şerafeddin 2008: 10).

Kitaba eklenen 36 sayfalık "Dizin"de hem kişilerin özel adları hem coğrafya isimleri verilmesine karşın, yine de neden Hıristiyanlık, Müslümanlık, Türk medeniyeti, İran medeniyeti, Prusya muharebesi gibi adların yer aldığını anlayamıyoruz. Kim bilir, belki de bu indeksin amacı yalnızca kişi ve coğrafya adlarını değil, konularla kavramları da listelemektir ama "Dizin"deki konu ve kavram adlarının da az olduğunu göz önüne aldığımız zaman, yalnızca bazılarına dikkat çekildiği tahmininde bulunabiliriz. Kitapta değinilen tüm kavramlara indekste yer verilseydi eğer, böyle bir indeks çok daha uzun olabilirdi.

Ahmet İhsan ve Şerafeddin Mağmumi'nin Hatıralarında Avrupa

XIX. yüzyılda Avrupa'yı ziyaret eden Türklerin rakamı Türkiye'yi gezen Avrupalıların rakamından çok daha düşüktü. Gezginlerin bıraktıkları gezi notları da oldukça azdır. Bu nedenle var olan eserlerin önemi büyük, taşıdıkları bilgi zenginliği yönüyle de değerleri tartışılmaz eserlerdir. Dolayısıyla Ahmet İhsan ve Şerafeddin Mağmumi'nin gezi hatıraları XIX. yüzyılın Türk gezginleri tarafından yazılmış diğer Avrupa gezi hatıraları gibi,[6]

[6] XIX. yüzyıl Avrupa'sını hatıralarında anlatan başlıca yazarlar arasında şunları sıralayabiliriz (parantez içinde gezi tarihi): Sadık Rifat Paşa (1830), Mehmet Rauf (1851) – Servet-i Fünuncu Mehmet Rauf ile karıştırmamak gerek, Abdülhak Hamit Tarhan (1876–1914), Ahmet Mithat Efendi (1889), Hüseyin Hulki (1891), Ahmet İhsan Tokgöz (1891), Mehmet Enisî (1894), Şerafeddin Mağmumi (1896–98).

günümüz araştırmacıları ve okurları için geçmişin Avrupa'sına dair önemli bilgi kaynaklarıdır. Ahmet İhsan'ın hatıralarında değinilen başlıca kentler arasında Paris, Le Havre, Londra, Brüksel, Amsterdam, Hannover, Hamburg, Berlin, Potsdam, Leipzig, Frankfurt, Freiburg, Zurich, Luzern, Bern, Geneve, Torino, Genova, Roma, Trieste, Viyana ve Budapeşte dikkat çekerken; Şerafeddin Mağmumi'nin anlattığı şehirler arasında da özellikle Brüksel, Londra, Paris, Lyon, Montpellier, Marsilya, Cannes, Nice, Monte Carlo, Genova, Roma, Napoli, Pompei, Venedik ve Grenoble yer alır. Şerafeddin Mağmumi'nin kitabının yeni baskısına eklenen 1914 yılı gezi anısında Hamburg ve Berlin izlenimlerini de bulabiliriz.

İki genç seyyahımız gezdikleri şehirler içerisinde en çok nelere dikkat ettiler, hangi yerlerde daha yoğunluğuna zaman geçirdiler ve daha kapsamlı notlar aldılar? Sorumuzun yanıtı için gezginlerin tercih ettikleri yerleri dikkatle incelediğimizde önemli sonuçlara varabiliyor, XIX. yüzyıl Türkiye'sinden Avrupa'ya gelen aydın gezginlerin beklentileriyle meraklarını öğrenebiliyoruz. Kuşkusuz, her ikisi de gezi yolculuklarına titizlikle hazırlanan "turistler" gibi çıkmışlar ve her ikisi de yine, bulunacakları şehirlerde görülmeye değer yerleri Fransız kaynaklarından önceden öğrenmişlerdir.

Ahmet İhsan'ın kitabından genç "turist"in – bu hatıraları yazarken – çok güzel bir amacının olduğunu anlarız: Türk okurlarına yalnızca gezdiği ve gördüğü yerleri ayrıntılarıyla anlatmıyor, aynı zamanda okurlarının Avrupa'ya dair bilgilerini zenginleştirmek yönünde de gidiyor. Bu açıdan bakıldığı zaman Ahmet İhsan'ın kitabı salt klasik bir "gezi hatıratı" olmaktan çıkıp biraz coğrafya kitabı, biraz rehber ve biraz da ansiklopedik eser niteliği kazanır. Örneğin Belçika kıyılarına vapurla yaklaştığı zaman not ettiği paragrafta

> Şimdi Belçika toprağına ayak atacağız; teferruat-ı seyahate başlamadan size memleket hakkında biraz malûmat-ı sathiye vereyim. [...] Belçika ahalisi iki takımdan müteşekkildir. Birincisine 'Valon'lar, ikincisine 'Flaman'lar derler fakat bunlar müsavi miktarda değildir; daima Valonların adedi Flamanlara nispeten üçün beşe nispeti gibidir (Ahmet 2007: 221).

derken, devamında da, Belçika'nın bir kısmının deniz seviyesinin altında bulunduğunu, araziye nispeten nüfus bakımından dünyanın en kalabalık ülkesi olduğunu, demiryolları en çok olan memleketler arasında yer aldığını, Belçika'da tren biletlerinin dünyanın en ucuz tren biletleri olduğunu not düşer; nüfusa dair istatistik bilgileri verir, konuşulan dilleri tanıtır ve Brüksel'in 1731 tarihli büyük yangından sonra yeniden ve çok daha düzenli bir şekilde inşa edildiğini aktarır. Kahvehanelerinin, bahçelerinin ve bulvarlarının güzellikleri nedeniyle bu şehrin "Paris'in bir yavrusu" olma durumu yazarın dikkatini çeker (Ahmet 2007: 231). Belçika'ya dair bilgiler kitabının 221'den 238'e uzanan sayfaları arasında yer alır ve bu bilgiler oldukça kapsamlı bir rehber niteliğindedir. Yazarın Belçika'da bir buçuk (!) gün kaldığını ve çok az yer gezebildiğini göz önüne aldığımız zaman, bu memlekete dair genişçe yer vermesindeki amacının gezi hatıralarından çok "hatıraları kapsayan rehber" yazmak olduğu gerçeği netlik kazanır.

Ahmet İhsan'dan altı yıl sonra (1897) Belçika'yı gören ve Brüksel'i gezen Şerafeddin Mağmumi de izlenimlerini benzer ayrıntılarla kâğıtlara aktarmış ve bu seyahatine o da aynı titizlikle hazırlanmıştı. Ancak, Ahmet İhsan'ın önceden detaylı olarak planlanmış üç aylık gezisine karşın Şerafeddin Mağmumi Avrupa'da mülteci olarak uzun müddet kalmış, gezilerini Avrupa'dayken planlamış ve şehir haritalarıyla rehber kitaplarını da Avrupa'da aramıştı. Tahmin edilebilir ki onun gezi hazırlıkları bu yüzden çok daha kolaydı. Paris'te bulunduğu günlerde Brüksel Dünya Sergisi'ni görme fikrine aniden karar verir, ertesi gün için tren biletini aldıktan sonra eve döner ve yolculuktan önceki son geceyi de Brüksel'e dair bilgileri toplamakla geçirir:

> Gece yarısına kadar meşguliyetim Brüksel planını, haritasını, rehber-i seyahatin kitabını tedkîk ve mütâlaa etmek, şâyân-ı ziyaret ve temâşâ mevâkii kayıt ve zabt eylemek, iki günde ikmâl olunacak hususî bir ziyaret haritası tanzîm etmekten ibaret oldu (Şerafeddin 2008: 22).

Herhalde bu "gecede haritayı tetkik" çok ciddî bir şekilde yapılmış olsa gerek ki, Brüksel'de sadece iki gün (!) kalan Şerafeddin Mağmumi bu seyahatini anlatan ve toplamı 75 sayfa tutarında tam 10 mektup yazmış. Belçika'ya dair izlenimleri, Ahmet İhsan'ınki gibi olumludur. Brüksel için "küçük Paris" der (Şerafeddin 2008: 89), şehrin ucuzluğunu ve düzenli mimarisini över, sayısız saraylarını, kiliselerini, parklarını ve müzeleri detaylı olarak anlatır. Her iki yazar da ilginç bir ayrıntıya dikkat etmiş; bu ortak ayrıntı, Brüksel sokaklarında mal satan esnafların küçücük arabalarına köpek koşmalarıdır.

Londra'ya ait anılar Ahmet İhsan'ın kitabında 40 sayfa, Şerafeddin Mağmumi'nin eserindeyse 16 mektup olmak üzere 100 sayfalık yer işgal eder. Biri sekiz gün, diğeri iki hafta süreyle Londra'da kalarak bu şehrin görülmeye değer yerlerini ayrıntılı olarak anlatırlar. Tarif edilen yerler arasında Thames nehri, nehir vapurları, köprüler, semtler ve Hyde Park başta olmak üzere Londra parkları, en ünlü müzelerle caddeler ve meydanlar, saraylar, kiliseler, kütüphaneler, hastaneler, garlar, anıtlar vb. bulunmaktadır. Şerafeddin Mağmumi, kitabının başka bölümlerinde de yaptığı gibi, bu bölümlerde de Türk okurlarına gördüğü yerleri anlatırken zaman zaman benzetmeler yapmaya çalışır. Örneğin Westminster Abbey'ye dair

> Haricen salîp şeklinde ve İngiliz Gotik tarz-ı mimarîsinde inşa olunmuş. Medhalin tarafeynindeki mütenâzır ve müteşâbih iki yüce çan kulesiyle Paris'in Notre Dame Kilisesi'ni andırıyor. Fakat ona nispeten nukuş ve müzeyyenâtı pek az, pek sadedir (Şerafeddin 2008: 160)

şeklinde bir karşılaştırma yaparken; Thames nehri altındaki tünel trenini anlatırken de

> Beheri bizim Galata tramvay arabaları gibi gayet dar beş vagon ile minimini bir lokomotiften mürekkep katar bizi bekledi" (Şerafeddin 2008: 169)

tanımlamasında bulunur. Ahmet İhsan'ın Londra hatıraları da aynı şekilde ilginç ve canlı bir üslupla kaleme alınmış. Ancak, ilk dikkat çeken yönü, Ahmet İhsan'ın, Mağmumi'den biraz daha çok tenkitçi olmasıdır. En çok şikâyet ettiği konuysa İngilizlerin kendi dillerinden başka dil bilmemeleridir:

> İngiltere'de seyahat etmek için velev sathî olsun İngiliz lisanına aşina olmak lâzım! [...] Meselâ Almanya'da, İtalya'da gezilirken Fransızca lisanla daima hall-i müşkil kabil olduğu hâlde Fransızcanın lisan-ı beynelmilel bulunduğuna ehemmiyet vermeyen İngiltere'de Fransızca ile değil İngilizceden gayrı lisan ile matlubu isaf ettirmek mümkün değildir! Londra cevelânımı yazarken nasıl eziyetlere düştüğümü gördüğünüz zaman hem güler hem şaşarsınız (Ahmet 2007: 166–167)

Şikâyet ettiği bir başka konu ise, İngiltere'deki para durumuyla ilgili. Örneğin, Avrupa'nın diğer ülkelerinde Fransız parası kullanılabildiği halde, burada yalnız İngiliz parası geçerli. Hem de, *pound*, *shilling* ve *pence* hesabı o kadar karışıktır ki, yazar,

> alış veriş zamanında şilin ve pena hesaplarının içinden çıkmak müşkilce olduğundan İngilizler bile ekseriya şaşırıyorlar! (Ahmet 2007: 168)

vurgulamasında bulunur. Yazarın "garaib-i âdâtı" olarak nitelendirdiği İngilizlerin tuhaflıklarından biri de, kendilerini her konuda üstün görmeleri. Bu konuda şöyle yazar:

> Bilâpervâ denilebilir ki İngiltere'nin hiçbir hareketi kimseye benzemez ve herkesten iyi yaparız davasındadırlar. Bundan dolayı İngiltere'nin nazar-ı ihtiramını kazanmak isteyenler onların âdât-ı garibesine uymalıdır" (Ahmet 2007: 168).

Ahmet İhsan için İngilizlerin mutfağı da son derecede kötüdür:

> Yemekleri de yenir hâlde değildir. [...] Londra'nın lokantaları hep İngiliz yemeği ihzar eyler; bunların müstahzaratı iştiha ile yenilir şeylerden değildir; İngiliz suret-i tabhından memnun olmak için İngiltereli olmalı. [...] Hele kaplumbağı çorbası, kurbağa yahnisi gibi şeylerini zikretmek bile istemem (Ahmet 2007: 168–170).

Sonuç

Yukarıda; özetle değinmeye, aktarmaya ve paylaşmaya çalıştığım gezi izlenimleri Ahmet İhsan'ın kitabında 500, Magmumi'nin kitabında ise 400 sayfadan fazla bilgilerle yer alırken gerçek bir kültür hazinesine dönüşmektedirler. Ne yazık ki, şimdiye değin bu eserlerden yalnızca Türk okurları yararlanabilmiş, yabancı dillere çeviri ve aktarımları yapılmadığı nedeniyle Avrupalı okurlarla araştırmacılar bu kaynak eserlere ulaşamamışlardır. Oysa, Avrupa gezi izlenimlerini Osmanlı seyyahlarının kalemlerinden okumak Avrupalı okurlar için kimi zaman eğlenceli, kimi zaman öğretici ve keyifli olabileceği gibi, araştırmacılar adına da büyük bir kazanç olacağını düşünmek yararlı olacaktır. Anı ve gezi türündeki eserlere ilgi duyanlar arasında yalnızca araştırmacılarla tarihçilerin değil, beraberinde, mimarî, teknoloji ve sanayi tarihçileri, çoğrafya, tiyatro, edebiyat uzmanları, sosyologlar, etnoğraflar ve hayatın başka alanlarındaki ilgililerinin de bulundukları unutulmamalıdır. Kanımca her iki eser – ihmal edilemeyecek değerde bilgiler içerdiklerinden – Avrupa dillerine çevrilmeye lâyık eserlerdir.

Bu makalenin ilk bölümünde örneklenen usulsüzlük ve yanlış editörlük yöntemlerinden kaçınılarak hazırlanan (ya da bundan sonra hazırlanacak olan) eski anılar, geçmişten bugüne, bugünden yarına taşınan değerleri tartışılmaz belgelerdir. Bu inanç ve düşünceden hareketle Türk araştırmacılarına ve yayıncılarına buradan seslenmek yerinde ise, henüz yeni baskıları gerçekleşmeyen eski hatıralarla gezi kitaplarını o unutulmuş oldukları tozlu gazete arşivleriyle kimi kişilere ait özel kütüphane raflarından bir an önce çıkararak gün ışığına kavuşturmalarının, en içtenlikli dileğinde bulunuyoruz.

Kaynakça

Ahmet İhsan. 2007. *Avrupa'da Ne Gördüm. Tuna'da Bir Hafta*. Servantie A., Gündoğdu F. (haz.). İstanbul.

Birinci A. 2005a. Canlanamayan Hâtıralar. *Müteferrika* 27: 73–88.

Birinci A. 2005b. Sultan Abdülhamid'in Hâtıra Defteri Meselesi. *Divan-İlmî Araştırmalar* 19: 177–194.

Birinci A. 2007. Hatıraların Bir Müdafaası. *Türkiye Kültür ve Sanat Yıllığı 2007*. Ankara: 580–601.

Şerafeddin Mağmumi. 2008. *Avrupa Seyahat Hatıraları*. Polat N. H., Fedai H. (haz.). İstanbul.

Studies on the Turkic World
A Festschrift for Professor St. Stachowski on the Occasion of His 80th Birthday
edited by E. Mańczak-Wohlfeld and B. Podolak, Kraków 2010: 223–230

Peter Zieme (Berlin)

Das türkische Vaterunser in syrischer Schrift

Kurze Einleitung

Das Vaterunser gehört zweifellos zu den berühmtesten Texten, die eine sehr weite Verbreitung auf der Welt erfahren haben. Auf einer Internetseite sind Versionen in 1449 Spachen und Dialekten verzeichnet, darunter auch mehrere türkische.[1] Ob die Jesu zugeschriebenen Worte in der heutigen Form tatsächlich auf ihn zurückgehen, ist eine Frage, die hier nicht zur Debatte steht. Die auf Matth. 6:9–13 basierende längere Fassung[2] liegt auch den türkischen Versionen zugrunde, die ich anläßlich des 80. Geburtstages von Stanisław Stachowski vorstellen möchte.

Christliche Texte aus den älteren Epochen der türkischen Welt kennen wir von den zentralasiatischen Regionen von Yedisu bis zur Turfanoase, von Xaraxoto sowie von mehreren Regionen Chinas bis einschließlich Quanzhou (etwa 10.–14. Jh.), aus dem Elhanidenreich (13.–14. Jh.) und dem kiptschakischen Wolgagebiet (15.–16. Jh.). Doch das Vaterunser begegnet uns erst in einem Denkmal der zuletzt genannten Region. Es ist wohl am ehesten der mangelhaften Überlieferung zuzuschreiben, daß die älteste türkische Version diejenige des Codex Comanicus[3] ist. Ein Vergleich dieser Fassung mit den osmanischen, dabei auch der hier vorgestellten in syrischer Schrift, sowie mit den modernen Versionen ist

[1] http://www.christusrex.org/www1/pater/JPN-turkish.html.

[2] Die kürzere Fassung hat Lukas 11:2–4.

[3] Codex Cumanicus, facs.: 63v27–32.

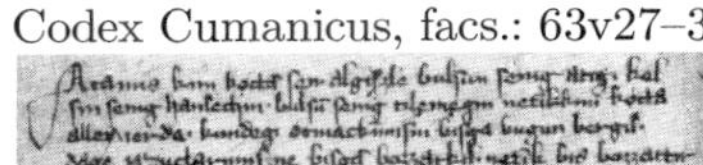

nicht angestrebt, wäre aber zweifellos ein interessantes Thema. Einzubeziehen wäre dann auch auch das kumanische Miatyánk aus Ungarn.[4]

Beschreibung der Handschriften

Die hier zu behandelnde osmanische Version gebe ich nach zwei syrischen Handschriften wieder. Die entsprechenden Kataloge geben folgende Auskünfte. Die erstere der beiden Handschriften ist Mingana 350, zu der der Sammler selbst in seinem Katalog schreibt:

> 110 × 89 mm. 246 leaves, generally nine and ten lines to the page. Miscellaneous extracts from the Office-Book and the Service-Book of the West Syrians. (...) On ff. 110–111 is the Lord's Prayer in Turkish, but in Syriac characters. Dated April, A.D. 1850, and written (probably at Mosul) by Joseph, son of Behnān (*sic*) al-Ḥaddād, in the time of the West Syrian Patriarch Ignatius Jacob; and of the Maphrian Gregory Behnam (written Behnān), Archbishop of Mosul; and of Cyril Matthew, Bishop of the monastery of St. Matthew (Shaikhs Matti). Negligent and bold West Syrian hand. Headings in red. Well rubricated.[5]

Die andere ist die von E. Sachau erwähnte Handschrift 191,[6] über sie schreibt W. Pertsch:

> Diese kleine Handschrift enthält christliche Gebete u. dgl., meist syrisch oder karschunisch, durchaus mit neuem gutem *P*ʰ*šiṯā* geschrieben; ganz am Ende stehen zwei kurze Abschnitte in türkischer Sprache, gleichfalls mit *P*ʰ*šiṯā* geschrieben, nämlich: 1. ein Glaubens-bekenntnis [...], 2. das Vaterunser [...] Grösse der Blätter: 11 × 8 cm.[7]

Beide Handschriften sind ihrer äußeren Erscheinung nach ähnlich, obwohl sich die Länge der Zeilen wesentlich unterscheidet. Das weist zumindest

[4] Mándoky Kongur I., *A kun nyelv magyarországi emlékei*, Karcag 1993.

[5] A. Mingana, *Catalogue of the Mingana Collection of manuscripts now in the possession of the Trustees of the Woodbrooke Settlement, Selly Oak, Birmingham*, I: *Syriac and Garshūni manuscripts*, Cambridge 1933, Sp. 648–649.

[6] E. Sachau, *Kurzes Verzeichnis der Sachau'schen Sammlung syrischer Handschriften*, Berlin 1885, Nr. 191: "(karsch[uni]. Brevarium eines Diaconus (...) (türk. Gebete in syrischer Schrift)".

[7] W. Pertsch, *Verzeichniss der türkischen Handschriften*, Berlin 1889 [*Die Handschriften-Verzeichnisse der Königlichen Bibliothek zu Berlin* VI], Nr. 514.

darauf hin, daß auch das Manuskript, für das nach der Katalogauskunft keine Zeitangabe zur Verfügung steht, etwa aus derselben Epoche stammen dürfte. Damit liegen Kopien vor, die in der Mitte des 19. Jahrhunderts in Mosul oder in dessen Nähe in Gebrauch gewesen sein mögen. Die Sprache jedenfalls ist osmanisch-türkisch, wenngleich es zumindest auch einen Hinweis auf syrische Beeinflussung gibt. Da das aramäisch-syrische Wort *malkut* "Königreich, Reich" kein gebräuchliches Lehnwort im Osmanischen war, kann man zumindest auf eine gewisse Nähe zu syrischen Christen schließen. Den stärksten Hinweis bietet natürlich der Gebrauch der syrischen Schrift.[8] Dennoch ist das Merkmal nicht stark genug, denn auch in osmanischen Bibeln in arabischer Schrift wird das Wort verwendet,[9] z. B. im *Kitabi Mukkades*[10] (*melekût-un gelsin*), in anderen wird *hükümranlık* oder *egemenlik* verwendet. Ein Text in arabischer Schrift von 1870 hat, wenn kein Fehler vorliegt, eine Doppelschreibung von initialem *m-* vor: *memlekūt*, die möglicherweise aus einer Kontamination mit *memleket* "Land" resultiert.[11]

Hier wäre zu erwähnen, daß das osmanische Wort *melkut* als eine Ableitung von *melek* eine ganz andere Bedeutung hat: "Yerden kaldırılıp alınan şey. Sokağa, virâneliğe, câmi veya kilise kapısına bırakılmış çocuk".[12]

Vergleichende Transliteration

In der folgenden Transliteration werden die beiden Handschriften Mingana 350 und Sachau 191 gegenübergestellt. Da die Zeilen der zweiten Handschrift auch angegeben werden, diese aber gegenüber der ersteren länger sind, ergibt sich keine völlige Zeilenkongruenz.

[8] B. Trigona-Harany hat kürzlich eine Bibliographie von osmanischen Peridioka veröffentlicht, unter denen viele, mindestens zum Teil, in syrischer Schrift gedruckt sind, vgl. B. Trigona-Harany, *A Bibliography of Süryânî Peridiocals in Ottoman Turkish*, in: Hugoye: Journal of Syriac Studies 12.2 (2009), 287–300. Zu ermitteln, wieweit handschriftliche Zeugnisse erhalten sind, bleibt künftiger Forschung vorbehalten, ich kenne bisher jedenfalls nur einen 1915 geschriebenen osmanischen Brief (nach einer Xeroxkopie, über die Professor Geng Shimin verfügt und die er mir zur Veröffentlichung zur Verfügung gestellt hat).

[9] Verwiesen sei auf die Internetseite (Fußn. 1).

[10] Istanbul 1976.

[11] Nach der oben zitierten Internetseite (Fußn. 1), die auf dem nicht nachgeprüften Buch The Lord's Prayer in ten languages of Russia, St. Peterburg 1870 basiert.

[12] Auch im Deutschen werden die Findelkinder als "Engel" bezeichnet.

Mingana 350	**Sachau 191**
110b	
04 ʾye	
05 g^{o}wgl^{a}rd^{ʾa} ʾw^{o}l^{ʾa}n[13]	01 ʾy$_{e}$ gw^{o}gl^{a}rdʾ ^{ʾo}wl^{aʾ}n p^{ʾa}p^{ʾa}
06 b^{ʾa}b^{a}mz – ʾ$_{i}$smy$_{i}$n̈	02 m^{e}yz . ʾsmy$_{i}$n m^{u}qd̃s ʾwlswn
07 m^{u}qd̃s ^{oʾ}wlswn[14]	
08 m^{a}lkwtyn̈ kʾlsw$_{i}$n	03 m^{a}lkw^{u}tyn g^{aʾ}lsy$_{i}$n m^{u}r^{aʾ}dy^{i}n
09 mrʾdyn̈ g^{o}wg^{a}dʾ	04 gw^{o}gd^{aʾ} ny^{e}ğ^{a}h qy^{i}ly^{i}nw^{u}rs^{aʾ}
10 n^{i}yğ^{a}h qylynwr ^{ʾi}	11 ^{i}ysh
111a	
01 ^{i}ysh y^{e}rd^{aʾ}[15] d^{a}ky	05 y^{e}rd^{ʾa} dky$_{i}$ b^{o}wy$_{i}$l^{a}h qy$_{i}$ly$_{i}$nw^{u}rs^{i}n
02 b^{o}w^{a}ylʾ qy$_{i}$l$_{i}$nsw^{o}n[16] .	
03 h^{a}r g^{o}wnky$_{i}$ -	06 h^{a}r gw^{u}nky$_{i}$ ^{ʾa}tm^{a}gm$_{i}$z^{i}y by$_{i}$z^{aʾ}
04 ^{ʾa}tm^{a}g$_{i}$mzy by$_{i}$z^{ʾa}	
05 bwgw^{o}n wy^{e}r -	07 bw^{u}gw^{u}n w^{e}yr w by$_{i}$z^{aʾ} sw^{u}ğl^{a}rm^{u}zy$_{i}$
06 w^{a} by^{i}z^{ʾa} sw^{o}ğl^{a}r -	
07 m̤zy̩ b^{ʾa}g̩šl^{ʾa} -	08 bg^{u}šl^{a}h ny^{e}ğ^{a}h ky$_{i}$ by^{i}z dky$_{i}$
08 ny^{e}ğh^{a} ky b[17]	
09 by$_{i}$z d^{a}ky b$_{i}$y$_{i}$z$_{i}$h^{a}	09 by$_{i}$zy^{i} sw^{u}ğlw^{u} ʾw^{o}lʾnl^{a}r^{a}
10 swğlwʾ[18] ʾwl^{aʾ} ::	
111b	
01 nl^{a}rʾ bʾgšlʾdyḥ	10 bg^{u}šl^{a}rz w by$_{i}$zy^{i} ʾmt^{a}h^{a}n^{aʾ}
02 – w by$_{i}$zy$_{i}$ ʾymt$_{i}$ḥ^{ʾa}nʾ	
03 ʾ$_{i}$dk̠ʾl ʾ$_{e}$ytm^{aʾ} -	01 ^{ʾe}tk̠^{aʾ}l ^{ʾe}ytm^{aʾ} . ^{ʾa}m̃ʾ by$_{i}$zy^{i} _
04 ʾm̃ʾ b$_{i}$y$_{i}$zy[19] _ šryr	
05 dʾn qwrṭ - -.	02 šr$_{i}$yd^{aʾ}n[20] qw^{u}rṭ^{a}t čw^{u}n m^{a}lk^{u}wt
06 č^{o}wn m^{ʾa}l^{a}kwt	
07 w q^{a}wʾt w ʿzt ʾ-	03 w qw̃ʾt w ʿz̃t ^{ʾa}b^{a}d^{ʾa} snndr
08 bdʾ snndr ʾmyn	04 ^{aʾ}my^{e}n

13 Das Diakritikon über dem w sieht wie ^{a} aus, sollte aber wohl ^{o} sein.

14 Das Diakritikon ^{a} steht vor dem Alif wie auch in vielen anderen Fällen.

15 Das Diakritikon ^{a} ist sehr lang, es erstreckt sich über drei Konsonanten.

16 Es gibt auch auf der Internetseite (Fußn. 1) eine Version in arabischer Schrift mit *k(ı)l(ı)nsun*.

17 Das b ist wohl zu tilgen.

18 Der Buchstabe nach dem w ist unklar, zusammen mit dem nachfolgenden ʾ wohl überflüssig.

19 Die Stellung des Diakritikons “arabisch i” unter dem y ist seltsam.

20 Das zweite -r- von šryr fehlt, dies dürfte jedoch einfach ein Fehler sein.

Einige Bemerkungen

In beiden Handschriften werden die diakritischen Zeichen für die Vokale nach dem Sertō-Usus angewendet, doch nicht durchgehend. Interessant ist auch der Umstand, daß der Schreiber an manchen Stellen zu den arabopersischen Diakritika überwechselt, was leicht erklärlich wird, wenn man an die vom Persischen beeinflußte Schreibung von *baba* als *papa* bedenkt.

Betrachten wir einige Unterschiede zwischen den beiden Handschriften, so ergibt sich der generelle Eindruck, daß Sachau 191 eine jüngere Orthographie repräsentiert. Dies fällt besonders am Beispiel k^{ʾ}lsw$_{i}$n (Mingana 350) gegenüber g^{aʾ}lsy$_{i}$n (Sachau 191) auf. Dabei ist allerdings nicht sicher, daß k- wirklich k- gesprochen wurde, denn es könnte ja einfach auch nach der arabischen Schrift reproduziert worden sein. Die Sachau-Schreibung läßt sich aber mit Sicherheit als *gelsin* interpretieren. Aber auch der Mingana-Beleg läßt sich wohl am besten als *gelsin* lesen, das Diakritikon unter dem -w- kann wohl nichts anderes bedeuten.

Die Schreibung in der Sachau-Hs. für *baba* "Vater" mit deutlichem *p* an beiden Stellen wurde bereits früher als seltsam angesehen. Die drei Punkte unter dem Buchstaben *b* sind dem persischen Usus entlehnt. Ob der Schreiber an dieser Stelle wirklich an den Papst (türk. *papa*) gedacht haben mag?

Der Aorist qy$_{i}$ly$_{i}$nw^{u}rs^{i}n der Sachau-Handschrift ist unik, ihm steht ein zu erwartender Optativ der 3. Person Singular in der Mingana-Handschrift wie auch der Versionen der Internetseite gegenüber.

Das Wort für "Brot" wird in beiden Handschriften *ätmäg* mit finalem *-g* (wie zu erwarten nach osmanischem *ğ* zwischen Vokalen) geschrieben.

Auffällig ist der Unterschied von *bizä suğlu olan* (Mingana) gegen *bizi suğlu olan* (Sachau), letztere Form muß ein Fehler sein.

Die unterschiedliche Schreibweise von *idhal* (Mingana) und *ethal* (Sachau) läßt auf den Übergang von -d- zu -t- schließen, zugrunde liegt arab.-pers. *idxāl*. Interessant ist aber die Schreibung mit unterstrichenem k für خ.[21] Die differierende Vokalisierung der ersten Silbe mag auch einen Hinweis auf unterschiedliche Aussprachen geben.

Die Formen qwrṭ (Mingana) und qw^{u}rṭ^{a}t (Sachau) für gemeintes *kurtar* "befreie (Imperativ)" der anderen Versionen bleiben mir unklar.

[21] Das ist die übliche Schreibweise für arabisch *x* in Karshuni, vgl. L. Costaz, *Grammaire syriaque*, Beyrouth 1992, p. 2 fn. 1.

Ein fast inhaltlicher Unterschied wird in dem Satz "wie wir vergeben unseren Schuldigern" deutlich. Die Mingana-Handschrift verwendet eine Vergangenheitsform, während die Form in der Sachauschen eben die Gegenwart (Aorist) ist.

Eine normierte Transkription

Eine normierte Transkription läßt sich in der folgenden Weise erstellen, nur stark abweichende Schreibungen der Sachau-Handschrift werden in Klammern wiedergegeben.

> Äy göglärdä olan babamız (papamız)! İsmin mukaddas olsun, malkutın gälsin, muradın gögdä nečä kılınur ise (kılınursa) yerde dähi böyle kılınsun (kılınursän), her günki ätmägimizi bizä bugün ver, wa bizä sučlarımızı bagıšla nečä ki biz dähi bizä (bizi) sučlu olanlara bagušladıx (bagušlarız), wa bizi imtihana idhal ätmä, amma bizi šärirdän kurt (sic!), čün malkut wa kuwwat wa izzat abdan sänindür amin.

Eine wörtliche Übersetzung

Schließen möchte ich die Vorstellung dieser Paternoster-Versionen mit einer wörtlichen Übersetzung

> O unser in den Himmeln seiender Vater! Dein Name geheiligt sei! Dein Reich komme, dein Wille im Himmel wie geschehe auf der Erde auch so sei! Unser tägliches Brot gib uns heute! Unsere Schuld vergib wie auch wir unseren Schuldigern vergeben (haben). Und uns in Prüfung führe nicht! Sondern uns von dem Bösen befreie! Denn das Reich und die Kraft und die Herrlichkeit sind ewiglich dein. Amen!

Abbildungen

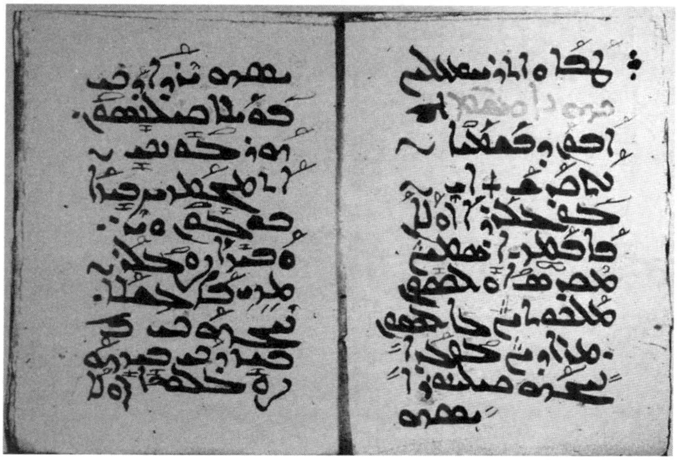

Abb. 1 *Mingana 350*, fol. 110b–111a (Reproduced by permission of Special Collections, University of Birmingham).

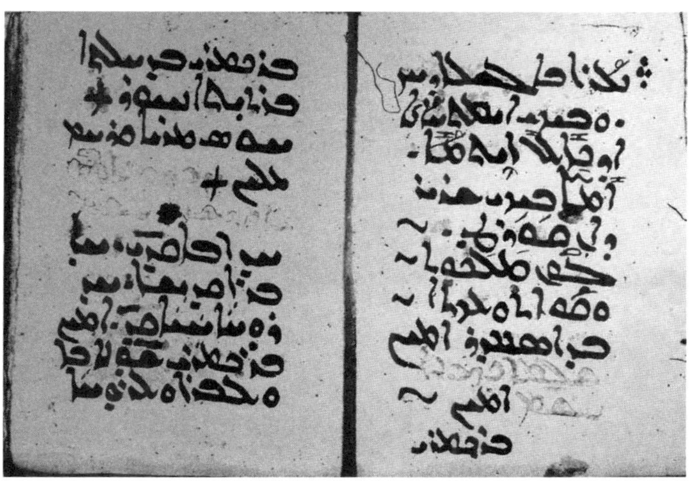

Abb. 2 *Mingana 350*, fol. 111b–112a (Reproduced by permission of Special Collections, University of Birmingham).

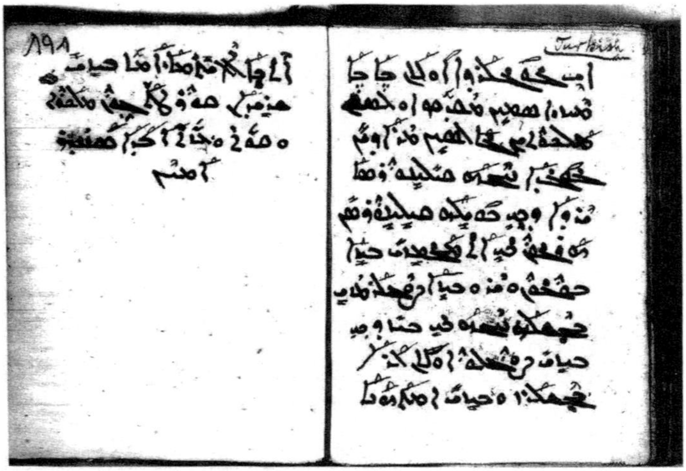

Abb. 3 *Sachau 191* (mit Genehmigung der Staatsbibliothek zu Berlin. Preussischer Kulturbesitz).

Invitation to Discussion

Studies on the Turkic World
A Festschrift for Professor St. Stachowski on the Occasion of His 80th Birthday
edited by E. Mańczak-Wohlfeld and B. Podolak, Kraków 2010: 233–239

Marek Stachowski (Kraków)

Türkisch *kulak* 'Ohr', *kul* 'Sklave', *kulun* 'Fohlen'

Vor 90 Jahren zählte W. Bang (1919: 6, Anm. 1) das atü. *kulkak* 'Ohr' zu denjenigen Wörtern, «deren Stammsilbe *etymologisch undeutbar* ist». Aber schon zwei Jahre später leitete er *kulkak* 'Ohr' < *kul* 'Knecht, Sklave' her und deutete es etymologisch als 'Knechtlein' (Bang 1921: 8, Anm. 2). Ähnlich sollte es sich auch mit *tamgak* 'Kehle' (eigentl. 'Wändlein') < *tam* 'Wand', *erngek* 'Finger' (eigentl. 'Männlein') < *eren* 'Mann' und *jangak* 'Backe' (eigentl. 'Seitlein') < *jan* 'Seite' (richtiger: **jān*) verhalten (op. cit.).[1] Die starke Seite dieser Erklärung ist ihr systemischer Charakter,[2] die schwache Seite dagegen die recht untriviale Bedeutungsentwicklung. Nur für *jangak* wird sie auch heute noch ohne viel Bedenken akzeptiert.

[1] Da Diminutivformen häufig keine diminutive, sondern eine übertragene Bedeutung haben, wäre hier angebracht, all die Wörter als 'Quasi-Knecht', 'Quasi-Wand', 'Quasi-Mann' und 'Quasi-Seite' zu übersetzen. Vgl. auch dt. *Ärmel*, eigentl. 'Quasi-Arm', nicht *'kleiner Arm'.

[2] Ein weiterer Vorteil der Etymologie von Bang (dabei auch für die Herkunft von *kulak* interessant) ist die Berücksichtigung des Langvokals im jak. Wort *kulgāx* 'Ohr', zu dem es heißt: «Wenn die Länge im Jak. *kulgāx* 'Ohr' berechtigt ist, so wird *-*qāq* eine gehäufte Bildung *-*qa-aq* sein» (Bang 1921: 8, Anm. 2). Die meisten Forscher nach Bang ignorierten diese Vokallänge oder konnten sie nicht mit dem vorhergehenden Konsonanten korrelieren. Poppe gibt entweder **kulgāk* (1959: 677) oder **kulgak* (1960: 18) an – beides müßte im Jak. zu **kulāx* werden. Starostin (1991: 52) kann sich zwischen **kulgak* (wie Poppe 1960) und **kulkak*, das aber ein jak. **kulgax* ergeben würde, nicht entscheiden – beides ist also falsch. In Wirklichkeit geht jak. *kulgāx* auf urtü. **kulkāk* zurück (GJV § 5.3d), und dieses weiter auf **kulka+ak* (s. hier den letzten Abschnitt).

Der Rest gilt als äußerst unsicher und wird heute zumeist ignoriert oder höchstens "aus Chronistenpflicht" erwähnt.

In ÈSTJa VI 126 wird – wie in allen neueren Bänden dieses Wörterbuchs – mehr Gewicht auf außer- als auf innertürkische Etymologisierungsmöglichkeiten gelegt. So wird hier auch tü. *kulak* in erster Linie mit dem mo. Wortschatz verglichen. Die Resultate können uns aber kaum weiterhelfen: die Zuverlässigkeit – heißt es dort – der Zusammenstellung des türkischen Wortes mit mo. *kulugu* 'Ohrenschmalz' sei hoch, genüge aber nicht, um eine Wortbildungsbasis zu rekonstruieren, so daß die kritische Beurteilung der Erklärungskraft der türkisch-mongolischen Zusammenstellung in TMEN IV Nr. 132 zum Teil berechtigt sei. Was eine hohe, aber unzureichende Zuverlässigkeit genau bedeutet, sowie warum G. Doerfers Kritik nur zum Teil berechtigt ist, wenn die Zuverlässigkeit der Zusammenstellung für eine etymologische Erklärung nicht ausreicht, das sind Fragen, die in ÈSTJa unbeantwortet bleiben.

Vergleicht man jedoch die unterschiedlichen Laut- und morphologischen Varianten des Wortes für 'Ohr', wie z.B. ttü. kirg. schor. tuw. oir. suig. *kulak*, MK. *kulak* ~ *kulkak*, chal. *kulāk*, jak. *kulgāx*, so kommt man zu dem Schluß, daß die Wortbildungsbasis hier gewiß ein **kul* oder **kul-* ist, obwohl man die Bedeutung schlecht rekonstruieren kann. Am günstigsten wäre ein Verb wie **kul-* oder **kulȳ-* 'hören'; nur, ein solches Verb konnte nirgendwo gefunden werden. Eine Verbindung mit **kul* 'Sklave' erscheint wenig glaubhaft, und sonst gibt es nur noch eine Möglichkeit: schon 1917 erschien ein Artikel von W. Bang, in dem er das Substantiv *kulun* 'Füllen, Fohlen' (tschag. auch 'Küchlein') als Diminutiv zu **kul* id. interpretierte (Bang 1916–1917: 131), worin er eine Parallele zu tschag. *kurtun* 'Wurm' < gtü. *kurt* id. sowie osm. *kojun* 'Schaf' < gtü. *koj* id. sah und auf dieser Grundlage ein Diminutivsuffix *+*un* rekonstruierte. Auf diese Weise erhalten wir einen dritten Stamm **kul*, und zwar einen mit einer weiteren Bedeutung. Ein Versuch, für die Bedeutungen 'Ohr', 'Sklave' und 'Fohlen' einen gemeinsamen Nenner zu finden, der es möglich machte, die ursprüngliche Bedeutung von **kul(-)* zu nennen, scheint ziemlich hoffnungslos zu sein. Und doch soll dieser Versuch hier unternommen werden.

Wir wollen zuerst ein paar Worte zu *kulun* sagen. Bangs Etymologie war weder die erste noch die letzte in der Erforschungsgeschichte dieser Wortsippe. Noch 1902 hat Z. Gombocz (NyK 32: 192; zit. nach Joki 1952: 209) tü. *kulun* mit ostjak. *kolaŋ* 'Rentier' zusammengestellt, was aber weder die Struktur noch die Etymologie des türkischen Wortes klärt. Joki (1952: 208f.) spielte mit dem Gedanken, tü. *kulun* mit akkad. *kudûnu*, *kudânu*, *kudannu*, *kudînu*

'Maultier' zu verbinden, «denn [...] *kudûnu* usw. ist urspr. kein semitisches Wort, und im Akkad. gibt es viele Fälle, wo *d* (?*δ*) mit *l* gewechselt hat». Nun, wenn *kudûnu* aber kein semitisches Wort ist, so müßte es in diesem Kontext ein türkisches Lehnwort gewesen sein, was nicht nur aus sachlichen Gründen (brauchten die Akkadier fremde Namen für Fohlen oder Maultiere?), sondern auch aus geographischen Gründen inakzeptabel ist, ganz zu schweigen davon, daß wir gar nichts über die Türksprachen im Zeitalter vor über 2000 Jahren v.u.Z. sagen können. Kurz gesagt: Bangs Etymologie ist weder die erste noch die letzte, aber sicher die einzige ernstzunehmende.[3]

Ein semantisches Detail mag in unserem Kontext von großer Bedeutung sein. Bang schreibt nämlich, daß das tü. Wort für 'Füllen', das im Tschag. auch 'Küchlein' bedeutet, von einem Stamm **kul* kommt, der ebenfalls 'Füllen' bedeutet. Man kann sich schlecht vorstellen, wieso die Tschagataier irgendwann begonnen hätten, ihre Küchlein 'Füllen' zu nennen. Offensichtlich war die ursprüngliche Bedeutung des Stammes doch anders, dabei aber vermutlich irgendwie mit 'Tierjunges' oder gar 'jung; Junges' verbunden. Diese Vermutung findet ihre Bestätigung in kzk. *kūluk*[4] *taj* 'junges Füllen' (Joki 1952: 208), wörtl. '*kūluk* Füllen' (*taj* ist ein anderes türkisches Wort für 'Füllen'). Die semantische Komponente 'jung' oder sogar 'sehr jung' tritt manchmal auch bei *kulun*-Belegen vor, so z.B. in azerb. *gulun* 'neugeborenes Füllen', tschag. *kulun* 'Fohlen in seinem ersten Lebensmonat', und das daraus entstandene tschuw. *xăm* ~ *xŏm* bedeutet gar 'Embryo, Leibesfrucht des Pferdes' (ÈSTJa VI 132). Die letztere Bedeutung findet sich auch in oir. tat.dial. *kulga* 'Embryo; Keim; Sproß', chak. *xulga* 'Keim; Sproß, Schößling' (Novikova 1979: 107) wieder.

Wie ersichtlich, drehen sich all diese Bedeutungen um die jüngste Lebensphase. Daher wäre ich geneigt, die ganze *kulun*-Sippe von einem gtü. Verb. **kul-* herzuleiten, dessen ursprüngliche Bedeutung vielleicht 'auf-/entsprießen' war. Dann ließen sich alle Substantive dieser Wortsippe auf eine ursprüngliche Bedeutung wie '1. Keim(ling); 2. Sproß, Schoß, Sprößling, Schößling' zurückführen.

Sollte auch ttü. *kulak* 'Ohr' auf dieselbe Wurzel zurückgehen, so wäre seine anfängliche Bedeutung 'Keimling, Sprößling' o.ä. gewesen, was eine interessante Art und Weise wäre, einen Inhalt wie etwa 'kleiner Abstecher' auszudrücken.

[3] Ščerbak (1961: 90f.) schlägt in seiner explizit den Bezeichnungen für Haustiere gewidmeten Studie keine eigene Etymologie von *kulun* vor, sondern verweist nur auf Bang und Joki.

[4] Die Vokallänge in *kūluk* ist sekundär vor dem hohen Vokal der Folgesilbe entstanden.

Das macht einen genetischen Zusammenhang zwischen 'Ohr' und 'Fohlen' möglich. Das *tertium comparationis* ist offensichtlich 'klein; Keim, Schößling'.

Dadurch läßt sich ein weiterer Beleg klären. In MKašg. Wörterbuch finden wir nämlich einen Ausdruck wie *kulak tōn* 'Kleid mit kurzen Ärmeln' vor (Dankoff 1985: 147). Da sein Zusammenhang mit *kulak* 'Ohr' unmöglich schien, wurde in ÈSTJa VI 126 jenes *kulak* in *kolak* geändert und dem Wort *kolak* '1. einarmig; 2. ohne beide Arme; 3. mit verkrüppeltem Arm' gleichgesetzt. Welche dieser Bedeutungen zu dem Beleg von MKašg. passen könnte, wurde nicht erklärt. Da dieses Kleid kurze Ärmel hat, kann der Ausdruck nicht 'Kleid ohne Ärmel' bedeutet haben. 'Einarmig' paßt ebenfalls nicht, da uns nichts davon bekannt ist, daß das Kleid nur einen Ärmel besitzen sollte. Am ehesten eignet sich hierfür die Bedeutung 'mit verkrüppeltem Arm', wenn man nur 'kurze Ärmel' als 'verkrüppelte Arme' zu deuten bereit ist. Es erscheint jedoch realistischer, die Erklärung in ÈSTJa l.c. beiseite zu lassen, das Wort nicht *kolak*, sondern wie bisher *kulak* zu lesen, und den Ausdruck *kulak tōn* als 'Kleid mit Schößlingen (*kulak*)' zu interpretieren.

Es fragt sich nun, ob auch *kul* 'Sklave'[5] zu derselben Sippe zu zählen ist. Bisher hat dies niemand vorgeschlagen. E. Littman wollte 1924 tü. *kul* 'Sklave' < ind. *kōlī* herleiten, was in TMEN III Nr. 1519 zurecht abgewiesen wurde, da weder die lautliche noch die chronologische Seite hier akzeptabel ist (*kul* ist schon im Orchontürkischen belegt, in einer Zeit also, in der die Orchontürken noch keinen Kontakt mit indischen Sprachen hatten).

A. Bernštams Versuch aus dem Jahr 1946 (zit. nach TMEN III, Nr. 1519; ÈSTJa VI 121), tü. *kul* 'Sklave' zu tü. *kol* 'Arm' und *kyl-* 'machen' zu stellen, mag semantisch überzeugend aussehen, läßt sich aber phonetisch nicht glaubhaft machen.

Auch TMEN und ÈSTJa konnten keine Etymologie anbieten. G. Doerfer sprach sich jedenfalls gegen eine Entlehnung und für eine einheimische Etymologie aus (TMEN l.c.).

Im ersten Augenblick erscheint ein semantischer Zusammenhang von 'Sklave' einerseits und 'Ohr' ~ 'Fohlen' andererseits ausgeschlossen. Bedenkt man aber, daß 'Ohr' und 'Fohlen' ursprünglich etwa 'Kleines, Junges; Schößling' bedeutet haben mußten, so ändert sich die Situation ganz wesentlich. Zu denken ist hier an ungefähr denselben Entwicklungsweg, den im Polnischen und generell im Westslavischen das Wort (im Polnischen – archaisch und

[5] Die jak. Entsprechung *kulut* id. ist eine semantisch depluralisierte Form: **kul* id. + jak. (< mo.) Pl.-Suffix *-t* (Kałużyński 1961: 117).

dialektal; im Tschechischen – literarisch) *otrok* durchlaufen hat:[6] (urspr.) ‘derjenige, der nichts zu sagen hat’ → (poln.arch.) ‘Säugling’ → **[a]** (slovinz.) ‘Fohlen, Füllen’; **[b]** (poln.dial.) ‘Jugendlicher’ → (poln.dial.) ‘Knecht; Landarbeiter; Diener’ → (tschech.) ‘Sklave’ (Kąś 2005).[7]

Auf Grund dieser Parallele können wir auch für die Türksprachen den folgenden Bedeutungswandel annehmen: **kul* ‘Kleines, Junges’ → *‘Jüngling’ ~ *‘derjenige, der schwer arbeitet’ → **[a]** ‘Arbeiter, Landarbeiter’; **[b]** ‘Sklave’.[8]

[6] In der semantischen Entwicklungskette stehen die Namen der einzelnen Sprachen in Klammern, da es hier nur um die semantische Entwicklung geht, deren einzelne Phasen sich unabhängig voneinander entwickelt haben und heute in verschiedenen Sprachen belegt sind (d.h. es wird nicht behauptet, daß z.B. die tschechische Bedeutung auf die polnische zurückgeht). Das Schema zeigt vielmehr potentielle Bedeutungswandel, die alle eventuell auch in ein und derselben Sprachen vorkommen könnten.

[7] Das Wort weist auch andere Bedeutungen wie ‘Sohn’ oder ‘Workoholic’ auf, die in unserem Kontext jedoch ohne Belang sind. Eine Kuriosität ist es, daß für das Wort *otrok* im polnischen Wörterbuch von Samuel B. Linde (1857) auch eine besondere Bedeutung notiert ist: ‘bei den Türken: Soldatenveteran, der ein Gnadengehalt bezieht’. Erstaunlich, denn ein Soldatenveteran ist gewiß kein junger Mann, noch ein schwer arbeitender Knecht – ganz im Gegenteil: er ist alt und arbeitet gar nicht mehr. Wie kann also *ein* Wort zwei entgegengesetzte Bedeutungen haben? Es kam hier natürlich zu einer Verwechslung: S. B. Linde hat das in einer polnischen Quelle vorkommende osmanische Wort *oturak* ‘Soldatenveteran’ (s. Stachowski 2005: 214: *oturak*, *otrak*) offensichtlich falsch gelesen oder notiert und es dann mit poln. *otrok* verwechselt und als eine spezielle Bedeutung des *otrok* in sein Wörterbuch aufgenommen (Kąś 2005: 163).

[8] Obwohl der Versuch, so unterschiedliche Bedeutungen wie ‘Ohr’, ‘Fohlen’ und ‘Sklave’ miteinander zu verbinden, ziemlich hoffnungslos aussieht, gibt es hierfür doch mehr als nur *eine* Möglichkeit. Ich habe mich davon sehr wohl überzeugen können, als Robert Woodhouse (Brisbane), dem ich über meine Arbeit an diesem Thema kurz schrieb, in seiner Antwort – zum Teil als Scherz – zu raten versuchte (allerdings ohne das Wortmaterial überhaupt gesehen zu haben, also wirklich “raten”), welche Bedeutung den gemeinsamen Nenner für alle Wörter dieser Sippe abgeben könnte. Seine Idee, daß es sich hier vielleicht um ‘hören, gehorchen’ handelt (d.h. etwa ‘Ohr’ ← *‘hören, gehorchen’ → ‘Sklave’ [= ‘der zu hören/gehorchen hat, gehorsam ist’] ~ ‘Fohlen’ [= ‘der erst hören/gehorchen lernen muß’]), zeigt eindeutig, daß es über die Möglichkeit ‘jung, klein; Sproß’ hinaus auch noch mindestens *eine* andere, wenngleich nur eine rein theoretische gibt. Dieser Umstand erhöht die Wahrscheinlichkeit, all diese Wörter, die hier genannt wurden, von *einer* Wurzel abzuleiten, zusätzlich. – R. Woodhouse machte mich dankenswerterweise auch auf die alte und bis heute ernstzunehmende Zusammenstellung von altkirchenslav. *rabъ* ~ *robъ* ‘Sklave’ < **orbъ* ‘klein, schwach’ (≫ russ. *ребёнок* ‘Kind’) :: dt. *Arbeit* :: gr. *ὀρφανός* > lat. *orphanus* > engl. *orphan* ‘Waisenkind’ = armen. *(v)orb* ‘Waisenkind’ aufmerksam. Für die Übersicht über verschiedene Etymologisierungsmöglich-

Die Entwicklung der ganzen Wortsippe stelle ich mir folgendermaßen vor:

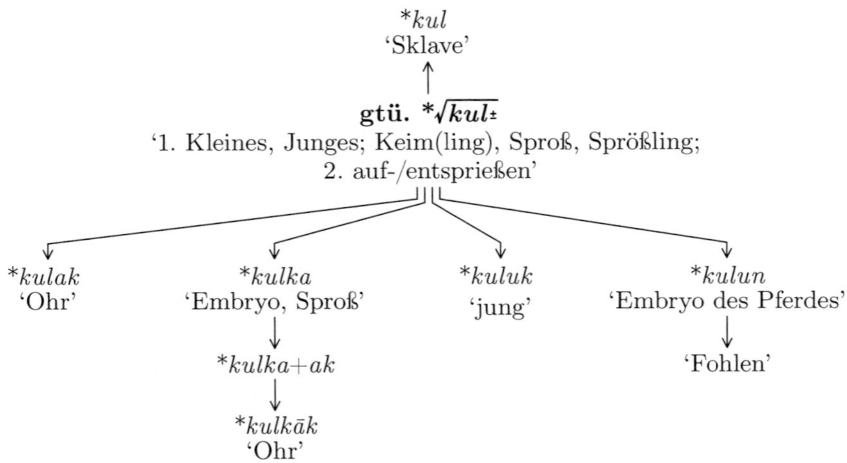

Literatur

ÈSTJa VI = [Sevortjan È. V. /] Blagova G. F. / Levitskaja L. S. / Dybo A. V., Rassadin V. I.: *Ètimologičeskij slovaŕ tjurkskich jazykov*, VI: к (Druckfehler für: ҡ), Moskva 2000.

GJV = Stachowski M.: *Geschichte des jakutischen Vokalismus*, Kraków 1993.

TMEN III = Doerfer G.: *Türkische und mongolische Elemente im Neupersischen unter besonderer Berücksichtigung älterer neupersischer Geschichtsquellen, vor allem der Mongolen- und Timuridenzeit*, III. Wiesbaden 1967.

TMEN IV = Doerfer G.: *Türkische und mongolische Elemente im Neupersischen unter besonderer Berücksichtigung älterer neupersischer Geschichtsquellen, vor allem der Mongolen- und Timuridenzeit*, IV. Wiesbaden 1975.

keiten und Benennungsmodelle, die für den Begriff 'Arbeit' erstellt werden können, s. Levickij 1995, wo auf S. 61 ebenfalls der Zusammenhang mit 'Sklave' unterstützt wird: «[...] значение 'мука, страдание' у герм. **arbē̯i̯iđiz* развилось, вероятнее всего, [...] из значения 'быть сиротой, невольником'».

Bang W. 1916–1917: Über die türkischen Namen einiger Grosskatzen. – *Keleti Szemle* 17: 112–146.

——— 1919: Vom Köktürkischen zum Osmanischen. Vorarbeiten zu einer vergleichenden Grammatik des Türkischen. Mitteilung 2–3. – *Abhandlungen der Preussischen Akademie der Wissenschaften. Phil.-Hist. Klasse 5*, Berlin: 1–79.

——— 1921: Vom Köktürkischen zum Osmanischen. Vorarbeiten zu einer vergleichenden Grammatik des Türkischen. Mitteilung 4. – *Abhandlungen der Preussischen Akademie der Wissenschaften. Phil.-Hist. Klasse 2*, Berlin: 1–26.

Dankoff R. 1985: *Maḥmūd al-Kāšγarī. Compendium of the Turkic dialects (Dīwān Luγāt at-Turk)*, III, Cambridge, Mass.

Joki A. J. 1952: *Die Lehnwörter des Sajansamojedischen*, Helsinki.

Kałużyński S. 1961: *Mongolische Elemente in der jakutischen Sprache*, Warszawa.

Kąś J. 2005: Polski *otrok* i turecki pseudo-*otrok* – 'chłopiec', 'pracoholik', 'weteran'? – Siemieniec-Gołaś E. / Pomorska M. (ed.): *Turks and non-Turks. Studies on the history of linguistic and cultural contacts* [FS S. Stachowski], Kraków: 159–164.

Levickij V. V. 1995: Ètimologija i istorija slova *Arbeit* v nemeckom jazyke. – *Movy jevropejśkoho kuĺturnoho arealu: Rozvitok i vzajemodija*, Kyjiv.

Novikova K. A. 1979: Nazvanija domašnich životnych v tunguso-mańčžurskich jazykach. – Cincius V. I. (ed.): *Issledovanija v oblasti ètimologii altajskich jazykov*, Leningrad: 53–134.

Poppe N. 1959: Das Jakutische. – Deny J. et al. (ed.): *Philologiae Turcicae Fundamenta*, I, Wiesbaden: 671–684.

——— 1960: *Vergleichende Grammatik der altaischen Sprachen*, I: *Vergleichende Lautlehre*, Wiesbaden.

Stachowski S. 2005: *Glosariusz turecko-polski*, Kraków.

Starostin S. A. 1991: *Altajskaja problema i proischoždenie japonskogo jazyka*, Moskva.

Ščerbak A. M. 1961: Nazvanija domašnich i dikich životnych v tjurkskich jazykach. – Ubrjatova E. I. (ed.): *Istoričeskoe razvitie leksiki tjurkskich jazykov*, Moskva: 82–172.

Studies on the Turkic World
A Festschrift for Professor St. Stachowski on the Occasion of His 80th Birthday
edited by E. Mańczak-Wohlfeld and B. Podolak, Kraków 2010: 241–265

Viktor Levickij (Černivci)

Semantische Struktur der ig. Wurzel **seH-* „Sehne“ und einige indogermanische und türkische Etymologien

1. Hypothesen und Ziele

In einer Reihe von etymologischen Untersuchungen (s. Trubačev 1966; Makovskij 1989; Levickij 1998; Lewizkij 1997; 2001 u.a.) wird die Hypothese über die Existenz des sogenannten semantischen Synkretismus in der ig. Ursprache besprochen. Dabei versteht man unter dem semantischen Synkretismus einen Vorgang, bei dem sich einige schwer vereinbare oder sogar entgegengesetzte Bedeutungen in einer einheitlichen Bedeutung vereinigen. Am deutlichsten zeigt sich ein solcher Synkretismus darin, daß die Derivate vermutlich derselben ig. Wurzel drei Grundbedeutungen zusammenbringen – „schneiden“, „verbinden“ und „biegen“. So vereinigt z.B. O.N. Trubačev in einer Wortsippe aisl. *skera* „schneiden“, ai. *kr̥nati* „schneidet“ und got. *haurds* (< **kr̥tis* „etwas geflochtenes“) „Tür“, indem er alle drei lexikalischen Einheiten auf eine einheitliche ig. Wz. **sker-* „schneiden/verbinden“ zurückführt (Trubačev 1966: 250).

Im Wörterbuch IEW (weiter Pokorny) kann man eine Menge von Wurzeln finden, die eine identische oder sehr ähnliche Form haben und dabei einen der aufgezählten Begriffe – „schneiden“, „verbinden“, „biegen“ – bezeichnen. Diese Wurzeln werden in Pokorny als Homonyme betrachtet; sie sind nummeriert – s. z.B. die Wurzeln **u̯er-*, deren Zahl 13 beträgt – Pokorny 1150–1166. Führen wir einige kennzeichnende Beispiele an: **u̯er-* „biegen, drehen“, **u̯er-* „binden“, **u̯er-* „aufreißen, ritzen“; **u̯el-* „drehen, winden“, **u̯el-* „reißen, ritzen, verwunden“;

**bher-* „mit scharfem Werkzeug schneiden"; **bher-* „flechten, weben"; **kel-* „schneiden", **kel-* „biegen".

Aber besonders oft lassen sich die Bedeutungen „schneiden", „reißen", „abhäuten", „verbinden", „biegen", „drehen", „nähen" usw. in den Wurzeln **sek-*, **skel-*, **sken-*, **smēi̯-*, **sēi̯-*, **snē-*, **seu̯-*, **su̯ēi̯-*, **sper-* uä. beobachten, d.h. in den Wurzeln mit dem anlautenden Element *s-*. Das hat uns ermöglicht (s. Lewizkij 1997: Levickij 1998), eine Hypothese darüber aufzustellen, daß in der ig. Ursprache eine Wurzel **sē-/se-* (in laryngaler Notation **seH-*) existieren konnte, die in ihrer synkretischen Bedeutung „Sehne; mit den Sehnen hantieren" alle drei oben erwähnten Komponenten [schneiden], [verbinden], [biegen] vereinigt hat. Diese Wurzel konnte, indem sie mit Hilfe verschiedener Determinative (vor allem der Sonanten) erweitert wurde, folgende Derivate ergeben: **sei̯-*, **seu̯-*, **sen-*, **sem-*, **sel-*, **ser-*, **sek-*, **set(h)-*, **sep(h)-*, die danach – entsprechend der Theorie von P. Persson[1] und der Theorie der ig. Wurzel, die von E. Benveniste ausgearbeitet wurde, – Formen wie **sekə-/skē-* > **skēi̯-*, **skēu̯-*, **sker-*, **skel-* usw. generieren konnten.[2]

Auf diese Weise konnte die von uns rekonstruierte Wurzel **seH-* „Sehne, mit den Sehnen hantieren" eine große Anzahl von Derivaten wie **sek-/sēk-, skē-, skei̯-, skeu̯-*, **sker-*, **skel-*, **sken-*, **sem-*, **smēi̯-*, **smer-*, **sen-*, **snē(i̯)-*, **sner-*, **sneu̯-* usw. hervorbringen, die von einem Satz semantischer Komponenten vereinigt wurden, die ihrerseits semantische Derivate einer synkretischen Bedeutung „schneiden/binden/biegen" sein konnten.

Als Ausgangsbedeutung für alle angeführten Formen könnte „Sehne" (als Gegenstand) und „mit Sehnen hantieren, manipulieren" (als Handlung) geltend gemacht werden. Dabei wurde vermutlich die ursprüngliche Handlung mit Sehnen als ein ungegliederter synkretischer Komplex von Operationen gedacht, aus dem sich später solche konkreten Handlungen wie „flechten", „drehen", „winden", „schneiden", „reißen", „nähen", „weben" usw., ausgegliedert haben (s. Levickij 1998: 211).

Es soll hervorgehoben werden, daß – im Unterschied zu den formalen Einheiten, die den Wortbestand der ig. Ursprache bilden (dieser Wortbestand ist insbesondere in Pokorny dargestellt) und, wie oben gezeigt, einer Derivationsanalyse und einer Berechnung unterzogen werden können, – die Derivationsverhältnisse zwischen den semantischen Einheiten einen

[1] S. weiter Abschnitt 2.

[2] Eine Möglichkeit für eine solche formale Umgestaltung wird einige Male in Pokorny bestätigt – s. S. 118, 988, 1108 ua. So kann nach Pokorny **sēi̯-* ein Derivat *(s)i̯ē-* generieren (s. 915); **bhel-* verhält sich zu **bhā-* wie **stel-* zu **st(h)ā-*, **del-* zu **dā-*, **u̯en-* zu **u̯ā-* usw.

komplizierteren und bizarren Charakter haben und die Anzahl von verschiedenen semantischen Einheiten (der „Bedeutungen“ der ig. Wurzeln) unvergleichlich größer ist als die Anzahl der in einem etymologischen Wörterbuch fixierten Wurzeln. Deshalb ist es viel schwerer und komplizierter, die semantische Derivation festzustellen und zu rekonstruieren als die formale (phono-morphologische) Derivation. Dessen ungeachtet hat die Etymologie auf diesem Gebiet etliche Erfahrungen gesammelt. So ist z.B. aus den etymologischen Quellen gut bekannt, daß das Sem [schneiden] mit Bedeutungen wie „Schwert“, „Axt“, „Messer“, „Wurfspieß“ (d.h. „stechender oder schneidender Gegenstand“) verbunden ist; „abschneiden, trennen“ (> „Schar“, „Menge“, „Schwarm“, „Menschengruppe“ usw.); „beschädigen“ (> „verwunden“, „verstümmeln“, „verderben“, „schaden“, „tadeln“ usw.) – s. Lewizkij 2001; s. auch Pokorny: 1099.

Damit ergibt sich eine neue Frage: Kann man auf irgendwelche Weise einen Kreis von formalen und semantischen Derivaten der Wz. *$s\bar{e}$-/*se*- „Sehne“ > „schneiden/binden/biegen“ genauer rekonstruieren und umreißen und dadurch die Realität der Existenz einer solchen Wurzel in der ig. Ursprache in einem bestimmten Maß bestätigen? Kein einziger Etymologe kann mit Hilfe der traditionellen Methoden der Analyse die ganze Vielfältigkeit von formalen und semantischen Zusammenhängen berücksichtigen, die vollzählig in einem etymologischen Wörterbuch vertreten sind.

Aber die vorhandenen quantitativen (statistischen) Verfahren ermöglichen uns, sich der Lösung der gestellten Aufgabe zu nähern.

2. Material und Methoden

Für die Bearbeitung der gestellten Aufgabe ist es zweckmäßig, ein Verzeichnis der ig. Wurzeln mit dem anlautenden *s*- zu benutzen. Am geeignetsten für die Erreichung dieses Ziels wäre unserer Meinung nach das Wörterbuch von J. Pokorny.

Dem geplanten statistischen Experiment gemäß wurden aus Pokorny alle „Basis-Wurzeln“ (mit dem anlautenden *s*-)[3] auf Zettel herausgeschrieben.

Die Wurzeln mit den Vokalen $a/\bar{a}$ (nach dem anlautenden *s*-), deren Anzahl in Pokorny 13 beträgt, wurden nicht herausgeschrieben. Folglich wurden aus Pokorny alle Wurzeln herausgezogen, die ein anlautendes *s*-, einen Vokal $e/\bar{e}$ oder *o* und ein primäres Determinativ (*d*, *g*, $\hat{g}h$, insge-

[3] „Basis-Wurzeln“ wollen wir solche invarianten Einheiten nennen, die in Pokorny mit Bedeutungen versehen sind, – im Unterschied zu den Derivaten dieser Wurzeln, deren Bedeutungen im Pokorny nicht rekonstruiert werden.

samt 5 Wurzeln), *i̯, k, k̑, kʷ, l, m, n, p, r, u̯* enthalten; nach solchen Wurzeln (wie **sek-*, **sē̆i̯-*) folgen in Pokorny die Einheiten mit den anlautenden Verbindungen *si̯-, sk- (-k̑-, -kʷ-), sl-, sm-, sn-, sp-, sr-, st(h)-, su̯-*. Auf diese Weise ergaben sich insgesamt 296 Wurzeln.

Um eine statistische Analyse der semantischen und phonetischen Zusammenhänge zwischen allen herausgezogenen Einheiten zu verwirklichen, muß man den ganzen Satz von *s*-Wurzeln einer inhaltlichen (semantischen) und formalen (phonetischen) Kategorisierung unterwerfen, d.h. man muß diese Wurzeln nach bestimmten semantischen und phonetischen Merkmalen gruppieren.

Leider existieren in der gegenwärtigen Linguistik keine objektiven (von dem Experimentator unabhängigen) Verfahren der Kategorisierung der inhaltlichen Spracheinheiten; sie wird daher intuitiv durchgeführt.

Die effektivste Prozedur der semantischen Kategorisierung des Wortschatzes ist unserer Ansicht nach die Komponentenanalyse, und zwar eine solche Prozedurvariante dieser sehr weit in der Semasiologie verbreiteten Methode, die die Komponentenanalyse maximal formalisiert vollzieht: jede Einheit der Wortbedeutung (außer den Dienstwörtern) wird als eine semantische Komponente betrachtet. Diese Variante der Komponentenanalyse scheint in unserem Fall auch deshalb besonders erfolgreich zu sein, weil in den Deutungen der ig. Wurzeln in Pokorny fast völlig Dienstwörter (Präpositionen, Konjunktionen usw.) fehlen; die Deutungen werden in der Regel mit Hilfe von sehr ähnlichen (synonymischen oder pseudosynonymischen) lexikalischen Einheiten, z.B.: **(s)nadh-* „einschneiden, schnitzen"; **su̯ei̯d-* „glänzen, schimmern"; **su̯ento-* „rege, rüstig, gesund"; **su̯el-* „schwelen, brennen" verwirklicht.

Nur in seltenen Fällen werden in den Deutungen Dienstwörter genutzt: **smē̆i̯-* „schnitzen, mit einem scharfen Werkzeug arbeiten".

Es ist verständlich, daß solche Dienstwörter nicht als semantische Komponenten betrachtet und daher auch nicht berücksichtigt werden. Wenn von J. Pokorny in einer Wortdeutung 2 und mehr Bedeutungen unterschieden werden, sind solche Deutungen entsprechend oft notiert worden; vgl.: **sp(h)ē̆i̯-* „spitz; spitzes Holzstück"; **smel-* „zermalmen, schlagen, mahlen; auch fein, zart, weich". Infolge dieser Vorgehensweise übersteigt die Anzahl der von uns erhaltenen Zettel (305) die Anzahl der Basis-Wurzeln mit *s*-Anlaut in Pokorny (296).

Auf solche Weise wurden aufgrund der Komponentenanalyse der Wortdeutungen 25 semantische Klassen gebildet; jede Klasse hat eine konventionelle Bezeichnung erhalten. Zu diesen Klassen gehören die folgenden (in den

Klammern sind die häufigsten oder typischen semantischen Komponenten, d.h. Wörter in den Pokorny-Deutungen aufgeführt):

1) schneiden (vereinigt die Wurzeln mit den Bedeutungen „schneiden“, „spalten“, „reißen“, „stechen“, „scharf“, „spitz“, „schnitzen“ ua.);
2) binden (binden, verbinden, knüpfen, zusammenschnüren, nähen, zusammendrehen);
3) biegen (biegen, drehen, krumm);
4) Bewegung (sich bewegen, zittern, vibrieren, zucken, eilen, sich hin und her bewegen, zappeln, springen, hüpfen, lebhafte Bewegung);
5) tönen (ertönen, rufen, sprechen, Schallwort, reden, zischen, donnern, surren, rauschen, stöhnen, schreien);
6) glänzen (glänzen, hell, leuchten, schimmern);
7) Farben (rot, färben, bläulich, grau, schwarz);
8) riechen, Rauch (stinken, rauchen, Rauch, riechen);
9) fließen, naß (fließen, Flüssigkeit, tröpfeln, rinnen, naß, strömen, Fluß, feucht);
10) Geschmack (schmecken, süß, salzig, bitter, an etwas Geschmack finden, sauer);
11) drücken, schlagen (schlagen, drücken);
12) beschädigen (beschädigen, Schaden, mißhandeln, Schmerz);
13) schützen, verschließen (decken, verdecken, schützen, bewahren, umhüllen, verschließen);
14) loslassen, werfen (lassen, werfen, säen, spritzen, schießen, entsenden, ausgießen, fallen lassen, schlaff herabhängen, nachlassen, loslassen);
15) ziehen (ziehen, spannen);
16) streifen, streichen (streichen, streifen, schmieren, Schmer);
17) fassen, ergreifen (greifen, fassen, nehmen);
18) wahrnehmen (hören, fühlen, worauf achten, bemerken, sehen, schauen);
19) stützen, Ruhe (stellen, starr, ruhig, träge, stützen);
20) brennen (verbrennen, schwelen, brennen);
21) Balken, Stange (Stange, Balken, Pfahl, Holzstück, Sparren, Stock);
22) Körperteile, „physiologische Prozesse“ (Mund, Schulter, Fußsohle, schwitzen, Kinn, Oberschenkel, Milz);
23) Fische, Vögel (Fischart, Vogelname, Specht, Sperling ua.);
24) Verwandtschaft (Mutter des Ehemanns, Schwester, Schwager, Schwiegertochter, Bruder der Frau);
25) übrige (Pronomen **so-s,* Num. **septm̥, sek̂s*; **sūs-* „Erzeuger“, **sēmi-* „halb“, **sem-* „Sommer“, **sp(h)er-* „Mistkügelchen“, **srīg-* „Kälte, Frost“, **spend-* „Trankopfer darbringen“ ua.)

Die erhaltenen semantischen Blöcke, die *Klassen* genannt wurden, kann man den großen semantischen Einheiten gleichsetzen, die wir mit dem Terminus *Hypersem* bezeichnen – im Unterschied zu den *Semen* (semantische Komponenten), aus denen jedes Hypersem besteht.

Bei der Aussonderung der formalen (phonetischen) Klassen ist es notwendig folgende Umstände zu berücksichtigen.

In Pokorny, wie schon in Abschnitt 1 gesagt ist, werden nicht selten solche Fälle beobachtet, in denen die Wurzeln wie **bher-* in die Wurzeln wie **bhrēi̯-*, **bhrēu̯-* „mit scharfem Werkzeug bearbeiten" transformiert werden; analogisch: **ĝer-/ĝrē-* „morsch, reif werden"; **k̂er-/k̂rē-* „versehren, zerfallen"; **sker-/skrē-* „schneiden" usw.

Eine ausführlichere Analyse solcher Transformationen wurde von P. Persson durchgeführt (Persson 1912).

So gibt z.B. ig. **ter-/terə-* die Derivate **trēi̯-*, **trī-*, **trēu̯-* (Persson 1912: 776). Auf eine analoge Weise ändert sich ig. **senə-* > **snē-* "binden, flechten": lit. *nýtis* „Weberkamm" (< **snēi̯-*), aber ai. *snāvan-* „Band, Sehne", aisl. *snūa* (< **snēu̯-*) „wenden, drehen" – s. Persson 1912: 813. Die auf solche Weise entstandenen Formen wie **trēi̯-/trēu̯-* können wieder erweitert werden oder auch ohne Erweiterung bleiben. So kann **bhelə-/bhlē-*, indem es mit Hilfe von *i̯* oder *u̯* erweitert wird, die Derivate **bhlēi̯-* und **bhlēu̯-* oder **bhle-* ergeben. Dann erfolgt eine sekundäre Erweiterung solcher Formen; z.B. geht dt. *bleich* auf ig. **bhlei̯-g-* und engl. *black* auf ig. **bhle-g-* zurück. So entstehen Formen mit den „Ablautentgleisungen" und Parallelwurzeln.

Daraus ergibt sich eine sehr wichtige Schlußfolgerung: die Wurzeln wie **sek-* und **sker-* können Varianten derselben Wurzel sein. In den Formen wie **sker-*, **snē-(i̯)-* usw. konnte die zweite Komponente der Anlautverbindung, *k*, *n* usw., ursprünglich ein Determinativ der Wz. **sē-/se-* sein.

Unabhängig davon, ob diese Hypothese richtig ist oder nicht, schließen wir in die zu untersuchende Lexik alle Wurzeln mit den anlautenden Komplexen *si̯-*, *sk-*, *sl-*, *sm-*, *sn-*, *sp(h)-*, *sr-* und *st(h)-* und alle Wurzeln mit der Struktur CVC (wie **sek-*, **sen-*, **sei̯-*) ein, die als eine potentielle Basis für die Bildung der Wurzeln mit dem Anlaut *si̯-*, *sk-*, *sl-* usw. dienen können.

Anders gesagt vereinigen wir in eine Klasse Wurzeln wie **sek-* und **sker-*, **sen-* und **snē-*, **seu̯-* und **su̯er-* usw. Solche phonetischen Klassen werden wir vereinfacht mit den Symbolen *sk-*, *si̯-*, *su̯-* usw. bezeichnen, obwohl diese Klassen eigentlich zwei Subklassen einschließen (**sek-* und **ske-*, **sei̯-* und **si̯-*, **seu̯-* und **su̯e-* usw.).

Da die Häufigkeit einiger Klassen mit *k̂* oder *ku̯* sehr niedrig ist (5 Wurzeln mit *sku̯-* und 7 Wurzeln mit *k̂-*) und unter Berücksichtigung dessen, daß in einigen Fällen *k* und *ku̯* wechseln können (vgl. **sku̯el-/skel-* „tönen"), wurden die Wurzeln mit *sk-*, *sk̂-* und *sku̯-* in eine formale Klasse mit einer konventionellen Bezeichnung *sk*-Klasse zusammengefasst. Auf diese Weise kann man alle von uns erhaltenen Basiswurzeln mit dem s-Anlaut in 10 phonetische Klassen gruppieren: *si̯-, su̯-, sl-, sr-, sm-, sn-, sk-, sp-, st(h),* übrige (*s* + Determinative *d, g, ĝh* oder Null-Determinativ).

Die erhaltenen Häufigkeitsverteilungen von phonetischen und semantischen Klassen sind in Tabelle 1 aufgeführt. Die Daten dieser Tabelle können einer Korrelationsanalyse unterworfen werden oder mit Hilfe von Chi-Quadrat-Tests oder der Kontingenzkoeffizienten bearbeitet werden (s. Zöfel 1985; Lewizkij 2007).

3. Semantische Zusammenhänge zwischen den ig. Wurzeln mit *s*-Anlaut

Um eine Methode für die Feststellung der semantischen Zusammenhänge zwischen den ig. Wurzeln auszuarbeiten, betrachten wir ausführlicher den phonetischen Bestand jener Wurzeln, die gleiche oder ähnliche Bedeutungen haben.

Die semantische Komponente [schneiden] finden wir z.B. in folgenden Wurzeln: **(s)kēp-* „mit scharfem Werkzeug schneiden", **(s)nerb-* „schneiden", **snei̯t-* „schneiden", **(s)ker-* „schneiden", **(s)kel-* „schneiden", **skēi̯-* „schneiden, trennen, scheiden", **skēu̯(t)-* „schneiden, trennen", **(s)nadh-* „einschneiden, schnitzen", **smēi̯-* „schnitzen, mit einem scharfen Werkzeug arbeiten", **su̯er-* „schneiden, stechen".

Von den 10 aufgezählten Wurzeln enthalten 5 Einheiten das anlautende *sk-*, 3 – *sn-*; außerdem sind Einheiten mit *sm-* und *su̯-* (je 1) vorhanden. Wenn wir aber eine analoge Liste von den Wurzeln betrachten, deren semantische Struktur das Sem [drehen] einschließt, so haben 4 von 11 dieser Wurzeln *sn-* in ihrem Lautbestand (**snēp-, *(s)nē-, *snēu̯-, *(s)ner-*), 3 – *su̯* und nur 2 – *sk* (**(s)ker-, (s)kerbh-*).

Die semantische Komponente [schlaff] enthalten 4 Wurzeln: **(s)leu̯p-, *(s)leu̯- (s)lēg-* und **(s)leb-* und, wie aus dem angeführten Verzeichnis zu sehen ist, haben alle 4 Wurzeln in ihrem Bestand die Anlautverbindung *sl-*. Von 5 Wurzeln mit der Komponente [spalten] haben 3 die Anlautverbindung *sp(h)-* (**(s)plei̯-, *(s)p(h)elg-, *(s)p(h)el-*).

Die erörterten Beispiele zeugen ganz unverkennbar davon, daß nach ihrer Semantik ähnliche oder identische Wurzeln eine unbezweifelbare phonetische Ähnlichkeit aufweisen und diese Ähnlichkeit sich vor allem im Zusammenfall der anlautenden Wurzelelemente zeigt. Vom Standpunkt der Etymologie läßt sich solch ein Verhältnis zwischen Form und Inhalt der betrachteten Wurzeln dadurch erklären, daß sie auf eine einheitliche ig. Grundform (in den behandelten Beispielen auf ig. **sek-, *sem-, *sel-, *sep(h)-*) zurückgehen.

Man kann also folgendes annehmen: Je mehr die Form der lexikalischen Einheiten zusammenfällt, desto größer ist die Wahrscheinlichkeit, daß diese Entitäten auf eine einheitliche Grundform zurückgehen und semantische Varianten oder Derivate dieser Grundform sind. Wenn man ein Messverfahren der phonetischen Ähnlichkeit zwischen den Wurzeln findet, kann man mit einem hohen Grad an Wahrscheinlichkeit über die semantisch-paradigmatische Ähnlichkeit dieser Wurzeln urteilen.

In der heutigen Linguostatistik existieren einige Verfahren für die Feststellung der Nähe und Ähnlichkeit zwischen lexikalischen Einheiten. Das verbreiteste von diesen Verfahren, das erlaubt, nicht nur die Zahl der gemeinsamen semantischen Komponenten, sondern auch ihre Häufigkeit zu berücksichtigen, ist die Korrelationsanalyse, die schon längst in der Semasiologie genutzt wird – für die Messung der semantischen Ähnlichkeit zwischen den lexikalischen Einheiten (Wörtern und Wortgruppen) aufgrund der formalen Eigenschaften dieser Einheiten (ihrer Kombinierbarkeit) – s. Suprun et al. 1969; Moskovič 1969; Lewizkij 1989.

Auf solche Weise können die Daten in Tabelle 1 der Korrelationsanalyse unterworfen werden. Die Größen der Korrelationskoeffizienten schwanken in den Grenzen von –1 bis +1 oder, anders gesagt, von 0 bis 1 mit dem Zeichen „+“ oder „–“. Die in der Tab. 1 vertretenen Häufigkeiten (Spalten) werden aufgrund der Häufigkeiten von formalen Einheiten (der phonetischen Klassen *sl-*, *sr-* usw.) paarweise verglichen. Die Zahl der sogenannten korrelierenden Paare (der Wertepaare) in der Tab. 1 ist 10 (die Zahl der phonetischen Klassen). Die Werte der erhaltenen Korrelationskoeffizienten können statistisch signifikant oder nicht signifikant sein. Bei der Zahl der korrelierenden Paare n = 10 sind die Koeffizienten mit den Werten 0,63 (Signifikanzniveau P = 0,05) und 0,77 (Signifikanzniveau P = 0,01) signifikant. Anders gesagt, wenn wir als minimales Signifikanzniveau P = 0,05 annehmen (das bedeutet, daß die Wahrscheinlichkeit eines Fehlers nur 5 % beträgt), so sind alle Koeffizienten mit dem Wert 0,63 und größer statistisch signifikant. Es ist verständlich, daß bei der Feststellung der semantischen

Zusammenhänge zwischen den semantischen Klassen (Hypersemen) nur positive Koeffizienten berücksichtigt sind.

Nach allen oben dargelegten Hypothesen und Erklärungen kann man zur Korrelationsanalyse selbst übergehen, die mit Hilfe eines Computerprogramms durchgeführt wird.

Um Platz zu sparen, führen wir die Tabelle mit erhaltenen Koeffizienten nicht an. Statt solch einer Tabelle ist es zweckmäßig, ein Schema der semantischen Verbindungen der ig. Wurzeln darzustellen, das aufgrund der erhaltenen Koeffizienten geschaffen ist (s. Schema 1). Im Schema 1 sind die zu untersuchenden semantischen Klassen mit den Kreisen bezeichnet; die Zusammenhänge zwischen diesen Klassen sind mit Hilfe von drei Arten der Linien dargestellt: zwei Linien repräsentieren sehr starke Zusammenhänge ($r \geq 0{,}77$); eine einfache Linie symbolisiert starke Zusammenhänge (von 0,63 bis 0,76); punktierte Linien bezeichnen solche Verbindungen („schwache“), die den Koeffizienten mit der Größe von 0,55 bis 0,62 entsprechen. Streng gesagt sind solche Größen (weniger als 0,63) vom Standpunkt der Statistik nicht signifikant, aber wir halten es für möglich, in unserem Fall von den strengen Anforderungen der statistischen Analyse abzuweichen, um die möglichen semantischen Zusammenhänge zwischen den zu analysierenden Einheiten zu demonstrieren.

Für die Interpretation der erhaltenen Resultate wollen wir zwei Termini ausnutzen – „qualitative Analyse“ und „quantitative Analyse“. Unter der qualitativen werden wir die etymologische Analyse verstehen und unter der quantitativen – die statistische Analyse.

Die Zusammenhänge, die im Schema 1 dargestellt sind, ermöglichen uns, über semantische Beziehungen zwischen den betrachteten Einheiten aufgrund der quantitativen Analyse zu urteilen.

Anscheinend ist eine zentrale Einheit im erhaltenen semantischen Paradigma das Hypersem [schneiden], das 8 Verbindungen mit allen anderen Einheiten hat (keine andere Einheit im Schema 1 hat eine solch hohe Anzahl von Verbindungen). Man kann annehmen, daß [schneiden] ein Kern der von uns rekonstruierten semantischen Struktur der Wurzel *$s\bar{e}$-/se- ist. Weiter könnte man daraus gehen, daß Hyperseme, die unmittelbare Verbindungen mit [schneiden] offenbaren, ein Zentrum in der semantischen Struktur der zu rekonstruierenden Wurzel bilden, und Hyperseme, die Verbindungen mit dem Zentrum haben, der nächsten Peripherie zugehören. Bei solchem Zugang gehören dem Zentrum des Paradigmas die Hyperseme [binden], [biegen], [warhnehmen], [glänzen], [Bewegung], [schützen] und [fließen] zu; die nächste Peripherie schließt die Hyperseme [beschädigen] und [loslassen] ein, der fernen Peripherie gehören [tönen] und [brennen] an. Was die Hyperseme [Balken], [Körperteile], [Vögel] und [Verwandtschaft] betrifft, so könnte man von Anfang an vermuten, daß diese Hyperseme nicht der semantischen Struktur der von uns betrachteten Wurzel „Sehne“ zugehören; deshalb könnte man diese Hyperseme von der statistischen Analyse ausschließen. Doch sind die Daten zu den Zusammenhängen der 4 genannten Hyperseme von einem bestimmten Interesse. So kann man annehmen, daß die Bezeichnungen von Fischen und Vögeln mit den Begriffen „glänzen“ und „Bewegung“, und die Hyperseme [Balken] und [Körperteile] mit dem Begriff „drücken“ verbunden sind (s. Schema 1).

Zugleich entsprechen die aufgefundenen Zusammenhänge zwischen [tönen] und [Balken], [Körperteile], zwischen [brennen] und [Verwandtschaft] unseren intuitiven Vorstellungen nicht und sind wahrscheinlich durch ein zufälliges Zusammenfallen des Lautbestands der Wurzeln entstanden, die Töne, Körperteile, Balken einerseits und Brennen, Verwandtschaft andererseits bezeichnen.

Wie aus dem Schema 1 zu sehen ist, sind Verwandtschaftsbezeichnungen mit [brennen] und [brennen] mit [binden] verbunden. Es wäre logisch zu vermuten, daß die Verwandtschaftstermini eher mit [binden] (gemeinsame formale Einheiten sind Wurzeln mit *sn-* und *su̯-*) verbunden sind. Tatsächlich sind für [binden] und [Verwandtschaft] positive Koeffizienten festzustellen: der Koeffizient r = 0,36; er hat aber die notwendige Signifikanz nicht.

Was andere mit Hilfe der statistischen Analyse festgestellte Tatsachen betrifft, so scheint ihre Interpretation erfolgreicher und zweckmäßiger zu sein, wenn wir die Daten der etymologischen und der statistischen Analyse miteinander vergleichen.

1. Vor allem hat die statistische Analyse die Hypothese bestätigt, daß die Begriffe „schneiden“, „binden“ und „biegen“ miteinander verbunden sind. Zahlreiche Belege der realen, in den etymologischen Wörterbüchern enthaltenen Verbindungen der Begriffe „schneiden, trennen“, „verbinden, vereinigen“ und „biegen, drehen“ sind teilweise oben illustriert; besonders überzeugend sind die Beispiele mit den anlautenden *sk-* und *sn-*.

Es ist hervorzuheben, daß die Verbindungen zwischen 3 Grundbegriffen, die die Semantik der rekonstruierten Wurzel **sē-/se-* bilden, auch in der semantischen Struktur vieler anderer Wurzeln betrachtet werden. So kann man z.B. aufgrund von Pokorny solche Verbindungen herausstellen: russ. *plesti* „flechten“ und lit. *plė̃šti* „reißen“ (< ig. **plēk̑-/plek̑-*); ig. **dhō-* „schärfen“ und **dhō-* „Strick“; ig. **u̯edh-* „stoßen, schlagen“ und **u̯edh-* „knüpfen, binden“; ig. **lēk-* „Strick, Schlinge“ und ig. **lēk-* „zerreißen“; ig. **u̯es-* „stechen“ und

**u̯es-* „drehen, wickeln“; ig. **i̯eu̯-* „verbinden“ und ig. **i̯eu̯-* „trennen“ (eine andere Erklärung der möglichen Identität dieser Wurzeln s. in Pokorny: 511); ig. **u̯el-* „drehen, winden“ und **u̯el-* „reißen“; ig. **u̯er-* „drehen, binden“ und **u̯er-* „aufreißen“; ig. **k̂er-* „flechten, knüpfen“ und **k̂er-* „zerfallen“.

Außer den oben erwähnten (s. S. 2) Derivationsbeziehungen „schneiden“ > „scharf“, „der schneidende Gegenstand“; „schneiden“ > „abschneiden, abtrennen“ > „Menge, Schar“ usw. kann das Hypersem [schneiden] mit vielen anderen Bedeutungen verbunden sein – „schnell“, „hastig“, „heftig“: russ. *rezvyj* „schnell, flink“ < *rezat'* „schneiden“; ahd. *skēro, skioro* „schnell“ (< **skei̯-* „schneiden“); lat. *recellō* „schnelle zurück“ (< **kel-* „schlagen, hauen“); russ. *skok*, ae. *sceacan* „schütteln“ (engl. *shake*), „eilen“; ahd. *scehan* „eilen, schnell fortgehen“; (< ig. **skek-* „springen, lebhafte Bewegung“).

Ähnliche Bedeutungen entwickeln sich auf der Basis „biegen, drehen“; vgl. lit. *skraidùs* „schnell“, *skraidýti* „hin und her im Bogen fliegen“ (< **sker-* „springen; sich drehend bewegen“ < **sker-* „drehen“.

Im Schema 1 ist die Verbindung zwischen „schneiden“ und „schnelle Bewegung“ und zwischen „biegen“ und „Bewegung“ mit Hilfe der Linien [schneiden] – [Bewegung] und [biegen] – [Bewegung] widergegeben, was völlig der etymologischen Analyse entspricht.

2. Das Hypersem [schneiden] generiert die Bedeutungen „verwunden“, „verstümmeln“, „verderben“, „Schaden“: ahd. *halz* „lahm“, gr. *κολοβός* „verstümmelt“, lat. *calamitas* „Schaden“, air. *coll* „Verderben, Schaden“, lat. *clādēs* „Verletzen, Schaden“ (< **kel-* „schlagen, hauen“); aisl. *skeina* „leicht verwunden“ (< **skei̯-* „schneiden“); mnd. *bat* „Schade, Unglück“ (< **bhāt-/bhət-* „schlagen“); aisl. *skarð* „Scharte, Loch, Mangel, Schade“, ksl. *krъnъ* „verstümmelt“ (< **sker-* „schneiden“); ae. *dolg,* ahd. *tolc* „Wunde“ (< **dhelgh-* „schlagen“);

Im Schema 1 ist zu sehen, daß nach den Resultaten der quantitativen Analyse [beschädigen] mit [biegen] und nicht [schneiden] statistisch signifikant verbunden ist. Aber die Korrelationsanalyse zeigt, daß [beschädigen] auch mit [schneiden] verbunden sein kann: der Korrelationskoeffizient ist ziemlich groß (+ 0,45); er verfehlt jedoch die notwendige Signifikanz.

Auf diese Weise kann die quantitative Analyse sui generis als ein Orientierungspunkt für Etymologen dienen: Es ist zu erwarten, daß in der Lexik der ig. Sprachen eine Derivationsverbindung „biegen, drehen“ > „beschädigen“ entdeckt werden kann. Es ist nicht z.B. ausgeschlossen, daß sich nach solchem semantischen Modell dt. *schwach* entwickelt hat, das genetisch mit *schwanken* (< ig. **su̯eg-/su̯eng-* „biegen, drehen“) verbunden ist, und engl. *worse* „schlechter", das mit dt. *wirren*, got. *wairs* „schlimmer" (< germ. **wers-/wurs-* < ig. **u̯er-* „drehen, biegen") verbunden ist. Vgl. ukr. *perekručuvaty* „entstellen, verdrehen", russ. *izvraščat'* dass., ukr. *kryvda* „Lüge" (< *kryvyj* „krumm").

3. Das Sem [schneiden, trennen] generiert nicht selten die Bedeutungen „wahrnehmen", „erkennen", „klug", „geschickt", „weise": lat. *cernere* „sichten, scheiden, deutlich wahrnehmen, erkennen"; lat. *scīre* „in Erfahrung gebracht haben, wissen", ahd. *skēri* „scharf, scharfsinnig" (< **skei̯-* „schneiden, trennen"). Zwischenglieder solcher semantischen Transformationen können, wie die angeführten Beispiele zeigen, „schneiden > Kerben machen > zählen, denken" oder „schneiden > scharf > scharfsinnig" sein. Eine andere, aber ähnliche semantische Linie lässt die Entwicklung der Bedeutungen „erfahren, forschen" vom Begriff „graben, wühlen" zu; vgl. dt. *Furche* und *forschen* – beide von den „homonymen" ig. Wurzeln **perk̑-*.

Im Schema 1 hat die betrachtete Gesetzmäßigkeit ihre Verkörperung in der Form einer starken Verbindung zwischen [schneiden] und [wahrnehmen] gefunden. Dieser mit Hilfe der statistischen Analyse bestätigte Zusammenhang kann in den etymologischen Untersuchungen nützlich werden.

So hat M. Stachowski eine interessante Hypothese aufgestellt, daß türk. *kulak* „Ohr", *kul* „Sklave" und *kulun* „Fohlen" genetisch miteinander verbunden sein können. Sich auf die semantische Typologie (semantische Parallelen in unterschiedlichen Sprachen, darunter auch in den slawischen und germanischen) stützend, ist M. Stachowski zum folgenden Schluß gelangt:

> Die Entwicklung der ganzen Wortsippe stelle ich mir folgendermaßen vor:

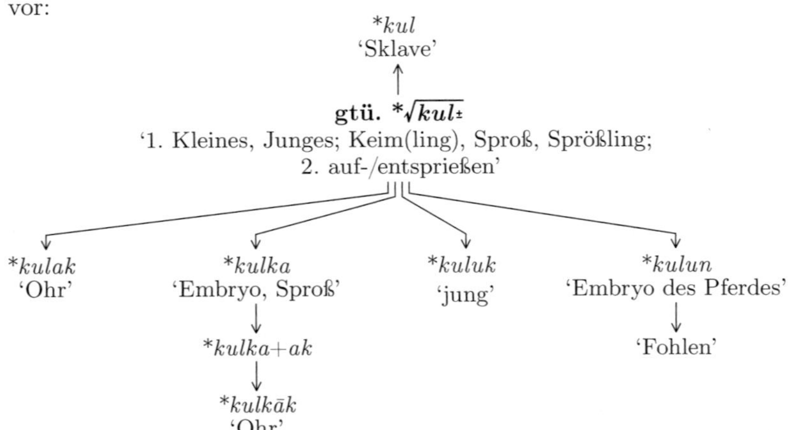

(Stachowski 2010: 238).

Wie aus der vorgeschlagenen Konstruktion zu sehen ist, wäre für „Ohr“, „Sklave“ und „Fohlen“ eine Ausgangsbedeutung „Keim, Sproß, Sprößling; auf-/entsprießen“ anzunehmen.

Da der Übergang „jung, klein“ > „Diener, Sklave“ in der Etymologie gut bekannt ist[4] und der Übergang „klein, jung“ > „junges Tier“ sich aufdrängt, wird in dem von M. Stachowski vorgeschlagenen Schema die Verbindung zwischen „Ohr“ und „Keim, Sproß“ bis zum Ende nicht klar. Der Autor erklärt diese Verbindung auf folgende Weise:

„Im ersten Augenblick erscheint ein semantischer Zusammenhang von, „Sklave“ einerseits und „Ohr“, „Fohlen“ andererseits ausgeschlossen. Bedenkt man aber, daß „Ohr“ und „Fohlen“ ursprünglich etwa „Kleines, Junges; Schößling“ bedeutet haben mußten, so ändert sich die Situation ganz wesentlich“ (s. 3).

Zweifellos ist eine solche Konstruktion für die Erklärung der von M. Stachowski aufgestellten Hypothese ganz annehmbar. Aber die Resultate der von uns durchgeführten quantitativen und qualitativen Analyse berücksichtigend könnte man ein anderes Schema der Zusammenhänge zwischen „Ohr“, „Sklave“ und „Fohlen“ anbieten (s. Schema 2).

Wie zu sehen ist, wäre die Ausgangsbedeutung für die ganze Wortsippe das Hypersem [schneiden], das solche Seme vereinigt wie [spalten], [reißen], [hauen], [zerkleinern], [durchbohren], [hervorstechen] – s. S. 241. Deshalb kann zweifellos [schneiden] auch das Sem [klein] generieren; eines der Derivate des Sems [schneiden] kann auch [sprießen, entsprießen] sein, das in unserem statistischen Experiment dem Hypersem [loslassen] zugehört.

Folglich ermöglicht, wie es scheint, die Rekonstruktion der Ausgangsbedeutung „schneiden“ es, die Verbindung von allen drei in den türkischen Sprachen vorhandenen Begriffen – „Sklave“, „Ohr“ und „Fohlen“ widerspruchsfrei zu erklären.

4. Von großem Interesse ist nach unserer Auffassung die Verbindung der Bedeutungen „schneiden“ und „fließen“, „loslassen, lassen, werfen, schleudern“, „biegen, drehen“, „zittern, vibrieren, sich ruckartig, abgebrochen, hin und her bewegen“. Die Verbindung zwischen den genannten Bedeutungen findet ihre Widerspiegelung in den fixierten lexikalischen Einheiten der ig. Sprachen.

[4] Vgl. aksl. *chlapъ* „Sklave, Knecht, Diener“, russ. *cholop* dass., ukr. *chlopecъ* „Bursche, Knabe“; < ig. **skol-* „schneiden“; russ. *rab* „Sklave“ und *rebjonok* „Kind“ < ig. **orbho-* „Waise“; ae. *mago* „Knabe, Sohn“, „Diener“, got. *magus* „Knecht, Knabe“; ahd. *scalch* „Sklave, Diener“, got. *skalks* „Knecht, Diener“, aisl. *skalkr* „Diener, Sklave“, dt. *Schalk*, aber aisl. *skalkr* „Schwert“; < ig. **skel-* „schneiden, zerspalten“.

So vereinigt gr. *σχάω* folgende Bedeutungen: „(ich) ritze, schlitze auf und lasse fallen, schlaff herabhängen“; *σχάσις* „das Ritzen, Schröpfen, Loslassen“ (s. Pokorny: 919). Folglich generiert die Bedeutung „zerspalten, zerreißen“ die Bedeutungen „schlaff“, „herabhängen“ > „fallen“; gr. *ἵημι* hat folgende Bedeutungen: „in schnelle Bewegung setzen; senden, schicken, absenden, entsenden; sich herablassen, hinabrutschen; ertönen lassen; mit Gewalt fortschicken, schleudern, werfen, schießen, abschießen; strömen lassen, fließen machen, ergießen; herabhängen lassen, herabrollen lassen; schnell bewegen, eilen, stürmen“.

Alle in der Semantik der griechischen Wörter feststellbaren Zusammenhänge sind auch gut im Schema 1 dargestellt. Die Bedeutung „schleudern, werfen“ kann auch aufgrund der Bedeutung „drehen, sich drehen“ entstehen: ahd. *zerben* „sich drehen, sich umdrehen“, ae. *torfian* „werfen, steinigen“ (vgl. dt. *drehen* und engl. *throw* – den Vergleich hat J. Pokorny angeführt) < **derbh-* (Pokorny: 212); ai. *kiráti* „streut aus, vergießt, wirft“ (< **skerə-* „springen“, auch und eigentlich „sich drehend bewegen, schwingen“; nicht zu trennen von **(s)ker-* „drehen“ – Pokorny: 933). Wie die letzte Bemerkung von J. Pokorny zeigt, kann aufgrund der Bedeutung „drehen“ auch die Bedeutung „springen“ entstehen, die ihrerseits mit der Bedeutung „sich hin und her bewegen, eilen, schnell“ verbunden ist.

Die Reflexe der Wurzel **sē(i̯)-* vereinigen die Bedeutungen „Sehne“ (dt. *Sehne*, engl. *sinew*), „verbinden, vereinigen“ (ai. *syáti, sinā́ti*), „Strick, Schlinge, Seil“ (ahd. *seita*, dt. *Seil*, russ. *silok*), „Saite“ (dt. *Saite*), „Band, Fessel“ (ai. *s6tu-h*, av. *hinu-*). Eine Variante dieser Wurzel ist **si̯ū-*, die als Ergebnis folgender Transformationen entstehen konnte: **sei̯-* > *si̯e* > *si̯eu̯-* > *si̯ū-*. Die Wurzel **sēi̯-/si̯ū-* hat die Bedeutungen „Sehne, Seil“ (ai. *syūman-* „Naht, Band“, *ὑμήν* „dünne Haut, Sehne“) und „nähen“ (lat. *suere*, russ. *šit’*, got. *siujan*).

Ig. **sē(i̯)-* „Sehne, mit Sehnen verbinden“ fällt formal mit ig. **sēi̯-* „werfen, säen, entsenden“ (lat. *serere*, dt. *säen*, russ. *sejat’*) zusammen. Der Zusammenhang zwischen den Bedeutungen „verbinden, flechten“ und „werfen, schleudern“ läßt sich mit den Handlungen erklären, die mit dem Weben (Zetteln) verbunden sind (s. Trubačev 1966: 113). Aber im Kontext der von uns aufgestellten Hypothese ist der Zusammenhang zwischen den genannten Bedeutungen in einer anderen Sphäre zu suchen. Das in der semantischen Kette „binden – werfen“ fehlende Verbindungsglied ist deutlich in der Semantik von ai. *sā́yaka-* „Pfeil, Wurfgeschoß“, *prá-siti* „Schuß, Wurf, Geschoß“ realisiert (vgl. ai. *prasiti-* „Schlinge, Netz, Falle“, *sāyáyati* „verbindet“ und *sinā́ti* „bindet“); gr. *ἵημι* wurde auch in der Bedeutung „schießen, Pfeile schleudern“ gebraucht.

Die Verbindbarkeit der aufgezählten Seme ist nicht nur für die Wurzel **sēi̯-*, sondern auch für andere Wurzeln kennzeichnend; z.B., **sen-/snē-* : lat. *nēre* „spinnen“, lit. *nýtis* „Weberkamm“, russ. *nit’* „Faden“, kymr. *nyddu* „nähen“, got. *nēþla* „Nadel“; ahd. *snarahha* „Schlinge“, aisl. *snara* „Strick, Schnur, Saite“, got. *snōrjō* „Korb, Flechtwerk“; lat. *nōdus* „Knoten“, got. *nati* „netz“, ae. *snōd* „Binde“; toch. B. *šñaura* (pl.) „Sehnen, Nerven“, ai. *snā́van-* „Band, Sehne“, av. *snāvarə* dass., lat. *nervus* „Sehne, Flechse, Bogensehne, Saite“, gr. *νευρά* „Sehne, Bogensehne“, arm. *neard* „Faser, Sehne, Fiber“, ae. *snēr* „Saite“.

Deshalb hat man allen Grund, für **sē(i̯)-* und breiter – für **sē/se-* die Ausgangsbedeutung „Sehne, Bogensehne; mit den Sehnen / Bogensehnen hantieren, manipulieren“ anzusetzen. Diese Rekonstruktion läßt sich durch den uralten Synkretismus der Semantik von **sē-/se-* erklären, welches die Komponenten [Sehne], [Bogensehne], [Saite], [verbinden], [schneiden], [biegen], [schleudern, werfen] enthalten hat, und die Widersprüche zwischen der Semantik einzelner Formen können beseitigt werden: vgl. germ. **snīþ-* „schneiden“ (> dt. *schneiden*) und russ. *nit’* „Faden“, lit. *nýtis* „Weberkamm“, mir. *snīm* „das Spinnen“. Die abgeleiteten Bedeutungen der „Bogensehne“ konnten auch „zittern, vibrieren“, „tönen“ ua. sein.

5. Aufgrund der Bedeutung „sich hin und her bewegen, zittern, vibrieren; lebhafte Bewegung“ entwickelt sich nicht selten die Bedeutung „glänzen, schimmern, funkeln“, da „lebhafte Bewegung – flimmern, funkeln“ ein häufiges Bedeutungsverhältnis ist“ (s. Pokorny: 1099). In Pokorny: 64 finden wir auch Hinweise auf die Beobachtungen einer Reihe von Etymologen, die „den Begriff des Leuchtens aus dem der schnellen Bewegung geflossen sein“ lassen.

In der von uns betrachteten Wurzel **sē-/se-* gründet sich der Zusammenhang zwischen „schneiden“, „Bewegung“ und „glänzen“ auf die formale Ähnlichkeit der Wurzeln mit den Anlautverbindungen *sk-* und *sp-*; vgl.: **skand-* „leuchten“, **(s)kāi-* „hell, leuchtend“, **skēu̯t-* „schneiden“, **skēi̯-* „schneiden“, **sp(h)e(n)d-* „glänzen, flackern“, **(s)p(h)el-* „glänzen, schimmern“, **(s)p(h)el-* „spalten“, **(s)kek-* „springen, lebhafte Bewegung“, **sperĝh-* „sich hastig bewegen“, **sp(h)eng-* „glänzen“.

Doch finden die Zusammenhänge solcher Art ihre Bestätigung in den formal-semantischen Verhältnissen vieler anderer ig. Wurzeln, die in Pokorny festgestellt sind: lat. *micāre* „sich zuckend bewegen“ und „funkeln“, ig. **tu̯ei̯-* „erregen, hin und her bewegen, schütteln, erschüttern“ und **tu̯ei̯s-* „funkeln“; mhd. *brehen* „plötzlich und stark aufleuchten“, aisl. *braga* „funkeln“, *bregða* „schnell bewegen, schwingen“, engl. *braid* „flechten“, ahd. *brettan*, mhd. *bretten* „ziehen, zucken, weben“ (Pokorny: 142).

Analoge Verhältnisse haben: ig. *ĝher-2* „kratzen, ritzen" und *ĝher-3* „strahlen, glänzen" (Pokorny: 441); *ĝhel-* „glänzen, schimmern" und *ĝhel-* „schneiden" (S. 429, 434); *dhel-2* „leuchten" und *dhel-3* „zittern, trippeln" (S. 246). Die Bedeutung „glänzen, schimmern" generiert ihrerseits verschiedene Farbbezeichnungen: **ĝhel-* „glänzen" und „gelb, grün, grau, blau" (S. 429); *bher-* „glänzen" und „hellbraun" (S. 136); **bhel-* „glänzen" und „weiß" (S. 118). Folglich kann das Hypersem [vibrieren, zittern, gebrochene Bewegung] mit einem weiteren Übergang zu [glänzen, schimmern, funkeln], [Licht, Farbe], [Geruch], [Schall, Tönen] sowohl aufgrund des Sems [schneiden, schlagen], als auch aufgrund des Sems [winden, drehen] entstehen. Das zeigt sich besonders klar im Verhältnis der Wurzeln **mer-1* „flechten, binden" (Pokorny: 733), **mer-2* „flimmern, funkeln" (ebenda), **mer-3* „dunkle Farben" (S. 734) und **mer-5* „aufreiben, reiben" (ebenda). Analoge Beobachtungen finden wir in Maciuszak 1996: 25; die Entwicklung der Farbbezeichnungen in den germanischen Sprachen entspricht den Konstruktionen, die in Berlin/Kay 1969 dargestellt sind: weiß/schwarz > rot > gelb/grün > blau > braun.

Alles Gesagte findet seine Bestätigung in den Ergebnissen der quantitativen Analyse. Die im Schema 1 fehlenden Zusammenhänge zwischen [Bewegung] und [tönen], [Geruch], [Farbe] zeitigen trotzdem einige Reflexe in den Ergebnissen der Korrelationsanalyse, obwohl – um noch einmal auf die Koeffizienten *r* hinzuweisen – in diesem Fall nicht signifikant ist. So kann man folgende Zusammenhänge anmerken: [Bewegung] + [tönen] – 0,41; [Geschmack] + [riechen] – 0,50; [Geschmack] + [tönen] – 0,40; [riechen] + [wahrnehmen] – 0,45; [tönen] + [Farben] – 0,34.[5]

In der oben erwähnten Arbeit äußert K. Maciuszak einen Zweifel an den möglischen Zusammenhang zwischen „dunkel" und „beschädigen". Sie schreibt:

> it is hard to imagine the relation between 'dark' and 'to hurt, shorten, cheat', as the reconstructed **dhebh-ro-* must have been traced to IE **dhebh-* 'beschädigen, verkürzen, betrügen' (Maciuszak 1996: 31).

Doch ist im Lichte der von uns erhaltenen quantitativen Angaben der Zusammenhang zwischen den genannten Bedeutungen ganz annehmbar.

6. Nicht selten entwickelt sich aufgrund der Bedeutung „schneiden" die Bedeutung „streifen, Spur, Furche ziehen usw.": russ. *borozda* „Furche"

[5] In einem anderen statistischen Experiment, das wir aufgrund nicht nur der *s*-Wurzeln, sondern auch der meisten in Pokorny fixierten Wurzeln (auch der oben aufgezählten) durchgeführt haben, ist das Sem [Farben] mit den Semen [Bewegung], [glänzen], [schneiden], [tönen], [brennen] stark verbunden.

(< **bher-* „schneiden“); serb. *díra* „Weg, den ein Heer gezogen ist oder zieht“, bulg. *dír'a* „Spur eines Menschen oder Tieres' (< **der-* „schinden, abspalten“); lett. *riewa* „Ritze, Falte, Furche“; lit. *raĩvė* „Streifen“; ai. *rēkhā* „Riß, Strich, Linie, ahd. *riga* „Linie“; < **rei̯-* „ritzen, reißen, schneiden“.

Weiter kann die Bedeutung „streifen, eine Linie ziehen“ in die Bedeutung „berühren“ übergehen – vgl. russ. *kasatьsja* „berühren“ < **kes-* „schneiden“ (s. Melničuk 1968), russ. *krenuti* „kaufen, nehmen“ < **sker-* „schneiden“ (Trubačev 1974, 13: 75).

Aufgrund dieser Gesetzmäßigkeit kann man die Etymologie von germ. **handuz* „Hand“ und **tāk-/tak-* „nehmen“ (engl. *take* „nehmen“, aisl. *taka* „berühren, nehmen“, got. *tēkan* „berühren“) präzisieren. Das erste Wort ist sicher mit dem got. *hinþan* „greifen, fassen“ zu verbinden und als eine Ableitung von ig. **skent-* „schneiden“ anzunehmen; das zweite Wort kann eine Ableitung der ig. Wurzel **dā/də-* „zertrennen, zerspalten“ sein (s. Lewizkij 2000, Bd. 1: 215; Bd. 2: 200).

Wie ist diese Gesetzmäßigkeit in den Resultaten der statistischen Analyse widergespiegelt? Im Schema 1 ist eine starke Korrelationsverbindung zwischen den Hypersemen [streichen, streifen] und [fassen] fixiert, was teilweise die obenerwähnte Gesetzmäßigkeit bestätigt. Beide Hyperseme [streifen] und [fassen] sind außerdem schwach mit [ziehen] (r = 0,38) verbunden; [ziehen] ist mit [binden] (r = 0,31) verbunden. Die aufgrund der etymologischen Analyse erwartete Verbindung zwischen [schneiden] und [streifen, streichen, ziehen] ist nur mit einem nicht signifikanten Korrelationskoeffizienten unterstützt: r (+0,16).

7. Der im Schema 1 dargestellte Zusammenhang zwischen [schützen] und [biegen] entsteht wahrscheinlich nach der Linie „biegen > umgeben, verschließen > schützen“. Doch zeigt die etymologische Analyse, daß zwischen den genannten Bedeutungen auch andere Derivationsverhältnisse möglich sind.

So haben eine ähnliche Form dt. *Schloße*, engl. *sleet* „Schloße, Schnee und Regen“, norw. (dial.) *slutr* „Schnee und Regen“ (< germ. **sliut-*) und dt. *schließen*, *Schlüssel* (< germ. **sliut-*); eine analoge Ähnlichkeit wird auch zwischen dt. *schießen*, *schützen* und engl. *shut* (< germ. **skeut-*) beobachtet. Eine gemeinsame Ausgangsbedeutung für alle angeführten Formen könnte „biegen, drehen“ (d.h. Hypersem [biegen]) sein. Diese Bedeutung generiert entweder das Sem [schließen] oder das Sem [schleudern]:

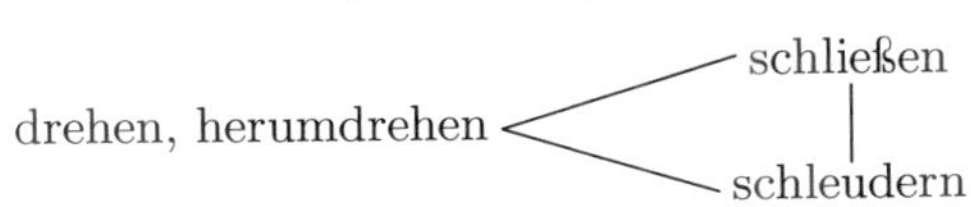

Im Ergebnis bildet sich auf den ersten Blick ein nicht bis zum Ende klarer Zusammenhang zwischen den Semen [schließen] und [werfen]. Dieser Zusammenhang hat, wie oben gezeigt, einen wiederholenden Charakter: dt. *schließen* – *Schloße* (< „werfen"); engl. *shut* „schließen" – dt. *schießen* (< „werfen"); dt. *werfen* – engl. *warp* „Zettel", „Werfen", russ. *metat'* „werfen" – *motat'* „wickeln, haspeln". Es ist unserer Meinung nach unmöglich, die angeführten Zusammenhänge nur mit den Weben-Handlungen zu erklären, wie O.N. Trubačev vorschlägt (s. oben). Das gemeinsame Verbindungsglied für beide Seme – [schließen] und [werfen] ist [drehen, biegen]. Im Schema 1 ist die Verbindung [biegen] + [schützen] ganz deutlich dargestellt; [biegen] und [loslassen] (d.h. „werfen") sind auch miteinander verbunden ($r = 0{,}59$ ist fast signifikant).

Auf solche Weise kann man behaupten, daß die Resultate der etymologischen und statistischen Analyse im Grunde genommen zusammenfallen. Die zentralen Bedeutungen der Wurzel **sē-/se-* konnten die miteinander eng verbundenen Bedeutungen „schneiden", „binden" und „biegen, drehen" sein. Diese Bedeutungen konnten ihrerseits eine ganze Reihe von semantischen Ableitungen generieren, denen die in diesem Artikel betrachteten „Bewegung", „glänzen, schimmern", „wahrnehmen", „fließen", „schützen, verschließen", „tönen", „loslassen, werfen, entsenden", „beschädigen", „streifen, streichen" ua. zugehören konnten. Außerdem können der etymologischen Analyse gemäß Derivate der Bedeutung „schneiden" auch „abtrennen" > „reinigen, rein"; „etwas abgeschnittenes, Stück, Fetzen, Balke", „Fleisch, Körper", „jung, klein" ua. sein.

4. Phonetische Zusammenhänge zwischen den möglichen Derivaten der ig. **sē-/se-* „Sehne, mit den Sehnen hantieren"

Um die Angaben über die phonetischen Zusammenhänge zwischen den Derivaten der Wurzel **sē-/se-* zu erhalten, kann man dasselbe Verfahren ausnutzen, das für die Feststellung der semantischen Zusammenhänge zwischen den ig. Wurzeln angewandt wurde. Wenn, wie auf Seite 6 gezeigt ist, die semantische Komponente [schneiden] mit den Wurzeln mit den anlautenden *sk-*, *sn-*, *sm-* und *su̯-* bezeichnet werden kann, so haben also diese Wurzeln gemeinsame semantische Funktionen.

Die Menge dieser Funktionen kann man nach der Häufigkeit jeder semantischen Klasse in Tabelle 1 feststellen. So können z.B. die *sk*-Wurzeln die folgenden semantischen Klassen bezeichnen: „schneiden" (11), „loslassen" (7),

„biegen“ (5), „binden“ (5), „beschädigen“ (4) usw. Die Hauptfunktion von *st*-Wurzeln, wie aus der Tabelle 1 zu sehen ist, ist die Bezeichnung des Hypersems [stützen], *sl* – [streifen] und [loslassen], *sn* – [binden] und [schneiden] usw.

Vom Standpunkt der Statistik wäre es richtiger, nicht nur die Vorkommenshäufigkeit der einen oder anderen phonetischen Klasse zu berücksichtigen, sondern auch die Tatsache, daß die entsprechenden empirischen (beobachteten) Häufigkeiten die theoretischen (erwarteten) Häufigkeiten übertreffen.

Ohne auf die Technik der benötigten Berechnungen einzugehen, führen wir nur die Daten an, die zeigen, in welchem Maße die empirischen Häufigkeiten die theoretischen übertreffen (s. Tabelle 2). Mit dem Zeichen „×“ sind solche Fälle kenntlich gemacht, bei denen die entsprechenden Werte um 1,3–1,9 mal die theoretischen übertreffen; das Zeichen „+“ zeigt ein Übertreffen um 2 und mehr Male an.

Die ganze Menge und Verschiedenheit dieser sich schneidenden semantischen Funktionen kann man mit Hilfe der Korrelationsanalyse feststellen. Für die Durchführung dieser Analyse wurde Tabelle 1 in eine andere Tabelle umgestaltet, so daß die Reihen und Spalten vertauscht wurden. Außerdem wurde in der neuentwickelten Tabelle die Anzahl der Spalten, d.h. der phonetischen Klassen, verkürzt (die Klasse [übrige] wurde ausgeschlossen), so dass nur 9 phonetische Klassen geblieben sind: *sl, sr, si̯, su̯, sm, sn, sk, sp, st*. Da die Zahl der Wertepaare n in der Ausgangstabelle gleich 24 ist (die Zahl der semantischen Klassen), sind Koeffizienten r mit den Werten 0,40 (P = 0,05) und größer (bei P = 0,01 ist r = 0,52) signifikant.

Die Resultate der Korrelationsanalyse sind im Schema 3 dargestellt. In diesem Schema sind mit 2 Linien Koeffizienten mit den Werten 0,52 und größer bezeichnet; eine Linie symbolisiert die Werte größer als 0,40 (signifikante Koeffizienten); punktierte Linien bezeichnen Werte unter 0,40, d.h. solche, die keine Signifikanz haben.

Wie aus dem Schema 3 zu sehen ist, ist das Kernelement in einem Satz der potentiellen Derivate der Wurzel **sē-/se-* die phonetische Klasse [sk]; den zentralen Elementen des rekonstruierten Systems gehören die Klassen [sn], und [sp] an, die sehr stark mit der Klasse [sk] verbunden sind. Sehr nahe einer signifikanten Größe ist der Koeffizient der Korrelation zwischen [sn] und [su̯] (r = 0,38, wobei r = 0,40 signifikant wäre); ziemlich hoch (aber nicht signifikant) sind die Koeffizienten für die Paare [sk] – [su̯] (r = 0,35), [si̯] – [sn] (r = 0,34) und [sk] – [sr] (r = 0,34). Am wenigsten wahrscheinlich ist die Zugehörigkeit der Klassen [st] (r = 0,29) und [sm] (r = 0,25) zu dem betrachteten System.

5. Schlußfolgerungen

Auf solche Weise ermöglichen die Resultate der etymologischen und statistischen Analyse es anzunehmen, daß in der ig. Ursprache eine Wurzel **sē-/se-* mit einer diffusen Semantik existieren konnte, die wir als „Sehne/ Bogensehne; mit den Sehne / Bogensehne hantieren" bestimmen. Die Derivate dieser Wurzel weisen einige gemeinsame Bedeutungen auf, indem sie eine Feldstruktur bilden. Der Kern des Feldes ist offensichtlich das Hypersem [schneiden]; dem Zentrum gehören die Hyperseme [binden], [biegen], [wahrnehmen], [glänzen], [Bewegung], [schützen, verschließen] und [fließen] an; die nächste Peripherie bilden [beschädigen] und [loslassen, lassen]. Die zentrale formale Einheit in der Struktur der Ableitungen der Wurzel **sē-/se-* ist, wie die statistische Analyse zeigt, die phonetische Klasse [sk]. Die Wurzeln mit *su̯-*, *st-*, *sr-* und *sm-* bilden eine fernere Peripherie in der formalen Struktur der Derivate der Wurzel **sē-/se-*.

Die Anwendung der statistischen Verfahren in der Etymologie kann, wie der in diesem Artikel dargestellte Versuch der Korrelationsanalyse zeigt, für die Feststellung der semantischen Zusammenhänge zwischen den formal ähnlichen lexikalischen Einheiten und für die Bestätigung der aufgestellten etymologischen Hypothesen nützlich sein. Das von uns betrachtete Material zeigt, daß alle in der Etymologie bekannten semantischen Zusammenhänge ihre Bestätigung in den Ergebnissen der quantitativen Analyse in einem gewissen Grad finden. Doch stimmen die auf dem quantitativen Weg erhaltenen Zusammenhänge nicht immer mit den Angaben der etymologischen Analyse und mit den intuitiven Vorstellungen des Forschers überein.

Phonetische Klassen	schneiden 1	binden 2	biegen 3	Bewegung 4	tönen 5	glänzen 6	Farben 7	riechen 8	fließen 9	Geschmack 10	drücken 11	beschädigen 12	schützen 13	loslassen 14	ziehen 15	streifen 16	fassen 17	wahrnehmen 18	stützen 19	brennen 20	Balken 21	Körperteile 22	Vögel 23	Verwandtschaft 24	übrige 25	gesamt
	Semantische Klassen																									
1 *sl*	2	2	1	1	1	0	1	0	1	1	1	2	0	4	1	5	2	0	0	0	2	0	0	0	1	28
2 *sr*	1	2	1	2	1	0	2	0	3	1	0	0	1	0	0	0	0	0	0	0	0	1	0	0	4	19
3 *si̯*	1	2	0	0	0	0	0	0	1	0	0	0	0	4	0	0	1	0	0	0	0	0	0	1	1	11
4 *su̯*	2	3	4	3	5	1	1	1	1	3	2	4	1	4	0	0	0	2	0	1	3	4	1	3	3	52
5 *sm*	1	1	0	0	0	0	1	2	0	1	1	0	0	1	0	2	0	2	0	1	0	1	0	0	5	19
6 *sn*	4	5	3	0	2	0	1	0	1	0	2	2	0	1	1	0	0	1	0	2	0	0	0	3	2	30
7 *sk*	11	5	5	5	3	3	1	0	3	0	1	4	3	7	0	0	0	3	2	1	0	1	1	0	2	61
8 *sp*	5	1	1	5	1	3	0	0	2	1	1	0	0	3	1	0	0	2	0	0	1	3	3	0	5	38
9 *st*	4	2	1	1	4	1	1	0	2	0	3	1	1	1	0	1	0	2	7	0	3	4	0	0	2	41
10 übrige	0	0	0	0	0	0	0	0	0	0	0	0	0	1	0	0	0	0	3	0	0	0	0	0	2	6
gesamt	31	23	16	17	17	8	8	3	14	7	11	13	6	26	3	8	3	12	12	5	9	14	5	7	27	305

Tabelle 1. Häufigkeitsverteilungen in den semantischen und phonetischen Klassen

Phonetische Klassen	Semantische Klassen 1	2	3	4	5	6	7	8	9	10	11	12	13	14	15	16	17	18	19	20	21	22	23	24
sl														×		+								
sr									+															
si̯														+										
su̯			+									+									+	×	+	
sm																								
sn	×	+																						+
sk	×		+	×		×						×	+	×										
sp	×			+		+																×	+	
st					×						×								+		+			

Tabelle 2. Semantische Funktionen der phonetischen Klassen

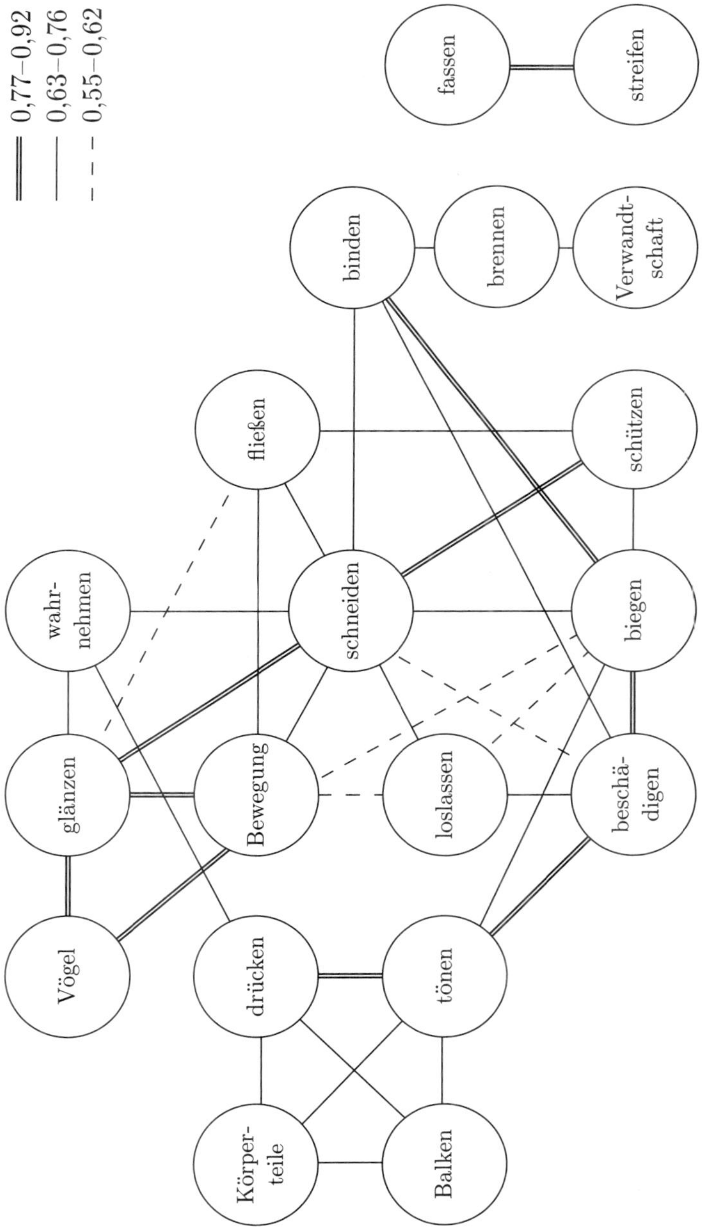

Schema 1. Semantische Zusammenhänge in der Struktur der Wurzel *$s\bar{e}$-/*se*-

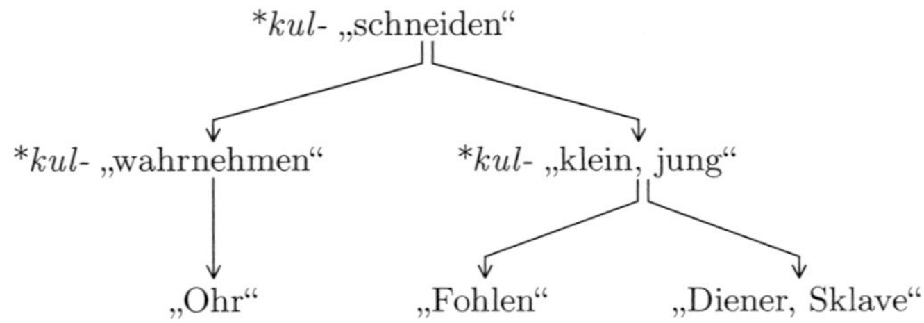

Schema 2

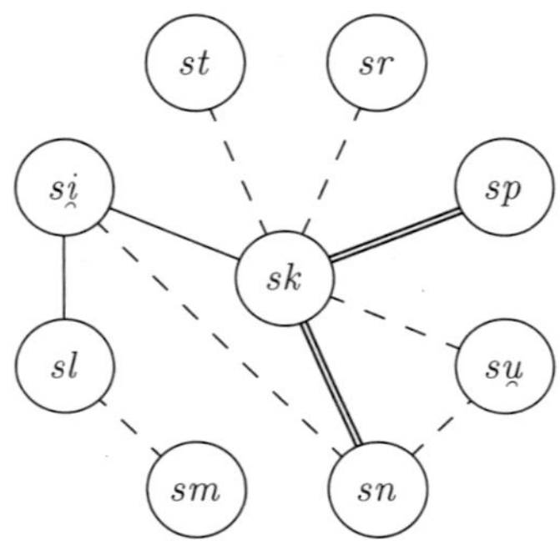

Schema 3. Phonetische Zusammenhänge zwischen den potentiellen Derivaten der Wurzel **se-/sē-*

Literatur

1. Benveniste E. 1935. *Origines de la formation des noms en indo-européen.* Paris: Librairie Adrien-Maisonneuve.
2. Berlin B., Kay P. 1969. *Basic Color Terms: 'Their' Universality and Evolution.* Berkley. Los Angeles: University of California Press. – 178 p.
3. Lewizkij V.V. 1989. *Statističeskoje izučenije leksičeskoj semantiki.* Kiev: UMK VO. – 156 S.
4. Lewizkij V.V. 1997. *Etimologičeskie i semasiologičeskie issledovanija v oblasti germanskix jazykov.* Černovzy: Ruta. – 276 S.
5. Levickij V.1998. Zur deutschen Etymologie. *Indogermanische Forschungen* 103: 210–226.
6. Lewizkij V.V. 2000. *Etimologičeskij slovar' germanskix jazykov*, 1–3, Černovzy: Ruta.
7. Lewizkij V.V. 2001. Semantičeskij sinkretizm v germanskom i indojevropejskom. *Voprosy jazykoznanija* 4: 94–106.

8. Lewizkij V.V. 2007. *Kvantitativnyje metody v lingvistike*. Vinniza: Nova knyha. – 259 S.
9. Maciuszak K. 1996. Notes on etymology of the New Persian colour names. *Studia Etymologica Cracoviensia* 1: 25–37.
10. Makovskij M.M. 1989. *Udivitelny mir slov i značenij: Illuzii i paradoksy v leksike i semantike*, Moskva: Vysšaja škola. – 199 S.
11. Mel'ničuk A.S. 1968. Koren' **kes-* i jego raznovidnosti v leksike slav'anskix i drugix indojevropeiskix jazykov, *Etimologija*, Moskva: Nauka: 194–240.
12. Moskovič V.A. 1969. *Statistika i semantika*. Moskva: Nauka. – 304 S.
13. Persson P. 1912. *Beiträge zur indogermanischen Wortforschung*. 1–2. Uppsala–Leipzig.
14. Pokorny J. 1959–1969. *Indogermanisches etymologisches Wörterbuch*. 1–2. Bern–München: Francke Verlag.
15. Stachowski M. 2010. Türkisch *kulak* 'Ohr', *kul* 'Sklave', *kulun* 'Fohlen'. In: Mańczak-Wohlfeld E., Podolak B., (red.) 2010. *Studies on the Turkic World. A Festschrift for Professor St. Stachowski on the Occasion of His 80th Birthday*. Kraków: Wydawnictwo Uniwersytetu Jagiellońskiego: 233–239.
16. Suprun A.E., Plotnikov B.A., Aladko Ž.G. 1969. K distributivno-korrel'azionnomu izučeniju leksičeskoj semantiki. In: *Aktual'nyje problemy leksikologiji*. Novosibirsk. – S. 17–19.
17. Trubačev O.N. 1966. *Remeslennaja terminologija v slav'anskix jazykax*. Moskva: Nauka. – 416 S.
18. Trubačev O.N., (red.) 1974 ff., *Etimologičeskij slovar' slav'anskix jazykov. Praslav'anskij leksičeskij fond,* Moskva: Nauka.
19. Zöfel P. 1985. *Statistik in der Praxis*. Stuttgart: Fischer Verlag. – 427 S.